Crown and Mitre

RELIGION AND SOCIETY IN
NORTHERN EUROPE
SINCE THE REFORMATION

The fifteen essays in this volume, papers delivered at a conference held at the University of Kent in September 1992, cover a number of common themes in the religious and social history of Northern Europe since the Reformation and include work by British, Dutch, French and German scholars; they exemplify the growing collaboration between scholars in different parts of Europe and a desire to achieve an international dimension in historical studies. The conference itself coincided with the opening of a major travelling exhibition on the same themes, organised by Kent County Council and partially financed by a Kaleidoscope Award from the European Community.

Crown and Mitre

RELIGION AND SOCIETY IN
NORTHERN EUROPE
SINCE THE REFORMATION

Edited by
W. M. JACOB and NIGEL YATES

THE BOYDELL PRESS

First published 1993
The Boydell Press, Woodbridge

ISBN 0 85115 346 1

The Boydell Press is an imprint of Boydell & Brewer Ltd
PO Box 9, Woodbridge, Suffolk IP12 3DF, UK
and of Boydell & Brewer Inc.
PO Box 41026, Rochester, NY 14604, USA

British Library Cataloguing-in-Publication Data
Crown and Mitre:Religion and Society in
Northern Europe Since the Reformation
    I. Jacob, W. M. II. Yates, Nigel
    274.8
    ISBN 0–85115–346–1

Library of Congress Cataloging-in-Publication Data
Crown and mitre : religion and society in northern Europe since the
    Reformation / edited by W.M. Jacob and Nigel Yates.
        p.   cm.
    Papers delivered at a conference held at the Univ. of Kent in Sept. 1992.
    Includes bibliographical references and index.
    ISBN 0–85115–346–1 (hard : alk. paper)
        1. Christianity – Europe, Northern – Congresses. 2. Sociology,
    Christian – Europe, Northern – Congresses. I. Jacob, W. M.
    II. Yates, Nigel.
    BR738.2.C76   1993
    274–dc20   93–35818

This publication is printed on acid-free paper

Printed in Great Britain by
St Edmundsbury Press Ltd, Bury St Edmunds, Suffolk

CONTENTS

ILLUSTRATIONS

NOTES ON CONTRIBUTORS

NIGEL ASTON is Course Tutor in Arts at the Open University and the author of *The End of an Elite: The French Bishops and The Coming of the Revolution, 1786–1790* (Oxford University Press, 1992).

VIVIANE BARRIE-CURIEN is Professor of Modern History at the University of Reims. She has published articles in *Revue Historique* and *Histoire, Economie et Société*; three chapters in *Histoire du Christianisme* (Paris-Tournai, 1992); *Guerre et Pouvoir en Europe au XVIIe Siècle* (Paris, 1991); and *Clergé et Pastorale en Angleterre au XVIIIe Siècle; le Diocese de Londres* (Paris, 1992).

DAVID BEBBINGTON is Reader in History at the University of Stirling. His most recent publications include *Evangelicalism in Modern Britain* (1989), *Victorian Non-conformity* (1992) and *William Ewart Gladstone: Faith and Politics in Victorian Britain* (1993).

CLYDE BINFIELD is Reader in History at the University of Sheffield. He is the author of numerous papers on Nonconformist history, attitudes and architecture. His major publications include *George Williams and the YMCA: A Study in Victorian Social Attitudes* (1973), *So Down to Prayers: Studies in English Nonconformity c.1760–1920* (1977), and *Pastors and People: The Biography of a Baptist Church: Queen's Road, Coventry* (1984).

LLEWELLYN BOGAERS took her Master's degree in history in 1983. In 1986–92 she held a scholarship awarded by the Netherlands Organisation for Scientific Research. From 1988 until 1991 she taught at the Faculty of History of Erasmus University of Rotterdam. She has published articles in Dutch learned journals and is currently completing her doctoral thesis on religious affiliations in Utrecht in the sixteenth century.

HUGH BOUDIN was appointed Pastor of the French Protestant Church of Canter-bury in 1991 having been previously Professor of Church History (1965–91) and Rector of the Protestant Faculty of Theology (1976–91) at Brussels. Between 1960 and 1970 he was a producer of religious and television programmes for Belgische Radio en Televisie.

STEWART BROWN is Professor of Ecclesasistical History at the University of Edin-burgh and co-editor of the *Scottish Historical Review*. He has published *Thomas Chalmers and the Godly Commonwealth in Scotland* (Oxford University Press, 1982) and jointly edited, with Michael Fry, *Scotland in the Age of the Disruption* (Edinburgh University Press, 1992).

FRANCOISE DECONINCK-BROSSARD is Professor of English at the University of Paris X-Nanterre, having previously lectured at the University of Picardie in Amiens.

She has published articles on eighteenth century shorthand, music and the homiletic use of the Bible, and her doctoral thesis was published as *Vie Politique, Sociale et Religieuse en Grande-Bretagne d'après les Sermons Prêchés au Publiés dans le Nord de l'Angleterre, 1738–1769* in 1984.

YVES-MARIE HILAIRE is Professor of Contemporary History at the Charles de Gaulle University in Lille. His publications include *Une Chrétienté au XIXe Siècle? La Vie Religieuse des Populations du Diocèse d'Arras, 1840–1914* (Lille, 1977) and, in collaboration with others, *Histoire Religieuse de la France Contemporaire, 1800–1988* (3 vols, Toulouse, 1985–8) and *Materiaux pour l'Histoire Religieuse de la France Contemporaire* (3 vols, Paris, 1982–92).

W.M. JACOB is Warden of Lincoln Theological College and Prebendary of Lincoln Cathedral. He has published several articles on eighteenth and nineteenth century church history and is currently working on lay Christian practice in the first half of the eighteenth century.

IAN MACHIN is Professor of Modern History at the University of Dundee. He has published many articles and books on aspects of religious history between 1820 and 1970 including *The Catholic Question in English Politics 1820–1830* and *Politics and the Churches in Great Britain 1832–1921*, the latter in two volumes dividing at 1868. His current field of research is the British Churches and social issues between 1918 and 1970.

ANNE OAKLEY is Senior Research Archivist at the Canterbury Cathedral Archives, having been Archivist to the Chapter, City and Diocese of Canterbury between 1970 and 1989. She has published *Actes du Consistoire de l'Eglise Francaise de Threadneedle Street, Londres* (1969), *The Freemen of Canterbury, 1800–1835* (1990) and several articles on aspects of Huguenot and Kentish history.

HANS OTTE is Head of the Archives of the Lutheran Church of Hannover and Lecturer in Church History at the University of Hannover. He has published *Milde Aufklärung: Theologie und Kirchenleitung bei J.H. Pratje, 1710–1791* (Göttingen, 1989), *Vernünftig und Christlich: Der Entwurf einer Brem-Verdischen Kirchenordnung von 1769* (Göttingen, 1989) and several articles on nineteenth and twentieth century church history.

W.R. WARD was Professor of Modern History at the University of Durham from 1965 until his retirement in 1986, and is an Honorary Doctor of Theology of the University of Basel. His many publications include *Religion and Society in England, 1790–1850* (1972), *The Early Correspondence of Jabez Bunting* (1972), *Early Victorian Methodism: the Correspondence of Jabez Bunting, 1830–58* (1976), *Theology, Sociology and Politics: The German Protestant Social Conscience, 1890–1933* (1979) and *The Protestant Evangelical Awakening* (1992). Since 1988 he has published five of the planned seven volumes of *The Journals and Diaries of John Wesley*.

NIGEL YATES is Consultant Historian to Kent County Council and Visiting Senior Research Fellow in Economic and Social History at the University of Kent. He was previously City Archivist of Portsmouth 1975–80 and County Archivist of Kent

1980–90. He has published many articles and books on religious and social history including *The Oxford Movement and Anglican Ritualism* (Historical Association, 1983) and *Buildings, Faith and Worship: the Liturgical Arrangement of Anglican Churches, 1600–1900* (Oxford University Press, 1991).

EDITORIAL PREFACE

All the papers included within this collection of essays were delivered at the University of Kent between 4 and 7 September 1992 at a conference on the theme of 'Religion and Society in Northern Europe since the Reformation'. The conference accompanied a major travelling exhibition on the same theme, opened during the conference by the Old Catholic Archbishop of Utrecht, the Most Revd Mgr Antonius Jan Glazemaker. The exhibition was held at the Royal Museum and Art Gallery in Canterbury and later travelled, in a somewhat truncated form, to venues in Folkestone and Maidstone, Utrecht and Bruges, a number of towns in the Nord-Pas de Calais region of France, ending up at Nuremburg in the autumn of 1993. The exhibition was made possible by the co-operation of archivists, librarians and museum curators throughout north-west Europe, especially in Bruges, Douai, Lund, Nuremburg and Utrecht, the five cities or towns in addition to Canterbury specially featured in the exhibition. For its opening venue the organisers, the Arts and Libraries Department of Kent County Council, were able to bring together some beautiful and rare items, including a seventeenth century cope and altar frontal, eighteenth century eucharistic vestments, Calvinist communion beaker, Lutheran chalice, Anglican flagons and baptismal bowl, Dutch and Scottish collecting shoes, a complete parochial library in its cupboard, as well as the cases of documents and the lavish panels bearing the main exhibition text which travelled to the other venues. The exhibition was made possible by substantial finding from the Kent County Council's European Fund together with an even more generous grant from the Kaleidoscope programme of the European Community. The main exhibition text was reproduced, together with an accompanying illustrated booklet, in four languages: Dutch, English, French and German.

The conference was chaired by the Dean of Canterbury, the Very Revd John Simpson, and attracted some forty scholars from Britain, mainland Europe and the United States of America. Over twenty papers were read at the conference of which fifteen appear in this volume. The exhibition was divided into six separate sections or sub-themes each of which is represented by at least one paper in this volume. The impact of the Reformation is shown on one community in Llewellyn Bogaers' paper on Utrecht; religious minorities in the papers of Anne Oakley, Hugh Boudin and David Bebbington; different aspects of the relationship between the religious and secular dimensions of society in the papers of Bill Jacob, Reg Ward, Viviane Barrie-Curien, Yves-Marie Hilaire, Stewart Brown and Ian Machin; the educational, or at least intellectual, impact of religion in the papers of Françoise Deconinck-Brossard and Nigel Aston, and its social impact in that of Hans Otte; buildings and worship in the papers of Nigel Yates and Clyde Binfield, together with some supporting illustrations. It was a very successful conference in which the common themes of church history in the post-Reformation period were vigorously and enthusiastically discussed and many new contacts made by those attending. It is the editors' hope that more conferences of this sort, aimed at exploring the common heritage of the northern European churches, will be held in the future on appropriate topics. They would like to record their appreciation to their contributors who have patiently met all their demands and to the publishers for producing such an excellent record of a major historical event.

W.M.J.
W.N.Y.

LLEWELLYN BOGAERS

Utrecht at a Crossroads: Religious affiliations in a sixteenth century Netherlandish city*

The quest for Christianity

In this paper I should like to show, by taking Utrecht as an example, that the development of denominations was a gradual process in the sixteenth century Netherlands, with distinctions only slowly emerging. It is only towards the end of the century that we can begin to talk of clear-cut denominations. Until then the demarcation lines between the various affiliations are rather transparent and fluid, not rigid or dogmatic.[1] In the town of Utrecht this shaping of denominations took place with very little excessive fanaticism, although of course at the critical moments pressure groups were at hand, as was the case with the iconoclasms, in Utrecht in 1566, 1579 and 1580, and with the ensuing alteration in 1580, when the reformed church was being favoured and public catholic worship forbidden. In

ABBREVIATIONS

AGN   *Algemene Geschiedenis der Nederlanden*
BHG   *Berigten van het Historisch Genootschap te Utrecht*
BMHG *Bijdragen en Medede(e)lingen van het Historisch Genootschap*
TvG   *Tijdschrift voor Geschiedenis*
UED   *Utrechters entre-deux*
WHG   *Werken van het Historisch Genootschap*

*   I would like to thank Marten Jan Bok, Prof. Dr W.Th.M. Frijhoff, Prof. Dr M.E.H.N. Mout, Dr B. Roest, Dr L. van Tongerloo and Prof. Dr J.J. Woltjer for their comments on an earlier draft of this paper. Rev. T.F. Taylor corrected the first English version. The investigations for this paper were supported by the Foundation for Historical Research, which is subsidized by the Netherlands Organisation for Scientific Research (NWO). This article can be seen as a preview of my forthcoming dissertation.

1   See *AGN*, vol. 6 (Haarlem, 1979), A.F. Mellink, 'Prereformatie en vroege reformatie 1517–1568'; J. Decavele, 'Reformatie en begin katholieke restauratie 1555–1568'; W. Nijenhuis, 'De publieke kerk veelkleurig en verdeeld, bevoorrecht en onvrij 1579–1621'. Alastair Duke, *Reformation and Revolt in the Low Countries* (London/Ronceverte, 1990), gives a wealth of information and a penetrating analysis of the interaction of revolt and reformation. In *De Dageraad van de Reformatie in Vlaanderen (1520–1565)* (Brussels, 1975), Johan Decavele subtly sketches the reformist movement in Flanders.

fact, it will be shown that in Utrecht throughout the sixteenth century there
existed a strong, steady undercurrent of belief in which the dominant motive was
how to live according to the example that Christ himself had set. In analyzing
reasons why people dissociated themselves from the catholic church and joined
another religious group, from 1530 onwards anabaptism or one of its more radical
offsprings, or later in the century the spiritually inclined parish around Hubert
Duifhuis or the more dogmatic reformed church, various motives can be detected,
political, economic, personal and religious.[2] For this paper I should like to focus
on the religious impulse, but when necessary I will dwell on other causes as well.

Marking out some international differences

To give some framework to those of you who may not be acquainted with the
position of church and state in the sixteenth century Netherlands I will briefly
mention in what aspects the Low Countries differ from what I have gathered is the
situation in Britain.

On a political level

In the sixteenth century the grip of the Habsburg government on the newly
acquired territories in the Northern Netherlands was not as firm as the central
authorities might have wished. Guelders had only come under Habsburg rule in
1543. Local powers everywhere were still quite strong, representing a force the
central government had to reckon with. This is, by the way, an outstanding feature
of the Netherlands: they have always been governed on the basis of *consensus*.
Never did a central authority succeed in gaining absolute control. This was very
much the case in the sixteenth century, and especially so in the *Nedersticht*, the
territory of which the city of Utrecht was the capital, which had only become part
of the Habsburg Netherlands in 1528. Until then the reigning bishop was head of
the diocese of Utrecht. In this function he had, until 1528, also exercised temporal
power over the *Nedersticht*. This did not mean, though, that he actually had much
influence in either the ecclesiastical or the political realm. From the 1450s onward
the bishops had been rather dependent on Burgundian, later Habsburg, support to
exercise some form of effective government. And due to the balance of power in
the *Nedersticht* itself the bishops from the fourteenth century onward gradually
had to recognize the influence of the Estates of Utrecht that assembled in the city.
In this political body that dealt with the more important issues of the country, like
war and peace and the collection of taxes, Utrecht's five chapters represented the
first Estate, the nobility and gentry the second, and the five towns of the
Nedersticht the third. Among the towns Utrecht's vote was often decisive. There
were strong personal ties between the members of the three Estates, and therefore

---

2   For an excellent analysis of how religion and politics interacted, see J.J. Woltjer, *Friesland
    in Hervormingstijd* (Leiden, 1962).

common interests, chief among them fighting off any influence the sovereign prince, until 1528 the residing bishop, and after 1528 the Habsburg princes Charles V and Philip II, might wish to exert. The princes could not make unilateral decisions in any of the matters mentioned above. For the collection of taxes, for instance, they needed the approval of the Estates each time.[3]

One does not need much imagination to envisage that this *privilege* or prerogative gave the Estates an excellent bargaining counter. In the course of the sixteenth century this issue would cause ever growing friction between the Estates and Brussels, the administrative centre of the Habsburg government that was in constant need of money.

Ecclesiastical affairs

In religious matters as well the bishop was not the dominant leader that one would expect, having lost all his spiritual tasks to other dignitaries and institutions within the church. The chapters, for instance, had certain areas in which they were entitled to nominate priests. For the city of Utrecht this right was *de facto* obtained by the Domchapter.

Religion could count on local interest. There are indications that local preferences were honoured in the appointment of priests, the most striking example being the nomination of Hubert Duifhuis as pastor of St. Jacob's church in 1575.[4] Also on other occasions consultation seemed to have taken place between canons of the Domchapter, clergymen and parishioners.[5] This need not surprise us at all: as all parties lived within the city of Utrecht they had plenty of opportunity to meet, in the street or at the inn, at mass, processions, and banquets, and in the frequent assemblies of the Estates of Utrecht.

On a personal level as well a lively communication was going on between priests and parishioners: in the Netherlands priests could write their own sermons and thus express a personal point of view from the pulpit. In this way they could attract a wide audience. In Utrecht we know this for a fact of the parish priest Dirck van Abcoude who preached in the church of St Geert's (1536/37–1542), of the *vice-cureit* of St Jacob's, Herman van Remundt (1541), and of Hubert Duifhuis, (vice-)pastor of St Jacob's from 1573 until his death in 1581.[6] In the

---

3 Cf. Rob van Drie, 'De Staten van Utrecht en Philips II', unpublished doctoral thesis (1983), available at the Bibliotheek der Letteren, Rijksuniversiteit of Utrecht, and at the Rijksarchief of Utrecht; Bram van den Hoven van Genderen, *Het Kapittel-Generaal en de Staten van het Nedersticht in de 15e eeuw*, Stichtse Historische Reeks, 13 (Zutphen, 1987), pp. 26–30 and 39–41.

4 See the articles of L. van Tongerloo and R.H. Pegel, in *Utrechters entre-deux* (Delft, 1992), pp. 84, 101 and pp. 130–132.

5 See the above-mentioned article by L. van Tongerloo in *UED, op. cit.*, pp. 75–84.

6 For Dirck van Abcoude and Herman van Remundt see 'Gedenkschriften van jhr. Herberen van Mijnden', in S. Muller Fz. (ed.), *BMHG*, 11 (1888), pp. 55–58. For Hubert Duifhuis, see J. Wiarda, *Huibert Duifhuis, de prediker van St. Jacob* (Amsterdam, 1858); B.J. Kaplan, *Calvinists and Libertines, The Reformation in Utrecht, 1578–1618*, Thesis

administration of the sacraments a personal communication between priest and parishioner could take place.

To summarize, in the city of Utrecht religion was not totally institutionalized from above. On quite a few levels room was left for personal involvement. This decentralized aspect seems to me one of the most characteristic features of the sixteenth century catholic church in the Netherlands. It may explain why so many people chose to stay within the catholic church, even after catholicism had been abolished in Utrecht in 1580 as a result of the war with catholic Spain. The reformed governments initially had not enough grip to force catholics to become reformed. Only when the Synod of Dordt (1618–19) had established a victory of the counterremonstrants upon the remonstrants, could the staunch protestants start exercising more pressure upon society.[7] Even then the balance of power was not reversed. All through the seventeenth century the catholics remained a power the reformed government had to reckon with.

Utrecht's impact
To return to Utrecht, I will first give you a rough idea of Utrecht's status in the middle ages. Being the bishop's see Utrecht was at that time the ecclesiastical heart of the Netherlands. The towery skyline of the city reflected its importance. As bishop's see it saw the establishment of five capitular churches, and also the erection of the impressive Domtower, three abbeys and numerous convents. As the town grew, four parishes were established. In the early sixteenth century around 20,000 people probably lived in the city.

Establishing the framework of this article
Concerning religious affiliations, historians from 1847 onwards until recently agreed that in the sixteenth century Utrecht was not prone to reformatory movements, let alone heretical adherence. The catholic church was so omnipresent, they say, that allegiance to the reformation could not have developed here.[8] They may

Harvard University 1989, facsimile Ann Arbor, 1990; B.J. Kaplan, 'Hubert Duifhuis and the nature of Dutch libertinism', *TvG*, 105 (1992); R.H. Pegel, in *UED*, *op. cit.*, pp. 132–134.

7 Cf. A. Duke, *Reformation and revolt*, *op. cit.*, p. xiv.
8 See H.J. Royaards, *Geschiedenis der Hervorming in de stad Utrecht* (Leiden, 1847), pp. 3–4. Here he states that being a bishop's see and having a strong clergy, Utrecht was not prone to reformist influence. An argument still being put forward: Stuart F.C. Moore writes in 'The Cathedral Chapter of St. Maarten at Utrecht before the Revolt', unpublished thesis (Southampton, 1988), 'Not that the area around Utrecht itself was especially prone to heresy, although as was to be clear in 1566, there was a determined minority of religious dissidents within the city itself, whose presence was to be significant in later decades.' In a note (n. 116) he then remarks that further study into the religious affiliations in Utrecht is necessary, because although 'Utrecht was a city Catholic at heart' this catholicism is not to be understood as univocal: too many layers within society can be discerned and they need to be further studied. In his chapter 'Building Heaven in Hell's Despite', *Reformation and*

have been influenced in this opinion by a statement of the Utrecht city magistracy in 1567, when in answer to a Spanish questionnaire with regard to the iconoclasm of 1566, it was said that before the hedgepreachings of that year only a few burgers were known to be adherents of the so-called new religion.[9] Did historians have sound evidence for this opinion?

Utrecht as a cultural centre

As was observed above, Utrecht was an important administrative centre, which required many trained clerks, especially in the field of both canonical and roman law. They were to be found among clergy and lay people alike, many of them with a university background, having studied mainly at Louvain, Cologne and Orléans. Would not these people take an interest in the intellectual debate of their time, a debate that examined the sources of Christianity, i.e. the bible and its translations and the various institutions and dogma which the church had built on behalf of them in the light of humanistic principles? Besides being a bishop's see, with all the wealth and political power that entailed, Utrecht was a rich city, providing opportunities not only for people working in the administrative field, but also in the trades and arts. Utrecht was known for its gold- and silversmiths, for its sculptors and painters.[10] The composer Jacob Obrecht had directed the Domchoir, in which Erasmus may have sung. Many of these highly qualified artisans were able to read and write, and among them were people who had travelled abroad. One would expect this complex body of clergy, gentry, politicians and artisans that was so highly involved in ecclesiastical and religious matters to be interested in the all-consuming debate that was launched by Luther's action in 1517.

Some methodological observations

To find an answer to these questions and hypotheses is not easy. This has to do with the intricacy of religion and politics in those days. For soon after Luther had proclaimed his theses, his teachings were condemned on all official levels: by the universities of Cologne and Louvain in 1519, the pope in 1520 and 1521, and the emperor Charles V in 1521. Thus, religion had become a political issue. Drawn into the heresy debate fairly soon, people felt no great need publicly to demonstrate

---

Revolt, op. cit., p. 98, Alastair Duke states that Utrecht 'was only lightly affected' (by the Reformation). In his thesis *Calvinists and Libertines, op. cit.*, Benjamin J. Kaplan ignores the local roots of the Utrecht reformation. Recent archival research presents a more nuanced picture. Of this new approach the above-mentioned articles by L. van Tongerloo and R.H. Pegel are good examples.

9   J.J. Dodt van Flensburg, *Archief voor kerkelijke en wereldsche geschiedenissen inzonderheid van Utrecht*, vol. V (Utrecht, 1846), p. 338, art. 9.

10   See *Kunst voor de Beeldenstorm, Noordnederlandse Kunst 1525–1580*, catalogue Rijksmuseum Amsterdam (The Hague, 1986), also available in English; Louise E. van den Bergh-Hoogterp, *Goud- en zilversmeden te Utrecht in de late middeleeuwen*, 2 vol. (The Hague, 1990).

their convictions or even to write about them. In Utrecht even the city magistrate and the Courts were reluctant to elaborate upon the theme.[11] So often historians find only indirect traces of what was going on in the field of religion, sources being judicial records, legislation, official and personal documents, the diaries of individual people, the books that were being written and published, and iconography. Scraping all these bits and pieces together produces a rather diversified picture.

The religious experience

First, religion never was a non-issue in the medieval Netherlands. From the days of Geert Groote (1340–1384) who was the founder of the *Devotia Moderna*, religion was a lively issue, less on an abstract theological level than because of its practical implications for daily life. How to follow Christ's example was a genuine question. Published for the first time in 1427, Thomas à Kempis' *Imitatio Christi* soon became a bestseller. In Utrecht this devotional attitude can be discerned in the reverence paid to sister Bertken, a nun who became a recluse in the Buurkerk, Utrecht's main parish church, in 1456/57, where she remained until her death in 1514. She left some beautiful poems and prayers, which all centre on the quest, later the experience, of how to attain to God. Within seven years after her death her writings were being published by *three* publishers in the Netherlands, including a publisher from Antwerp. Between 1516 and 1520 *eight* editions are known.[12] This concern with leading one's life style according to the Gospel was reinforced by the humanists' achievements. The retracing of the original sources of the bible and its translations opened the way to the examination of some of the institutions and dogma of the catholic church, notably the sacraments. Thus genuine involvement with religion and criticism of the church became entwined.

The reformist debate

In Utrecht the humanists' proceedings were being followed at the bishop's court, among the clergy, both secular and regular, and by the teachers of the Hieronymusschool, the Utrecht grammar school. Laypeople got information through books, sermons and travelling, to Antwerp for instance, and from hear-say. Although no overt allegiance to the reformist cause can be ascribed to bishop Philip of Burgundy (1517–1524), he did support a humanist, even renaissance, courtlife. The famous painter Jan Gossaert van Maubeuge belonged to his house-

---

11 For instance when people leave prison on bail, often either their names or their alleged crimes are not mentioned. Often the historian has to combine several sources to get some basic understanding of the event.

12 Sister Bertken left some texts that were published as two booklets. The first book is called *Boecxken van die passie o.l. heeren*, see W. Nijhoff and M.E. Kronenberg, *Nederlandsche bibliographie van 1500 tot 1540*, 3 vols (The Hague, 1923–1971), numbers 308, 2408–2409, 4187–4188; for the second book, called *Boec tracterende van desen puncten*, see Nijhoff and Kronenberg, *op. cit.*, numbers 309, 2407 and 4186.

hold. His secretary Gerard Geldenhouwer was personally acquainted with Erasmus with whom he corresponded. In 1517 Erasmus dedicated his book *Querimonia Pacis* to bishop Philip of Burgundy. Later Geldenhouwer would write about himself that as early as 1518 he had taken an interest in Luther's works. Having followed as early as 1521 the Habsburg example of banning and burning books considered heretical, bishop Philip was neither a man to pursue an active anti-heretical policy, nor to resist Habsburg in this matter.

Several teachers of the Latin or Hieronymusschool participated in the reformist debate of the day: as early as 1521 the rector of this school, Hinne Rode, a Brother of the Common Life, is said to have travelled to Luther to discuss the meaning of the eucharist with him, since this was a popular subject for discussion among theologians and lay-people.[13] Hinne Rode himself tended to a symbolic interpretation of the communion, conceiving of bread and wine as *images* of Christ's body and blood, rather than assuming, as was the belief within the catholic church, that through the act of consecration bread and wine literally transformed into Christ's body and blood. Accused of Lutheranism, Rode had to leave Utrecht in 1522, after which he visited reformers like Oecolampadius, Zwingli and Bucer.[14] Rode was a strong advocate of the reformist cause, which at first did not take the shape of a struggle *pro* or *contra* Rome, but was more concerned with the true meaning of doctrines such as those surrounding the holy communion. In this he followed Wessel Gansfort's and Cornelis Hoen's opinions. Through Rode Zwingli came to understand the eucharist as a symbolical act.[15]

It was not only Rode who left the Netherlands. Others who were involved in the reformist debate, and thus under suspicion of heresy, did so as well. Among them was Gerard Geldenhauwer. After such experiences people were less inclined to express their religious convictions openly, but teachers of the grammar school were

---

[13] B.J. Spruyt in *UED*, *op. cit.*, p. 31. Although it is often questioned whether Rode truly was the rector of the Hieronymusschool, I tend to be in favour of this opinion. By a contemporary, Gulielmus Gnaphaeus, who knew him well, Rode is both called 'praeceptor' (teacher) and 'percelebri Hieronymiani collegii praefectus' (rector of the famous Hieronymusschool). Authors, (f.i. B.J. Spruyt, *op. cit.* p. 22) tend to interpret this statement as 'rector of the House of the Brethren of the Common Life', but in the argument itself they often leave out the – in my view crucial – word 'percelebri'. I cannot see any reason why a convent would be called 'perceleber', whereas this term makes sense when applied to a school. In his insistence that Rode was not the rector of the school, but of the Brotherhouse, R.R. Post does not refer to the description by Gnaphaeus, but to the description in a chronicle of the Doesburg Brotherhouse, namely 'rector domus clericorum', see *The Modern Devotion. Confrontation with Reformation and Humanism*, Studies in Medieval and Reformation Thought vol. III (Leiden, 1968), pp. 571, 575, notably note 2.

[14] In the Netherlands of the first half of the sixteenth century 'lutheranism' was the common accusation for people suspected of heresy. The term itself, however, does not give any information on the actual content of the suspect's beliefs, which may in fact be lutheran or sacramentarial or anabaptist.

[15] For literature on Hinne Rode, see C.C. de Bruin, in *Jaarboek Oud-Utrecht*, 1981, pp. 191–208; B.J. Spruyt, in *UED*, pp. 21–43.

never totally successful in hiding their enthusiasm for humanistic approaches, which often entailed a critical view of Rome and its institutions.[16]

The religious debate which was being encouraged by Luther's action in 1517 also reached secular priests who talked about it from the pulpit. Already in 1522 a priest had to renounce convictions which were much inspired by Luther.[17]

Even laypeople talked about religious issues in public. They questioned the validity of the eucharist and of saints, even the sanctity of the mother Mary. Sometimes they acted out their convictions, making a mockery of a procession or a ritual.[18]

Religion and politics

How did the government react to this? It has already been indicated that the Habsburg government did not tolerate any deviations from the catholic path. Hence its strong condemnation of Luther's opinions, which started off an anti-heretical campaign. Although not incorporated into the Habsburg empire until 1528, Utrecht had already before this date followed its policy, establishing in 1524 a board consisting of four magistrates to prevent the spreading of the so called Lutheran heresy. On this occasion the city council also forbade the reading and selling of Lutheran and other heretical scripts. When people were accused of heresy the magistrates did not follow Habsburg prescriptions. The people that had been arrested got off fairly lightly, seen at least from the perspective of the death penalties that were later executed: they 'only' had to publicly renounce their so-called heretical convictions and to repent and worship in front of the community, sanctions which in effect may have been experienced as a social

---

[16] Lambertus Hortensius, rector at Utrecht c.1527–1534, was nicknamed 'the lutheran papist', see G.H.M. Delprat, *Verhandeling van de Broederschap van G. Groote* (Arnhem, 1856), p. 156. Did Hortensius write his treatise *Tumultuum anabaptisticarum* (Bazel, 1548), which is directed against the anabaptists, out of fear he might be accused of having sympathized with them? Hortensius was familiar with Henric Niclaes, the founding father of the Family of Love, and 'deeply enough involved to translate some of Hendrik Niclaes' writings into Latin in the late 1550s.' Quotation out of Alastair Hamilton, *Cronica*, Kerkhistorische Bijdragen 15, Documenta Anabaptistica Neerlandica VI (Leiden, 1988), p. x.

The humanistic approach of Macropedius, rector from 1537 until 1552, is widely acclaimed. Many of his pupils became leading scholars, often displaying an enlightened attitude towards religion. Outstanding examples are Johannes Saskerides, Willem Canter, Johannes Heurnius, Georgius Rataller and Cornelius Valerius, Delprat, *op. cit.*, pp. 157–58.

[17] On 13 January 1522 the priest Herman Gerritsz. had to publicly renounce nine so-called heretical convictions, *Corpus Documentorum Inquisitionis Haeretici Pravitatis Neerlandicae*, ed. by Paul Frédéricq (Ghent/The Hague, 1900), vol. IV, n. 62, pp. 86–87.

[18] Read the 13 testimonies, made in 1525, on the city's cooper Willem Dircsz., in Paul Frédéricq, *Corpus op. cit*, vol. IV, n. 330, pp. 368–373, or the indictment by the Court of Utrecht against the Utrecht burger Dirck Weyman, *BHG*, 1851, pp. 124–25, on 25 April 1534.

humiliation.[19] This pattern of moderate government interference in religious affairs was characteristic of the *Nedersticht*, even after Habsburg had taken over power in 1528. In the jurisdiction of Utrecht at least, people were generally not condemned to death for their convictions. The authorities were well aware that too severe a punishment or a dismissal of a priest would also have a disturbing effect upon the community. This tolerant attitude only broke down when society was considered endangered, as was the case in 1533 when a priest refused to renounce the reformed and seditious opinions he had expressed from the pulpit,[20] and even more explicitly so during the Münster upheaval (1534–35) and after, when radical sects were found to have a stronghold in Utrecht, as was the case both in 1539 and in 1544/45. For transgression of heresy legislation a total of 38 people were condemned to death in Utrecht prior to the executions that followed the iconoclasm of 1566.[21] All but two, possibly three convicts were born outside the *Nedersticht*. One observes that the magistrates protected their own citizens against the encroachment and sanctions of Brussels. Native leaders and adherents of dissident opinions, often citizens or people of considerable *status*, were given the opportunity to flee, as was the case with Hinne Rode. By the late 1520s all the main leaders of the early reform movement had left Utrecht, leaving the city bereft of experienced spiritual teachers. This may be one reason why people opened themselves up to radical or anabaptist influence in the 1530s and 1540s.

Utrecht and Münster

In 1534–35 the anabaptist upheaval at Münster took place. Only a few Utrechters had actually gone there. Some were arrested *en route*. Among the latter was Dominicus Abelsz., a young goldsmith, the son of the then famous Utrecht goldsmith, Abel van de Vechte, who had made shrines and chalices for the Dom-chapter.[22] What turned Dominicus into a zealous anabaptist we will probably never know. But he had the gift of the tongue. An eye-witness of his execution on 30 March 1534 described him as one of the most important and certainly the

---

19 The above mentioned cooper Willem Dircsz., for instance, was sentenced to sit on a heightened chair in the Domchurch and listen to a sermon in which his convictions were condemned, Paul Frédéricq, *Corpus op. cit.*, vol. IV, nn. 362 and 363, pp. 395–97.

20 This death sentence befell Jan Winter, vice-pastor at Hoorn, *BHG*, 1851, pp. 117–19.

21 Of these 38 death penalties 33 were for adherents of radical groups. Three men had refused to abjure. And two men combined another crime, repeated theft and cheating, with heretical ideas or behaviour, f.i. the seduction of a nun. This figure is excluding those who were condemned to death for church robbery without an ideological connotation being linked to the crime.

22 Louise E. van den Bergh-Hoogterp, *op. cit.*, vol. II, pp. 554–559, 576–585. In this thesis biographies are dedicated to both Abel van de Vechte and his son Dominicus (nn. 89 and 138). See for more detailed information on Dominicus Abelsz. my forthcoming articles in both the *Doopsgezinde Bijdragen*, 1993, and *Jaarboek Oud-Utrecht*, 1993.

most learned of the baptizers. He had heard Dominicus' fellow-prisoners state that they could not believe St Paul had been more learned or a better preacher in his days.[23] In Utrecht he had inspired at least 18 men and women, the men all being craftsmen, among them well-respected and well-to-do burgers. Thirteen members of this group appealed for mercy after Dominicus' execution, and this they all obtained.[24]

What is amazing though is that only a handful of Utrechters felt an urge to go to Münster. Compared to the thousands out of Holland and Frisia it is a negligible figure.[25] For this I can detect three grounds, although at this stage of my research it is hard to evaluate them. First of all, I believe that the economic structure of Utrecht was totally different from that of Holland. Being dominated by commerce Holland was susceptible to fluctuations in the market. We all know that the grain trade through the Sont was at this time very difficult due to political tensions. The uncertainties of employment may have reverberated in the appeal that came from Münster with its announcement of the millenium. By contrast, as a city of trade and handicrafts Utrecht essentially was a corporate unit, the guilds representing a rather monolithic structure with its emphasis on traditions, rules and hierarchy. Besides, Utrecht produced for a local market and for a large hinterland, notably the German Rhinecountries. With trade relations relatively undisturbed Utrecht was less susceptible to the vibrations of the market, although of course it did experience the dearth in the supply of grain and the consequent rise in price. Compared with Holland though Utrecht's economy seems quite stable at this time.

Another reason why anabaptism did not get support in the *Nedersticht* may be that reformist ideas, including anabaptist ones, were not being stimulated by the local magistrates or by rural lords, whereas in numerous towns of Holland these ideas received, if not overt support, at least a moderate toleration. This was certainly the case in Amsterdam.[26] We have already seen, that the Utrecht courts did not punish so-called heretics severely. But they did follow a policy of discouragement. The unity of society could after all not be disturbed.

An important reason why anabaptism did not appeal to Utrechters may be the state of spiritual care in Utrecht. Contrary to the received view of the priests of those days as unlearned, adulterous and unconcerned,[27] from their sermons and/or

---

23 *Documenta Anabaptistica Neerlandica V,* Amsterdam (1531–1536), ed. by A.F. Mellink (Leiden, 1985), p. 29.

24 Rijksarchief Utrecht, inv. Hof van Utrecht, n. 99, Criminele Sententiën, vol. I, ff. 197–214v, all sentences given between 20 and 30 June 1534.

25 Cf. A.F. Mellink, *De Wederdopers in de Noordelijke Nederlanden, 1531–1544* (Groningen, 1953); and J.J. Woltjer, *Friesland in Hervormingstijd, op. cit.*

26 Cf. G. Grosheide, *Bijdrage tot de Geschiedenis der Anabaptisten in Amsterdam* (Hilversum, 1938), pp. 87–94; and Albert F. Mellink, *Amsterdam en de wederdopers in de zestiende eeuw* (Nijmegen, 1978).

27 Cf. R.R. Post, *Kerkelijke verhoudingen in Nederland vóór de Reformatie* (Utrecht, 1954), pp. 48–64, 97–145.

their reading it can be gathered that most of Utrecht's parish priests were educated men who took their tasks seriously.[28] As has been observed, a highly involved dialogue was going on between priests and parishioners. The wide range of beliefs within the Utrecht clergy may have encouraged this. A few examples will suffice: before 1540 reformist sermons were being preached in the church of St Geert by the pastor Dirck van Abcoude and in St Jacob by the vice-pastor Herman van Remundt. They both attracted an ever growing audience, among them members of the well-to-do, and even the magistracy. These two priests got into a competition, so states one eye-witness, for the favour of the public. Ever bolder statements were being hurled from the pulpit. This did not go by unnoticed, as it also disturbed the unity of the community. As a result of a royal visit in 1540 these priests were questioned by inquisitors, imprisoned, and eventually given the choice to renounce their opinions or die. Both opted for the first of these choices. After being banned in 1542, Dirck van Abcoude settled himself in the nearby city of Vianen in the virtually independent territory of the Lord of Brederode. Until 1550 he continued to have a say in who was to represent him as a pastor of St Geert's.[29] As long as he lived – he died before 23 March 1576 – he got paid for the various vicariates he possessed in Utrecht, although there are no indications he ever visited the town again. This is by the way a striking example of how vested interests were respected. More examples of priests who proclaimed new ideas in the city of Utrecht can be given. Among them were Steven van Loon, pastor of St Geert's from 1556 until 1561, and Ricoud Jansz. van Rees, Nicolaas Rol and Johannes van Haller, all *vicecureit* at St Jacob's, respectively in 1550, in 1554 and from 1559 until 1572.[30] Although the reform orientated priests could express their opinions for some time, in the end they were all deprived of their pastoral cures. Some were even imprisoned as happened to curates of the Buur- and Jacobichurches in 1557.[31] Among them was Nicolaas Rol who had to renounce his beliefs and flee. This was the fate of other priests too. And yet at the same time it happened that the *vicecureit* of St James' Ricoud Jansz. van Rees, dismissed in 1550, not long afterwards obtained an official position at St John's chapter in Utrecht, first becoming a *presbyter animarum* in 1553 and later an honorary canon.

In Utrecht were also priests who adhered to the Tridentine view. The best known of these was Joachim van Oprode, pastor of the Buurkerk (1557–c.1571),

---

[28] Particularly illuminating in this respect is the above-mentioned article by L. van Tongerloo in *UED, op. cit.*, pp. 75–112. The little biographies give a wealth of detail.

[29] For information on Dirck van Abcoude and Herman van Remunt, see the 'Gedenkschriften van Herberen van Mynden', as mentioned under note 6. For biographical details on Dirck van Abcoude, see L. van Tongerloo in *UED, op. cit.*, pp. 79–81, 86–87 (n. 21), pp. 108–09, and on Herman van Remunt, *op. cit.*, p. 102.

[30] For the biographies of Steven van Loon, Ricoud Jansz. van Rees and Nicolaas Rol, see L. van Tongerloo in *UED, op. cit.*, pp. 81–82, 102 and 103.

[31] RAU, inv. Domkapittel, 1, acta on 17 February 1557 (information from Arie de Groot).

Utrecht's main parish church, who sympathized with the counter-reformation.[32]
He also had a wide audience.[33]

To summarize, throughout these decades, there had always been priests – next
to the many who took a more neutral or traditional view – who shared an interest
in reforming the catholic church from within, some inclining to protestant reformed ideas, others to counter-reformational solutions. In the end most priests
who tended to so-called heretical views were forced to resign or chose to do so, the
striking exception being Hubert Duifhuis who nearly always enjoyed official
support. The fact that these dissident priests eventually had to leave did not mean,
though, that all doors were closed for them: after all the pastor Dirck van
Abcoude, banned in 1542, officially remained in post until 1550, receiving his
vicariate pensions until his death, and the dismissed Ricoud van Rees later became
a canon in Utrecht. This mixture of a firm stand where society's integrity was
considered endangered and yet a lenient, tolerant, almost Erasmian attitude towards dissident opinions is typical of the way in which religious affairs were
handled in the city of Utrecht. A reason for this seemingly inconsistent policy may
be found in the personal interest some members of the magistracy and chapters
took in religion.

Another, and perhaps more important inference of this overview is that nearly
all through the sixteenth century reform orientated priests held posts in Utrecht,
expressing their ideas within the framework of the catholic church. Time and
again Utrecht parish priests offered such a wide range of religious affiliations that a
Utrechter could choose whatever kind of priest he or she wished to hear. Finding
gratification of one's spiritual needs within the catholic church may have been a
very important reason why so few Utrechters chose to break away from the
motherchurch throughout the sixteenth century.

Growing awareness . . .

And yet, in spite of the anabaptist upheaval in Münster and the disturbances
caused by the *Davidjoristen* and the *Batenburgers*, radical sects that operated in the
Netherlands after the fall of Münster, the new ideas gained ground among all
strata of society. The government's usual prudent administration of justice could
not prevent this. An ever widening circle of people responded to the spirit that was
mentioned before, being concerned not so much with a radical reshaping of
society, as the leaders of the anabaptists or radical sects were, nor with institutions

---

32 During a visitation in 1569 he stated he had the Trent resolutions proclaimed as soon as
   this was asked of him ('Verslagen van Kerkvisitatiën in het Bisdom Utrecht in de 16de
   Eeuw', *WHG* (1911), p. 59). On request of King Philip II he revised the Dutch translation of the Catechism by the Jesuit Petrus Canisius and had it published for the third
   time in 1576, *Batavia Sacra* (Antwerp, 1716), vol. II, p. 656.
33 During a visitation in 1569 Joachim van Oprode estimated the number of communicants
   at 8000, see the 'Verslagen van Kerkvisitatiën', *op. cit.*, p. 57.

and dogma as the later reformed church was, as with an inner devotion to God. The quest for a vital christianity was very strong in this century. Metaphors used of Jesus express this longing for the living Christ: the Word Incarnate, the Life Giving Water, the Fountain of Life. This all-pervasive search finds expression in many spiritual treatises, covering all angles of sixteenth century christianity. In the Netherlands it is nearly impossible to classify these people as being within or without the catholic church until the iconoclasm in 1566, with the exception of course of the radical anabaptists and the mennonites. As I said before, boundaries were very thin at this time and virtually non-existent. In his Dutch rhymed version of the psalter of 1534 the Utrecht nobleman Willem van Zuylen van Nyevelt asks a fatherly God to try him so he can purify his ways.[34] And in his *Play of the Christian Church* (1540) the rhetorician Reynier Pouwelsz. emphasizes that neither good deeds nor outwardly displayed belief matter, but only the intentions of the heart, the inwardly felt convictions: this is what God observes. The Holy Scripture can in his view be a guide on this path.[35] All these authors can be seen as representatives of that quest that already for so long had such a strong appeal in the Netherlands: truly to live according to Christ's example of charity.

. . . leading to growing dissent

While awareness grew, society was not likely to remain unaffected. In the 1550s people were less inclined to have their children baptised. In a public an-nouncement of 1551 the city council ordered the parents that had not had their children baptized, to do so immediately.[36] We know of mennonites preaching and baptising in the city.[37] In these decades prior to the iconoclasm at least eight conventicles had existed in the *Nedersticht* and its immediate surroundings.[38] In the end they were all dismantled. As mentioned before, the government did not allow any infringement of the structure of society, the unity of both citizenry and church having to remain intact. Most participants came off lightly though, as was mentioned before, having to do public penance only. Three men were put to death in the years immediately preceding the iconoclasm of 1566. One of them refused to abjure his dissident opinions. In this period we repeatedly find prison guards helping prisoners who were arrested for the sake of religion escape, sometimes even

---

34 W. van Zuylen van Nyevelt, *Souterliedekens*, s.l., 1540, the last verse of psalm 138. Another book by W. van Zuylen van Nyevelt is called *Die Fonteyne des Levens*, s.l., 1533. C.f S.J. Lenselink, *De Nederlandse Psalmberijmingen in de 16de eeuw* (Assen, 1959).

35 Reynier Pouwelsz., *'tSpel van de Cristenkercke*, c.1540, manuscript number 1336 at the university library of Utrecht. This view is strongly expressed in the prologue, cf. G.A. Brands, *Tspel van de Cristenkercke* (Utrecht, 1921).

36 Gemeentelijke Archiefdienst Utrecht, Stadsarchief I, n. 16, Buurspraakboek, f. 170, on 10 March 1551.

37 See the record of baptisms performed by Lenaert Bouwens, *BMHG*, vol. 36 (1915), pp. 39–71; *Doopsgezinde Bijdragen*, 1903, pp. 11, 13, 14, 39, 41, 42.

38 They will all be presented in my forthcoming thesis on religious affiliations in the city of Utrecht in the 16th century.

fleeing with them. Should we map the dissidents we should find that the mennonites formed the greater party before 1566.

Iconoclasm and revolt

The reform-orientated priests and the books that were being read prepared the minds of those who wanted a reformed church. In 1566 150 men and women were actively involved in the hedgepreachings around Utrecht. Once the iconoclasm found a response in Antwerp, on 20 August 1566, it flared out all over the Netherlands. It also reached Utrecht. In three days, from 24 to 26 August, the interiors of the four parish churches and the churches of the hated dominican and franciscan friars were demolished. The social background of iconoclasts all over the Netherlands showed many similar features. They did not come from the rabble of the populace, as is still too often assumed. Most of them were well-to-do craftsmen, the leaders being of noble rank.[39]

The issues at stake were not only of a religious nature, although we should not underestimate the impact of religion as a motive. What bound the participants together was a variety of dissatisfactions which found unifying force in the religious issue: the abhorrence of the religious policy of the Habsburg government as expressed in the heresy legislation or *plakkaten*, the – in Utrecht not so real – threat of the Inquisition, the many death penalties, notably in Antwerp, and Philip's unwillingness to relent. What also found expression in the iconoclasm was the resentment against the centralist policy of the Habsburgs. The transference of the temporal power over the Nedersticht to Charles V in 1528 had been experienced as a loss of autonomy. From that time the Estates of Utrecht had resisted any Habsburg intrusion in the field of jurisdiction, taxation and *privileges*.[40]

Alva's punishment

After an initial hesitation the Habsburg government fought back, forcing the leaders of the movement to flee, among them William of Orange and Hendrik van Brederode who had both backed up the reform movement.[41] The latter had even

---

39 For Utrecht read Sherrin Marshall Wyntjes 'The lesser nobility of Utrecht in the Revolt of the Netherlands', thesis (Tufts University, 1972), facsimile Ann Arbor, 1980. For Holland see H.F.K. van Nierop, *Van ridders tot regenten* (Amsterdam, 1990).

40 See note 3. Cf. Ferdinand H.M. Grapperhaus, *Alva en de tiende penning* (Zutphen, 1982), pp. 115–17.

41 It is often questioned whether Prince William of Orange was involved in the iconoclasm and early revolt. In Utrecht at least William took an active stand. In his capacity as *stadhouder* he stayed in Utrecht from 19 October until 15 December 1566 in order to restore peace in town. In this period he visited the well-known leader of the malcontented noblemen, Henrick van Brederode, Lord of Vianen, twice. Brederode in his turn visited William two or three times. In the same period William's brothers saw Brederode several times. On top of this William of Orange supported the Lord of Brederode with guns late in 1566. In Utrecht William lodged with a nobleman who had been a leader of the

attempted to initiate a revolt. With the arrival of the duke of Alva in 1567 severe punishment awaited the iconoclasts and the soldiers in Brederode's army. Many of them fled to England and Germany, Utrechters often finding refuge in the Rhine-countries. Those who had not fled were nearly all condemned to death or to serve in the galleys. The refugees were all banned for life. The goods of these people were confiscated. The aftermath of the iconoclasm can be seen as the starting point of the Dutch revolt.[42]

As war dragged on, less attention was paid to the issue of religion. Since 1569 the city of Utrecht had been heavily plagued by billeted soldiers who had to be lodged, fed and even paid. Religion was not on the magistrates' mind. In 1575 a priest was installed as pastor or *cureit* of the *Jacobikerk* by the name of Hubert Duifhuis, having already served as a *vicecureit* at the same parish in 1573. Yet this man was not without a reputation: in 1572 as pastor of St Lawrence's church in Rotterdam he was summoned for interrogation by the Inquisition. He fled rather than appear. Duifhuis was later said to have spiritually *libertine* opinions.[43] In Utrecht the responsible people must have known of his position, yet he was installed.

With the billeting continuing, life in Utrecht became very strained. There was the constant danger of looting and mutineering soldiers. The Utrecht people were being squeezed out to keep the soldiers contented.

Reaction

In this predicament Utrecht was ready for peace. Negotiations with the provinces in revolt, Holland and Zeeland, seemed the best way to provide this. However, their leader, William of Orange was looked upon with suspicion in Utrecht. His support in 1566/67 for the new religion and for the rebellious Lord of Brederode had not been forgotten. Yet he was the leader since 1572 of the successful revolt against the central government. In Utrecht also the anti-catholic policy pursued by the *Geuzen* was mistrusted. And yet, the loyal provinces had to come to terms with these forces in order to obtain peace. War on the side of the central government had brought too many risks and costs that people became less willing to bear.

iconoclasm in Utrecht, Jan van Renesse, Lord of Wilp. While in Utrecht William was looking for a rapprochement with the Utrecht protestants. In *Utrecht in 1566 en 1567* (Groningen/Batavia, 1932), A. van Hulzen strongly advocates the view that Prince William of Orange was openly supporting the iconoclasm and ensuing revolt and knew all along of the movement and intentions of the malcontented nobles, see chapters II, III and IV.

[42] For those readers who require further insight into this Revolt I recommend *Texts concerning the Revolt of the Netherlands*, ed. E.H. Kossmann and A.F. Mellink (Cambridge, 1974).

[43] The consistorialists called Hubert Duifhuis a *libertine*. This is another way of saying he held undogmatic views. Hubert Duifhuis can be rightly called a *spiritualist*. See both Alastair Hamilton, *Cronica, op. cit.*, and Benjamin J. Kaplan, 'Hubert Duifhuis', *op. cit.* In both these works the relationship between Henric Niclaes, the founding father of the Family of Love, and Hubert Duifhuis is elaborately dealt with.

In the absence of a Spanish governor, the Estates General started peace negotiations with Holland and Zeeland in 1576. In Ghent it was agreed that war should come to an end. Since the question of religion was one of the obstacles, it was decided that Holland and Zeeland could remain reformed. Once this treaty had been implemented, and thus the ties between all the Netherlandish provinces formally restored, Utrecht had to ensure itself that it would be effectively out of the warzone, regardless of how Philip would react to the treaty. This meant getting rid of the billeted soldiers. Siege was laid to the castle Vredenburg, the stronghold of the Spaniards in Utrecht. After three months the Spaniards surrendered. After another successful battle, this time with German mercenaries who had been lodged in the city, Utrecht was free of foreign soldiers in 1577. The only military force that remained was the *burgerwacht*, the guard consisting of Utrecht citizens themselves, of which a hard core happened to be devoted to the reformist cause, be it spiritual or reformed. The *burgerwacht* forced the Estates to conclude negotiations with William of Orange and to accept him again as a *stadhouder*. This was effectuated on 31 October 1577.

Catholic worship forbidden

Although William of Orange and the Estates aimed at establishing peace between the various denominations, which were now rapidly taking distinct shapes, this goal was not to be reached. The main cause was the war situation which perverted all internal relationships. 'Catholic' was associated with 'Spanish' and therefore with inquisition and betrayal.[44] The majority of the catholics had no way of defending themselves against this charge, as they were not so much advocating the counter-reformist cause, but rather continued the traditional type of catholicism, which was quite undogmatic, leaving room for local and personal preferences. Utrecht catholics did not submit to being subjugated without resistance, though. In the negotiations for the Union of Utrecht (1579), Utrecht catholics tried to introduce political guarantees that would safeguard catholic worship, once the Union between the revolting provinces had been established. The spokesmen of this so-called Counter-Union were, however, arrested and put in jail. The mastermind behind the movement, the *scholaster* of the chapter of Oudmunster, Jacob Cuynretorff, even remained in prison until the treaty was signed.[45] No guarantees for catholic worship were included in the final version of the Union. Tension between the various denominations however grew, fed by the war with Spain. When catholicism was officially abolished, in Utrecht in 1580, catholics were formally excluded from public functions. Catholicism was driven into the private realm, as all churches were taken from the catholics and no public worship was to take place. Catholic education was forbidden. And yet, being the largest denomination

---

[44] Cf. A. Duke, *Reformation and revolt, op. cit.*, pp. vii, xiii.
[45] See 'Stukken over den tegenstand der Utrechtsche katholieken, onder leiding van den scholaster van Oudmunster Jacob Cuynretorff, tegen de Unie van Utrecht', as assembled by P.L. Mulder, in *BMHG*, 9 (1886), pp. 393–472.

and having very influential people among its members catholicism *de facto* survived in Utrecht, as it did in other places where it could not be subjugated, yet
under a considerable financial strain and unfavourable conditions.[46]

Strife among the protestants

Among the protestants themselves relationships were very ambiguous. After the
Satisfaction with William of Orange had been concluded in October 1577, the
spiritualist Hubert Duifhuis started to worship in a moderately reformed fashion,
but without introducing a consistory, or internal discipline. In this decision he was
supported by some magistrates and captains and members of the *burgerwacht*. In
1578 the magistracy had not been willing to fulfil the urgent request of the
reformed people for a church of their own, where they could worship after their
own fashion. This group included the Utrecht refugees who had fled in 1567 but
had now returned, many of them having become staunch calvinists in the exile
communities abroad, as well as refugees from the Southern Netherlands. Of course
these people could not tolerate being harassed once again. Some of the captains
and members of the *burgerwacht* supported their appeal. When the magistracy was
not willing to grant a church, in August 1578 the reformed took what was not
being given to them, occupying the vacant church of the franciscan community
who as staunch catholics had been forced to leave the city some weeks before.
After the Treaty of Utrecht had been signed in January 1579, the reformed soon
started to officially celebrate communion. They then began recording their members.[47] They also set up a consistory from which they took the title consistorialists.
All along they felt a bitter resentment towards the parish of Hubert Duifhuis
which had such strong support from the magistracy and did not wish to adopt
ordained reformed institutions. Vehemently they fought its policy which they
considered to be *libertine*. When Leicester was captain-general of the Netherlands
he supported the reformed cause, in 1586 forcing the independent parish of St
Jacob's to become part of the consistory. Now this faction felt frustrated. When
Leicester had left the country and the magistracy that had been deposed was back
in power, they, in 1589, in one stroke dismissed all reformed parsons, including
the moderate ones. Thus the magistracy consolidated a breach within society that
was already hard to mend.[48]

Conclusion

Unity could not be maintained in this multi-religious society, one of the reasons
being that religion itself had become a political issue, and thus part of political
propaganda. After 1577 religion was a source of internal strife. And this was the
more so because none of the protestant denominations could assert themselves and

---

[46] Compare A.Th. van Deursen, *Bavianen en Slijkgeuzen* (Assen, 1974), pp. 129–160.
[47] Gemeentelijke Archiefdienst Utrecht, arch. Nederlands Hervormde Gemeente, 404, list of
members 1579–1589.
[48] See Benjamin J. Kaplan, *Calvinists and Libertines, op. cit.*

the catholics, although subjugated as a result of the war, were still the major economic force behind the political scene.

Since 1577 there had been repeated breaches in confidence between the city council and groups within society, which were not easily to be undone. To this should be added that the religious debate itself had hardened. Theological issues were being treated from the pulpit. Opponents, whether clergymen, magistrates or institutions could be personally attacked. In a way a schism had occurred within society. Initially the parsons whom the magistracy eventually appointed in 1590 did not receive the support of the reformed community. For years the situation remained strained, and this made it very difficult for the reformed church to consolidate its position. Due to internal and external debates, often made more difficult by an entanglement with theological issues, many reformed goals like the diaconate, education, and even internal discipline, did not get firmly rooted before 1620, all energy being devoted to arguing and surviving. It was only after stadtholder Maurice of Orange had in 1617 replaced the *libertine* inclined magistracy by a more orthodox council and after the Synod of Dordt had taken place in 1618–19, that the reformed church in Utrecht could begin to consolidate itself. Even then, in a society which was so divided between denominations, the catholics still being an important part of the populace, not only in number, but also in wealth, and the battle between reformed and remonstrants continuing, this was not an easy task.

Epilogue

Let us return to the question that was posed in the beginning: were historians justified in proclaiming that the reformation had triumphed totally in Utrecht? In my opinion, many of them looked upon the sixteenth century with the frame of mind that is characteristic of a nineteenth or twentieth century Dutchman, being acquainted with *verzuiling* or the compartmentalization of society into various religious denominations. They may have expected as clearcut a situation in Utrecht as in Holland and Frisia, where the anabaptists and also at a later stage the reformed had quite a strong following. As we have seen, this was not the case in Utrecht. Yet, this bias hindered a thorough investigation of the abundant, though dispersed, archival material. The record publications that ensued and the commentaries that were written upon them also betrayed this prejudice.[49] It hindered historians from seeing the specific nature of the early reformation in Utrecht,

---

49 For instance in the *BHG* 1851, a collection of *data* on the early reformist movement in
    Utrecht has been published. This record was the basis of later historical research. Of the
    events in 1534 only the abjuration of 4 heretics was listed in the *BHG*, but not the
    subsequent amnesty for 13 men and women who had actually been rebaptized. Until now
    all historians failed to detect them. Next to this there are many mistakes in the interpreta-
    tion of these recordings, due to the fact that the editors were not well enough informed on
    the situation in Utrecht. Later historians often repeated these mistakes, as they did not
    check the published data. Especially on the history of the early reformation in Utrecht
    there circulate many views which are simply not factual.

where a lively interest in humanist and evangelical ideas and ideals coincided with a tolerant and prudent government policy in religious affairs that consequently did not emphasize heretical events.[50] Only through new research in the archives could opinions be adjusted. This process led to a reevaluation of the actual functioning of the catholic church and to a new understanding of the impact of religion at a local level in an important sixteenth century Netherlandish city: more light was shed on the circulation of religious ideas and on the interaction between the authorities and the inhabitants of the city. In my opinion the advantage of this analysis is that it leads to a more nuanced appreciation of Dutch sixteenth century society. Put in relationship to present-day society, which is burdened by growing cultural and religious differences and conflicts, and above all by mutual misunderstanding, such a nuanced attitude is of great importance. It may help to get a more balanced view of the historical roots of internal relationships, and as a result put local events in a wider perspective.

---

[50] See note 11.

HUGH BOUDIN

Protestant Bankers and Financiers in Belgium: Max Weber Revisited

Some years ago the proceedings of two conferences touched the subject which we would like to deal with.

The first was the *Internationale Historikertag* held in Stuttgart in 1985[1] which dealt with Max Weber the historian. The participants were reminded that Weber started his career as a lawyer. He taught political economy and was a consultant to the German Armistice Commission at Versailles, but was later considered a sociologist although his approach was mainly historical: an early example of interdisciplinarity. The conference tried to go further than what is now the traditional and still the most debated study of Weber on Protestantism. Some considered it as a practical joke to include in the programme a paper about Weber methodology seen in taoistic perspective! Increased international attention has been devoted to Weber as an inspirational source for the history of society.

The second conference brings us even nearer to our topic. It was one of the numerous gatherings held to commemorate the Revocation of the Edict of Nantes. In *International Calvinism 1541–1715* Henry Lüthi contributed *Variations on a theme by Max Weber*, a shortened version of his previously published papers. Nothing essentially new transpired.

What did Weber really contribute?

In his two famous essays published in 1904 and 1905 Weber presented an interpretation of the historical relations between capitalism and reformed Protestantism, even extending his concept of ascetic Protestantism to include Puritans, Pietists, Methodists, Baptists and Quakers. For him it is the spirit of capitalism which enters into play, not the rational organization of labour geared to produce gain for the entrepreneurs.

The scope of this paper does not permit us to deal with what has been termed the *Weber thesis controversy* which still occupies historians, as a decisive pronouncement has still to be uttered on the subject.

In this controversy the arguments which have been marshalled for and against

---

[1] *Max Weber als historicus*, J. Kocka (ed.), Max Weber, der Historiker. Kritische Studien zur Geschichtewissenschaft 73 (Göttingen, 1986), 284 pp.

have been called 'the long and intense dialogue of Max Weber with the ghost of Karl Marx'. His source material, with an astonishing lack of primary sources, omits the strongholds of reformed Protestantism such as Geneva and Scotland and excludes also reformed correspondence and auto-biography. He does, however, use the literature of those considered to be Protestant casuists. Essentially the criticisms levelled at Weber's thesis concern the content of Protestantism and the definition of capitalism. In the view of certain critics Weber surrendered the particularities of history to the tyranny of the sociological model. Weber is credited with being the inventor of the ideal type as a means of highlighting patterns of behaviour, even if he, in a certain sense, is doing violence to historical reality.

Weber considers his topic only after 1600.

Even if capitalism – considered as the control of financial resources yealding riches as a result of speculation or money lending – is as old as history, even if capitalism predates Protestantism as Rachfall and Sombart have pertinently re-marked, Weber is looking for a new devotion to maximizing profits. The capitalist spirit was thriving in medieval Italy long before the Reformation and even in the Papal States as Jean Delumeau has shown with the alum mines of Tolfa. In the very heartland of catholicism, within 80 km. of Rome, 800 workers mined the precious mineral. The merchants of Florence and Genoa sold alum loaves to the whole of Europe including the Protestant nations and created a capitalist industry very important for the dyeing of cloth.[2]

Three Tests

Notwithstanding all the negative criticims of the Weber thesis, we nevertheless would like to test its validity by an enquiry of three different groups.

> 1. The Swedish Connexion,
> 2. The Geneva Connexion,
> 3. The Belgian group

The Swedish Connexion is composed of those entrepreneurs who came from the Low Countries in the sixteenth and seventeenth centuries and settled in the Sweden of Gustavus-Adolphus II. He bears our first crown.

The Geneva Connexion includes those financiers who, arriving from Switzerland, established their trade in the Austrian Netherlands (present day Belgium) and who, thanks to the timid liberalisation of religious freedom proclaimed by the *Toleranz Patent* of the Austrian Emperor Joseph II, settled there after 1782. He wears our second crown.

The third group of bankers did not leave Belgium, nor arrive in Belgium, they were in Belgium in the nineteenth and twentieth centuries partly during the reign of Leopold I. He presents our third crown. Unfortunately I am not able to produce a mitre: Presbyterians do not seem to favour such headgear.

---

2   Delumeau, J., *L'alun de Rome* (Paris, 1962).

Three groups, three periods and three tests of the Weber thesis.

To avoid resorting to a rather fastidious enumeration of names, a kind of reformed *Who's who*, in each instance we shall pick out a leading figure embodying its characteristics and follow up with some prominent members of the group.

The Swedish Connexion

The story starts in a dramatic way. On a dark evening of 1595, a barge covered with peat slowly floats down the river Meuse sailing from Liège to Dordrecht. In this vessel a family, two parents and four children, is hiding. A reformed Christian, Louis de Geer, is fleeing from the regime of the Prince-archbishop of Liège, Ernst of Bavaria. Louis de Geer, who later was called the Father of Swedish Industry was born on 17 November 1587 in Liège.[3]

Wanting to obey Gods will and desiring to organize his life de Geer decided at the start to involve God in his business. He wrote in his diary:

> I have taken the vow to consecrate to God 10% of all the Lord will let me acquire begging Him to help me with His Holy Spirit, preserving me from bad company and from all fraud , not granting me superfluous riches which would make me forget the Lord. May He above all etch His fear and His love in my heart.[4]

After his father's death and after having left Dordrecht for Amsterdam he entertained a lively trade relationship with Sweden and finally settled there in the mining district of Uppland at Finspång. He started making iron bars, copper plate and cable. He thanked the Lord for all the blessings for family and firm. Indulging in his audacious undertakings, he preferred to put his trust in God. On 15 May 1628 he wrote:

> We pray God that He may keep our vessels and bring them safely to port. We promise a bounty of one thousand florins to the poor.

No longer was he the money-lender counting his gold whilst his wife looked on, immortalized by the painting of Quentin Metsijs; Louis de Geer had become an international banker dealing with kings and states, and controlling the extensive network of his vast entreprises.

With the help of his compatriot and co-religionist Velam Gillison de Besche, de

---

3   There exists an idealized portrait of Louis de Geer in the simple dress of a Reformed gentleman which is a copperplate engraving by Jeremias Falck. Original in the Royal Library, Stockholm. Cfr Dahlgren, E.W., *Louis de Geer, 1587–1652. Hans liv och verk*, 2 vols (Uppsala, 1923).

4   The original French text is: J'ai fait vœu de consacrer à Dieu la dixième partie de tout ce que le Seigneur me ferait acquérir, le suppliant qu'il voulût m'assister de son Saint Esprit, me préserver de toute mauvaise société et contre toute fraude, ne point me donner des richesses superflues qui me fassent oublier le Seigneur et qu'il daignât graver avant toutes choses dans mon cœur sa crainte et son amour.

Geer modernized the manufacturing of iron products by introducing new machinery and improving techniques. As Sweden got deeply enmeshed in European politics and continental warfare, de Geer increased his production, going in for the making of cannon and other military material such as uniforms.[5]

In order to accomplish all his plans and to maintain his output, he needed an effective workforce. He sent emissaries to his native country, especially to Liège and Namur, to recruit smiths and metal workers for his forges. This provoked opposition in those provinces. The King of Spain, Philip IV, published a placard forbidding smiths from Namur to be recruited by these agents from Sweden as this would not only damage their own country but also endanger their souls.[6] This interdiction was repeated in 1627 because the recruiting had increased.

The Walloon emigration to Sweden was twofold: the leading industrialists and the technicians of the metal industry. In 1968 E. Appelgren identified 600 Walloon families.[7] In 1985 Bernt Douhan revised this estimate to 1,000 to 1,200 families including single individuals without family. About 20% seem to have returned after their first contract. The number of Swedes of Walloon origin is nowadays estimated at 50,000.[8]

The de Geer family also made investments of a cultural nature. They set up an extensive library of more than 30,000 books, which is still to been seen in Löfsta, the family castle in Uppland. They got together a collection of old masters, the biggest and the oldest in the country. De Geer built a chapel for the reformed congregation and saw to it that a pastor and a schoolteacher were at hand to effectively preserve faith and culture for the ensuing generation.

His partner Gilles de Besche thrived also and is reputed to have been one of the richest iron-masters in Sweden. Wilhelm van Wijck,[9] a resident of Antwerp between 1566 and 1571 before moving to Sweden, was a merchant who developed skills which made him in 1580, the highest supervisor for the Swedish Crowns Ironworks (*Kronones Järnbergsverk*) Dahlgren[10] thinks that van Wijck laid the foundations for the development of forges in Uppland, whilst Heckscher[11] estimates that the new drive which placed the Swedish metal industry on a world level, came from the Southern Netherlands of which its formost representative was Wilhelm van Wijck.[12]

5   Brzezinski, R. and Hook, R., *The Army of Gustavus Adolphus 1. Infantry*, Men-at-Arms Series, no. 235 (London, 1991).
6   6 mai 1624, A.E. Namur, fol. 239 (1602–1629), Conseil provincial.
7   Appelgren, E.W., *Vallonernas namn* (Stockholm, 1968).
8   Douhan, B., *Arbete, kapital och migration – Valloninvandringen till Sverige under 1600-talet*. Acta Universitatis Upsaliensis (Uppsala, 1985).
9   Kilbom, K., *Vem war Wilhelm van Wijck?* in *Vallonerna, Valloninvandringen, Stormaktsväldet och den Svenska Järnhanteringen* (Stockolm, 1958), pp. 151–67.
10 Dahlgren, E.W., *De upländska bruken Osterby, Forsmark, Leufsta och Gimo under äldre tider* (Uppsala, 1933).
11 Heckscher, E.F., *Sveriges ekonomiska historia fran Gustav Vasa*, Vol. I (Stockholm, 1935).
12 Kilbom, *op. cit.*, p. 166.

Johan Palmstruch (1611–1671), originally Hans Wittmacher, the son of an emigrant from the Low Countries, contributed two important features in banking. First he is credited with the invention of the bank note. He started by introducing credit letters as certificates for sums that clients had deposited. They were negotiable and produced interest. The inconvenience was that they were no longer valid after a certain date. Very soon Palmstruch discovered the principle of the bank note. He removed the interest and the prescription. This became Sweden's first paper money. His downfall was the release of too many bank notes. In 1668 he had to stop operations, being insolvent. In 1657 he received authorization to found the *Palmstruchska Banken* in Stockholm under state control. The privilege was granted for 30 years. His Bank was the origin of the Royal Swedish Bank, the *Riksens Ständers Bank*, which was to be the first Central bank in the world.[13]

The Geneva Connexion

On the world trading scene a Protestant Westphalian, Johan Bernhard Friedrich Romberg, became a sort of legend.[14] In 1759 after his marriage with Sophie Luise Huyssen, he made Brussels his commercial headquarters. He created a series of trading firms, one with his younger brother Christian the *Cie Romberg Frères*, later called *F. Romberg et Fils*. In 1762 the goods which he sold were mentioned as being merchandise from Silesia, Saxony and Persia, muslin, silk and wool. Slowly he moved from textiles to transport, bringing for example the steel production from Klagenfurt into the Netherlands.[15] In 1780 he acquired a cotton mill in Brussels, which was taken over later by the brothers Basse.

In 1782 Romberg is supposed to have had 94 vessels sailing the high seas with about 2,000 sailors manning these ships. He had offices in Ostend and in Ghent, he used the harbours of Le Havre and La Rochelle and sent his son to Bordeaux where a new firm was set up *Henry Romberg, Bapst et Cie*. He imported sugar from the West Indies and furnished building materials to the French Navy. He delved into a specific trade which then seemingly was acceptable, without much hesitation. He took up the slave trade. The first slave ship which left Ostend for Africa, called the *Marie-Antoinette*, could transport 290 negroes. Later Romberg armed 10 more ships, providing room for 5,000 slaves. He organized several trips to the Gold Coast and Guinea and to the French Islands of the Americas, especially Saint-Domingue. He also pursued trade relations with the young Republic of the United States where he had contacts in Carolina and Virginia. He spearheaded

---

[13] Meyer, J., *Les capitalismes*, Collection L'Historien, PUF (Paris, 1981). Origine du billet de banque, p. 162.
[14] *Le Voyageur dans les Pays-Bas autrichiens ou Lettres sur l'état actuel de ces Pays*; Lettres XII, Malines, ce . . . Avril 1783, 6 tomes (Amsterdam, 1782).
[15] Reininghaus, W., *Kooplieden uit Iserlohn in de Zuidelijke Nederlanden tijdens de achttiende eeuw*, in Handelingen der Maatschappij voor Gechiedenis en Oudheid te Gent, Nieuwe reeks, Deel XLIV, 1990, p. 145.

commerce for other traders opening up new fields of commerce. Romberg was a master in the art of camouflageing his ships to pose as neutral traders and thus avoid the inspection of the British Navy.

In Ostend a new Protestant Congregation was officialy instituted on 18 December 1783 with at its head a committee of five trustees which appointed a minister Dr John Trevor, lately from the parish of Otterhampton in Somerset. This creation was a direct consequence of the *Toleranz Patent* of Emperor Joseph II. When one peruses the Church Registers one finds names of Americans, Danes, Englishmen, Germans, Irishmen, Norwegians, Scots, Swedes, Swiss and Welsh, among whom are several bankers (William Herries, William Kerr and William Boyd).[16] This multinational and interconfessional congregation mainly, but not exclusively, catered for the needs of a commercial, maritime and financial constituency.

In 1782 pretending to be incognito the Emperor Joseph II visited the Austrian Netherlands. Everbody knew he was around, but kept up the fiction of his absence. He used this opportunity to have long conversations with Romberg and other merchants from Antwerp, Ostend and Brussels.

In Brussels the Romberg family participated in the life of the congregation which met on the premises of the Diplomatic Representative of the United Provinces. This was one way of getting around the interdiction of holding public Protestant services. It gave rise to the extra-territoriality first of the Embassy chapel, then of the whole Embassy buildings.[17]

The commercial success of the Austrian Netherlands owed a lot to the Romberg firm, whose head was the one who bore all the brunt and took all the risks. There was even a proposal to erect his statue for the development he gave to the activities of other merchants. Eventually, the Emperor made him a baron and granted him a coat of arms depicting a large sailing vessel. His letters patent were dated at Vienna, 28 July 1784.

When the Emperor declared Ostend a free port, he acknowledged that the memoranda of Frederic Romberg about this matter had served to convince him to have the fortifications and ramparts of the town levelled in order to increase the area of the docks. The war had attracted to Ostend many trading firms. In less than a year the number of broad and attractive streets had doubled, the spacious

16 Original Registers of the Anglican (Protestant) Church in Ostend, Austrian Netherlands, 1784–1794, 4 vols, paper, fo, 1. Baptisms, Marriages and Burials 1784–1786; 2. Baptisms 1787–1794; 3. Marriages 1787–1794; 4. Burials 1787–1794. Ms 10,457/1–4 in Guildhall Library, London. The Registers of burials are currently being published Boudin, H.R. (ed.), *The Register for the Protestant Parish of Ostend in the Austrian Netherlands*, in Biographies Protestantes Belges, L–14, pp. 1–19. The Registers also contain an account of the foundation of the chapel and parish and minutes of meetings of the Protestant inhabitants held at the English hotel in Ostend 1783–1785. This account has been published Boudin, H.R. (ed.), *The Protestant Chapel of Ostend in the Austrian Netherlands (1783–1794), ibidem*, L–14/2, pp. 1–4.
17 Boudin, H.R., *L'extraterritorialité des chapelles d'ambassades*, in Ad veritatem, no. 27, September 1990, pp. 42–48.

warehouses were full of goods from cellar to loft and the whole city thrived and boomed.

It was Romberg who, hearing about the political difficulties in Geneva, advised a group of important Genevese merchants to come to Brussels, where they could engage from a central location in their trade with the Netherlands, England, France and Germany.

Three main reasons existed for the influx of Genevese capitalists in the Austrian Netherlands.

1. The political situation in Geneva itself caused strongly opposed parties to clash, with the consequence that an important group of well-to-do financiers left the wide open lakescape of Geneva and headed some to Ireland, where their linen industrial settlement ended in a fiasco, and some to Constance on the shore of the Bodensee, where a watchmaker colony was established and vegetated for some years, and lastly to what is now present-day Belgium where they had a roaring success and became even more prosperous.

2. The religious situation in the Austrian Netherlands attracted the fugitives. Empress Maria-Theresa's son Joseph II, imbued with the ideas of the Enlightenment, gave the Protestant and orthodox citizens of his Empire freedom of worship, and granted permisson for the opening of Church buildings provided the exterior architectural decoration would not betray the religious use to which the buildings were being put. Existing semi-clandestine congregations came out from the shadows. In Brussels the Genevese Group practised freely their reformed religion. They had with them their own pastor, Isaac-Salomon Anspach, a forefather of a later famous Brussels burgomaster.

3. The choice of Belgium as a settling country was determined not only by the religious but also by the economic situation. The American War of Independence made the British Admiralty decree a blockade of the North American Colonies not only in respect of munitions but also in respect of timber, tar, seeds and vegetables.

However the neutral countries tried to uphold the axiom *Neutral flag makes neutral cargo*. From 1780 to 1783 nine countries (Austria, Denmark, France, Portugal, Prussia, Spain, Sweden, the Two-Sicilies, and the United Provinces) got together to form the *League of maritime neutrality of non-belligerant nations*. The Austrian Netherlands were in the hub of the conflict when France concluded a treaty of alliance with the young Republic of the United States and when Britain declared war on the United Provinces.

Two figures illustrate the importance of maritime trafic in Ostend. In 1778, 81 boats entered the harbour; in 1781 more than 3,000 sailed from it when it had been declared a freeport.

Ready to leave their country and homestead to stay faithful to their political opinions, these traders were anxious to remain true to their faith by ensuring the presence of a pastor capable of instructing them and their children in biblical knowledge and reformed doctrine. They did not hesitate to invest their accumulated capital in new ventures, applying their financial skills to fructify what they had already acquired.

One of them was Jacques Bidermann,[18] associated with his brother Antoine as a dealer in printed cotton goods, the so-called *indiennes*. Jacques had brought the textile industry over from east Switzerland to Geneva where he boosted the manufacture of printed calico. The political situation forced him to leave the city in 1782 because of the Genevese Revolution of 8 April 1782 and its repression by the French troops on 2 July. He started a commercial establishment in Brussels and worked closely with his compatriots Etienne Claviere, Jean-Jacques Claviere, François Gros and Pierre-François Vieusseux. Bidermann was even accused by Bonnal des Granges of being Jewish in the group of speculators and officials guilty of misappropriation (*un individu israélite dans la tourbe des agioteurs et concussionnaires aux armées*). Some historians – if you choose to call them so – always seem to find a Jew in the background, others uncover a Genevese lurking in a dark conspiracy.[19]

Thanks to the advice of Romberg, the Swiss concentrated their living quarters in a residential part of the city at the rue Ducale on the border of the Royal Park, which become known as the *Quartier des Suisses*. It was and still is the fashionable place to live, including the residences of the Swiss and British ambassadors to Belgium.

A list dated 30 December 1785 gives us the occupancy of the different lodges in the covered market of Brussels held by the merchants. Numbers 1 and 2 are for Romberg, 3 and 4 for Jean-Théodore Rivier & Cie, a subsidiary of the Genevese firm Plantamour, Rillet & Cie, 5 for the Brothers Overmann with offices in Ostend headed by Guillaume Deonna, a Genevese associate, 6–7 Pourtales & Cie from Neuchâtel, 8–9 for Senn, Bidermann & Cie.[20] All this activity was in the hands of Protestant merchants whose trade was really extra-territorial moving between Ostend and Germany, France and Switzerland.[21]

Their activity has to be placed in front of the backdrop of an essentially agricultural economy. The government, as we have seen, favoured Ostend as a port of national and international importance unaffected by the closure of the Scheldt and the paralysis of Antwerp. Their trade thrived even if the opportunities for big

---

18 Lüthi, Henri, *La Banque Protestante en France de la Révocation de l'Edit de Nantes à la Révolution*, vol. 2, pp. 667–73. Born in 1751 at Winterthur, he died in Paris in 1817.

19 Lüthi, *ibidem*, p. 629, note 63.

20 Lüthi, *ibidem*, pp. 668–69.

21 Other names of Genevese traders and financiers are: Bethmann, Meinicken & Overman, Bordeaux; Bidermann Jacques from Winthertur; Boyd Walter, trader in Brussels; Claviere Etienne; Claviere Jean-Jacques; Deonna Guillaume, trader in Ostend; Gros François; Herries Guillaume; Herries Keith & Cie trader in Ostend; Keith Georges & Cie, trader in Ostend; Odier Antoine Jacques, trader in Ostend; Odier Jean-Louis Lombard, trader in Brussels and Geneva; Overmann frères, trader in Ostend; Riviere-Vieusseux, trader in Ostend and Brussels; Roman Jacques, trader in Geneva and Brussels; Sautter Jean-François, trader in Geneva and Brussels; Senn-Bidermann, trader in Geneva and Brussels; Vieusseux Pierre-François.

scale capitalist enterprises were curtailed by the lack of funds. The nobility, the landed gentry and the clergy were infinitely better off and better provided with capital than the merchants or industrialists. None of them were, however, willing to invest in these entreprises and were reluctant to entrust their money to Protestant financiers. Against these odds, this group of rich entrepreneurs, keen to use technical improvements, helped banking in its infancy and forshadowed the industrial revolution.[22]

Unfortunately jealousy erupted among the indigenous traders. The Protestant merchants were obliged to send a delegation to Vienna to lodge a complaint against the quibbling and chicanery of the excise department, to whom false reports of smuggling had been leaked. The outcome of this long struggle resulted in the lifting of all their privileges – but by then the Genevese were already packing to return to Geneva which welcomed them back.

The Belgian Group

The third group is chosen because of the minority situation of Protestantism in Belgium. The nineteenth century is pinpointed, because it was only then that Protestantism in Belgium was able to enjoy complete freedom.

May I introduce Jacques Engler? He is a classical example of an entrepreneur according to Weber. As a member of an important group of industialists, insurance brokers, ship owners, traders and bankers, he mixed financial acumen with Protestant faith.[23]

In seeking associates for new endeavours as well as for matrimonial alliances, the members of this socio-religious group wove a network of relationships so as to ensure simultaneously the preservation of wealth and the maintenance of reformed religion. Marriages permitted them to keep their wealth in a circle of trusted colleagues and friends.[24]

---

22 Kossmann, R.H., *The Low Countries 1780–1940*, p. 51.
23 Boudin, H.R., *Engler Jacques*, in Biographie Nationale publiée par l'Académie royale des Sciences, Lettres et Beaux-Arts de Belgique, tome XL (Bruxelles, 1978), cols 6–12.
24 Other members of this entrepreneurs, industrialists and bankers group were: Anspach Frédéric, Balser Charles, Basse Frédéric Chrétien, Borel Frédéric, Born George Hartmann, Brugmann A.V.M., Brugmann Fréderic G.A., Bunge Edouard, Cockerill Charles James, Cockerill John, Duden Guillaume, Ellermann Abraham, Ellermann Charles Frederic, Faber Frédéric, Fester Geo Henri Emile, Flemmich A., Grellet Jacques, Guillaume Jean, Jones Henri, Kreglinger Alfred Eugène, Kreglinger Alfred Thédore, Kreglinger Auguste Fréderic, Kreglinger Chrérien, Kreglinger Théodore Paul, Kreglinger Gustave, Lausberg Jean-Pierre, Lemme Chrétien Liévin, Luning Diederich, Lynen William, Marsily William James, Mertens Louis Joseph, Mettenius Jean Guillaume, Morel Auguste, Overman Jacques, Overman Gustave Adolphe, Overman Henri Jacques, Peltzer Auguste, Peltzer Edouard Henri, Rahlenbeck Chrétien Guillaume, Rivier Theodore, Romberg Maurice, Ronstorff Jean-Englebert, Schumacher Félix, Schumacher Henri Georges, Schumacher Thierry Ernest, Stuttberg Jean-Pierre, Van Goethem Guillaume.

Jacques Engler knew how to appreciate the talent and encourage the zeal of his co-workers. He helped several to acquire their own personal fortunes. He was quick to grasp the economic potentialities of an enterprise. He contributed to the commercial and industrial development of Belgium at a decisive moment. In the first half of the nineteenth century the increasing dependancy of technology on the full expansion of capital, highlights his contribution as a significant financial developer.

Engler cames from the Eifel region in the east of Belgium straddling the German-Belgian frontier. His family moved deeper into the country and set up its textile firm in Verviers, the leading centre for wool processing. His career showed the evolution from trader to industrialist and then onwards to banker. At each step he put to use his wealth accumulated during his previous occupation. His vast experience made him a useful person to know. King William I of the United Kingdom of the Netherlands consulted him. The king pursued a policy of encouragment to the founding of new industries and the opening of an important market in the Dutch Asiatic colonies. He created the *Société générale pour favoriser l'industrie nationale* which still exists to day. The sovereign was its principal shareholder; he consulted Engler for advice on how to proceed successfully.

As a supple and subtle manufacturer Engler was able to weather political storms from the Napoleonic era, to the independent Kingdom of Belgium and through the Belgian-Dutch united regime.

Leopold, the first King of the Belgians, also often invited Engler to participate in working dinners organized at the Brussels Royal Palace. Engler was elected senator and was the first Protestant member the Belgian Parliament had in the 1840s.

In order to assert a socio-professional picture of Belgian Protestantism, an analysis of official census returns has been made. The available statistical material giving the possibility of comparing profession with confession is dated 1816 and 1829, during the United Kingdom of the Netherlands and 1835 and 1842 during the Kingdom of Belgium.

The archives of the city of Brussels show that in 1816 its population was 70,735 strong and the Protestant percentage was 0.63. The lowest percentage in the rather poor Section III was 0.23 and the highest in the well-to-do section VII with 1.25.[25]

The number of Protestants, including Lutherans and Anglicans as well as the reformed majority was

in 1816	447
in 1829	2,228
in 1835	416
in 1842	1,058.

25 Archives de la Ville de Bruxelles, Recensements 1816: 5 tables; 1829: 8 tables; 1835: 7 tables; 1842: 8 tables.

The Revolution of 1830 drove many away. Twelve years had to pass before their number reached half of those present in 1829. Census returns show that 20% of the male Protestant population were active in non-manual professions (liberal professions, proprietors, bankers, doctors, etc.). This was higher than the overall Brussels average.

Concluding Remarks

It has been said that Protestantism only let capitalism develop in as far as it lost its religious fervour and that in the Protestant bourgeoisie the religion of work took over and replaced the religion of the Reformers, so that in being unfaithful to Calvin's theology, the reformed Christian merchant became capitalist.

In Belgium there seemed to be no lack of commitment on the part of the reformed businessmen and financiers as they identified with the Protestant congregations and were willing to be elected onto the different church councils. It would have been far more convenient for financial activities to blend with the prevailing confession and to dissappear among the majority. This did not happen and they went out of their way to be known as members of a minority group. So the balance between the weakening of faith feeding the capitalist strain is not applicable in these test cases, especially the last.

Although his thesis made a big impression, Weber of course was not the first to have linked Protestantism to capitalism. Bossuet had already formulated it in his *Traité de l'usure*. So this was not a new discovery of historians, but evidence perceived afresh by observers of economic questions.

Protestant ethics as well as the capitalist spirit have taken form in real human beings of flesh and blood whom we cannot reduce to their religious beliefs nor to their professional occupation. They have tried to bring these elements together and sought to reconcile them, if need be. We cannot forget that the Reformation also had its Lutheran and Anglican forms with an equally decisive impact on the economy: the confiscation of church property, the dissolution of the monastries, and the secularization of assistance to the poor.

What the Reformation brought into the lives of its believers was what has been called the secularization of holiness. This discipline does not apply to the happy few who have taken vows, but ideally speaking to the whole of society. There is no longer a functional separation between those who pray and those who work. There is no longer a hierarchy between those high up who keep their hands clean in prayer and those who down below dirty themselves, even if it is with the counting of gold coins.

The idea now is that working is also praying. Service to fellow men becomes worship to God in a life of faith.

The house of the Lord has many dwellings, it now contains a workshop, a shipyard, a forge, a cannon foundry and a dockyard.

In the sixteenth and seventeenth century all Protestants were far from being capitalists, but many capitalists were Protestant more than the average in the population as a whole.

ANNE OAKLEY

Archbishop Laud and
the Walloons in Canterbury

On 13 April 1635 William Somner, registrar of the diocese of Canterbury, stood
before the commissary court under the north west tower of Canterbury cathedral
with William Kingsley, archdeacon of Canterbury, and Prebendary John Jeffray.
Also present were the Dean, Isaac Bargrave, and Prebendary Thomas Jackson, two
of Archbishop William Laud's commissaries for the metropolitical visitation; John
Bulteel and Philip Delmé, ministers of the Canterbury Walloon church with John
de Bever and Quintin Galmar, the elders there; and Gaspar van Nierne, minister
of the Dutch church in Sandwich with two elders, Peter Maes and Isaac Rickeseys.
There was no-one from the Dutch church in Maidstone.

The commissaries handed Somner a mandate from the Archbishop and ordered
him to read it. The mandate read as follows:

> . . . The two injunctions of William Laud, archbishop of Canterbury, concern-
> ing the Dutch and Walloon Churches within his diocese Anno 1635. 1. That all
> natives of the Dutch and Walloon Congregations in his Graces diocese are to
> resort to their severall parish Churches wherein they inhabit, to heare divine
> servise and Sermons, and performe all duties as parishioners required in that
> behalfe; 2. That the Ministers and all others of the Dutch and Walloon Congre-
> gations which are not Natives, and born subjects to the Kings Majesty, or any
> other strangers that shall come over to them, while they remaine strangers, may
> have and use their owne discipline as formerly they have done; yet it is thought
> fit that the English liturgy should be translated into French and Dutch for the
> better fitting of their children to the English government . . .

After the reading the commissaries ordered the ministers, priests and elders of
their respective congregations to conform, and to warn all the parishes in Canterbury and Sandwich to receive them as if they were parishioners.

On 26 September following Somner sent a note of these proceedings to the
Archbishop as proof that his order had been carried out, which was recorded in his
register. And in the following October, Anthony Denis, the Clerk to the Canterbury Politic Men met the Canterbury congregation to explain that it was not the
king's intent, nor of the Council of State to dissolve their congregation. Natives of
the first degree were to continue members of the congregation but natives after the
first descent were enjoined to obey the Archbishop's injunction and conform

themselves to the English discipline and liturgy, 'everyone in his parish; without inhibitting them notwithstanding, that they may resort sometimes to our Assemblies.' Denis continued, 'My Lord Archbishop of Canterburie's Grace meanes notwithstanding that the said Natives shall continue to contribute to the maintenance of the Ministry and of the poore of their Church for the subsisting thereof; and promiseth to obtain an order from the Counsell if need be, and they require it to maintaine them in their manufactures against those that would trouble them by informations.' He ended, 'All which is notified unto you, that none may pretend ignorance and thereby fall into inconveniences.'

These negotiations had been in progress since Laud's first metropolitical visitation of 1633 when he had issued an enquiry to discover how many strangers there were in his diocese, and what liturgy they used. Fear of dissolution led the ministers to confer together and practise delaying tactics of all sorts, demanding time to compose their answers. There were three foreign churches in Kent at this time: the Walloon church which met in the crypt of Canterbury cathedral; and the two Dutch churches in Maidstone and Sandwich.

In most of the negotiations it was Canterbury which took the lead. Sandwich followed; but Maidstone collapsed. In his return to the Archbishop, Somner reported in April 1635 that the commissaries had not called on the Dutch church in Maidstone, 'because they are informed that they have broken up their congregation on the former monition [of 1633], and all resort to the English Church, being but a few of them and having abode so long among the English, that they are hardly to be known by face or language from them'.[1] Somner added, however, that he thought the Maidstone church had capitulated because it could not afford to pay for a minister, and had taken the path of least resistance.

What led to this state of affairs where a disciplined refugee group which had been well received and had been practising its own religion under the aegis of the Crown for the past 60 years or so, should again have found itself persecuted, this time by its former benefactors?

The answer is complex. One might say times change. It lies in the characters and ideals of two persons, Charles I and his archbishop of Canterbury, William Laud; to a certain extent in the attitudes of the refugees themselves, and of the Mayor and Corporation of Canterbury; and the economic position of Kent.

Charles I was a generally well-intentioned man, but weak. As with many of his European contemporaries, he was always in debt and looking for ways out of an impossible situation. At the beginning of his reign Charles had been quite prepared to renew Edward VI's charter of 1550 of freedom to practise their own religion and trades to the refugee strangers in his kingdom, as his predecessors had done, but failed to keep his word when his archbishop persuaded him that those same refugees were nothing but spies and informers.

Catholics were feared, and the king had married a French princess, Henrietta Maria, daughter of Henri IV, in 1625. Despite her ancestry, she was undoubtedly

---

1   *Calendar of State Papers Domestic 1635* (London, 1865), p. 26.

a Roman Catholic with no love for the Calvinists. Some men about the court, Sir Thomas Windebanke, one of the king's principal secretaries of state, for instance, and one of the Privy Council, were known and tolerated catholics. John Bulteel, the Canterbury minister, firmly believed that Laud intended to reintroduce the Roman faith. In his narrative of the proceedings with the foreign churches, admittedly written some time later, he wrote of 'the malice and disaffection of the Archbishop of Canterbury to the Dutch and French Churches in this Kingdome which stood in his way, intending to the dissipation and exstirpation of them, so that his fine designe of bringing Popery might have taken effect and surefooting in religion'.[2]

The activities of merchant factors in the port of Dover supported Bulteel's idea. There were considerable numbers of French, both catholic and Calvinist living in Dover who when presented for entertaining strangers in their houses, not attending church, nor receiving communion, fell back on the excuse that they were factors in the port exempt as subjects of the king of Spain, and freed by the articles of peace between the kings of England and Spain. More seriously, in June 1637 twelve inhabitants of St Mary Dover, some accompanied by their wives, but all strangers borne out of England, were presented 'for being at Mass at the house of Thomas Garrett dwelling at the Signe of the George . . .' They all replied that 'the Queene of Englands Bishopp comming from London to Dover to pass beyond the Seas . . . did say Masse' in Mr Garrett's house, and each one of them 'heard it, he being a stranger borne, a subject of the king of Spaine and a factor for the merchants beyond Seas'.[3]

It may have been true that the merchants and their factors were protected catholics, but some at least who entertained them, Mantle, Hugesson and Bing, were Calvinists who had been refugees in Canterbury for some years. These isolated cases do not prove that Dover was a den of recusancy, but it does go some way to point the problem of the presence of catholics in the port who may have been in contact with Calvinists coming from and going to France. If they were not catholics or spies, they may well have been informers.

William Laud first came into contact with the refugee congregations when he was bishop of London, and he had no love for them. His dislike of them is well documented. He told the king that they were 'great nurseries of inconformity' and as such a danger to the kingdom. He spoke slightingly of the way they conducted their communion services, 'that their churches used irreverence at their communion' and 'sat altogether as if it were in a tavern or alehouse with their hats on their heads'. As indeed they did. During his 1633 visitation of the Canterbury diocese, the churchwardens of St Mildred, Canterbury presented 47 persons 'that sit with their hats on in service time'.[4] Not all of them were strangers, and this served to

2 B. Magen, *Die Wallonengemeinde in Canterbury von ihrer Gründung bis zum Jahre 1635* (Frankfurt/M, 1973), p. 257 note 12.
3 Canterbury Cathedral Archives (hereafter cited as CCA) Z.4.6, fo 65.
4 CCA X.6.10, fo 238.

reinforce the archbishop's view that the manners of the refugees were affecting the native English to no good purpose.

From an early date Laud opposed the prevailing Calvinist theology. 'A parity they would have, no bishop, no governor, but a parochial consistory and that should be lay enough too' he argued in a sermon at the opening of Parliament in 1626, and continued, '. . . first this parity was never left to the Church by Christ; he left Apostles, and disciples under them. It was never in use with the Church since Christ; no Church ever, anywhere (till this last age) without a bishop'.[5] He again expressed his intolerance of any diversity of views within the church in a speech in the Star Chamber on 16 June 1637 at the censure of John Bastwick, Henry Burton and William Prynne[6] which was circulated throughout Europe.

Puritan opposition was aroused by Laud's conviction that the communion table, and not the pulpit, was the centre of the church; his insistence on the fixing of the communion table at the east end of the churches; and his attempt to stamp out the practice of appointing puritan lecturers, who preached but were not compelled to read the services to which they objected, made him easy ammunition for his enemies who saw in it more than was perhaps intended.

Everitt points out that there was at first little united opposition to Charles I in Kent. There was economic complaint among the clothiers, but generally speaking little agrarian opposition among the farmers and gentry in what was a prosperous county. None of the Kent members of the Long Parliament was of much conse-quence politically with the exception of Sir Edward Dering, and there was no dominant county family around which any rebellion might localise.[7] Apart from the gifted Sir Edward Dering, who might have led the ecclesiastical opposition, men like Sir Peter Heyman of Somerfield, Sir Dudley Digges of Chilham Castle, Sir Edward Boys of Fredville Court and Sir Edwin Sandys of Northbourne Abbey were motivated by family concerns alone, particularly in respect of the collection of Ship Money.[8]

There were powerful puritan groups, but according to Everitt, the type of puritanism to be found in Kent seems to have been less clear cut that was to be found elsewhere. Ecclesiastical discontent came to the fore on Laud's appointment as archbishop in 1633 but was directed not specifically at Laud, but at the consequences of his acts. It was felt that he did not understand Kent, or was too impatient to do so.

Laud himself feared that the Walloons in Kent with their undoubted privileges would become the target of an opposition party, as they had in France in earlier

5 R. Gwynn, *Huguenot Heritage, the History and Contribution of the Huguenots in Britain* (London, 1985), p. 54.
6 William Laud, *A Speech delivered in the Star Chamber XVIth of June MDCXXXVII at the censure of John Bastwick, Henry Burton and William Prinn* (London, 1637).
7 Sir Edward Dering represented Dover in Parliament during the early part of the reign of Charles I. He owned property in many of the parishes around Dover.
8 A. Everitt, *The Community of Kent and the Great Rebellion 1640–60* (Leicester, 1966), pp. 62–64.

religious conflicts. He complained to the king that there were 'yet very many refractory persons to the government of the Church of England about Maidstone and Ashford',[9] and that those who believed in parity would never support the monarchy in the state. In consequence he intended to hinder schism in Kent before it became a problem.[10]

But he failed to understand the consternation his actions would cause among the Walloon and the Dutch churches, or to recognise that there was in reality little need for uniformity, or indeed conformity. For the refugees their faith was not only a matter of the heart, but a way of life. It lay outside the law by charter. It is small wonder that faced with the demands of an archbishop who saw uniformity as a way of purifying the Church of England and ridding it of opposing sects, that the refugee congregations were concerned about their future.

After the dissolution of the religious houses in Canterbury, the city had been left in a parlous state. Local industries and tradesmen had lost the major part of their steady custom; the city had lost its place as a European centre of pilgrimage; and no pilgrims came to the shrine of Thomas Becket or other holy places. Admittedly such visits had been tailing off over the past 100 years or so prior to the dissolution; the 1420 jubilee had attracted barely 600 pilgrims, but in the following years numbers dropped to less than 50. Lodging houses and dwellings were empty. There was also unemployment.

Against this background the city had petitioned the crown for a refugee community, such as had been settled at Sandwich before 1561 and Maidstone in 1567, to boost its economy. Eventually a group settled in Canterbury in 1574. They were allowed to set up their own churches and to ply their trades without having first served an apprenticeship, but by toleration or the payment of a small yearly fine. Because these alien churches were an effective link with protestant churches in Europe and acted as their own welfare agencies, the government and the city was happy to see them flourish.[11] Although circumscribed by the inhibitions placed upon them by the English (particularly in Canterbury) with regard to trading, imposed for fear of competition with trades in which the English specialised, many like the Six and Lepine families became wealthy and acted as money lenders to the English as well as their own merchants.[12]

It is highly doubtful, however, that it was the intention of the refugees to remain permanent exiles, and in this lies part of their own problem. They had fled from religious persecution in France and Flanders, but large numbers of them retained their family properties in Europe, often visited them, certainly drew rents from them, and bequeathed them in their wills to other members of their families. Michael le Grand of Holy Cross, Canterbury had a house in Leauwerke in

9   C.W. Chalklin, *Seventeenth Century Kent, A Social and Economic History* (London and Southampton, 1965), p. 225.
10   See Gwynn, *op. cit.*, p. 54.
11   See G Davies, *The Early Stuarts 1603–1660* (Oxford 1952), pp. 70–110.
12   See inventories for these families in the Centre for Kentish Studies, Maidstone (hereafter cited as CKS).

Flanders.[13] Catherine Brills was not provided for in the will of her husband Adrian van de Brooke in 1607 because she already had her own inheritance in Flanders.[14] Catherine de Thoor and John Verbruge of Sandwich had property in Ypres and Zealand.[15] Mary le Houcq of St Mildred, Canterbury had interests in Calais, Guines and Marke in Flanders;[16] and Matthieu Jombart of St Peter, Canterbury had goods in Richebourg which he had divided in his will between his children.[17] Others indicated in their wills that their Flemish property was to be divided according to the custom of the particular town or castelry where it lay, and there are several references to the customs of Belle in Flanders.[18]

Evidence from the Canterbury congregation deacons' accounts suggests that there was considerable traffic to and from the continent, and most notably between 1630–1647 when many of these *passants*, as they were called, were given money for their journeys. The deacons give names and numbers of persons travelling through Canterbury to and from the continent of Europe to Holland, France and Antwerp, as well as to other cities in England. In September 1632 Pia Louche went back to Holland with her children to rejoin her husband. In April 1635 Jacques de Wuider, his wife and three children on their way to St Christophe landed at St Pierre where one of the children died. They were given 4s and lent a further 6s to go back to France. Men, women and children, poor students, ministers, even some friars minor who had renounced catholicism and joined the calvinist church at Dieppe, were helped on their way.[19] These are references to those who could not afford to travel without help. There were probably many more who could.

Many refugees had relatives in France and Flanders with whom they kept in constant contact. Gilles Guerin of Canterbury had a son Peter in Holland.[20] Michelle Nutient of St Mildred, Canterbury had a brother Peter and two sisters Joan and Margaret living in Flanders;[21] Parnelle Parren of St Mary Magdalene, Canterbury, a widowed sister Franchoise living in Tournai;[22] and Jane Vassell of St Mary Northgate, Canterbury a brother James abroad.[23] Willemine Caesteker of Sandwich had relatives on her mother's side in Kemmele in Flanders, and a relative of her father's, Peter de Caesteker living at Belle in Flanders who drove a waggon between Belle and Ryssell.[24]

Some of these people went home, but others took their places on the understanding that they too would always have freedom of worship under the charter of King Edward VI. In such a situation the refugees were living in an ideal world. There was no reason to integrate with the English if they did not intend to stay,

13 CKS PRC16/227/1394, 1639/40.
14 CKS PRC16/130, 1607.
15 CKS PRC16/154, 1614/15; 233/A134, 1637.
16 CKS PRC16/226/A1365, 1640.
17 CKS PRC16/130, 1607/8.
18 CKS PRC16/155, 1616 for instance.
19 CCA U47 C1, 2.
20 CKS PRC16/175, 1622/3.
21 CKS PRC16/150, 1612.
22 CKS PRC16/168, 1620.
23 CKS PRC16/171, 1621.
24 CKS PRC16/155, 1616.

and could travel backwards and forwards at will maintaining a base in both England and Europe.

An enquiry carried out by the London church in the early seventeenth century found that many had taken the opportunity offered by the war to travel abroad and trade in peace, and see a bit of the world outside Europe.[25] There is no reason to suppose that some of them did not come to Canterbury for the same reasons. As early as 1582 the Canterbury City Corporation had been concerned at the large numbers of refugees living in the city and had decided to send away all those who had come, not for conscience sake, but to escape the war. In this they were supported by the Weavers company[26] but the move had little effect.

If one assumes a steady growth in the population of Canterbury, there were probably just over 6000 persons living in the city in 1633. Of these, according to Bulteel, 1080 were members of the French church in Canterbury. The official return states that there were 900, but these were probably the adult communicants. There were 500 Dutch in Sandwich and 50 Dutch in Maidstone. Canterbury was the largest refugee group outside London where there were 1400 Walloons and 840 Dutch refugees.[27]

Those refugees who were received in Canterbury were allowed to practise their manufacture of textiles without serving an apprenticeship, but were not allowed to become freemen of the city. Between 1550 and 1649 no French or Dutch names occur in the lists of freemen, although there are considerable numbers of weavers, woollen drapers and linendrapers, as well as nine silkweavers. The freedom was kept exclusively for the natives. Aliens could not buy or marry into it, nor be given it. Nor in consequence could they inherit it. Some did try to become freemen but were rigidly excluded. There are no alien freemen by apprenticeship until the 1670s. This exclusion seems to be peculiar to Canterbury. In Norwich the strangers did enter the system in the second generation so that by 1675 Robert Taylor and Francis Barton could move to Chester from Norwich only on the 'assurance of their being made freemen.'[28] This exclusion left the Canterbury refugee community totally outside its local government. They were allowed no vote or say in city administration and their sole liaison with it was through the twelve Politic Men. Since there was nothing they could do about the system, this encouraged the refugees to think of themselves more as a separate unit rather than otherwise.

Intermarriage might have solved the problem, and it was one of Laud's major annoyances that the strangers did not intermarry with the English. In London, and particularly in Canterbury intermarriage was frowned upon by the refugee community. Those who did attempt to marry with the English were brought before their consistory and admonished. Canterbury marriage contracts suggest that the number of marriages contracted between refugees in the first and second

25 E. Kerridge, *Textiles in Early Modern England* (Manchester, 1985), p. 230.
26 CCA Burghmote book 1582, p. 44; and Kerridge, *op. cit.*, p. 230.
27 Chalklin, *op. cit.*, p. 10; and *CSP Domestic 1640* (London, 1880), p. 526.
28 Kerridge, *op. cit.*, p. 232.

generations was far larger than in the third. This process was reinforced by the City Corporation who refused to allow strangers to intermarry with the daughters of freemen, and so enter that privileged group of citizens who could trade freely. Left to themselves, those in the third generation might have readily intermarried had not Laud's interference caused a temporary tightening of the rules within the Canterbury congregation. When intermarriage became commoner in the early eighteenth century, the inevitable happened, and many strangers joined the ranks of the freemen.

The strangers had always supported their own poor and so relieved the city of the problem. When Archbishop Laud ordered that the strangers should join their local parish churches, and by inference, break up their local congregations, the city assumed that it would be responsible for the foreign poor as well. It is therefore hardly surprising that the city Corporation did all it could to support the walloon textile industry; it took away the need for the refugees to be supported by their parishes. In their petition addressed to Archbishop Laud in 1634 the Corporation pointed out that the Walloons spent more than £153 yearly on the relief of their poor, a sum which the city could not afford. Greater charges would fall on the parishes, especially the poorer ones, which might prove dangerous, 'the English poor being all ready to quarrel with them' for fear of competition in relief. In addition, the city claimed that many poor persons would be put out of work, and that 'Many inconveniences will also arise in the way of trading, to the danger of overthrowing trades of which no Englishman in their city has ever had any knowledge.'[29]

Laud dismissed the allegation that many poor would be put out of work. He thought it ungrounded and that it had nothing to do with the injunctions. He was, however, concerned about provision for the poor, and determined that the strangers should continue to provide for their poor as they had always done while also contributing to their parishes.

The city of Canterbury was divided into four quarters by the Walloon administration: London, North, Dover and Rie. Each quarter had about 200 families, though there were more in North which was the poorest area. In comparison with the £153 raised by the Walloons in 1634, the scale of poor relief in the English parishes was extremely small. Unfortunately there are few figures prior to 1642, but for the years 1642–1650 in Holy Cross parish, for instance, an average of just over £30 a year was raised for poor relief.[30] In any year the largest sum was £53 18s 8d. The average payment was 6d a week, whereas the Walloon deacons often offered as much as 2s a week or more.

The Walloons were almost certainly the largest employer of labour in Canterbury in the seventeenth century. In 1630 they employed 1000 jersey spinners; and in 1636 in Holy Cross parish alone 150 spinners, mostly poor English. Because

29 *CSP Domestic 1635* (London, 1865), p. 77, 19 May 1635.
30 J. Campbell, *The Walloon Community in Canterbury 1625–1649* (Wisconsin, 1970), p. 99.

they worked outside the apprenticeship system, they could use labour more flexibly, and inevitably pay less. Crop failures in the 1630s had driven up the prices of wheat and barley to famine levels and caused corn riots in the city. Money was scarce, but despite this, and the general disenchantment among the Walloon journeymen and their other labourers with the government of the Walloon congregation and the city of Canterbury at this time, the major cloth dealers among the Walloons thrived. Food prices in Europe were higher than in Canterbury, and the refugees could undersell the Flemings on their own ground in Europe.[31]

The Walloons in Canterbury were not exempt from the payment of city rates such as murage and watch. Those they paid. But they had always assumed that they were exempt from the payment of local parish rates. Laud's advisers claimed that the Act of 1601 superseded all other poor law acts and made them liable. Further, their persecution by Laud effectively established the principle that Walloons born in England were English subjects, subject to English law, and so liable to pay English taxes.

Many were expected to, and did pay their poor and church rates long before 1633. John de Bever was successfully prosecuted in the church court in December 1628 'for refusing to pay 9s being sessed towards the reparacions and ornaments of the church' of St Peter, Canterbury. He claimed he was not liable but paid the tax;[32] likewise John Gesquier in 1625.[33]

After 1633 examples of non-payment of church rates become more common. In 1636 Joel de Peere of St Peter, Canterbury was presented. In 1637 and 1639 James le Rooke and John Cokewe of St Mary Northgate were presented both for non-payment and for detaining money. They were described as 'two principall parishioners of our parish and strangers belonging to the French congregation' who were appointed to collect money from the strangers because they knew them.[34] Despite this, thirty persons, all Walloons from Northgate parish were presented for non-payment of sums ranging from 5s 2d to 6d in 1639. Le Rooke complained to the court 'that the Wallons congregation or the Chiefe of them did allott to him and John Coquu 5s for their paynes in collectinge Le Cesse' which they had kept, and so had handed over less than the churchwardens were expecting. They were forced to give up the 5s, and each of the 30 Walloons was presented many times. After twelve months many had still not paid.[35] Mordechay Renard of Holy Cross, William Lampard of St Mary Bredman, and Simon and John Oudart of All Saints were presented in 1635; Stephen Telyer of All Saints in 1636; and John Capitt of St Alphege and John Capit of St Margaret in 1637. All owed sums ranging from 6d to 18d.[36] Others in the Dover parishes were also

31 See Kerridge, *loc. cit.*
32 CCA X.6.5, F190, 191.
33 CCA X.6.5, F62.
34 CCA X.6.10, F155.
35 CCA X.6.10, fo 165.
36 CCA X.6.10, fos 47, 49, 68, 81, 103; and CCA Z.4.6, fo 153.

presented, including William Grill of St James who said 'he would see them hanged before he would pay it' in May 1639.[37]

Apart from the negative evidence of non-payment of rates, there is evidence that some Walloons took their parish duties seriously, both before and after 1633. Many, if not all, had their children's baptisms recorded in the parish register where they lived, as well as in the French church register, from 1574 onwards.[38] Registration was enforced after 1633. However, James Puttoo and his wife, when admonished for not having their child baptised in Holy Cross in January 1636 said 'that his Child was baptised in the Duch congregation by the Duch Minister, and that it was ignorantly donne of him for if he had knowne my Lords Grace of Canterbury his pleasure in that Case he would have had his Child Christened in the parish Churche'. Perhaps the Puttoos had arrived after the proclamation of the injunctions. These do not appear to have been repeated.

Other strangers acted as churchwardens. John Verrier and Nicholas Terry were churchwardens at St Paul, Canterbury in 1638. In the same year twelve Walloons including Joell de-Peere, Andrew Pator, Philip Hanna, Peter van-Acre and John Bode 'all strangers, parishioners and free denizens' attended the Easter Monday vestry meeting at St Peter, Canterbury to choose the new churchwardens. Later that same year they protested in court at the rector, Rufus Rogers' refusal to accept their decision, but instead to appoint someone 'of meane Capacity and not fitt to undergoe that office, not to be trusted with the parishes stocke.'[39]

The fact that the Canterbury congregation did not collapse at this particular time owes much to the quality of their minister John Bulteel; the general and very real fear of Roman Catholicism among the refugees; and the peculiar precautions taken by the Mayor and Corporation of Canterbury to protect their own tradesmen. Bulteel was the chief spokesman for the strangers in the South East, and a very real support to his own congregation. He spoke of his own fear of Roman Catholicism and reinforced the views of his own members. They had fled from Roman Catholic persecution and had put their trust in the charter of Edward VI which they believed guaranteed them freedom to practise their own religion and to pursue their own trades in peace. Neither Bulteel nor the members of his congregation would have agreed lightly to any alteration in those liberties which they considered their sole reason for fleeing France and the Low Countries. The actions of the catholics in Dover did nothing to allay their fears. The strangers learned English, but little attempt was made to translate their liturgy into English.

The attitude taken by the Mayor and Corporation of Canterbury reinforced in the strangers the idea that they were different, and seemed more to set them apart from the local community rather than encouraging them to integrate. To protect their own tradesman, the Corporation had inadvertently created a select group of trading merchants who although they had no voice in the government of the city,

---

[37]   CCA Z.4.6, fo 267. He paid before the end of the month.
[38]   See All Saints and St Alphege church registers, CCA U3/9 and CCA U3/8.
[39]   CCA X.6.10, fo 159.

used Canterbury as a safe base from which to trade extensively in Europe where they had maintained many family contacts.

In some ways William Laud's interference and attempt to disperse this close knit community came too late. Left to themselves, the Canterbury strangers would eventually have integrated naturally with the native population in Canterbury and Kent. Those who intended to stay had begun to settle in Canterbury, leasing property from major landowners such as the Dean and Chapter of Canterbury and the City Corporation, paying for weekly stalls in the markets, and actively travelling between Canterbury, London and Europe in support of their trading enterprises. Some had become members of their local parish communities, and men like Joel de-Peere had already proved their worth in their parish vestry meetings. In the 1620s and 1630s other members of the congregation were already beginning to spread out into the parishes around Canterbury, and to make their homes in parishes such as Herne and Bekesbourne.

Instead of achieving their desired effect, Laud's injunctions acted as an impetous and encouraged the strangers to retain their independence from their hosts for far longer than might otherwise have been the case. Had Laud been less intolerant and more patient, even less ambitious in pursuing his own career and his narrow bigoted ideology and fears, he could have achieved his aim of dispersing the foreign congregations without the injunctions. Anthony Denis' statement to the congregation proved more correct in the long run than might have been supposed at the time. Although the strangers obeyed the archbishop's injunctions, they also continued to attend the services in the crypt and to maintain their minister and congregation. They still do.

NIGEL YATES

Unity in Diversity:
Attitudes to the Liturgical Arrangement of Church Buildings between the Late Seventeenth and Early Nineteenth Centuries

In the Danish Lutheran church at Thorslunde there used to be an altar frontal of 1561 which is now displayed in the National Museum at Copenhagen.[1] The frontal has a double significance. It illustrates the liturgical conservatism of the Danish church, in which the clergy still wore eucharistic vestments, used unleavened bread and celebrated the Holy Communion at altars with a crucifix and two lighted candles. But the greater significance of the frontal is that it also illustrates the balance between word and sacrament that some reformers strove to achieve, and the implications of this for the liturgical arrangement of church buildings. In the embroidery on the Thorslunde frontal the altar is balanced on either side by the font, in which a baptism is taking place and the pulpit, in which the preacher is expounding the word of God.

Achieving this balance was the desire of all churches in the post-Reformation period, yet how to do so in practical terms was not always easy. Nevertheless, by the end of the seventeenth century a number of interesting parallels had begun to emerge in the arrangement of church buildings of different denominational groupings in North-West Europe. The aim of this paper is to build on some recent work looking at liturgical experimentation in the Anglican churches within the British Isles,[2] as well as some comparisons between liturgical arrangements in Anglican churches in Wales and in Presbyterian churches in Scotland,[3] and to extend these to cover a wider geographical area and all the main religious

---

1 *The Danish Church*, ed. P. Hartling (Copenhagen, 1965), between pages 48 and 49.
2 W.N. Yates, *Buildings, Faith and Worship: The Liturgical Arrangement of Anglican Churches 1600–1900* (Oxford, 1991).
3 *Idem*, 'Church Buildings of the Protestant Establishments in Wales and Scotland: Some Points of Comparison', *Journal of Welsh Ecclesiastical History* ix (1992), pp. 1–19. This is an area in which Professor George Yule is also doing some interesting comparative work.

groupings in North-West Europe. This paper is essentially an exploratory statement, posing very many more questions than it offers answers, in the hope that it
will lead to a more extensive study of the issues raised in the future.

In the first century after the Reformation diversity was probably at its greatest.
The initial response of reformers on liturgical matters, and on the adaptation of
the church buildings they had inherited, was either very conservative or destruc-
tively radical. The difference was usually based on theology though it may not
have been that simple. It is instructive to compare the impact of Calvinism in
Holland or Switzerland with that in Scotland. Whereas in Scotland churches were
ruthlessly stripped of all their fittings and the larger buildings divided up to be
used by separate congregations, in Holland and Switzerland churches were
adapted for reformed worship whilst retaining many fittings which did not ham-
per this. Indeed in Holland the process of adaptation seems to have been particularly slow, with alterations only gradually taking place during the seventeenth
century and even later. The element of continuity is revealed at Gouda in the
remarkable series of stained glass windows that span both the Catholic and
Calvinist régimes of the late sixteenth century. In many large Dutch town
churches, such as that at Breda (Plate Ia), pre-Reformation fonts, screens and stalls
have been retained, and mix indiscriminately with the post-Reformation pulpits,
communion tables and canopied pews. In Scotland the dearth of medieval fittings
is virtually complete and the few medieval buildings still in use were mostly
rebuilt, either from ruin or with extensive internal modification, in the nineteenth
or twentieth centuries.

After the initial impact of the Reformation, when the new national churches
began to define their liturgical positions, it would appear that, despite doctrinal
differences, a number of common initiatives were developed, in some cases by
emulation, in most by accident, and that in some areas similar challenges elicited a
similar response. Those areas which it is intended to explore in this paper concern
attitudes to preaching and reading the service, to seating the congregation and to
means of achieving an improved liturgical focus through alternative ways of ar-
ranging or designing church buildings. These are all areas in which interesting
experiments took place in the British Isles and in which there appear to be some
parallels in other churches on the neighbouring mainland.

Preaching and Reading the Service

The fundamental problem was the difficulty of providing a convenient focus for
preaching and reading the service, whilst at the same time maintaining reverence
for the altar. If the seating was designed to face the pulpit in the position in which
the preacher was most audible, usually in the middle of the building, then the
inevitable consequence was that part of the congregation would be facing away
from, and probably sitting with its back to, the altar. If seating remained focussed
on the altar then the inevitable consequence was either that the pulpit had to be
positioned where the preacher could not be conveniently heard by the whole
congregation, or else that part of the congregation had to sit with its back to the

pulpit. The attempt to resolve this fundamental problem was a prime concern for all those involved in adapting existing churches or building new ones in the post-Reformation period.

Some differences between churches in attempting to resolve this problem were inevitable but they may have been less than the doctrinal divisions would suggest. For Roman Catholics and Lutherans, where most of the service took place at the altar, the pulpit was inevitably a secondary liturgical focus. The requirement in the Anglican church that Holy Communion should only be celebrated if there were sufficient communicants,together with the fact that the liturgy was based more on the breviary than the missal meant that the altar became secondary to the pulpit and reading desk. For Calvinists, most of whom did not require a permanent communion table as any sort of liturgical focus, the ability to make the pulpit the only focal point in their buildings was very much simpler. It is a matter of debate as to how far the new liturgical focus on the pulpit was really determined by the Reformation. It has been argued that the creation of a separate liturgical centre for preaching began in the planning of the churches of the mendicant friars in the late medieval period[4] but how far this influenced other buildings is not clear. The location of most medieval pulpits in the eastern part of the nave, and the fact that this position was also favoured by the more conservative reformers, suggests that the creation of a separate liturgical centre for preaching was largely a post-Reformation innovation. Indeed the evidence points to it being a development of the early seventeenth century. The focus could be created either by placing the pulpit well down the nave in the centre of the congregation or by making it part of the traditional focus at the ritual east end of the building; both methods of achieving this focus seem to have been adopted before 1650, but became particularly widespread thereafter. The situation was further complicated by the need in some Protestant churches to provide for a place in which the service could be read or singing led, separate from both the pulpit and the altar. This was the practice in all Anglican and many Calvinist churches. In Lutheran churches the whole service was usually conducted from the altar or the pulpit but clearly reading desks were provided in some churches, for instance in Germany at Stolzenau, Oiste and Brelingen, all churches built to designs by F.A.L. Hellner between 1828 and 1849.[5]

Of the two types of experiment, the pulpit on the long wall, to which one or more desks for reading the service or leading the singing might be attached, seems to have been widespread throughout north-west Europe. The earliest known Anglican example would appear to be that at Wilby (Norfolk), a church refitted after a fire in 1637–8.[6] It was the normal arrangement for single cell churches in Scotland. Though the current fittings at Glenbuchat date from 1792 the evidence

4   C-G. Bergman, 'Predikan och Kyrkorummet', in *Predikohistoria Perspektiv*, ed. A. Andrién (Stockholm, 1982), pp. 96–132.
5   *Friedrich August Ludwig Hellner 1791–1862*, ed. U. Müller (Hanover, 1991), pp. 83, 87, 126.
6   Yates, *Buildings, Faith and Worship*, p. 79.

Plate Ia Church of Our Lady (Grote Kerk), Breda

Plate Ib Schermerhorn Church, North Holland

suggests that they largely replicate those installed when the church was rebuilt in 1629.[7] In Dutch Calvinist churches the pulpit was frequently placed well down the nave if the church was not cruciform; this arrangement is seen in the painting of the Nieuwezijds chapel in Amsterdam in the late 1650s[8] and the roughly contemporary interior of St Bavo's church at Haarlem.[9] At Schermerhorn church (Plate Ib) the pulpit was similarly placed and the seating arranged to face it from three different directions. Perhaps more surprisingly the position was widely adopted by Roman Catholics in Belgium and Northern France despite the fact that the pulpit was clearly a secondary liturgical focus compared with the high altar. A particularly splendid example of such a pulpit can be found in Ghent cathedral. It was erected in 1745, occupies the whole of the middle bay on the south side of the interior west of the chancel screen, and is reached by a gently curving double staircase.[10] Elaborate pulpits in a similar position can also be found in the cathedrals at Amiens[11] and Tournai,[12] where they date from 1773 and 1754 respectively. Among Lutherans, placing the pulpit on the long wall was less common but certainly not unknown. It occupied this position at Ubby[13] and in the cathedral at Maribo.[14] It was shown in this position in the plans of Holy Trinity Church, Copenhagen, built between 1637 and 1657,[15] and in an early illustration of the Church of Our Lady in the same city, a handsome, neo-classical building designed by C.F. Hansen, and built between 1810 and 1829.[16] More normally Lutherans preferred to place the pulpit in the eastern part of the nave. A good Danish example is the church at Slangerup, built in 1588, where the contemporary fittings remain intact. The short apsidal chancel with its elaborate reredos is separated from the nave by a low screen. The pulpit is placed in the north wall with only a few pews to the east of it.[17]

Placing the pulpit well down the nave worked reasonably well either if no alternative focus was needed for a permanent altar or if the seats in the nave were moveable. The former applied in Calvinist churches and the latter, to a greater or lesser extent, in Roman Catholic ones. In the former cathedral of St Donatian at Bruges, a painting of the interior in the late seventeenth century showed the nave completely devoid of either pulpit or seating.[18] The churches at Plomion and St Riquier (Plate II) in Northern France, however, retain fixed benches and elaborate

---

7   Research undertaken by the former Aberdeenshire County Council who restored the church in 1948 and 1964. See also Yates, *op. cit.*, pp. 182–3.
8   Rijksmuseum Het Catharijneconvent, Utrecht (hereafter cited as RHC), RMCC s 11.
9   K.H.D. Haley, *The Dutch in the Seventeenth Century* (London, 1972), p. 87.
10   R. Van de Wielle, *St Bavo's Cathedral* (Ghent, 1988), p. 12.
11   J. Brandicourt and J. Desobry, *La Cathédrale d'Amiens*, p. 20.
12   J. Dumoulin and J. Pycke, *La Cathédrale Notre Dame et son Trésor* (Tournai, 1990), p. 31.
13   Hartling, *loc. cit.*. This shows a mid-nineteenth century view of the church's interior with the distinguished Danish preacher, Vilhelm Beck, occupying the pulpit.
14   T. Paulsson, *Scandinavian Architecture* (London, 1958), pl. 15
15   H. Johannsen and C.M. Smidt, *Danmarks Arkitektur: Kirkens Huse*, pp. 133–4.
16   Johannsen and Smidt, *op. cit.*, p. 116.
17   Paulsson, *op. cit.*, pl. 86b and p. 188.
18   Stadsbibliotheek, Bruges, hs 449.

pulpits of the eighteenth century. In Anglican and Lutheran churches the placing of the pulpit well down the nave usually meant either that part of the congregation was forced to sit with its back to the preacher or that some seating had to face westwards or inwards in the eastern part of the nave. Neither arrangement was considered entirely satisfactory. At St Mary's, Sandwich, the seats directly in front of the sanctuary were occupied by the mayor and the members of the corporation who had to face west for the main part of the service and east for the communion. In some Danish churches the seats between the pulpit and the altar were made reversible so that the congregation could face whichever end the liturgical action was taking place without difficulty.[19]

Placing the pulpit centrally at the ritual east end of the building therefore had its attractions for Anglicans and Lutherans, though in fact the practice seems to have been pioneered by Calvinists. The French Calvinist church at Charenton, near Paris, shown in a watercolour of 1623,[20] was a tall rectangular building with two galleries around the interior and the pulpit placed in the middle of one of the short sides. A similar arrangement is shown in Pieter de Bloot's painting of an unnamed Dutch village church in 1624. Here the pulpit and a desk for the precentor are placed against what appears to be the entrance to the chancel.[21] At the Remonstrants' church in Rotterdam a painting of 1660 shows the pulpit placed against one of the short walls with canopied seats on either side, double galleries along the two long walls and an empty space in the middle of the building.[22] An early Lutheran example of a church in which the pulpit was placed centrally at the east end of the nave in front of the altar was Holy Trinity, Kristianstad, in Sweden. This arrangement, shown in the plan of the church, which was built between 1618 and 1628, has now been altered and the pulpit moved to one side.[23] Clearly it obscured the altar completely, which was invariably the case in the many Anglican churches which adopted this arrangement from the middle of the eighteenth century.[24] Anglicans found a way around this difficulty by breaking up the combined pulpit and reading desk and placing them, as separate pieces of furniture either one on each side of the altar in small churches, or else at the entrance to the chancel.[25] Lutherans looked for a different solution and found it either by raising the altar higher than the central pulpit so that both were visible to the congregation, or by placing the pulpit over the altar. The former solution was adopted at the Frauenkirche in Dresden.[26] The latter became very common throughout Germany, and to a lesser extent in Scandinavia, from the middle of the eighteenth century. Two Danish examples of this arrangement are shown in plans of

[19] Hartling, *op. cit.*, p. 34. Photograph of St Mary's, Sandwich, in 1869 held at Centre for Kentish Studies, Maidstone.
[20] Original in Royal Library, Copenhagen.
[21] RHC, RMCC s 28.
[22] RHC, SPKK s 25.
[23] Johannsen and Smidt, *op. cit.*, pp. 130–1.
[24] Yates, *op. cit.*, pp. 84–93.
[25] *Ibid.*, pp. 115–23.
[26] Bergman, *op. cit.*, p. 112.

Plate II   Abbatial Church of St Riquier, Somme Département

Frederiksberg church, Copenhagen, in 1734 and the chapel of the Hirschholm Palace in 1735, and there is an Icelandic example at Reynistadur.[27]

In Germany what was commonly referred to as the pulpit-altar seems to have become the normal method of providing for the convenient celebration of the liturgy from the middle of the eighteenth to the middle of the nineteenth centuries, at exactly the same time as the central pulpit was popular in Anglican churches. At St John's church in Hanover a photograph of the interior in 1913 shows the pulpit as part of a single architectural composition with the altar surmounted by an elaborate canopy.[28] The popularity of the pulpit-altar can be seen in the new churches designed by the German architect, F.A.L. Hellner, in the first half of the nineteenth century. Of some 45 surviving buildings no fewer than 39 had the pulpit placed over the altar.[29] In most cases the interiors either had galleries on all four sides, or galleries at the ritual east and west ends, with the pulpit entered from the gallery behind the altar. In several churches the altar was placed in an internal apse so that the gallery behind it was curved and the area underneath screened off to form vestries; in some cases the internal apse was complete with the gallery itself glazed to provide family pews similar to boxes in a theatre, as at Bülitz (Plate IIIa). An alternative arrangement, dispensing with the gallery behind the altar, was also popular. In this case there was a vestry behind the altar from which stairs led to the pulpit. At Walsrode there was a spectacular internal arrangement. The whole of the east end was apsidal with an octagonal vestry created behind the altar. The lower gallery does not surround the whole of the interior, the area over the vestry serving as an ante room to the pulpit, placed over the altar. The upper gallery, however, completes the circuit of the external walls including the area behind the altar. At Walsrode and also at Biennenbutel, Bülitz and Himbergen the single liturgical focus is completed by placing the font directly in front of the altar.[30] After 1850 the popularity of the pulpit-altar seems to have dwindled and this is reflected in the design of Hellner's later churches. At Suderbruch the pulpit is placed on the south side of the entrance to the sanctuary, though still entered through the wall from the vestry.[31] A further refinement came at Molzen and Gross Lobke (Plate IIIb) where the pulpit staircase itself was incorporated in the main body of the church, though still with access from the vestry.[32] It is instructive to compare these developments with similar ones in Anglican churches which had begun a generation or so earlier. At Gross Lobke the sanctuary arrangement was completed with a reading desk on the opposite side from the pulpit, and by placing the font directly in front of the altar. Exactly the

27 Johannsen and Smidt, *op. cit.*, pp. 146, 149. G. Kristjansson, *Churches of Iceland* (Reykjavik, 1988), p. 31.
28 H. Von Poser, 'Kirche und Kunst in Luthertum', in *Reformation und Kirchentag: Kirche und Laienbeeregung in Hannover*, ed. W.R. Röhrbeim (Hanover, 1983), p. 75.
29 Müller, *op. cit.*, pp. 75–150.
30 *Ibid.*, pp. 98, 104, 122, 129.
31 *Ibid.*, p. 131.
32 *Ibid.*, pp. 136, 146.

Plate IIIa   Bulitz Church, Lower Saxony, before 1939

Plate IIIb   Gross Lobke Church, Lower Saxony, before 1939

same arrangements are shown in early nineteenth century water colours of the interiors of Anglican churches at Egham and Hastings.[33]

Seating in Churches

This was an area where there seems to have been a high degree of uniformity throughout North-West Europe between the late seventeenth and early nineteenth centuries. The common elements were the introduction of box pews, special seats for important people and galleries. Apart from among Roman Catholics, box pews had replaced open benches or loose chairs and stools almost everywhere by the end of the seventeenth century. Yet even among Roman Catholics they were not unknown. The church of St Peter and St Paul at Rotterdam, shown in a drawing of c.1800, had galleries along its north and south walls and box pews under the galleries. The main nave space was empty of seating.[34] A similar arrangement survives at the church of Our Lord in the Attic at Amsterdam, though here the middle of the nave is filled with chairs. Box pews are shown in an engraving of the Roman Catholic chapel at Edinburgh in 1831,[35] and in a watercolour of the Roman Catholic chapel at Brighton in 1853.[36] At the former they only occupied the side walls and there was a wide central aisle, but at the latter they were arranged in front of the altar and pulpit in three blocks as they might have been in a Protestant church. Box pews had many advantages over other forms of seating. They created order in the building, they were comfortable by the standards of the age and above all they helped to exclude draughts, a necessity for the enjoyment of long sermons on cold days. In Lutheran churches box pews, with seats on one side only, usually faced towards the altar irrespective of the position of the pulpit. Pews of this type are shown in the two plans of 1827–8 for Hellner's church at Stolzenau, where they still survive, and in his plan of 1826 for the church at Gross Solschen, where open benches were actually installed.[37] A photograph of the interior of the church at Nienhagen in 1900 shows a mixture of box pews and open benches.[38] At Rone church, on the Swedish island of Gotland, the box pews form three blocks in a virtually square nave, with the pulpit in the south-east corner and a large stove in the north-east corner.[39] In Anglican churches box pews were frequently square with seats on three sides but if they followed the smaller Lutheran shape they might be arranged to face in any convenient direction, the pulpit normally taking precedence over the altar in determining the arrangement.

---

33 Original watercolours in the museums at Egham and Hastings: see Yates, *op. cit.*, pp. 106, 119; also D.B. Robinson, *Pastors, Parishes and People in Surrey* (Guildford, 1989), pl. xii, and *Sussex Churches and Chapels*, ed. D. Beevers, R. Marks and J. Roles (Brighton, 1989), p. 59.
34 RHC, ABM t 77.
35 P.F. Anson, *Fashions in Church Furnishings*, rev. edn (London, 1965), pl. 2.
36 *Sussex Churches and Chapels*, p. 27. The original is in Brighton Museum.
37 Müller, *op. cit.*, pp. 80–5.
38 *Ibid.*, p. 115.
39 Paulsson, *op. cit.*, p. 70 and pl. 33a.

Calvinist churches needed to make provision for the long communion tables that were the norm everywhere outside Switzerland. This might be done in the redundant chancels or else by maintaining an open space in another part of the church in which the tables could be put up when required, as is shown in a 1784 engraving of a communion service in the Oude Kerk at Amsterdam.[40] This could be between the pews, as appears to have been the case in the Dutch Reformed church at Schermerhorn (Plate Ib), an area later occupied by movable chairs, though in cruciform churches in Holland it was usually under the crossing. This Dutch arrangement was deliberately copied by the architect of St Saviour's church in Copenhagen, as shown in the plans of 1682, despite the fact that the open space under the crossing served no useful purpose, since one of the arms of this cruciform church contained the altar with a classical reredos of ultimate extravagance.[41] In Scottish churches by the end of the eighteenth century the erection of temporary tables had given way to incorporating them in the seating.[42] Sometimes, as at Durisdeer or Glenbuchat, the tables were fixed in a row of ordinary box pews, separated by partitions which could be removed to create one long table. In churches where the pulpit and precentor's desk were placed on one of the short walls it was possible, as at Ardchattan (Plates IVa, IVb), to design a building in which a long table pew ran from the pulpit and precentor's desk to the doors on the opposite wall; blocks of normal seating were then provided along the long walls and the available accommodation increased by galleries on three sides, excluding the pulpit wall. There were other variants to these arrangements. In two Skye churches, Duirinish and Snizort, the table pews are placed on either side of the pulpit and precentors' desk, as was the custom in some early nonconformist chapels in England and Wales. In another Skye church, Sleat, the table pew is square not long and is placed at the pulpit end of a central pew block, an arrangement that dates from as late as 1876–7. At St Peter's church on South Ronaldsay there are three table pews, a square one in front of the pulpit with the more traditional long ones on either side. At Lochbroom church there are two long table pews between the pulpit and precentor's desk on one of the short walls and the entrance on the opposite short wall.[43]

Special seats for important people were provided in all established churches in North-West Europe, including Roman Catholic ones. The position of the mayoral pew, in the middle of the nave opposite the pulpit, was identical in the former Roman Catholic cathedral at St Omer, at the Anglican parish church of Saffron Waldon (shown in a plan of 1793),[44] and at the Calvinist Nieuwezijds chapel in

---

[40] RHC, St CC g 46.
[41] Johannsen and Smidt, *op. cit.*, pp. 136, 138–40.
[42] G. Hay, *The Architecture of Post-Reformation Scottish Churches* (Oxford, 1957), pp. 180–1.
[43] J. Gifford, *Buildings of Scotland: Highland and Islands* (London, 1992), pp. 310, 433, 540. The photographs of Ardchattan church are reproduced by kind permission of the Royal Commission on the Ancient and Historical Monuments of Scotland.
[44] Essex Record Office, D/P192/8/9.

Plate IV   St Modan's Church, Ardchatten

(a) pulpit and precentor's desk

(b) long communion table

Amsterdam.[45] In this church, as in many in Holland, the special seats, sometimes with canopies, were placed around the pillars of the nave and along the walls of the outer aisles. A comparable arrangement can however be seen in a Scottish Calvinist church at Burntisland where the magistrates' pew of 1606 is built around the north-east pier supporting the roof of this square building, itself an interesting early example of Protestant design and liturgical arrangement.[46] The special seats might be on the ground floor of the church but they were more often placed in galleries or lofts, such as those in the north aisle of the Swedish Lutheran church at Genarp[47] or opposite the pulpit in the Norwegian stave church of Lom,[48] the Hopetoun loft of 1708 at Abercorn,[49] or the Newcastle pew of 1725–6 at St George's, Esher.[50]

The provision of galleries was also widespread throughout North-West Europe, certainly in all Protestant churches. They were less common in Roman Catholic churches where they tended to be restricted to use for organs and choirs. It is, however, worth noting that an exception to this rule can be found in the Basque region along the Franco-Spanish border where several churches, including those of Aïnhoa, Espelette, Itxassou and St Jean de Luz have up to three tiers of galleries lining the walls of their naves; these galleries date from the seventeenth century and were reserved for the use of male parishioners. The theatrical effect of galleries could be quite marked. At Evercreech (Somerset), where they are the main surviving feature of a reordering shown in a plan of 1843,[51] they have steeply tiered seating and bulge out from both the north and south arcades of the nave very much as boxes do in a theatre. The curved arrangement of the double galleries in the Marktkirche at Hanover, shown in a watercolour of 1850,[52] and of many other Lutheran churches in Germany produced a similar effect. In Christian's church, Copenhagen, completed after the death of its architect, Niels Eigtved, in 1754, the galleries, again on two levels, are glazed in and placed around three sides of the interior, the exception being the wall containing the pulpit placed over the altar as part of an elaborate reredos. It is perhaps no surprise that this interior was planned at the same time that Eigtved was designing the Royal Theatre in Copenhagen.[53] A similar effect was achieved at the Norwegian church of Kongsberg, which has three tiers of galleries and both the pulpit and organ case placed over the altar, in an interior notable for its extravagant decorations in white and gold.[54]

---

45 RHC, RMCC s 11. For special seats in churches see also Yates, *op. cit.*, pp. 38–40, 84, and G.W.O. Addleshaw and F. Etchells, *The Architectural Setting of Anglican Worship* (London, 1948), pp. 92–7.
46 J. Gifford, *Buildings of Scotland: Fife* (London, 1988), p. 112.
47 S. Fernland, *Kyrkor i Skåne* (Lund, 1980), p. 141.
48 Paulsson, *op. cit.*, pl. 34a.
49 C. McWilliam, *Buildings of Scotland: Lothian* (Harmondsworth, 1978), pp. 69–70.
50 I. Nairn and N. Pevsner, *Buildings of England: Surrey*, 2nd edn rev. B. Cherry (Harmondsworth, 1971), pp. 220–1.
51 Somerset Record Office, D/P/eve/6/3/1.
52 F.R. Zankl, 'Die Kirchen in der Alt-und Neustadt Hannovers', in *Reformation und Kirchentag*, p. 56.
53 Johannsen and Smidt, *op. cit.*, p. 153.
54 Paulsson, *op. cit.*, pl. 80 and p. 167.

Some particularly interesting comparisons can be made between the seating arrangements of some Anglican and Lutheran cathedrals in the early nineteenth centuries. Neither was exempt from the practice in other churches of installing galleries and box pews. In most Anglican cathedrals the naves remained devoid of seating until the late nineteenth century when cathedrals became the venue for diocesan functions and more popular services.[55] Choirs were fitted up for worship much as contemporary parish churches. At Gloucester the medieval choir stalls were made to resemble box pews by the addition of new fronts, and loose benches were placed down the middle of the choir for the congregation; at Lichfield, before its restoration in 1860, the choir was fitted up with box pews with a large pulpit and reading desk in the middle of the north side; all this was swept away in 1860 when new choir stalls were introduced, since no vestiges of the medieval stalls remained.[56] At Chichester cathedral an early nineteenth century illustration of the choir shows not only box pews in front of the stalls but also galleries on top of the stall canopies, with projecting galleries in the eastern part of the choir.[57] Until 1829 a further gallery ran across the east end of the choir over the top of the altar screen.[58] These arrangements were almost replicated in the Lutheran cathedrals at Lund and Odense. At Lund, before its restoration in 1833, the choir was separated from the nave by a solid screen. The choir itself was used for university lectures, and the nave was fitted up for worship. The nave had box pews with a wide central aisle, and galleries projected from the nave arcades. The pulpit was placed well down the nave. The altar stood in front of the screen on its western side, with a gallery containing the organ occupying the top of the screen.[59] At Odense the whole cathedral was used for worship; an illustration of 1840 shows pews in the nave and a double set of galleries ranged along its north and south sides, with a three-tier gallery at the west end, the uppermost tier containing the organ.[60] At Ribe cathedral the nave was pewed from about 1600; a painting of the interior in 1836 shows box pews in the nave painted white but no galleries, though it is likely that these had only recently been removed in a major restoration which took place between 1830 and 1845.[61]

Another interesting comparison can be made between the placing of the Ten Commandments in Anglican churches in England and Wales and in Calvinist churches in Holland. In Anglican churches the commandments were usually placed in the chancel, either as part of the reredos or in some other convenient position, but they might also be placed over the chancel arch or on top of a

55 See W.O. Chadwick, *The Victorian Church*, vol. ii (London, 1970), pp. 366–95.
56 R.J. King, *Handbook to the Cathedrals of England: Western Division* (London, 1864), pp. 286–95.
57 Reproduced as the cover of the Southern Cathedrals Festival Brochure in 1983. I am grateful to the Cathedral Librarian, Dr Mary Hobbs, for supplying me with a copy of this illustration.
58 H.C. Corlette, *The Cathedral Church of Chichester* (London, 1901), p. 43.
59 O. Rydbeck, *Lunds Domkyrkas Byggnadshistoria* (Lund, 1923), pls III and IV.
60 Johanssen and Smidt, *op. cit.*, p. 113.
61 E. Nyborg, *Ribe Cathedral*, pp. 20, 28.

chancel screen as part of a tympanum. In Dutch churches paintings of the Ten Commandments, frequently of considerable elaboration, usually hung in the main body of the building. However, this was not always so. In St Gertrude's church at Bergen-op-Zoom, a painting of the interior in 1693 shows the nave and aisles fully pewed with the pulpit in the middle of the nave on its north side. The chancel is screened off and on top of the screen are placed the Ten Commandments in exactly the same position as in some Anglican churches of the late seventeenth and eighteenth centuries.[62]

Improved Design and Focus

Except in Ireland and Scotland, where surviving medieval churches are few and far between, most established churches had to adapt buildings they had inherited from previous generations with significantly different liturgical requirements. The number of new buildings dating from the seventeenth and eighteenth centuries is therefore comparatively small. The number of substantial adaptations or enlargements is very much greater. Where new churches were built there was a good deal of comparable experimentation across doctrinal and geographical boundaries. This included the construction of circular, elliptical or octagonal buildings, examples of which can be found among all Protestant groups. Among the earliest such buildings were some French Calvinist churches including those at Lyons (1564), La Rochelle (1577), Rouen (1601) and Caen (1611).[63] The church at Lyons, which was circular, was probably designed by Jean Perrisin (1536–1611); an undated painting, attributed to the reputed architect, shows a galleried interior with the congregation gathered around the pulpit.[64] St Anne's church in Copenhagen, begun in 1641 but never completed, the partial structure being demolished in 1668, was also circular.[65] The earliest British example of a circular church was the Scottish Presbyterian one at Hamilton, built in 1732. It has to be emphasised that although examples of circular, elliptical or octagonal churches can be found throughout North-West Europe the total numbers are very small.[66]

Very much more common are the T-plan churches, created either by the internal re-arrangement of cruciform buildings or by the addition of a transept or transepts to an existing building. The significance of such buildings in Scotland has long been recognised, but the large number of Anglican examples had been largely overlooked.[67] Although examples of such buildings are also known outside

---

[62] RHC, St CC s 29.
[63] Bergman, *op. cit.*, p. 115; L. Carrive, 'Le Temple des Anglicans', in *Liturgie et Espace Liturgique*, ed. C. d'Haussy (Paris, 1987), p. 65.
[64] *The Quiet Conquest*, ed. T. Murdoch (London, 1985), pp. 26–7.
[65] Johannsen and Smidt, *op. cit.*, p. 132.
[66] Yates, *op. cit.*, pp. 27, 30, 103–7.
[67] *Ibid.*, pp. 93–103. Since writing this paper my attention has been drawn to examples of T-plan churches in eastern Hungary, where the majority of the church going population is Calvinist. A Channel Four documentary on the Hungarian Calvinists, broadcast on 14 December 1992, showed examples of three church interiors. Of these the two city

the British Isles there may well be more than is generally realised. In some cases, as in Britain, T-plan buildings may have been obscured by later alterations. This was certainly the case at Valleberga in Skåne, formerly in Denmark but part of Sweden since 1658. The church was rebuilt in 1791 in the shape of a cross with the altar in an apsidal chancel. The elaborate pulpit was placed at the north-eastern part of the crossing with box pews facing it in both nave and transepts,[68] though the T-plan arrangement was somewhat disguised by the liturgical focus from the nave being on an equally elaborate reredos, both that and the pulpit being re-used from an earlier building. In 1908–10 the T-plan interior was destroyed when the transepts were shortened and the nave lengthened by a new building at its western end. Most of the furnishings were replaced though parts of the reredos of 1742 were preserved and the pulpit of 1619 was retained but relocated.[69] The T-plan arrangement has been retained in the Danish Lutheran church of St James at Varde, where the transepts were added in 1812 for precisely this purpose. Nave and transepts were fitted out at the same time with painted box-pews, all facing the canopied seventeenth century pulpit. There are galleries at the west end of the nave and in each transept. The arrangement is identical to the Anglican one at Hartley Wintney (Hants), refitted when the transepts were added in 1834, or the Scottish Presbyterian churches at Cromarty and Golspie, or cruciform churches in Holland adapted for Calvinist worship. One of the new churches designed by F.A.L. Hellner in Germany, the church of St Nicholas at Kirchdof, dating from 1829–32, was designed as a T-plan. The pulpit was placed over the altar entered from an apsidal vestry. There were galleries around all three walls of the nave and in the two transepts, with all the seating facing the altar and pulpit.[70] Two earlier Swedish examples of churches designed as cruciform externally, but as T-plans in their internal arrangement, are St Catherine's, Stockholm, built in 1656,[71] and the late seventeenth century cathedral at Kalmar.[72]

A fine Dutch example of a T-plan interior can be found at the Dom church, the former cathedral of St Martin, in Utrecht. This building was first adapted for Calvinist worship in 1580 and the nave appears to have been fitted up as the main worship area.[73] In 1672–3, during the French occupation of Utrecht, these fittings

churches, which were post-Reformation buildings, were rectangular with a centrally placed pulpit, in one case on one of the long walls and in the other on one of the short walls. The village church, which was clearly of pre-Reformation origin, had a nave and chancel treated as a single liturgical space with the pulpit and seat for the minister in the middle of one of the long sides; opposite this was a transept, so that the seating faced the pulpit from three different directions. The liturgical arrangement of this building was remarkably similar, both in its lay-out and in its austerity, to Calvinist churches in the remoter parts of Scotland.

68 Fernland, *op. cit.*, p. 220.
69 A. Hörlén, *Valleberga Kyrka* (Ystad, 1990), pp. 2, 8, 11, 14,
70 Müller, *op. cit.*, p. 90.
71 Paulsson, *op. cit.*, pl. 74b and pp. 163–6.
72 *Ibid.*, pl. 76a and pp. 164–6.
73 Drawing in Gemeente Archief, Utrecht, T.A. He 22.

appear to have been cleared away when the cathedral was used once again for Roman Catholic worship.[74] In 1674 the impact of a freak tornado was sufficient to cause the complete collapse of the nave shortly after the resumption of Calvinist services. Advantage was taken of this collapse to re-order the surviving choir and transepts. The choir stalls were moved into the north transept, the organ and pulpit were placed against the wall now erected across the western end of the crossing, and seating in the chancel was arranged to face westwards towards the pulpit. The south transept could be used for additional seating or as a space for the communion tables when required. Thus a classic T-plan interior was created. Although refurnishings took place in 1831, when a new organ was installed, and 1926, when the pulpit and most of the seating was replaced, this arrangement remained unaltered until 1986 when a new altar was placed at the east end of the choir and the seating was made to face inwards as in a medieval cathedral choir.[75] An approach comparable to that at Utrecht had also taken place when the former cathedral at Geneva was adapted for Protestant worship by John Calvin. All the seating was rearranged to face a central pulpit under the crossing in the choir, transepts and eastern part of the nave, and the transepts were provided with galleries to increase the available accommodation. No seating was provided in the western part of the nave or its aisles since the occupant of the pulpit could be neither seen nor heard from there.[76] An even more unusual example of a T-plan interior can be found at Christ Church, Dromard (Co. Sligo) in the Republic of Ireland. Here the pulpit and reading desk are placed at what is ritually the west end of the church, against the wall of the tower, the lower part of which acts as a vestry. Seating faces the pulpit in what are transepts at the west end of the nave, and in the nave itself. The altar is placed at the east end of the nave and forms no part of the main liturgical focus.[77]

Concluding Remarks

The examples given in this paper, which illustrate liturgical developments in the various churches of North-West Europe, provide no more than a preliminary indication of the type of parallels which can be made between liturgical developments in churches of differing doctrinal standpoints. The fact that ecclesiastical historians have tended, at least in the post-Reformation period, to concentrate on developments in their own countries, has encouraged a narrow view of religious

---

74 Painting in Centraal Museum, Utrecht.
75 M.H. van Haeringen-t'Hart and A.C. Voogt, *The Dom Church of Utrecht* (Utrecht, 1992), p. 14. See also *Van Willibrord tot Wereldraad*, ed. J. Bouvy (Utrecht, 1972).
76 Carrive, *loc. cit.* Compare the arrangement with that at Basel where it was the nave and aisles that were fitted up for worship and the choir of the former cathedral that was not used.
77 Information kindly supplied by the Rt. Revd. J.R.W. Neill, Bishop of Tuam, Killala and Achonry, in a letter to the present writer dated 13 April 1992.

attitudes which has obscured, and indeed served to misinterpret, movements that crossed both denominational and geographical boundaries; developments that have been seen purely in one national context turn out in reality to have been international developments after all.[78]

---

[78] Where no footnote reference is given to information in this paper, it is based upon knowledge of the building as a result of a personal visit by the present writer. In some cases the date and places of ephemeral publications are not known and have therefore been omitted. I am most grateful to those whose help has added greatly to my ability to widen the evidence for the views expressed in this paper, especially Carsten Bach-Nielsen of Århus, Llewellyn Bogaers of Utrecht, Göran Larsson of Lund and Hans Otte of Hanover, though they must be absolved from any complicity in the arguments put forward, for which I alone take full responsibility.

W. M. JACOB

Church and Borough: King's Lynn 1700–1750

Among the civic portraits displayed in Blackfriars Hall in Norwich is one inscribed 'Portrait of Thomas Hall Esq, who in the Year 1715 founded the Sacramental Lecture in this City and gave the Gold Chain now worn by the Mayor Elect'. This appositely illustrates the aim of this paper, to demonstrate the interaction of the church and state at the level of the corporate borough. In the first half of the eighteenth century in England there was little conceptual separation between issues of Church and state, religion and politics. Religion was not a matter of private belief peculiar to the individual but a matter of corporate identity within which ideas about social reality were conceived and debated. Few people drew a particular distinction between Church and state. The continuing favour of the God, in whom virtually everyone believed, towards the English nation was seen as related to the virtue and faith of the English people. The abuse of God's gifts, the practice of immorality and impiety by the individual citizen, as well as by the borough or nation, might well endanger prosperity and the maintenance of the constitution in Church and state, under God's beneficent rule.

Such interaction has frequently been interpreted as the subjection of the Church to the state, or, locally, as the manipulation of the Church in the interests of local politicians and grandees. On the contrary, it was an expression of a particular form of Christianity, a response to the perceived threat from the spread of immorality and vice and a way of bringing their fellow citizens and themselves to salvation. Its principles are set out and summed up in an epitaph in Bath Abbey to 'Richard Ford . . . Senior Alderman of the Corporation, Twice Mayor and Treasurer of the Charity School . . . He was a Vigilant Magistrate and an Orthodox Member of the Church of England, an Affectionate Husband and a Tender Father, a daily Frequentor of Public Worship, and a Generous Promoter of every Good Work' who died on 27 May 1733.[1]

In the first half of the eighteenth century English towns were growing and prospering. The provincial towns and ports in particular were thriving. Bristol increased from about 20,000 inhabitants in 1700 to about 50,000 in 1750, Norwich from about 30,000 in 1700 to about 36,000 in 1752, Newcastle from about 16,000 in the 1660s to 29,000 in 1750, Hull from 7,000 in 1700 to 13,000

---

[1] Inscription in South Transept of Bath Abbey.

in the late 1760s, Leeds from 6,000 in 1700 to 12,000 by 1750. During these years there was a burst of civic and commercial investment in public buildings. Towns became a social focus where the gentry, professional people and men of commerce met together on common ground.[2]

Incorporated boroughs with a mayor, aldermen and common council were independent oligarchies, governed by royal charters, which permitted them to raise rates, charge rents and tolls and regulate markets and fairs, and to administer justice as magistrates under a recorder. The Test and Corporation Acts required that all office holders in an incorporated borough should demonstrate their allegiance to the rites and ceremonies of the established Church by having received holy communion a year before election. After 1719 this was somewhat modified by the Act for Quieting and Establishing Corporations which provided that anyone elected to a town corporation whose tenure was not questioned for six months thereafter was freed from the need for a sacramental qualification and from any fear of prosecution. In 1726 an Indemnity Act was passed which permitted a person to qualify for corporation office after taking office, by then receiving the sacrament.[3] There was thus a strong presumption in favour of all elected members of corporations being conforming Anglicans or, at least, Dissenters who attended the parish church as well as their meeting house.

The relationship between Church and state at borough level can be illustrated by reference to the borough of King's Lynn but frequent reference will be made to evidence from other boroughs. King's Lynn is particularly interesting as a flourishing east coast port with good communications with other east coast ports, notably Hull and Newcastle, and especially with London. It was also the local power base of Sir Robert Walpole, who represented the borough in the House of Commons from 1702 and held office as High Steward of the borough. His sister had married the son of a leading merchant of King's Lynn, Sir John Turner, who served alongside Walpole as its M.P.[4] This then is a borough with clear Whig sympathies but as will become clear, the activities of the corporation illustrating that Whigs as well as Tories had a care for the Church and its mission. Walpole may not have been much interested in theology but his local dealings in King's Lynn suggest he spoke the truth when he pointed out to Edward Harley that he took 'care of the Church'.[5]

The Webbs noted that in Leeds in the early eighteenth century the membership of the Common Council and the Vestry was almost coterminus, and that the

---

2   See Peter Borsay, *The English Urban Renaissance: Culture and Society in the Provincial Town 1660–1760* (Oxford, 1989), ch. 1.
3   The provisions of the Test and Corporation Acts are fully discussed in James E. Bradley, *Religion, Revolution and English Radicalism: Nonconformity in Eighteenth Century Politics & Society* (Cambridge, 1990), pp. 69–70.
4   H.L. Bradfer Lawrence, The Merchants of Lynn, *A Supplement to Blomefield's Norfolk*, ed. Clement Ingleby 1929, p. 160. For Walpole's relations with King's Lynn see J.H. Plumb, *Sir Robert Walpole: The Making of a Statesman* (London, 1956), pp. 102–105.
5   Jeremy Black, *Robert Walpole and the Nature of Politics in Early Eighteenth Century Britain* (Basingstoke, 1990), pp. 15–16.

vestry minutes were signed not only by the vicar and the churchwardens but also by the mayor.[6] This practice seems to have been general; at Wigan in 1717 when the vestry agreed twelve church leyes amounting to £120 to be levied for the repair of the Church the mayor was the first signatory, at Boston the mayor regularly headed the list of signatories, as also at Hull and Beverley.[7] However, in boroughs where there was a multiplicity of parishes and the mayor and members of the common council would be likely to be members of a number of parishes, for example in Norwich, York and Lincoln, the mayor does not regularly sign any parish's vestry minutes. Indeed there may even have been rivalry among the parishes to have the mayor as a parishioner, as witnessed by lists of mayors surviving on sword rests in parish churches in these towns. Although King's Lynn possessed two medieval churches in addition to St Margaret's, St Nicholas, which though a large and splendid fourteenth century building was only a chapel of ease to St Margaret's, and All Saints which was in fact outside the borough boundary, St Margaret's was therefore the parish church of the borough and the Common Council and Vestry seem to have been coterminus.

When the common council came to assume that the appointment of a church warden for the parish was a perquisite of the council there could be tension with an incumbent as at Wigan in 1709. The mayor informed the Rector at the beginning of the vestry meeting that 'according to custom', the common council had 'met in the Hall' and chosen Sir Roger Bradshaugh as church warden. The rector interrupted him to tell the mayor that he was president of the meeting and that the accounts of the present wardens should be read before new wardens were elected. When he ordered the clerk to read the eighty-ninth and nintieth Canons, one of the council men asserted that 'Custom and law overrule them'. The rector ignored this and ordered the canons read, at which the interrupter orchestrated a disturbance which the mayor, at the rector's request, quelled after which the retiring church wardens proposed three candidates, one of which, the mayor voting for him, was elected.[8] In South West England there were also major power struggles between religious factions for control of the vestry and borough, for instance at Dartmouth, Tiverton, Totnes, Bridgewater and Taunton.[9]

At King's Lynn there was less likely to be such a dispute given that the Corporation appear to have effectively acquired the right to present the minister to the

6   Sidney and Beatrice Webb, *The Parish and the County* (London, 1906), reprinted 1963, p. 50.
7   George T. Bridgeman, *The History of the Church and Manor of Wigan Pt III*, Chetham Society, vol. 17, NS 1889; Lincolnshire Archives Office [LAO] Boston 10/1 Vestry Minute Book 1705–1776; Doncaster Archives Department [DAD] P1 4A1 Vestry Minute Book 1691–1847; Humberside County Archive Office (HCAO) PE/158 temp 61 Holy Trinity Hull Order Book 1690–1797; PE 1/86 St Mary's Beverley Church Wardens Account 1687–8.
8   *The Diary of Henry Prescott LLB Deputy Registrar of Chester Diocese Vol. 1, 1704–1711*, ed. John Addy, Record Society of Lancashire and Cheshire, cxxvii (1987) p. 232.
9   Jonathan Barry, 'The Seventeenth and Eighteenth Centuries', *Unity and Variety: A History of the Church in Devon & Cornwall*, ed. Nicholas Orme (Exeter, 1991), p. 99.

patrons, the Dean and Chapter of Norwich. On 28 March 1702 it is noted in the Borough Hall Book 'the Revd Thomas Littell DD, Prebendary of Norwich is unanimously elected Lecturer or Preacher. To preach every Sunday and in course on all Solemn Festivals . . . at a salary of £50'. In an entry on 20 November that year Dr Littell is described as 'curate of the Dean and Chapter' and it was agreed to make his salary a total of £100, 'he preaching alternately at St Margaret's and St Nicholas Chapel with Mr Thomas Pile', who had been appointed Minister and Preacher at St Nicholas Chapel, in August 1701, having been curate since 1698, 'to preach there every Sunday and to Read divine Service every day of the Week except Sundays at St Margaret's Church' at a salary of £50 p.a. Both appointments were to be 'during the pleasure of the Hall'.[10] In addition Dr Littell was 'to have the house usually enjoyed by the Minister of St Margaret's'. Dr Littell was also required 'to find and provide two sufficient Curates and Readers'. As the income with which the living was endowed consisted only of the surplice fees and Easter offerings and other perquisites amounting in 1731–2 to £105 6 8, and the curate was then paid £80 p.a.,[11] the Borough's salary was essential to provide the minister with an adequate income.

It was not unusual for corporations to augment an incumbent's stipend. The Vicar of St Nicholas Newcastle, the parish church of the town, in 1721 received a quarterly 'Salary' from the Chamberlain of £22 10 0.[12] At Beverley Minster, the mayor, aldermen and burgesses contributed £10 a year to the minister's income and eventually, on the petition of the minister with the encouragement of the Archbishop, they granted £200 from the 'Old Minster Estate' to Queen Anne's Bounty to attract a similar grant to augment the benefice income.[13] At Holy Trinity Hull the reader was appointed and paid by the corporation.[14] The situation at St Mary's Warwick was similar to that at King's Lynn, the mayor and corporation being responsible for paying the vicar's stipend.[15]

The drawback for the minister of being paid by the corporation was that they

---

[10] King's Lynn Borough Archives [KL] C 7/12 Hall Book 1684–1731.

[11] Norfolk and Norwich Record Office [NNRO] PD 39/67 St Margaret's Lynn Ministers Account Book 1731–55.

[12] Northumberland County Record Office [NCRO] EP 86/65 St Nicholas Newcastle Vicars Accounts 1721–28.

[13] HCRO PE 1/842/40, Volume of Documents Relating to Beverley Minster. Only two other boroughs took advantage of this means of augmenting their incumbent's income – Wootton under Edge and Launceston in 1721 and 1746 respectively see C. Hodgson, *An Account of the Augmentation of Small Livings by the Governers of Queen Anne's Bounty* (London, 1826), pp. 140 and 165.

[14] *The Diary of Abraham de la Prynne*, Surtees Society, liv (1869).

[15] Philip B. Chatwin, 'The Rebuilding of St Mary's Church Warwick', *Birmingham Archaeological Society Transactions and Proceedings* lxv (1949), p. 10. The reason for the poverty of the livings in some incorporated towns, was that they had been impropriated to religious houses, the lands and revenues of which had been disposed of at the Dissolution. In the case of King's Lynn the revenues had been purchased by the Corporation but the revenues seem to have been very small see B. Mackerell, *The History and Antiquities of the Flourishing Corporation of King's Lynn* (London, 1738), p. 88.

called the tune. They required daily prayers to be read in St Margaret's church. They indicated when special sermons were to be preached, for example they 'desir'd Dr Littell to preach a Commemoration Sermon on 8 March 1708 being the Day of Accession of her Sacred Majesty to the Throne'. In 1725 it was noted in the Hall Book that 'It is agreed that Mr Aubury and Mr Scarlett Aldermen do communicate to the Revd Dr Littell the sentiment of this Society and of the parish in general of the unsuitable behaviour of some of his late curates in their offices and to request his kinder care on that behalf for the future'. Dr Littell's reply reveals commendable tact in defending his independence in a small world where the tension between independence and inter-dependence was all important

> You will believe (I hope) that it must be very acceptable to me to find your worshipful body express such concern for the honour and services of Religion as appears in the Message delivered to me by Mr Aubury it being what I have (as in Duty and Inclination bound) very much at heart and was willing to hope, it would not have been questioned but that the misfortune complained of was a very sensible grievance to me and so far from being my fault that I have taken a great deal of pains and been at trouble and charge to remedy and provide against such misfortune for the future.[16]

The cause of the grievance is not revealed in the Hall Book. If it were political, this may hint at the difficulties a minister, paid by the corporation, might experience in the ebb and flow of borough politics.

The corporation, however, seem not to have been unappreciative of the service of their ministers. When Richard Salter, Lecturer at St Margaret's resigned in September 1695,

> under some disposition of health . . . this House in response to his great merit, and as a signal of the true Value and Esteem they retain of him. In consideration thereof with one Ascent and consent have granted And do Give and grant to the said Mr Salter, an an Annuity of twenty pounds . . . [to] continue for five years if he shall soe long live and if he shall not in that time have other preferment.[17]

In hiring and retiring their ministers the members of the Corporation had much greater flexibility and control than most bishops and patrons.

The Corporation were not only concerned with the appointment of their ministers and the maintenance of daily worship and weekly sermons; they also had a concern for godly learning. First they managed the town's free Grammar School appointing and paying the master and usher who were, of course, in holy orders. This was a matter of considerable importance for them, for the master's salary of £40 p.a. and a house and garden worth £20 was to pay him for teaching the sons of freemen, their sons. To encourage a wider mix of boys, the house provided for the master was capable of accommodating twenty boarders and he received

---

16 KL C 7/12 Hall Book 1684–1731.
17 *Ibid.*

'40s p ann; over and above his Salary for every Scholar who is not a Freeman's son' in addition to the fee of £16 p.a. paid by parents for each boarder.[18] They also regularly elected scholars from the Grammar School to Emmanuel and Christ's Colleges, Cambridge on closed scholarships. This was an important service to the Church for the most usual destination for boys who went on to the university from the Grammar School was ordination.

A further concern was to provide elementary education. From at least 1692 the corporation was supporting four poor boys at a writing school which was regularly inspected by two aldermen. In 1699 a new master was appointed to 'the Towne Writing School to instruct Youth in the Arts of Writing and Arithmetic during the Pleasure of the House . . . and he is to instruct all Children in the Church Catechism contained in the Liturgie of the Church of England'.[19] Later, in 1704 the Corporation

> For the Incouraging and better carrying on a Public Schoole intended by the pious and charitable contributions of well disposed persons to be set up for instructing Children freely in Reading, Writing and Arithmetic. It is this day ordered and agreed that the Chamber over the East end of the Shambles in the Saturday Market Place . . . be granted . . . under an annual Rent of one Shilling payable yearly.[20]

Whether or not this is one of the charity schools mentioned by Dr Littell in his correspondence with SPCK,[21] it shows the Corporation encouraging the godly and Christian education which is such a feature of early eighteenth century church and charitable life.[22] King's Lynn was not unique in this support for elementary education, both Beverley and Newcastle corporations were similarly supporting schools. Newcastle corporation paid for catechetical lectures to be given every week that did not have a holy day in it at St Nicholas for both scholars at the Grammar School and the charity schools.[23]

More surprisingly, the corporation of King's Lynn had a great care for another important aspect of the renewal of the Church in the early eighteenth century, the town Library.[24] The Library, which consisted almost entirely of theology books, was kept by the usher of the Grammar School who was paid 40 shillings a year by the Corporation for this task. In May 1708 the Corporation established a committee 'to inspect and inquire into the Condition of the Library at St Margaret's and which Bookes are missing. And to consider Methods for better looking after them.' In September 1712 a further committee was appointed to inspect the

---

[18] KL C 7/13 Hall Book 1731–1761.
[19] KL C 7/12.
[20] *Ibid.*
[21] SPCK Archives CR 1/4 Abstract Letter Books, Vol. IV.
[22] See, for example C.M. Rose, 'Politics, Religion and Charity in Augustan London, c.1680 – c.1720', unpublished Cambridge Ph.D. thesis, 1988.
[23] NCRO DDBC/3/105, and J.C. Shuler, 'The Pastoral and Ecclesiastical Administration of the Diocese of Durham 1721–1771', unpublished Durham Ph.D. thesis, 1975, p. 50.

Plate V   St Margaret's Church, King's Lynn, before restoration in 1874. Interior of
the nave looking west showing the original position of the Snetzler organ.

Library and 'order the Binding such bookes as are necessary and to call in those which are lent out'. The following month the Library Keeper was desired 'that for the future better care may be taken in keeping the Library'. It seems that the north porch of St Margaret's, where the Library was kept was a 'moist and damp situation'. When therefore the Corporation received a bequest for the Library of 441 volumes from Thomas Thurlyn, late President of St John's College Cambridge, a former scholar of the Grammar School, it was clear that the existing space was neither large enough nor suitable for the storage of the books. They therefore, in 1714 appointed another committee 'to consider a proper place to erect a new Library . . . and the proper means of ordering the Library'. The mayor, Dr Littell and the churchwardens applied for a faculty to build a new free standing Library to the south of the Church, which was granted on condition that a catalogue of the books be deposited with the diocesan registrar. A subscription was set on foot to raise £244 to build the Library to which Lord Townshend gave £50 and Walpole and his brother-in-law, Sir Charles Turner, as MPs each gave £25. It was described as 'a grand structure with a portico and elaborate free standing bookcases'.

Effective management of the Library was a continuing problem for the corporation. In 1720 the committee appointed in 1714 was revived 'to inspect the number and order of the books that all be called in and to consider methods for better regulating, well ordering and preserving the same for the future and for payment of the arrears still due to tradesmen and workmen'. Again in 1732 a new usher of the Grammar School and keeper of the Library was ordered 'to make a Catalogue of the Books now in the Library'. In 1737 it was ordered that the Mayor, Recorder, Minister and [numerous others] form a Committee 'to inspect the Books and Manuscripts in St Margaret's Library and to

> dispose of such books of which duplicates shall be found there and to buy with the money arising from such disposition other books which they shall think proper to be placed in the said Library to and for the use of the Mayor and Burgesses and that the Committee propose and report to the Hall such Regulations as they shall find convenient for the future preservation of the Library.[25]

If practically minded men of business like the merchants of King's Lynn who were the allies and beneficiaries of the policies of Walpole, were prepared to contribute both public money and their time as members of the corporation to the management of a largely theological library, then matters of religion are likely to have been important to them.

There are other incidental references which suggest the significance of the Church and religious matters in the corporate life of the borough. When meetings of the Hall fall on a 'red letter' saint's day, that is noted e.g. the Beheading of St

---

[24] See *The Parochial Libraries of the Church of England: Report of a Committee appointed by the Central Council for the Care of Churches* (London, 1959), pp. 18–24.

[25] KL C 7/12 and 13.

Plate VI   St Margaret's Church, King's Lynn, before restoration in 1874. Interior of the nave looking east showing the seats for the Mayor and Corporation.

John the Baptist. On 24 October 1745 it was 'Resolved by the House nem:con: that the Justices of the Corporation be, and they are now desired, strictly to put down the Laws in Execution against all persons who shall Exercise their Callings or Trades on the Lord's Day within this Borough and the Liberties thereof'.[26] When the Bishop of Norwich visited the town during the course of his visitation he was entertained by the Mayor at the expense of the corporation. Similarly at Doncaster the mayor and aldermen entertained the Archbishop of York during his visitation[27] and at Macclesfield the bishop of Chester was met in 1705 by the mayor and a 'considerable fraternity' at the 'end of the Town' where the bishop alighted from his coach and 'walks with the Magistrates thro' a Crowd to the Mayors'.[28]

Borsay has pointed out the important part played by music in the life of the eighteenth century towns.[29] Musicians of high calibre were appointed as parish church organists and paid by town corporations. At Hull an organ was purchased in 1711 for £586, the money being raised by subscription through the efforts of the mayor and the MPs. At Doncaster in 1738-9 the organ cost £525 with the mayor heading the subscription list.[30] At King's Lynn the Mayor and corporation had secured a faculty for an organ in the first instance in 1677 but in 1752 they again erected a new organ in the rebuilt parish church at their own charge.[31] The corporation subsequently employed the distinguished musician, Dr Charles Burney, as their organist.

The most dramatic evidence of the concern of corporate boroughs for the well being of the established Church is in the field of church building and repairs. The first half of the eighteenth century was a major period of church building. In the provincial towns alone some fifty churches were built or substantially recon- structed between 1700 and 1750[32] and a glance at the churches in towns well provided with medieval churches like York, Norwich and Bristol shows that few medieval churches escaped some eighteenth century improvement in the way of reredoses, altar rails, and chandeliers, let alone the ubiquitous galleries. Church building was a central aspect of early eighteenth century town planning. The rebuilt St Mary's Warwick, after the town fire of 1696, with a commanding tower and spacious nave, was the high spot of the whole town rebuilding programme, absorbing about two thirds of the relief money. St Ann's Manchester was the focus of a new development of a square as was St George's in Liverpool. Mostly the mayor and corporation, as the leading citizens, played a prominent part in furthering

---

26   KL C 7/13.
27   DAD P 1/4/A1 St George's Doncaster Vestry Minutes 1691–1847.
28   Addy, *op. cit.*, p. 54.
29   Borsay, *op. cit.*, p. 122.
30   Nicholas Temperley, *The Music of the English Parish Church Vol. 1* (Cambridge, 1979), p. 110.
31   KL, unnumbered, St Margaret's Church Book 1741.
32   C.W. Chalklin, 'The Financing of Church Building in the Provincial Towns of Eighteenth Century England', in *The Transformation of English Provincial Towns 1600–1800*, ed. Peter Clark (London, 1984), p. 285.

such important communal projects. At Leeds, when it was proposed to build a third church to accommodate the increasing population the mayor headed the subscription list with a promise of £100 and other aldermen made this up to £580 before they sought subscriptions more widely.[33] At Bristol in 1732 the Common Council contributed £100 to the £1,000 raised to restore St Stephen's parish church.[34] The mayor and corporation of Beverley, as trustees of Sir Michael Warton's Benefaction of £4,000 for the repair of the Minster were presented with an estimate of £3,500 for the renovation of the Minster in 1716 by Nicholas Hawksmoor. In the twenty years 1726–45 they spent £3,720 on the Minster fabric using income from Warton's benefaction.[35] A corporation that was at the sole charge of building a church was Lincoln where they rebuilt the parish church of the Stonebow, their meeting place, St Peter at Arches in 1724. In 1728 they went to further expense and gave a peel of eight bells and commissioned Damiani to paint the altar piece.[36]

The mayor and corporation of King's Lynn therefore were doing nothing unusual when they took up the task of rebuilding the nave of the parish church after a disastrous storm on 8 September 1741. Their reaction was immediate. At a meeting on 9 September it was minuted

> That the hurricane yesterday blew down the Spire and Body of the Church of St Margaret and also the spire of St Nicholas Chapel and very much damaged the body of the Chapel. That the Shipping as well as the small Craft of the Harbour were greatly damaged thereby. That several Persons have received insupportable Losses in their houses. Desired that Mr Mayor, Mr Recorder, Mr Mayor-elect and Mr Alderman Goodwin do attend and represent the fact above to serve Sir Robert Walpole, now at Houghton and beg his Direction and Assistance for getting an Act of Parliament for rebuilding the Church and Chapel, and amending and preserving the Port and Harbour, and that the Chamberlain provide them a Coach and Four to go to Houghton to Morrow Morning'.[37]

Walpoles's intervention proved invaluable for he assisted them in 'interceding with His Majesty for his Royal Bounty to this Corporation towards rebuilding the Church and repairing the Chapel'. In March 1742 they ordered their 'Compliments of thanks' be returned to Walpole for 'procuring £1,000 from his Majesty'. All the business acumen of the town's leading citizens and merchants was applied to the task of rebuilding their parish church. At a general meeting of the parishioners on 23 November 1741, the Mayor, Recorder, one MP, 7 Aldermen, the Vicar, thirteen Gentlemen and two Churchwardens or any eleven of them were authorised to act on behalf of the parishioners until Easter Monday 1745 to

---

33 *The Diary of Ralph Thoresby FRS 1677–1724*, ed. Joseph Hunter, vol. II (1830), p. 203.

34 John Latimer, *The Annals of Bristol in the Eighteenth Century* (Bristol, 1893), p. 180.

35 HCRO DDBC/3/104 Account Book of Benefaction of Sir Michael Warton to Beverley Minster.

36 E. Mansel Sympson, *Lincoln: A Historical and Topographical Account of the City* (London, 1906), p. 336.

37 KL/C7/13.

rebuild the Church, appointing a Treasurer and a Receiver.[38] The committee carefully researched the market as to when best to sell the fifty tons of lead from the church roofs and commissioned Matthew Brettingham, who was collaborating with Kent on the building of Holkham Hall, to draw up plans and estimates for rebuilding the Church. Brettingham's estimate for the rebuilding was £5,000 not including the spire and repairing the towers. £650 could be raised from the sale of lead, stone and timber from the old building not required for the new. However, even with the King's gift of £1,000, a further £3,350 was required to be raised.

To give them guidance in this complex task the Committee secured a copy of the minutes of the Trustees appointed to enable the Parishioners of St Botolph without Aldgate to rebuild their Church in 1741 at a cost of £4,700. This provided them with copies of all agreements and indentures with contractors and seems to have proved invaluable in assisting them in their task. Money raising posed a formidable problem. Over £3,000 could not be expected from voluntary subscriptions, especially given the losses that many citizens had suffered in the storms, – by 1747 only £745 12s 10d had been raised in this way. As an alternative an Act of Parliament was secured in 1742, to enable 'the Parishioners of St Margaret's King's Lynn to raise money by Rates upon themselves for finishing the Church'. It allowed for the appointment of trustees one of whom must be the Mayor and the others had to be Aldermen, members of the Common Council or the Bishop or Chancellor of the diocese, or the Dean of Norwich or the two churchwardens, who were empowered to raise a rate not exceeding 1s 6d in the pound, to fund the payments of interest on annuities valued at up to £350 each, which the trustees were authorised to sell at 8% interest. They were also authorised to rent pews in the new church for the benefit of the parish.[39] After advertising widely, annuities were sold raising a total of £3,000.[40]

In June 1744 there was a major crisis when funds ran out and work on the building was suspended. Alderman Sir John Turner was desired to wait upon Lord Orford (formerly Sir Robert Walpole) for his promised subscription of £200 and his brother, Lord Walpole for his £100. By April 1745 enough money had been obtained from the sale of annuities to recommence work and Mr Brettingham was recalled to do so. He replied that he was detained in London for 'three or four days longer, after which I will fly to Lynn with the Speed of a Lover to carry on the work of the Church as fast as possible'. The relationship did not continue sweet for long. In September 1746 it was minuted that Matthew Brettingham was suing two former mayors for monies on account of building the church.

When the work was completed and the church was ready for reopening in September 1747, the final task awaiting the Trustees was the allocation of pews in the new (and smaller) building. The allocation of pews was a highly significant

38 KL unnumbered St Margaret's Church Book 1741.
39 NNRO Bradfer Lawrence Collection II e 28.
40 NNRO Bradfer Lawrence Collection VII a Register for Annuities to Contributors for building St Margaret's Church in King's Lynn. Five annuitants were from Lynn and seven from London. The last surviving annuitant died in July 1816.

process for it needed to reflect the social and power structure of the community. The Mayor and Recorder were allocated the most elevated pew on the north side and 'the Knights, other Gentlemen and Strangers', the highest elevated seat on the south side. The two pews below the mayor's seat and the knights' seat were for the Aldermen, the large seat on the north side fronting the pulpit was for the mayoress and 'aldresses', the two pews on each side of the Aldermen's seats were for the town clerk and common council. The two seats east and west of the mayoress's seat were for the wives of the town clerk and common council. The seat under the pulpit on the east side was for the minister and lecturer and the north part of the same seat was for their wives and families; the seat next to the reading desk was for the church wardens. The two seats in the back of the mayor's seat were for the sword bearer, sergeants-at-mace, cryer, gaoler and beadles and the four pews on the north side against the chancel were for the Master, usher and scholars of the Grammar School. The dignitaries of the borough having been placed in due order before God, for the rest it was agreed that

> for the avoiding any uneasiness and Discontent that may arise among the Parishioners at large or any imputation of undue preference or partiality in the Disposal of . . . Seats . . . the Trustees will make [the Voluntary Contributions for the finishing and completing the Church] their Rule in the following manner. That the Subscribers shall be divided in to four classes viz 20, 15, 10 and 5 pound subscribers. That the Subscribers shall ballot for the choice of the Seats according to their classes. The £20 to ballot first and afterwards each according to their Order and Degrees.

Simple and appropriate though this solution for allocating seats in church for a mercantile and trading community was, some people tried to disturb it. On 24 October, a month after the Church was opened it was noted 'if anyone appropriates an unappropriated pew they will be reported to the Mayor' and 'the Pew for Knights and Gentlemen strangers being the highest elevated seat on the southside be opened to none but strangers and such gentlemen of the town as shall introduce strangers'.

New criteria for the allocation of seats were needed when in 1754 new galleries were completed as part of the re-arrangement for the installation of the new organ all at the charge of the Mayor and Burgesses. It was now

> Ordered that those parishioners who pay £6 p.a. or more in church rate be listed and the list given to the Sword Bearer who is hereby ordered to attend at the Doors of the New Organ and Gallery . . . before Divine Service and permit the said Parishioners named on the said list and their Wives and Children and None others to go up, into the same Gallery and there sit during the times of Divine Service.[41]

---

41   KL unnumbered St Margaret's Church Book 1741.

When it transpired that the Gallery would hold more than all the £6 rate payers and their families it was opened to £5 rate payers as well.

The rebuilding of the parish church by the Corporation, vividly illustrates the centrality of the Church in the life of the borough. It was far and away the most expensive project that the borough undertook during the period. The task was undertaken with great care and attention to detail by the corporation and their minutes suggest that they took the initiatives and that the incumbent and church-wardens were not seen as having a distinctive role. The church building, the appointment of ministers and lecturers and their income, the maintenance of the library of theological works, the administration of Christian education through the Grammar School and the writing school were all in the hands of the corpora-tion. Their power is made plain when the mayor applies to the bishop for a faculty, when they complain to the incumbent about the curates, when they allocate the seats in the church, above all when they nominate a son or son-in-law of one of their number as vicar or lecturer.

The form of religion was central to the life of the borough. In every borough the mayor and common council attended church in state with sword and maces on Sundays and the holy days of Church and State. The parish church rather than the town hall was the arena for the enacting of the rituals of the borough; it was the only covered space large enough for representatives of the whole population to meet to worship God and to hear his word interpreted. The nave of the church was built and fitted out in the best of contemporary taste as the chancel had been by their fathers at the end of the previous century.[42] The common council had specified the nature of the worship, daily morning and evening prayer to be accompanied on Sundays and holy days by a sermon and on the first Sunday in the month to include a celebration of the holy communion.[43]

But what of the content of the worship? What spirituality enlivened it? Difficult though it is to penetrate behind the evidence of extensive support for formal religious life there is some indication that in King's Lynn, as in many other places, extensive church building programmes, support for education under the aegis of the established church, provision of theological libraries and financial support for the provision of daily prayers and regular sermons was mirrored by a movement for deepening the spiritual and the devotional life of citizens.

In 1697 the vicar of St Margaret's, Dr Thomas Littell applied to John Moore, the Bishop of Norwich for permission to hold 'private meetings for free discussion or serious conference' so that his parishioners might 'improve themselves in relig-ious knowledge'. In his reply the bishop pointed out that he did not have any power by law to constitute and authorise such assemblies. He was willing to allow the experiment but he cautioned the meeting to 'avoid all discussion about state

---

[42] Mackerell, *op. cit.*, pp. 13–16. The altar piece had been designed in 1684 by the distin-guished gentleman architect of King's Lynn, Henry Bell at a cost of more than £186.
[43] *Ibid.* p. 16.

affairs and whatever might tend to give umbrage to government'; and he advised them to meet in small rather than large companies.[44]

Initially the meetings seem to have been held in private houses, but in 1704 'Orders to be observed at the Society when met together' were drawn up and thereafter meetings seem to have been held in St Margaret's vestry. The Orders required that the members should meet 'every Lord's day evening after divine service for religious conference'. The meeting should begin with the Collect for the Second Sunday in Advent, followed by another collect from the Prayer Book, 'if a chapter be read out of the New Testament, then the Society to discourse of the contents of that chapter, aiming thereby each to improve himself in the undertaking thereof and in the lively application thereof to his own heart and conscience, and to render the influence more powerful to the mind both of himself and his conscience'. Members were also required to contribute generously to the poorbox. The meeting closed with two further collects. In addition members

> might raise any argument of a spiritual or religious nature, providing it be not above our reach and capacity, nor leading to doubtful disputations, but such as may conduce to general benefit and advantage, to counselling the doubtful, and instructing the ignorant, confirming the weak, and encouraging one another. . . But matters of controversy to be avoided, especially state affairs. . . . whosoever shall pretend to start anything of debate or controversy concerning state affairs, after the first or second admonition shall be excluded from the society; also all discourse of such matters of trade or other temporal matters to be forborne.

Absentees without due cause, from meetings were to be fined 6d. Two stewards were to be elected from the members of the society. Members were required to 'take the holy sacrament together' six times a year at St Margaret's church. It may not be co-incidental that also in 1704 a very handsome pair of large silver gilt candlesticks were given for the use of the altar of St Margaret's.[45] After Dr Littell's death in 1732 this religious society seems to have declined until in 1744 it was reduce to six members and appears to have been dissolved soon after.[46]

No sermons that were preached in King's Lynn by Dr Littell survive. However it is possible to speculate on the nature of the sermons preached by Thomas Pyle who succeeded him as vicar and was curate and lecturer for the whole of the period under consideration. He presumably owed his appointment to his marriage to Mary, the daughter of Charles Rolfe, a member of a distinguished merchant family of the town. But he was not just a poor relation requiring patronage. When he was ordained in 1697 the examining chaplain, William Whiston, described

44 William Richards, *The History of Lynn, Civil, Ecclesiastical, Political, Commercial, Biographical, Municipal and Military from the Earliest Accounts to the Present Time*, vol. II (Lynn, 1812), p. 1009.
45 Nikolaus Pevsner, *The Buildings of England: North West and South Norfolk* (Harmondsworth, 1962), p. 226. During this period an alms dish was also given in 1716, and St Nicholas Chapel was given a silver gilt flagon in 1714.
46 Richards, *op. cit.*, pp. 1010–1012.

Pyle as one of the best scholars he had ever examined.[47] Nor was Whiston an average examining chaplain. He was a pupil of Newton and was Newton's choice as his successor as Lucasian Professor of Mathematics at Cambridge. His translation of *The Genuine Works of Flavius Josephus the Jewish Historian* was reprinted as recently as 1981. Pyle was obviously well regarded by the Bishop, John Moore, for when he was translated, to Ely he presented Pyle as Rector of Bexwell in 1709 and of Outwel[1] in 1710. He resigned Bexwell in 1711 when the Common Council nominated him to the lectureship of King's Lynn and Outwell in 1717 when Moore presented him to the Vicarage of All Saints Lynn.[48]

Pyle clearly remained in touch with Whiston who achieved considerable notoriety through his publication of the results of his research in the primitive church which showed that he regarded Athanasius as a forger and the Church's adoption of Athanasius' doctrine of the Trinity as a mistake. Because of his forthrightness in the publication of his anti-Trinitarian views, Whiston was deprived of his Chair in 1710.[49] In spite of this Pyle appears to have assisted Whiston in his *Liturgy of the Church of England Reduced Nearer to the Primitive Standard* which was written in 1713 but not published until 1750 in which, throughout, pre-eminence is given to the Father over the Son and the Holy Spirit. Dr Samuel Clarke, another notorious anti-Trinitarian succeeded Whiston as chaplain to Bishop Moore. It was claimed that Clarke never used the Athanasian Creed in his parish near Norwich. Indeed Clarke had set out the precept in his *The Scripture Doctrine of the Holy Trinity, 1712* that

> All communications from God to the creation are conveyed through the intercession of the Son, and by the inspiration and sanctification of the Holy Ghost so, on the contrary, all Returns from the creation, of Prayer and Praise, of Reconciliation and Obedience, of Honour and Duty to God, are made by the guidance and assistance of the Holy Ghost, through the mediation of the Son to the Supreme Father and Author of All Things.[50]

When in 1717 Bishop Hoadly of Bangor became the focus for high church attacks following his sermon, preached before the King and printed by the King's

---

47 *Memoirs of a Royal Chaplain, 1729–63. The Correspondence of Edmund Pyle DD Chaplain in Ordinary to George II with Samuel Kerrich DD Vicar of Dersingham, Rector of Wolferton, and Rector of West Newton*, ed. Albert Hartshorne (London, 1905), p. 1.

48 Francis Blomefield and Charles Parkin, *An Essay Towards a Topographical History of the County of Norfolk*, vol. IV (Lynn, 1775), passim and Hartshorne, *op. cit.*, p. 2. He had also been presented to the rectory of Watlington in 1710, by Edmund Rolfe. He pursued his pluralism by being appointed to the livings of Tydd St Mary and Gedney in Lincolnshire in the 1720s which he resigned in favour of his son Edmund in 1743 who had been appointed lecturer at St Nicholas Lynn by the Common Council in 1730. In 1726 Pyle was made a Prebendary of Salisbury Cathedral by Bishop Hoadly, on which he resigned Watlington.

49 Eamon Duffy, ' "Whiston's Affair": The Trials of a Primitive Christian 1709–14', *Journal of Ecclesiastical History* xxvii (1972), p. 137.

50 See J.P. Ferguson, *Dr Samuel Clarke: An Eighteenth Century Heretic* (Kineton, 1976), ch. 5.

order, on the text 'My kingdom is not of this world' in which he denied any independent spiritual authority to the Church, and provoked a thunderous response from William Law, Pyle identified himself with Hoadly and his extreme Latitudinarian position in his pamphlet *A Vindication of the Bishop of Bangor in Answer to the Exception of Mr Law* which he followed up later in 1717 with *A Second Vindication*.[51]

In 1725 Pyle published his *Paraphrase of the Acts and the Epistles in the Manner of Dr Clarke* which brought him considerable further notoriety and involved him in a controversy over the doctrine of the Resurrection of the Body in his paraphrase of 1 Corinthians 15.[52]

Their vicar's views on the Trinity must have been well known to his congregation and the Common Council. If they had not read his publications they could not have avoided knowledge of his public involvement in contemporary theological controversy and of the favour he enjoyed from Bishop Hoadly who, in his short time as Bishop of Salisbury, made Pyle a prebendary of Salisbury. That he expressed himself candidly and forcefully is shown in an anecdote told by his son about his reactions to the furnishing of the nave of his rebuilt parish church. His son noted that he had been

> out of order with a violent hoarseness and oppression upon his lungs and found little relief from medicines, but going abroad has set all to rights, He walked, t'other day to see his new church wherein a magnificent pulpit is putting up, as the finishing stroke. In going down the middle isle he started back, on a sudden, at the sight of the Trinity in Unity emblematically displayed on the front panel of the said pulpit, and what with distemper and indignation was almost suffocated. But nature, God be praised, got the better both of the mystery and the disease, and the conflict produced what physic had in vain attempted, a free and large expectoration, which was succeeded by a fit of as clear and audible raving as a man would wish to hear from a sound Protestant divine upon so provoking an occasion.[53]

Whether by accident or design, after listening to Pyle's anti-Trinitarian sermons for nearly fifty years, the pulpit the Corporation set up for him to preach from in their new church proclaimed, in its decoration, the doctrine he detested. It may well be that in spite of preaching week in and week out for so many years Pyle had failed to carry his congregation, even the most literate and influential of them, with him in his theological speculations [which may speak volumes about the claimed power of the pulpit]. Perhaps Hoadly was right to claim

> his Good Life . . . his Religion . . . mix'd up with Fasts and Feasts, which he observes with the greatest Devotion, . . . the use of Oyl and the Trine Immersion in Baptism. . . . Water mixed with Wine in the other Sacraments. . . . Believing

---

51 C.L.S. Linnell, *Some East Anglican Clergy* (London, 1961), p. 82.
52 Linnell, *op. cit.*, p. 83.
53 Hartshorne, *op. cit.*, p. 86, Hartshorne dates this letter 1743 but it must be 1747 when the interior of St Margaret's was being refitted.

in Christ towards the East were not incompatible with believing the Son, to be Inferior and Created by Him'.[54]

Perhaps too, congregations were more influenced by the words of the Catechism which they had learned in their school days and the words of the liturgy that they heard and repeated daily and weekly and perhaps by their membership of a religious society than by any sermons. In a Church where authority was diffuse and where the bishop's power was largely restricted to selecting or rejecting ordination candidates, the power of the lay elite of a borough would appear to have been used in the service of the Church to ensure that the outward form of religion was maintained, not only to ensure the proper maintenance of good order in the borough under its mayor and corporation, but also to ensure that the citizens could worship God, receive the grace of his sacraments and hear his word interpreted in their parish church.

What is indisputable is that the Church was central in the civic life of the borough. It was unquestioned that the common council and the rate payers should accept responsibility for the maintenance of the parish church, and its library, and for the payment of numerous clergy, including the master of the grammar school. The evidence strongly suggests that by the late seventeenth century, in corporate boroughs the leading laity, as represented by the common council men and aldermen, had come to assume responsibility for the ordering of church as well as civic life in their boroughs, and that they saw provision for the spiritual welfare of their citizens as a high priority.

---

[54] Benjamin Hoadly, 'To His Holiness Clement XI', in Richard Steele, *An Account of the State of the Roman Catholic Religion throughout the World* (London, 1715), pp. xiii–xv quoted in James E. Force, *William Whiston: Honest Newtonian* (Cambridge, 1985), p. 30. Hoadley is describing Whiston but the description could well be applied to Pyle in what we know of the liturgical practices at King's Lynn.

W. R. WARD

Anglicanism and Assimilation; or Mysticism and Mayhem in the Eighteenth Century

The English church in the eighteenth century is not in common perception a very good candidate for inclusion in a conference devoted to the theme of church and society in northern Europe. A by-word for isolation and torpor, it has not been quite restored to life by either Dean Sykes's insistence that things were not as bad as nineteenth-century zealots found it convenient to make out, or the more recent refurbishments of Jonathan Clark. Today without entering dialogue with them or going over too much of the ground I have covered recently in delineating the European context of all the Protestant churches, including the churches in America, I would like to talk about another side of Anglican life, very international in its bearings, and not lacking in vigour though rather unpredictable in its outcome.

Social Christianity is more problematic now than it was in the early eighteenth century. The fact that statesmen could assume with ease that the business of churches was to provide an ideological platform for the great game of international politics and to assimilate restive populations, owed much to the fact that everyone thought that the best way to care for the welfare of peasants, for example, was to Christianise them more thoroughly, and to put down at any rate those superstitious observances which they did not share with their social betters.

The two great aims of the statesmen were of course often incompatible, or at least inconvenient for each other. The Counter-Reformation provided an ideology for both Habsburg and Bourbon, but it did not illuminate their mutual hostility, nor solely determine their relations with their own churches or even the Pope. Lutheran Orthodoxy provided a platform for the aggression of Sweden and Saxony against Prussia, even after the Saxon Elector had turned Catholic, and in some respects hampered what either could do for the savagely oppressed Protestants of the Habsburg lands and Hungary. By the early eighteenth century what was left of the Reformed confessional interest was taken up with keeping anti-French propaganda at fever heat, with providing for a mass of refugees, and with salvaging something from the wreck of the Reformed interest in Rhinelands.

It was at points like this that the ideological interests of the states linked up with their domestic interests or conflicted with them in new ways. The whole of eastern Europe was very short of labour, and the simple solution of fixing what labour there was to the soil by ever more rigourous forms of serfdom created problems as well as solved them; labour resistance might take the form of peasant revolts which in the Habsburg lands were frequent, or more frequently still, of peasant flight to Poland, to the Baltic where there were thousands of vacant peasant lots, or to the Ukraine. Labour shortages, and still more shortages of skilled labour were damaging to to the confessional purity of states which took most pride in it. The sudden Habsburg acquisition of an enormous empire in the south-east at the expense of the Turks created a tremendous demand for settlers and for skilled assistance. Narrowly Catholic as was the Habsburg dynasty it did not mind lining the Turkish frontier with Protestants, and using the plums of empire as a bait for selected Protestant conversions. Altogether they absorbed far more German immigrants, many of them Protestant, than even the American colonies, creating problems in Croatia and elsewhere which are still with us.

The Tsars stiffly defended the privileges of the Russian Orthodox establishment, but they could not modernize their empire without German Protestant assistance, govern the provinces they acquired along the Baltic littoral without the German Protestant gentry, nor populate the lower Volga without German settlers. The first two cases opened the door to German Pietism and the last to German-speaking Mennonites. The whole business was most skilfully managed by the kings of Prussia who advertised for settlers every year, and took them in on a basis of state-managed toleration by the thousands annually. Most of them were Reformed, but in 1731 they acquired 20,000 Salzburgers, those fascinating revivalistic Lutherans, and fished hard and treasonably in Bohemia for Czechs, and acquired some, though not the scores of thousands with whom they conspired and who were kept at home by an eighteenth-century version of the Iron Curtain.

What states could do, private enterprise could also do. If the Protestant gentry of Saxony's most recently acquired and restive province in Upper Lusatia sought to develop their own estates (and incidentally resist assimilation by Saxony) by Christianising their own suppressed populations of Wends and Sorbs, and smuggling out Czechs and Moravians from the old kingdom of Bohemia, the von Dietrichstein estates across that border were busy smuggling settlers in the opposite direction. If Oglethorpe, the governor of Georgia in the 1730s, who had served with Prince Eugene in the great campaign in which the Habsburgs had routed the Turks and knew all about their frontier settlement policies, advertised in German Pietist journals for settlers to man the Georgia frontier against the Spanish in Florida, the Spanish sought to disrupt the process from within, just like the kings of Prussia in Bohemia, by promoting the mass flight of negro slaves.

There was, moreover, a further complication. If settlement policies could only be carried through in defiance of the claims to confessional purity which so frequently were used to justify the international policies of states, attempts at assimilation proved much more difficult than anyone expected at first, and often generated a religious response which no-one quite knew how to handle, what we call religious revival. This first became obvious in the Habsburg lands, where Protestant populations deprived of their church systems and of the inherited leadership of nobility and clergy, began forcibly to pull themselves up by their own bootstraps, but it also was prepared in the most pagan part of Europe, east of the Baltic. Here the Swedish church, given the task of assimilating those territories to Sweden, made a determined assault on the old deities of nature and of fire. Its work was not complete when those territories fell to Russia, but the old paganism seems to have been fatally undermined, and when in the 'thirties Pietists and Moravians whose expectations were shaped by places where religious revival was breaking out, arrived, one of the most dramatic of all religious revivals took place. And it was this change in expectations which affected the whole religious situation, not only in the West of Europe, but in America as well. For here was another division of spirits. Everywhere the Orthodox parties tried to convict Pietists and revivalists on the score of false doctrine, a charge vehemently repudiated, or of breach of discipline. On this latter point the more enthusiastic spirits on the other side convinced themselves not merely that revival was the normal condition of the church, but that since New Testament times the true church was the *Wanderkirche* or itinerant church. If anyone was in breach of discipline it was the Orthodox devotees of the parish pump.

So far I have hardly mentioned the British situation, but if anyone were to imagine that the picture I have painted is somehow remote from the British experience, he would simply be confessing to the way the isolation of the modern Church of England has imposed itself upon its historiography. For if Anglicanism was hardly a crusading platform for British courts, British support for the threatened Greek Orthodox interest at Constantinople and the menaced Protestant interest in Europe was implied by their guarantees to successive peace settlements, and was expected by friends abroad, some of whom like the Swiss could give little in return. Even the Lutheran Orthodox who had limited sympathy with the Church of England, did not, from the standpoint of their own interests, want to see the triumph of Jacobitism; and even the Lutheran Orthodox exposed themselves voluntarily to the biggest bombardment of English devotional, theological and exegetical literature ever mounted. Moreover British courts and ministers had the same work of assimilation for the Church to do as had their colleagues abroad. In England the field for assimilation was in one direction limited by the creation of a second-class establishment for dissenters under the Toleration Act. But the standard continental work of assimilation remained where the large contingent of Huguenots, and the smaller contingents of Palatines who had mostly been established upon estates in southern Ireland were concerned; and there were two major additional works in getting the Welsh on to the broader and safer paths of English Christianity, and making something of the American colonies. There was a fourth major work of assimilation of critical immediate importance, the defeat of Jacobitism in the Scottish Highlands and their conquest for Lowland religion and the English Bible, but this fell to the Church of Scotland.

Mention of America and Scotland brings out a complication in the position of the Church of England which had its parallel in various parts of Protestant Europe, but was made by that fact no easier to cope with. The churches of England and Scotland were not made partners by their sharing a common head and having some common tasks. In fact in the long and bitter struggle in which the Kirk fought its way north of the Tay and into the Highlands, episcopalianism was one of the persecuted parties. Nor was it endeared to the Presbyterian zealots by the fact that their own pressure made Scottish episcopalians look more to England than they ever had before, nor that in 1712 it obtained legalised dissenting status under a Toleration Act passed during a rabid Tory reaction. This concession apparently infringed the terms of the Act of Union, and went in the teeth of that rabid minority in Scotland which still aspired to the full severity of the Solemn League and Covenant. The embarrassments of the Kirk, at once assimilating and threatened with assimilation are not my theme today; the very unusual Anglican experience of persecution is. Before turning to that subject, however, I would ask you to hold in mind the fact that although the Church approached its work in America through the same organisations as it employed in Wales, the S.P.C.K. and S.P.G., it had here to face the consequences of the fact that the Protestant succession had only been saved by importing a series of foreign monarchs, and that even good Queen Anne had been happily married to a Lutheran, Prince George of Denmark. He it was who appointed as his court chaplain a Halle Pietist, Anton Wilhelm Böhme; Böhme was retained in office by George I, and succeeded on his death in 1722 by a still more important chaplain, Friedrich Wilhelm Ziegenhagen. These gentlemen not only linked the S.P.C.K. with the Halle policies of universal regeneration, and steered the Hanoverian court away from the policies of narrow Orthodoxy they maintained in the electorate, but did it major service in helping to populate the American colonies with Germans and civilising those who settled, and had an impact on the Church in England which reinforced that already made by Scotland. Thus the work of the Church in America was complicated not just by a Puritan establishment in New England, a minuscule Dutch establishment in New York secured by treaty, and continuous Presbyterian immigration from Ulster and Scotland, but by the informal representation of the Lutheran establishments at the London court.

The peculiarity of the north-east of Scotland was that in spite of hard times episcopalianism went on working normally for some twenty years after the Revolution, supported by a good deal of unanimity between clergy, gentry and people. Most of the clergy qualified themselves by taking oaths of loyalty to the government, but some like George Garden who did not, went on ministering. Where churches were claimed for the Presbyterians, heritors would refuse access to the building and keep hold of the communion vessels and the session records. There was no Presbyterian communion in Aberdeen between 1690 and 1704. It was clear that the episcopalians of the north-east would not be got out without a fight, for which the Presbyterians were only too ready. In this fight they had one powerful political weapon, to pin the charge of Jacobitism upon their opponents. This charge stuck only too well, for when it came to rebellion in 1715, virtually all the spiritual leaders and gentry of north-eastern episcopalianism came out for the Pretender. George Garden returned to the pulpit from which he had been expelled to announce that a Stuart victory would lead to the reintroduction of episcopacy, he and his brother James presented an address of loyalty when the Pretender arrived, and the earl of Mar who set up the Pretender's standard at Braemar, promised to restore episcopacy, and amongst his troops used only the English liturgy. Whatever one may think of the political judgment of the Scots episcopalians, all this was perhaps only to be expected from men who had all along been stout defenders of episcopacy and opponents of the Covenant. What is interesting about the spiritual leaders of this movement, however, and eventually made them important for the church south of the border, was that they were not simply Scottish Sacheverells, but had developed a distinctive religious position.

Like so many in the early eighteenth-century the north-eastern episcopalians reacted hard against against the religious controversy of the previous century, against the notion that the core of Christian belief and practice could be encompassed in systematic statements like the Westminster confession, or indeed, unyielding apologists for episcopacy as they might be, in forms of church government. Their reaction against Presbyterianism was centred on worship and took the double form of an interest in liturgy and a propensity to mysticism. The interest in liturgy was something new. Scottish episcopal services in the seventeenth century differed little from Presbyterian ones, though they did make use of the Lord's Prayer, Ten Commandments, and the Baptismal Service. After the Toleration Act of 1712, however, the English Prayer Book, came into very general use, much furthered by George Garden, now deprived of the cathedral parish in Aberdeen, and his brother James, deprived of a divinity professorship there. Once into liturgy, however, the episcopalians could display as much of the Old Adam as the Presbyterians, and the Gardens together with Principal George Middleton soon became leading supporters in the north-east of Laud's prayer book, divisive as this was and has remained among episcopalians of the north.

Their roots in mysticism go further back and produced in the end more palatable fruit. The north-east made three special contributions to the literature of mysticism, the *Spiritual Exercises* of John Forbes of Corse, Henry Scougall's *Life of God in the Soul of Man*, and James Garden's *Comparative Theology*. All these authors were professors of theology at King's College, Aberdeen, and the spiritual leaders of the region were intimately involved with them all. George Garden, the soul of that movement, translated Forbes's *Spiritual Exercises* into Latin and published them in the collected edition of Forbes's works which he brought out in Amsterdam in 1702–3, and remains the chief authority on Forbes's life and character. With the Scougalls Garden was intimately associated. Bishop Patrick Scougall, Henry's father, ordained Garden, Henry preached at Garden's first induction to a parish, when Henry became a professor in 1673 Garden was recalled to his old college, and, in 1678 when Henry died at the early age of 28, Garden preached his funeral sermon. James Garden, as we have seen, was George's brother, and the full title of his work, *Comparative Theology, or the True and Solid Grounds of a Pure and Peacable Theology* represented the objects of them both. They were buried side by side in the churchyard of Old Machar, Aberdeen.

Garden's title represented a frame of mind which the group had inherited from Forbes, a stout champion of episcopacy and opponent of the Covenant, indeed, but a man who preserved the proportion of faith, did not dabble in the technical language of mysticism, and insisted that what came first was personal communion with a faithful and loving God. In Scougall's *Life of God in the Soul of Man*, the best known Scottish contribution to devotional literature, the net was cast wider. The book was first published by Bishop Burnet in 1677, and a fifth edition was eventually produced by the S.P.C.K.. Sixty years ago Professor Henderson described it as the work of a lover of Thomas à Kempis and S. Teresa, a great admirer of M. de Renty, a friend of the saintly Archbishop Leighton, and disciple of the Cambridge Platonists. With George Garden, a man esteemed equally for learning and gentleness and influential as a spiritual director to the gentry, the net was cast wider again. He was a devotee of a catholic spiritual tradition to which Protestants in various parts of Europe were turning for a new spiritual impetus and escape from polemic, Augustine and Bernard, Tauler and S. Teresa, de Renty and John of the Cross, François de Sales and Thomas à Kempis. Indeed, as the bibliographers have now made clear, the old reaches of this tradition had always been common to Protestant and Catholic, and had been the mainstay for the former during a terrible century; and those now seeking new ways to Christianise their world were all of them middlemen seeking to mediate between the world of ecclesiastical precision and this common stock of spiritual nutriment. And it was at this point that Garden got into a conflict with his church which was never resolved.

Garden came to look with favour on two contemporary Catholic mystics who, partly because they got into severe trouble with their own church authorities, became the object of intense Protestant interest, Antoinette Bourignon and Mme Guyon. To the former he was introduced by her editor, that curious hypermarket of mysticism, Pierre Poiret, and himself published and introduced translations of a number of her works. It was *An Apology for M. Antonia Bourignon* (1699) attributed to him and not disavowed, which brought about his condemnation by the General Assembly, a verdict in practice upheld by the Scottish bishops after the Hanoverian accession. The connexion with Poiret brought the Gardens into an entirely different religious world which had also been under the hammer. Poiret had begun as a Reformed pastor in the Rhineland, and his forsaking that vocation for mysticism had been in part a statement that the sacrifices the Reformed community had made to maintain their shibboleths against Louis XIV had been more than the cause was worth. He followed Bourignon around, published her works, collected a great library of mystical texts, and left it after his death to the most notable of his followers, Gerhard Tersteegen, by whom it was transmuted into a saintly life of the finest water, and into his peculiar contribution to the Protestant heritage, three huge volumes of *Select Lives of Holy Souls*, all of them Catholic and mostly Counter-Reformation saints. There was mutual give-and-take between Poiret and the Jacobite mystics of the north-east. He introduced them to Bourignon as the way of life; they made her works available to their countrymen. Poiret learnedly defended James Garden's *Comparative Theology*, describing its author as 'vir doctrina solida, . . . vir integer, pius, pacificus' and again as 'auctorem innocentissimum, admirabilemque, et amabilem'; they made arrangements for the circulation of Poiret's works at home. The key figure here was a medical doctor, John Keith, who was also part of the Gardens' circle. His father had succeeded George Garden in the ministry of Old Machar, and he had been introduced by

Garden to the mystics. By the time of his death he had acquired a valuable collection of mystical literature in Dutch, German, Spanish, Polish and other languages, and used it to cultivate an attitude of complete passivity, abandonment and acquiescence in God's will. But he was not passive in daily life; he helped Garden with his English editions of Bourignon and did more than anyone to get Poiret's output into the gentry libraries of the north-east.

Above all when Poiret turned from Bourignon to Mme Guyon, he took Garden and his Scottish circle with him. The great contests which had earlier raged round Mme Guyon, in which she had been accused by Bossuet, and defended by Fénelon who was finally disgraced, were now past, as was her own imprisonment in the Bastille; but their general European resonance had been felt even in Scotland. For Fénelon's secretary before he died in 1715, who then wrote an idealized *Life* of his hero and edited his works, was a Scot who had gone over to Rome, Andrew Michael Ramsay. Ramsay's *Life* of Fénelon deeply impressed Alexander, 4th Lord Forbes of Pitsligo, whose house at Rosehearty became George Garden's headquarters for spreading the influence of Bourignon. From all this Pitsligo concluded that 'God was All, and the whole creation in itself . . . was nothing', perhaps an appropriate inspiration for a man who came out for the Stuarts in the both the '15 and the '45, and lost all the family estates. But Ramsay operated directly upon the Scottish situation. Having lost Fénelon he came to assist Mme Guyon. She dictated to him letters to her Scottish followers, while their letters for her were directed to him and translated into French for her to read.

Such was sway which Mme Guyon came to exercise over the Scottish group, that contact between them could not be confined to book and letter. Ramsay stayed three years with her at Blois, Lord Forbes of Pitsligo and the brothers William and James Forbes made very long stays; Lord Deskford confessed to her his secret penchant for Jacobitism, and was described by Ramsay as one of Mme Guyon's dearest children. George Garden was present at her death bed. The sight of Mme Guyon holding court at home to a crowd of Protestant Scottish Jacobites is I think one of the most extraordinary images of the early eighteenth century, even more than their making off with copies of the *Lettres Spirituelles* and the *Life of Gregory Lopez*.

At this point I can imagine your saying that you have heard all this before, and that it is part of the conventional background to the young John Wesley. It is quite true that the whole body of literature we have been discussing from Scougal to Gregory Lopez, from M. de Renty to Bourignon and Mme Guyon, formed part of the furniture of Wesley's mind in his earnest pursuit of sanctity, and stayed with him and his propaganda lifelong. The connexion between the Scottish story and Wesley is indeed closer than a mere literary one. One of the medical friends of Dr Keith, the distribution agent for the works of Poiret, was the celebrated George Cheyne. Cheyne is remembered for having increased in weight to 33 stones, and having to be followed by a man-servant bearing a stool for him to sit on every few yards; however he got his weight down to viable proportions by a strict diet, and made a good thing out of becoming a gout specialist at Bath. He was, however also a member of the mystical circle of the north-east, and an admirer of Poiret's work for the mystics. Wesley as a young man, followed Cheyne's dietary prescriptions, and always remembered them with gratitude; he read his *Natural Method of curing diseases* (1742) with enthusiasm, and was touched by a private account of his good death. Still closer to home, the northeastern group were intimate with John Heylyn, 'the mystic doctor', rector of St Mary-le-Strand 1724–59, the favourite preacher of the London religious societies at the time when they formed the context of the work of Whitefield and Wesley, and a man at that time admired by Wesley himself. Still closer to home Wesley records having been led in the early 'thirties deeper into the mystics by 'a contemplative man'; and prominent on a very short list for identification with this character is James Garden, a familiar of the Byrom circle in Manchester and a neighbour in Lincolnshire.

However, what I want to argue is not the rather implausible case that Wesley was what he was because the Scottish circle were what they were, but that the cycle of experience of the Scottish Jacobite episcopalians was very closely recapitulated in the next generation among Anglicans of Jacobite propensities. Here Wesley affords a very striking illustration. His parents, though both former dissenters, were both very high Tories and almost equally high royalists. Samuel, however, accepted William III as king; Susanna did not. This difference of opinion had a practical bearing upon the obligation to pray for the king, and, as is now well known, led to a breach of conjugal relations which was not healed by the death of William III. The fruit of the ultimate reconciliation was the birth of John Wesley himself, and, if he may be believed, old Samuel made good any defect in his toryism by helping to write the defence speech in the trial of Sacheverell. This tradition the young Wesleys maintained. Educated in Oxford at its most treasonable, John's elder brother was a protégé of Bishop Atterbury, and believed his preferment had been blocked by the Walpole interest, while John himself had a lifelong hostility to Walpole, and in the 'thirties sought preferment through the Jacobite Bolingbroke. Unlike the Scots, episcopalians of Wesley's hue were not subject to persecution, but they had the vision that Walpole was corrupting the fabric of church and state from the top, and although by origin Little Englanders of the narrowest stripe, found consolation for their defeat in the church they loved in the Quietism which had suffered like defeat upon the continent.

The fact that, unlike the Scots, men like the Wesleys were still within the establishment rather than outside it exposed them to court influence in unexpected ways. The S.P.C.K. had been intended to put down Quakerism at home and dissent generally in America, but from a very early stage had been consumed by enthusiasm for Francke's schemes of universal regeneration, and had been kept up to the mark in this by successive German court chaplains and a strong Halle Pietist influence in the distaff side at the court of George I. The great moment for this alliance came over the winter of 1731–2 when international rescue schemes had to be mounted to save some 30,000 Protestants who resolved to leave the diocese and principality of Salzburg. A small party of them were settled in the new colony of Georgia through the efforts of the S.P.C.K. and the Georgia trustees. The S.P.C.K. had to involve many more people in the rescue operation, approaching old Samuel Wesley, his curate, John Whitelamb, John's pupil, and finally John himself to go out and provide pastoral oversight. The extraordinary feature of this nexus, inspired by 'the genuine fruit of a true saving faith' among the non-episcopalian Salzburgers, is the strong Jacobite influence it reveals. Sir John Philipps, the Welsh baronet who was the moving spirit in the S.P.C.K. was a Jacobite; Oglethorpe, the governor of Georgia, had been christened James Edward for the Old Pretender, and his sisters devoted themselves to Jacobite conspiracy. This time, however, Wesley received an introduction to the outside world more powerful than the mysticism he had so far taken on board. He learned German and Spanish, in the case of the former, also acquiring an introduction to the main schools of current Lutheran spirituality, by translating hymns from the Moravian hymnbooks; he picked up the new Lutheran view of the religious significance of the New World, and the Pietist understanding of children's and heathen missions; he was indoctrinated with the significance of the great international feud between Halle and Herrnhut. And he returned to England so overburdened with religious claims and counterclaims as to be enabled to find escape only through conversion. In other respects things had only changed in his absence for the worse. The alliance between Walpole and Bishop Gibson had broken down humiliatingly. Clearly the church would be saved by private enterprise or not at all; the radical programme of reform envisaged by the Jacobite-country party alliance needed its religious counterpart, a spreading of scriptural holiness through the land. And it is worth noting that Wesley's brand of red-blooded religion proved more successful than that of the establishment as a whole in one of that institution's main tasks, that of assimilation first of the Huguenots and later of the Palatines settled in Ireland. And his friend Whitefield was much more successful than the S.P.C.K. in Wales, though Welshness rather than Englishness rode on the back of revival.

There was one more surprise to be sprung by Scottish Jacobitism, this time Presbyterian, on behalf of the great cause of a national revival of religion. The great hope of the English revivalists lay in the fact that not only did it prove possible to pull Walpole down, but that there was now once again an alternative centre of political influence, the Leicester House interest led by Frederick, Prince of Wales, which seemed to have the future before it. By the early forties, the prince's secretary, James Erskine, Lord Grange, was building up a broad-bottomed Methodist coalition of alternative religion around the skirts of Leicester House, including the Countess of Huntingdon, Howell Harris and the Wesleys, not to mention Whitefield, of whose prospective elevation to the bench of bishops there were constant rumours. Grange was invited to Wesley's Conference in 1745, and actually attended in 1748. He and Charles Wesley seemed able to reduce each other to happy tears at will; he helped to get John Nelson out of pressed army service by providing a substitute; Charles Wesley rescued a lost daughter of his from Deism and reconciled her with her father. The extraordinary feature of all this was that Grange was one of the most equivocal figures of the age. The younger brother of the Old Pretender's general, the earl of Mar, Grange kept just on the side of legitimacy in the interests of the family estates, but recent scholars have no doubt of his Jacobite involvement; even in 1745 he encouraged the Young Pretender's adventure, whilst condemning his arrival without an army. Mar's wife suffered from occasional insanity, and Grange was thwarted in an attempt to carry her off to Scotland in 1731 by her sister, Lady Mary Wortley Montagu, armed with a warrant from the King's Bench. At the same time Grange's relations with his own wife reached a stormy climax. Violent, drunken and an occasional imbecile, she is said to have accused him of treason and stolen letters to prove it. At any rate in 1732, Grange celebrated her death, having in fact had her abducted by men in Lovat (Jacobite) tartan to confinement for many years in St Kilda, and later in Assynt and Skye, where she truly died in 1745. The simplest explanation of these adventures is that both wives had access to secrets ruinous to the Erskine family. Grange, however, was not only engaged in an attempt to shift the balance in the English church prior to the succession of the reversionary interest. He also endeavoured to shift the balance in Scotland by bringing in Zinzendorf and the Moravians in the wake of Whitefield's successes at Cambuslang, and sent the Count a huge 23-page analysis of the Scots religious situation, seeking to show that the time was now ripe. Zinzendorf was too preoccupied with other things to take the opportunity, and the original Methodist hope of political as well as religious regeneration came to an end with the untimely death of Frederick Prince of Wales in 1751, almost a decade before his father. Bishops and others in possession could breathe easy again.

There is a moral in this tangled story. Like most of the religious establishments of Europe (though unlike the Kirk) the Church of England failed in the tasks of assimilation which it was set in the eighteenth century; but those parts of the church which were, or felt themselves, painfully subject to assimilation, generated remarkable energies of both a spiritual and practical kind. In this respect what I have called the mayhem of mysticism was a parable of religious revival all over Europe, and among the European diaspora in America.

Further Reading

Footnotes are hardly appropriate to a paper which represents the fruits of reflection on the subject rather than the pursuit of new material. The general background and the particular point relating to James Erskine, however, is more thoroughly treated, with references, in my *Protestant Evangelical Awakening* (Cambridge, 1992) and there is much more about Poiret and the influence of the French mystics outside France, also with full references, in Gustav A. Krieg, *Der mystische Kreis. Wesen und Werden der Theologie Pierre Poirets* (Göttingen, 1979) and in two forthcoming papers of my own, 'Mysticism and revival: the case of Gerhard Tersteegen' to appear in the Festschrift for Dr J.D. Walsh, and 'Is Martyrdom Mandatory? The case of Gottfried Arnold', to appear in *Studies in Church History*. The modern literature on Mme. Guyon is usefully surveyed in Marie-Louise Gondal, *Madame Guyon (1648–1717). Un nouveau visage* (Paris, 1989). The struggle in north-east Scotland is ably treated from opposite sides in G.D. Henderson, *Mystics of the North-East* (Third Spalding Club, Aberdeen, 1934), and

John MacInnes, *The Evangelical Movement in the Highlands of Scotland, 1688 to 1800* (Aberdeen, 1951). Wesley and the literature about him are notably handled by Henry D. Rack, *Reasonable Enthusiast. John Wesley and the Rise of Methodism* (London, 1989).

VIVIANE BARRIE-CURIEN

Clerical Recruitment and Career Patterns in the Church of England during the Eighteenth Century

This essay does not attempt an exhaustive study of all ecclesiastical careers in England in the eighteenth century; it merely aims at describing their chief characteristics within the Church of England based on the evidence of one particular diocese. The diocese of London, which included then, besides the City itself, the counties of Essex and Middlesex and about two-thirds of Hertfordshire, numbered just over 600 parishes, as well as the cathedral and collegial churches of St Paul's, Westminster and Windsor;[1] it was therefore an area of strong contrasts, with some densely-populated and wealthy parishes in the City and Westminster, and others in the countryside surprisingly isolated and almost deserted. About 2,000 clergymen were beneficed in this diocese from 1714 till 1800, and a random sample of 500 was selected for the purpose of this study. In fact, the analysis of their careers covers about a century and a half, since many clerics already present at the time of Queen Anne's death had been nominated under the previous reigns, sometimes as early as that of Charles II, while others who were instituted in the last years of the eighteenth century lived on well into the nineteenth century. The data about these 500 clergy have been gathered chiefly out of the Institution Books which are part of the Exchequer archives,[2] and out of J.A. Venn and J. Foster's registers of Cambridge and Oxford graduates, since by the eighteenth century all the personnel of the London diocese held a degree, or several, from one or the other university.[3]

1 R. Newcourt, *Repertorium Ecclesiasticum Parochiale Londinense*, 2 volumes (London, 1710); G. Hennessy, *Novum Repertorium Ecclesiasticum Parochiale Londinense; or, London Diocesan Clergy Succession from the Earliest Times to the Year 1898, with Copious Notes* (London, 1898).
2 Public Record Office, London; Exchequer MSS, Institution Books, diocese of London; index B, volume V, pp. 230–259, 1660–1720; index C, volume I, part I, pp. 200–248, 1720–1838.
3 J. Foster, *Alumni Oxonienses, the Members of the University of Oxford, Being the Matriculation Register of the University, Alphabetically Arranged, Revised and Annotated*, 8 volumes (Oxford, 1887–1892); J.A. Venn, *Alumni Cantabrigienses, a Biographical List of all Known Students, Graduates and Holders of Office in the University of Cambridge, from the Earliest Times to 1900*, 10 volumes (Cambridge, 1922–1954).

A first question concerning any clerical career is the number of benefices held by each cleric together or in succession. The majority of the 500 men studied here led rather static careers, in the sense that they were not preferred to a great number of livings: 47% of them never held more than two preferments, and over a fifth of them had only one; two-thirds could not go beyond three. These figures include of course preferments all over England, outside as well as within the diocese of London. This striking lack of mobility could be called double-edged: clergymen stayed for years in the same parishes, and could become well integrated within the local community, while parishioners knew their parsons very well; on the other hand, clerical careers offered very few opportunities for professional change and promotion; besides, many parishes had little hope of getting rid of their incumbents should they find them unsatisfactory. At any rate, since numerous institutions remained exceptional, these figures partly dispose of the black legend of widespread pluralism among the English clergy: most of them could neither hold more than two livings at a time, nor accumulate valuable preferments, even if they wished to.

The second and the most important feature of clerical careers is the nature of the highest preferment that could be reached. Of course, only *ecclesiastical* appointments are considered here, while a number of clerics also taught in schools, private families or universities, or, though less often, had political and judicial activities. However, within the Church alone, more than 60% of the 500 clergymen studied did not rise above parish appointments, even if 46% were beneficed in rectories; 21% became canons, but this figure includes minor canons as well as prebendaries; just over 5% ended their careers as archdeacons, and the same proportion as bishops or archbishops: one, Matthew Hutton, became primate of all England in 1757.[4] On the whole, clerics did not lead outstandingly distinguished careers, since the majority were to be content with mere parishes; but that is not very surprising given the small number of dioceses in eighteenth century England – twenty-six in all – and therefore the rarity of vacancies among them, as well as among their canonries and prebends.

In fact, very few clergymen were called to important functions upon their first institution, as is disclosed by comparing the number of posts a clergyman held in the course of his career and the rank he could hope to rise to within the ecclesiastical hierarchy. Almost a third of those who were beneficed only once ended their lives as mere vicars; cases such as that of William Bingham, who was nominated archdeacon of London in 1789 without any previous preferment,[5] were exceptional: altogether, only 35 clergymen out of 500 became either dean, archdeacon or canon as soon as they entered the ministry. Second appointments meant a rectory to more than half of the newly promoted, so that it must have been a crucial stage for most parish clergy, since being a rector implied at least a measure of financial security that vicars could not hope for. 'Middle of the road' careers,

4   Venn, I, 2, p. 442; *Dictionary of National Biography*; Institution Books, C, I.
5   Foster, II, 1, p. 110; Hennessy, p. xviii, p. 8.

numbering from three to six appointments, generally allowed one to rise above the parish level, and to reach at least a canonry, if not a deanery or a bishopric; nobody could hope to become a prelate of the Church of England before his fourth or his fifth appointment. 'Long' careers, with six institutions or more, usually meant becoming a bishop: Robert Lowth, later to become bishop of London, obtained his first bishopric upon his seventh preferment, at St David's in Wales.[6] To be preferred to more than two posts, therefore, gave one reasonable chances of becoming a canon, and more than five were necessary to be promoted to a bishopric. Important and prestigious functions were not conferred upon clergy-men at the beginning of their career, at least from a statistical point of view. It means that in an age of patronage, such nominations were not solely determined by political friendship or family connections, despite accusations long levelled at the Hanoverian Church: some pastoral experience in parishes, or as a chaplain, was also demanded.

This pattern underwent variations during the late Stuart and Hanoverian age, which can be broken down into twenty-year periods, with the last years of the seventeenth century included in the first one up to 1720; the 500 clergymen are divided between each of them according to the date of their first institution in the diocese of London. It turns out that the posts enjoyed by clerics were more numerous if their nomination in this diocese occurred before 1720 and after 1760, than if it took place between 1721 and 1760. Till 1720, nearly 12% of them held seven different preferments; this collapsed to 4½% between 1721 and 1740, and to 1% between 1741 and 1760; during the last twenty years of the century, it stood at 3½%. On the other hand, clerics beneficed to only one living in the course of their career were very few at the end of the seventeenth century and before 1720, their numbers increasing between 1721 and 1760, but reducing again in the last forty years of the century; of course, these figures are relevant only for the diocese of London. But it must be sufficiently representative, especially as its clergymen held benefices in other parts of England as well, to show that the clerical profession was facing paralysis in the middle of the eighteenth century, while the reigns of the later Stuarts and of George III were times of a reduced pressure on livings, and of a greater mobility of careers. The same applies, of course, to the possibility of entering the high clergy: people ended their careers as archbishops, bishops or deans more often if they entered the diocese of London between the end of the seventeenth century and 1740, than when their first nomination in the diocese took place during the 1740s and 1750s; it became easier in the 1760s, and less frequent again in the 1780s. Canons and archdeacons could be found mainly among clergymen who came into the diocese before 1721. It is needless to add that the parish clergy met with an exactly reverse fate: few people stayed at this level when first appointed in the diocese before 1721; but from half to two-thirds of the ecclesiastics nominated between 1721 and 1760

---

6   *Dictionary of National Biography.*

would never go beyond the posts of vicar, perpetual curate or rector; an improvement started in the 1760s, when many parish clergy could hope to become at least canons some day.

These changes can be interpreted easily enough, provided one allows for the effects of time gap; many clerics who were ordained after the Restoration entered the higher clergy between the end of the seventeenth century and the 1730s; this was a time for easy promotion,[7] owing to the political and ecclesiastical upheavals under the later Stuarts and the first Hanoverians. So that the years 1740–1760 were, by contrast, those of slow and unpromising careers, as all the more important posts had already been filled by the previous generation of ecclesiastics, particularly under Walpole's ministry and on the advice of Bishop Gibson of London. The end of the century, and chiefly the first twenty years of George III's reign, was a time of renewal for the bench of bishops, as well as for canonries and prebends. Fluctuations in career patterns partly explain why the Church was disregarded and unpopular in the middle of the eighteenth century, and became attractive again in the 1760s. Political and social factors must also have played a part: the Church of England lost a great deal of credit after the Restoration and at the beginning of the eighteenth century through changes in patronage and policy: the exclusion of the Dissenters, quarrels between Whigs and Tories and divisions between the low church and high church parties, and the non-jurors' crisis, all tended to destabilize the episcopate as well as the parish clergy.[8] Clerical careers were also unattractive for economic reasons: the government and ruling classes had just become aware of the extreme poverty of some livings, Queen Anne's Bounty had not yet started to improve them, so that few young people wished to enter the profession; paradoxically, the lack of vocations allowed some clergymen easy promotions and opportunities for pluralism, since there was no particular pressure on livings.[9] On the contrary, the Church in the 1740s and 1750s suffered from no shortage of personnel, as parishes as well as higher preferments were occupied, often by pluralists, so that many new ordinands who had been attracted by the prospects the previous generation had enjoyed, found themselves disappointed. George III's reign implied a renewal of mobility, as many vacancies occurred when older people began to disappear, but also as new professional openings in trade and industry offered themselves to middle class young men; fewer people entered the Church,

---

7   Eric J. Evans, 'The Anglican Clergy of Northern England', in Clyve Jones ed., *Britain in the First Age of Party: Essays Presented to Geoffrey Holmes* (London, 1987), p. 222; Geoffrey Holmes, *Augustan England: Professions, State and Society, 1680–1730* (London, 1982), pp. 83–84.

8   John Walsh, 'Origins of the Evangelical Revival', in G.V. Bennett and J.D. Walsh eds, *Essays in Modern Church History, in Memory of Norman Sykes* (London, 1966), pp. 139–140.

9   The same phenomenon seems to have occured in Leicestershire, where young clerics ordained in the 1660s, even though they were not always preferred to the best livings immediately, did not desperately outnumber the available parishes in the course of the following fifty years; J.H. Pruett, *The Parish Clergy under the Later Stuarts; the Leicestershire Experience* (Urbana, Chicago, London, 1978), pp. 53–54.

pluralism could and did increase, at least for a time, thus solving some of the economic problems of the clergy, while moving from one post to another became easier; it turned the Church into a more profitable career, which it continued to be in the early nineteenth century.

The second part of this essay will focus on the various paths to successful ecclesiastical careers. A crucial factor was the social background of ordinands. This issue has often been raised, and it is frequently assumed that the social origins of the clergy improved in the second part of the century, so that 'plebeians', as they were termed in university registers, were ousted by the sons of the gentry and of the aristocracy from the most important posts, and even from Church careers themselves.[10] But our analysis of the Institution Books and of the Venn and Foster registers points to a slightly different conclusion, and it does not support the idea of the Church as an elitist profession.[11] Three main groups can be identified among these 500 men who entered the Church during the eighteenth century: the sons of the gentry, those of clergymen, and those of 'plebeians': the nobility does not represent more than 1.2% of the total sample. The gentry accounts for nearly 38% of it, but the sons of the clergy are almost as numerous – over 35%. Over 19%, almost a fifth, are sons of 'plebeians', probably shopkeepers, traders, free-holders, husbandmen, yeomen and small farmers. Moreover, in the break-down into sub-groups, 'gentry' here means the sons of mere gentlemen, who amount to more than a quarter of the whole sample; the sons of esquires, knights and baronets represent no more than 12½%. Among the sons of clergymen, only 6% have a father belonging to the higher clergy. The personnel of the diocese of London does not therefore appear as particularly aristocratic; on the contrary, one of its striking features is the high percentages of sons of parish clergy, of 'plebeians' and of mere gentlemen. The diocese then went on integrating a large proportion of working-class or lower middle-class people – in nineteenth-century terms.

The social recruitment of the clergy naturally underwent changes; if broken down in the same twenty year periods as previously, it does indeed reveal how between the beginning and the end of the century, the gentry increased from 31% to almost 57%, the sons of 'plebeians' went down from 28½% to just over 12%, and those of the parish clergy decreased from almost 26% to 19½%, while those of the higher clergy rose from under 3% to over 5%. The nobility became more numerous at the same time, and the sons of peers and baronets taken together constituted 4% of the sample in the last twenty years of the century. But the

---

[10] Norman Sykes, *Church and State in England in the Eighteenth Century* (Cambridge, 1934), pp. 156–157; G.M. Trevelyan, *A Social History of England* (London, 1944), pp. 359–360; G.E. Mingay, *The Gentry; the Rise and Fall of a Ruling Class* (London, 1976), p. 138; Peter Virgin, *The Church in an Age of Negligence* (Cambridge, 1989), pp. 110–111.

[11] For a detailed analysis of the social and geographical recruitment of the clergy of the diocese of London during the eighteenth century, see Viviane Barrie-Curien, *Clergé et Pastorale en Angleterre au XVIIIe Siècle; le Diocese de Londres* (Paris, 1992), chapters II and III, pp. 59–116.

Church was still nothing like an exclusively aristocratic body; even at the end of the century, it contained a fair proportion of sons of 'plebeians', who were managing to enter an ecclesiastical career. It is likely that in other, poorer dioceses in the north and west of England, the increase of the gentry class was not yet perceptible in the eighteenth century.

These 500 clergymen, particularly those born in the gentry, can be further characterized through their geographical origins. 57% came from London, the county of Middlesex, and from provincial towns, the population of which reached 2,000 inhabitants or more in 1801, according to the census taken in that year. This already very high proportion reaches 67% when it comes to the sons of the gentry, 30% of whom were born in provincial towns and the rest in London and Middlesex. So that the Church did not attract a majority of landed gentry, not even enlisting their younger sons. It recruited rather the sons of professional people – doctors, lawyers, merchants and traders – whose wealth and respectability earned them the status of gentlemen or even of esquires, but who could not on any account be classified as country squires. Thus it is obvious that 'professions' or 'urban gentry' amounted to such a proportion in the recruitment of the clergy of the Church of England, that the link between the latter and the landed gentry could not be sustained, at least as far as the London diocese is concerned. As for the 'plebeians', nearly two-thirds of them came from towns, which suggests how education, then a urban phenomenon, had helped them on in the course of their careers. The sons of clerics, on the other hand, were mostly the children of country clergymen, very often beneficed in the county of Essex, a fact which emphazises the degree of self-recruitment and the extent to which sons succeeded to their fathers' livings, therefore founding clerical dynasties.

Was the social rank of ordinands a major factor in the course of their ecclesiastical career? It certainly played a part, but the highest functions in the Church were not monopolized by the sons of the gentry and of the nobility to the extent that has sometimes been assumed.[12] It is true that the two men in the sample who were to become archbishops belonged to the gentry – Matthew Hutton's father was termed an esquire – and to the nobility – Robert Hay Drummond was the second son of the earl of Kinoull and the grandson of Robert Harley, first earl of Oxford.[13] But on the whole, the upper classes' advantages were not so obvious. The 18½% of the sons of 'plebeians' who remained mere vicars were only marginally more numerous than those of the gentry who numbered 16%; and the sons of clergymen did best of all – only 11% were never preferred to any other living than a vicarage. In fact, there is no major difference in the proportions of young gentlemen and of 'plebeians' who stayed parish clergymen all their lives, while sons of clergymen rose more often above the rank of vicar or rector. As for the higher clergy, a greater percentage of canons, deans and bishops can be found among the sons of the clergy or of 'plebeians' than among the sons of the gentry; on the other

---

12 Virgin, p. 139.
13 Venn, I, 2, p. 442; *Dictionary of National Biography*; Institution Books, C, I; Hennessy, p. 449.

hand, the latter become archdeacons more often than the former. But when dividing these 500 men into two main groups, – first those who did not succeed in rising above the ranks of the parish clergy, then those who reached at least one of the functions available in the higher clergy, from canon to archbishop –, one finds that 63% of the sons of the gentry ended their career in mere parishes – ranging from perpetual curacies to rectories –, and 31% among the higher ranks of the hierarchy, compared with respectively 58% and 37% of the sons of clergymen, and 65% and 34% of the sons of humble people. The most important factor of success was thus heredity, and to belong to an ecclesiastical family mattered more than to be born in the gentry. Of course, noblemen could be almost sure of being always promoted to the highest posts, but their numbers were so few that they could not stand seriously in the way of other ordinands. As for the gentry, particularly the urban gentry, they did not, from a statititical point of view, enjoy any outstanding favours from the Church; nor did the 'plebeians' meet with any marked professional failure.

Of course, some sons of the gentry may have stayed in mere parishes of their own free will, and may not have even tried to obtain higher and more lucrative preferment, not because they could not reach them, but because they did not need them, as they had private means to support themselves. Moreover, it cannot be denied that patronage and local connections were very useful to them: it seems obvious, for instance, that William Brampton became rector of several parishes in Essex because his father, Sir Mundeford Brampton, had his residence at Little Baddow in the same county;[14] Graham Hanmer, third son of Sir Walden Hanmer, held as his first preferment the vicarage of Hanmer in Flintshire, where his father and his elder brother were settled.[15] But the same kind of influence can be traced in ecclesiastical families: Denison Cumberland, bishop of Clonfert in 1763, was a grand-son of Richard Cumberland, bishop of Peterborough, and the son of another Richard Cumberland, a canon of Peterborough and of Lincoln, and the archdeacon of Northampton in the diocese of Lincoln;[16] in the Tanner family, the great-grandfather and the grandfather held parishes in Wiltshire; the father became in turn chancellor of the diocese of Norwich, archdeacon of Norfolk, and bishop of St Asaph, while his brothers had less brilliant careers in the dioceses of Norwich and St Asaph, no doubt under his protection; the last of the family, Thomas, was rector in the three dioceses of London, Norwich and Canterbury, and ended his life as canon of Canterbury.[17]

Did the eighteenth century bring about significant changes in the influence of

14 Venn, I, 1, pp. 203–205; John Le Neve and T.D. Hardy, *Fasti Ecclesiae Anglicanae, or a Calendar of the Principal Dignitaries of England and Wales and of the Chief Officers of the Universities of Oxford and Cambridge, from the Earliest Times to the Year 1715, Corrected and Continued from 1715 to the Present Time*, 3 volumes (Oxford, 1854), volume III, p. 81.
15 Venn, II, 3, p. 227; Hennessy, p. cxxix.
16 Venn, I, 1, p. 432; Hennessy, p. xliv, p. 161; Le Neve and Hardy, volume II, p. 215; Institution Books, C, I.
17 Foster, I, 4, pp. 1455–1456; Foster, II, 2, p. 1387; Hennessy, p. lxxx; Institution Books, C, I and II.

social origins on ecclesiastical careers? It is true that the sons of the gentry and of the nobility made their presence increasingly felt under the reign of George III, but not before the last twenty years of the century. Till 1780, clerics from humble families did succeed in obtaining deaneries and bishoprics, chiefly through the channels of private patronage and with the help of school and university scholarships. As for the sons of clergymen, their influence reached its highest point between the beginning of the century and 1740 or 1750, when many became deans or bishops, but they could still hope for canonries or archdeaconries afterwards. The increase of the nobility and gentry on the episcopal bench, or in deaneries, after 1780, proves of course that the Church had become a much more respectable profession at the end of the century than under Queen Anne or the first Hanoverians; however, an important proportion of sons of clerics and of 'plebeians' could still enter the higher clergy, though at a lower level, so that the Church of the early nineteenth century can be termed an 'open élite'.

The geographical origins of the 500 men of the sample have shown the importance of local recruitment, especially among sons of the gentry and of clergymen, who came chiefly from the diocese itself or the south-east of England; did they play a part in terms of professional success too? A first point concerns the clergy born within the diocese itself; people from London became chiefly either vicars, or archdeacons and bishops; Essex and Middlesex provided numerous rectors, as well as archdeacons and deans, but few bishops. Parish self-recruitment was thus especially important in the provincial part of the diocese, where many sons of clergymen succeeded their fathers, or where sons of the gentry could be helped on by their local connections; but the upper ranks of the Church came from the capital city itself, as well as from other parts of England. Besides, the clergy recruited within the diocese displayed three types of career patterns: some were fairly detached from their native place, held one or two benefices in the diocese but were also appointed elsewhere; such was Richard Lockwood, the son of the vicar of Fifield in Essex, who held the rectory of Willingale Doe in the same county for three years, but left it to be preferred to several livings in the diocese of Norwich, as well as to a prebend of Peterborough cathedral;[18] others were deeply rooted within the diocese which they never left, such as Samuel Angier, the son of a mercer born in Colchester, who became rector both of Layer Bretton in Essex and of St Michael Cornhill in London;[19] a third type of career reveals how clerical dynasties controlled some parishes; a particularly significant instance of this phenomenon is the Altham family: Thomas Altham succeeded his father James as rector of Latton in Essex in 1758, being nominated by William Altham, his uncle or cousin, before taking also ten years later the rectory of Magdalen Laver in the same county; but Latton seems to have been in the family for several generations:

[18] Foster, II, 3, p. 867; Venn, II, 4, p. 198; Institution Books, C, I; his father William
     Lockwood had been presented to the rectory of Fifield in 1754 by his own father Richard
     Lockwood, esquire, from London.
[19] Venn, I, 1, p. 32; Hennessy, p. cxxxiii; Institution Books, C, I.

Michael Altham was rector there from 1681 till 1705, when his son Roger, also a canon of St Paul's and the archdeacon of Middlesex, 'inherited' it.[20]

When looking at all regions of England and Wales who 'sent' ecclesiastics into the diocese of London, the most striking feature is that over a third of those who came from the North, the South and East Anglia, eventually entered the higher clergy; at the other end of the spectrum, over two-thirds and up to three-quarters of those from Wales, and from the East and the West Midlands, were to remain parish clergymen; while those from London, the Home Counties, the South Midlands and the South-West, led 'average' careers, with two-thirds of them in parishes all their lives, while a third obtained at least a canonry. However, the majority of the highest posts, that is bishoprics and deaneries, went to clerics born in the south and the east of England, which stresses the importance of this part of the country in ecclesiastical and cultural history, as it had developed parishes, towns and schools in greater numbers and an earlier date than any other.

It is easy enough to explain why clergymen from the South or from East Anglia who came into the diocese of London had brilliant careers: these were densely populated regions, provided with numerous parishes, among the oldest and wealthiest in England; their ordinands did not need to leave their native counties to be preferred to vicarages or rectories, they came into another diocese to do better. The explanation is different where the North is concerned; parishes were few, large and poor, and the pressure upon benefices very high; the clergy who came down south from Yorkshire or Lancashire were usually sons of 'plebeians', outstandingly able, ambitious, hard-working, and protected by powerful patrons. On the other hand, Welsh people did not do well: 76% of them did not rise above the ranks of parish clergy, the highest percentage among all regions; they probably suffered from prejudice, but also from the lack of towns and therefore of good schools in Wales during the first half of the eighteenth century. The East and West Midlands were a different case; they did not have such numerous and rich preferments as East Anglia or the South, but enough nevertheless to satisfy the best among their ordinands; those who came into the diocese of London were therefore probably less talented than those from the North.

However there were variations in the eighteenth century, which matched those already analyzed concerning the clergy's social origins. Brilliant careers favoured people from the south and the east of England chiefly when they came into the diocese of London before 1720 or after 1760; the forty-years interval was the time when ecclesiastics from the north and the west came into their own; from George III's reign onwards, East Anglia, the South and the South-West reappeared as 'successful regions', while London and the Home Counties were more and more turned towards parish careers. These variations are easily interpreted according to the changing social prestige of the Church: when at its lowest point under the first

---

20 Foster, II, 1, p. 20; I, 1, p. 21; Venn, I, 1, p. 26; Hennessy, p. xix, pp. 9, 12, 53, 57, 90; Institution Books, C, I. A similar dynasty is the Smythies family, who, though originally from East Anglia, came into Essex and managed to dominate parishes and schools in and around Colchester for several generations in the eighteenth century.

Hanoverians, the recruitment of worthy bishops and other dignitaries had to take place among the most talented 'plebeians' who came from poor regions with few other openings besides the Church; after 1760, its renewed popularity encouraged the sons of the gentry and of the clergy, who came chiefly from the south and the east, to enter it and to use their connections to reach high appointments. Besides, the north and some parts of the west of England had begun to develop new opportunities in trade and industry for ambitious and able people.

This analysis does not do justice to the complexities of the links which bound together, particularly in the diocese of London itself and at its periphery, the various families who entered an ecclesiastical career, be they gentry or clergy, nor to the intricate workings of patronage. It is obvious, though, that entering the Church could imply either a great social and geographical mobility, or a deep attachment to a family tradition and to a particular region, the latter attitude being of course met more frequently among the sons of clerics.

A last factor needs to be taken into account to explain Church careers. Ever since the Reformation, ecclesiastical and political authorities alike had stressed the need for an educated clergy, and by the eigheenth century, practically all ordinands were possessed of at least one university degree. Did the university they had attended and the nature of their degree affect a clergyman's success or failure?

As a matter of fact, since canons, deans, bishops and archbishops, were automatically awarded an MA or a DD by the king or by the archbishop of Canterbury upon their taking up these posts, the degrees themselves did not mean anything regarding the learning of the higher clergy.[21] But the choice of their university, and even of their college, implied a great deal for the future ordinands' careers. In absolute numbers, clergymen came more often from Oxford than from Cambridge, if only because the former foundation was larger. But among the Oxford graduates, 16% became vicars and 48% rectors, compared with 12% and 42% respectively among those from Cambridge; on the other hand, 24% of Cambridge graduates ended their careers as canons, 4% as deans, and 7½% as bishops or archbishops, against 19%, 4%, and 3½% among those from Oxford. The higher clergy were thus chosen by governement and Church authorities preferably from among Cambridge men, while the ranks of parish clergy were filled with Oxford men. The reasons for this policy are complex, and a classification of the clergy according to the colleges they went to would be necessary to explore them to the full, but they seem in a large measure political, as becomes clear from the changes which occurred between Queen Anne's reign and that of George III.

Oxford men who started their career in the diocese of London before 1740 had little chance of entering the higher clergy later; but they were more successful

---

21 D.A. Winstanley, *Unreformed Cambridge; a Study of Certain Aspects of the University in the Eighteenth Century* (Cambridge, 1935), pp. 79 and seq.; for instance Edward Cobden left Oxford with a BA in 1706, but a BD and a DD were granted to him simultaneously in 1723, two years after his appointment as canon of Lincoln.

when they entered it between 1740 and 1780; meanwhile, Cambridge men could hope for important appointments if their career began between 1720 and 1740, then again if they came into the London diocese during the last twenty years of the century. In fact, and allowing again for the effects of the time gap, the difficulties met by Oxford graduates till the middle of the century were due to the university's deserved reputation of Toryism, whereas Cambridge had supported the Whig party, the 'Glorious Revolution' and the Hanoverian settlement; some confusion may have occurred during Anne's reign, since the queen's high church sympathies went with the Tories, but on the whole, she and the first Hanoverian kings followed William III's policy, which was to promote Whig prelates, and even parish clergy when the Crown was patron of the living. It might well be also that during Walpole's ministry, when members of the administration had strong personal links with Norfolk and Suffolk, Cambridge graduates found themselves favoured by the government because many, besides being Whigs, came from East Anglia according to the rule of local recruitment. The following years must also have spelled success for Cambridge men, as the duke of Newcastle was chancellor of the university, and would, when able to exercise his patronage as chief minister, appoint men from its colleges till his resignation in 1757. On the other hand, Oxford graduates were preferred to parish livings by local patrons, many of whom belonged to a sometimes Tory-inclined gentry. However, from 1750 onwards, Oxford gave up its old policies, and sided with the government; after George III's accession in 1760, his ministers turned again towards Oxford graduates for crucial ecclesiastical nominations;[22] so that clergymen from this university first beneficed within the diocese of London between 1740 and 1780 ended their careers between 1760 and 1800 in higher positions than their predecessors. As for the change which occurred after 1780, it probably had little to do with politics, but more with the attraction of the Evangelical movement in the first decades of the nineteenth century, when men appointed for the first time between 1780 and 1800 reached their highest preferments; the movement had developed in Cambridge earlier than in Oxford, and even if all bishops or archbishops of Evangelical persuasion who were nominated then were not from the former university, they must have turned towards it for many appointments within their patronage, and advised the governement to do so when political authorities intervened in ecclesiastical matters.[23]

---

22 G.V. Bennett, 'Against the Tide: Oxford under William III', in L.S. Sutherland and L.G. Mitchell eds, *The History of the University of Oxford*, volume V (Oxford, 1986); Bennett, 'Loyalist Oxford and the Revolution', *idem*; Bennett, 'The Era of Party Zeal, 1702–1714', *idem*; Paul Langford, 'Tories and Jacobites, 1714–1751', *idem*; L.S. Sutherland, 'Political Stability, 1751–1777', *idem*; L.G. Mitchell, 'Politics and Revolution, 1772–1800', *idem*; Paul Langford, *A Polite and Commercial People; England, 1727–1783* (Oxford, 1989), pp. 342–343.

23 D.W. Bebbington, *Evangelicalism in Modern Britain; a History from 1730s to the 1980s*, London, 1989, pp. 106–107, 138–139. Apparently the renewal of successful careers among Cambridge graduates cannot be explained by the rekindling of liberalism and by the campaign in favour of the emancipation of Dissenters and of the repeal of the Test and Corporation Acts at the end of the eighteenth century, as both movements took place in

On the evidence of one particular diocese, it seems that for a long time, an essential condition to rise within the Church of England in the Hanoverian age, was to have been born and educated in a clerical family, and that a kind of heredity, so to speak, drove one to the highest ranks of the clergy more often than gentry origins, particularly as the gentry which gave its sons to the Church was chiefly urban and professional. The workings of patronage, be it private or public, lay or ecclesiastical, need to be more closely investigated. But it seems to have favoured also people born in the south and the east of the country, thus giving a good example of local self-recruitment; for the same reason these clerics had been educated at Cambridge, and had therefore acquired a Whig and latitudinarian ideology, which guaranteed, at least for the major part of the century, their attachment to the political and ecclesiastical establishment. Altogether, these career patterns helped to turn the Church into a closely-bound, homogeneous, and specific professional body, and to give it a gentility which had still been doubtful in the first years of the century.

both universities, and met with a very cold reception at their beginning; Winstanley, pp. 300, 304, and Mitchell, pp. 166, 190.

FRANÇOISE DECONINCK-BROSSARD

Eighteenth-Century Sermons and the Age

As a human discourse interpreting, at a particular moment in history, the Scripture text from which it takes its point of departure and receives its ultimate authority, a sermon cannot but reflect the contemporary world that, by definition, it also wants to influence or reform. When the climate of opinion and the habits of society are different, the role of the pulpit changes accordingly. The very few histories of the genre written so far underline this dialectical movement exemplified by the history of homiletics throughout the ages.[1]

To take but a relatively recent example, one may say that the controversial service held at the end of the Falklands hostilities had very little in common with the thanksgiving sermons preached in the aftermath of the 1745 Jacobite rebellion. The former was not devoid of pity for the Argentinian victims of the conflict, whereas the latter triumphantly insisted that the Hanoverian establishment had been granted victory in a just war against what was regarded as 'unnatural', i.e. unjustified, subversion.[2]

The one permanent feature is the wish to appeal to the hearts or the minds of the audience through the devices of the art of persuasion. In order to arouse a

---

1 On the history of homiletics, see for instance Charles Smyth, *The Art of Preaching: A Practical Survey of Preaching in the Church of England 747–1939* (London: SPCK, 1940), Edwin Charles Dargan, *A History of Preaching* (New York: Hodder & Stoughton, 1912); for specific periods, W. Fraser Mitchell, *English Pulpit Oratory from Andrewes to Tillotson: A Study of its Literary Aspect* (London: SPCK, 1932) can be contrasted with Peter Bayley, *French Pulpit Oratory 1598–1650: A Study in Themes and Styles, with a Descriptive Catalogue of Printed Texts* (Cambridge UP, 1980); on the eighteenth century, Rolf P. Lessenich, *Elements of Pulpit Oratory in Eighteenth-Century England (1600–1800)* (Köln: Böhlau Verlag, 1972) complements James Downey, *The Eighteenth Century Pulpit: A Study of the Sermons of Butler, Berkeley, Secker, Sterne, Whitefield and Wesley* (Oxford: Clarendon Press, 1969).
2 Robert Runcie's controversial 8 May 1992 letter to *The Times*, 'When the Price of Even a Just War Becomes Too High' (p. 8, cols 1–7) had already shown the anglican primate's stance. The text of his sermon at the Falklands Islands service at St Paul's Cathedral was reproduced *in extenso* in *The Times* of the following day (27 July 1982): 'Runcie Praises Courage in the Falklands and remembers Ulster and Argentina'. On anti-Jacobite sermons, see my article on 'The Churches and the '45', *Studies in Church History Volume 20 The Church and War*, ed. W.J. Sheils (Oxford: Basil Blackwell for the Ecclesiastical History Society, 1983).

sympathetic response to the demands of the Biblical message, the preacher has to translate the implications of the Scripture text into terms applicable to contemporary society. As a result, the sermon becomes a *topos* for the conscious or unconscious reproduction of the prevailing outlook or ideology in a given commmunity. This phenomenon can be traced in the often misrepresented eighteenth-century pulpit literature.[3]

In 1753, an almost obscure compiler, Sampson Letsome, published a catalogue of all the sermons printed since the Restoration, entitled *The Preacher's Assistant*, for the benefit of those preachers who might like to find inspiration in their predecessors' work.[4] This 13,734 entry bibliography, providing data in table form, gives invaluable information to the modern historian. Its successor, John Cooke's 1783 edition,[5] extended the period of coverage by thirty years, while increasing the amount of references for the earlier period fourfold. The total number of items recorded in the later list thus exceeds 24,000. The figure compares well with holdings in the British Library ESTC database.[6] It is therefore reasonable to assume that the catalogues compiled by Cooke and – maybe to a lesser extent – by Letsome survey the output of printed sermons in eighteenth-century Britain with a reliable degree of accuracy.[7]

[3]   This is what I have tried to do in *Vie politique, sociale et religieuse en Grande-Bretagne d'après les sermons prêchés ou publiés dans le Nord de l'Angleterre, 1738–1760* (Paris: Didier-Erudition, 1984) 2 vols.

[4]   Sampson Letsome, *The Preacher's Assistant, In Two Parts. Part I. A Series of the Texts of All the Sermons & Discourses Preached upon, and Published since the Restoration to the Present Time. Part II, An Historical Register of all the Authors in the Series, containing, A Succinct View of their Several Works. To Which are Added, Two Lists of the Archbishops and Bishops of England and Ireland, from 1660 to 1753* (London: for the Author, 1753). Very little is known about Letsome, apart from the information given on the title-page: 'Vicar of *Thame* in Oxfordshire, and chaplain to the Right Honourable John Earl of *Granville*, Lord President of his Majesty's most Honourable Privy-Council'; he had matriculated at Magdalen Hall, Oxford, in February 1722, aged 18, passed his B.A. in 1725 and his M.A. in 1728 and was therefore in his late forties at the time of the publication of the book. How long he had spent compiling the data is anyone's guess.

[5]   *The Preacher's Assistant, (After the Manner of Mr. Letsome), Containing a Series of the Texts of Sermons and Discourses Published Either Singly, or in volumes, by Divines of the Church of England, and by the Dissenting Clergy, since the Restoration to the Present Time, Specifying Also the Several Authors Alphabetically Arranged Under Each Text – with the Size, Date, Occasion, or Subject-matter of Each Sermon or Discourse* (Oxford: Clarendon Press, 1783).

[6]   The Eighteenth-Century Short Title Catalogue includes 21,398 records with sermon titles (online query, February 1992). One should bear in mind that the ESTC database covers the whole of the eighteenth century for publications in the English language, thus including works written and printed in America.

[7]   Professor Spaulding, from the University of Vancouver, B.C., who completed the computerisation of Cooke's catalogue, known as 'Spaulding's Cooke,' in 1988, kindly sent me his data on loan in 1992, when I was spending part of my sabbatical leave at the IBM Almaden Research Center in San Jose, California, so that I might compare such information with the database that I had designed in the mid-1980s from Letsome's bibliography.
      I am very grateful, not only to professor Spaulding, but also to the generous hospitality

**Sermons
1660–1753**

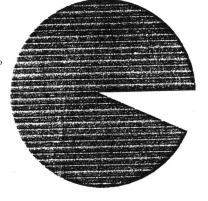

C.o.E. 13,734 93.3%

Dissenters 991 6.7%

1660–1782

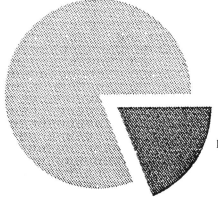

C.o.E. 24,295 81.0%

Dissenters 5,704 19.0%

Figure 1

extended to me by the computing department at the IBM research center. Without their unfailing help, I would have been unable to read Professor Spaulding's data, which was laid out in a format hitherto unknown to me and required much memory. It would be too long for me to list the names of all the members of staff to whom I owe a debt of gratitude, but I wish to give special thanks to my manager there, Dr K.M. Mohiuddin, and also to Raymond A. Lorie for his assistance with SQL.

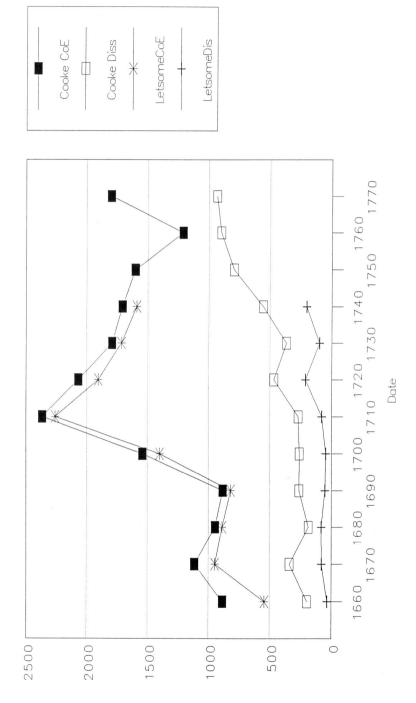

Figure 2 Sermons 1660–1782

The major biographical data include the preachers' names, degrees and titles, together with a very rough denominational indicator, dissenters being singled out by italics. This crude criterion only mirrors the contemporary perception of the unity of non-conformity underlying the subtle differences between the three denominations of 'the dissenting interest'.[8] Besides, as the Wesleyan schism had not yet officially taken place, most of the preachers considered, either by their contemporaries or by later generations, as 'methodists', were, strictly speaking, ministers of the established Church. Their names are therefore printed in Roman type, like those of their anglican colleagues.

The Church of England's hegemony appears at first sight, even though Cooke was obviously able to find three times as much information about the dissenting pulpit as his predecessor (figure 1). However, the figures may be misleading. The ratio of non-conformist to anglican sermons seems disproportionately high, particularly in Cooke, compared with population statistics. If dissenters were able to print one fifth of the overall sermon output at a time when they numbered about five per cent of the population,[9] one may say that their influence went far beyond their numerical strength. Besides, the much-publicised 'decline of dissent' is blatantly belied by the data to be found in Cooke (figure 2), as though non-conformists had been most productive when they were fewest in numbers.

One can notice the amazing similarity in the use of the Bible by anglican and dissenting preachers. They found their inspiration in the same books, appealed to the same examples and even the same quotations, particularly in political and charity sermons, as if they had been guided by the same political and religious blueprints. It was a matter of defending the social and political status quo that could guarantee the spirit of moderation so desperately sought by these preachers of the Enlightenment. This explains the consensus, before the period of the American revolution,[10] on the need to fight the obscurantism of the Roman church and the French absolute monarchy, to defend free trade and constitutional monarchy, and to promote a form of charity that could not sap the providential interdependence of rich and poor.[11]

However, there was a marked difference in emphasis, not only in doctrinal or polemical sermons (figures 3 and 3A). In the earlier period, members of the established Church found proportionately twice as many opportunities to preach on political themes as their non-conformist counterparts, who were but rarely asked to address assize sessions or royal audiences for instance. Elaboration on the

---

8 On the unity of 'the dissenting interest,' see James E. Bradley, *Religion, Revolution and English Radicalism: Non-Conformity in Eighteenth Century Politics and Society* (Cambridge UP, 1990) 50–4.

9 On the demography of dissent, see Bradley, *Religion, Revolution and English Radicalism*, 92–3.

10 On the change of attitude from the time of the American revolution, see Bradley, *Religion, Revolution and English Radicalism, passim* and Robert Hole, *Pulpits, Politics and Public Order in England 1760–1832* (Cambridge UP, 1989).

11 For charity sermons, see Donna Andrew, *Philanthropy and Police: London Charity in the Eighteenth Century* (Princeton UP, 1989).

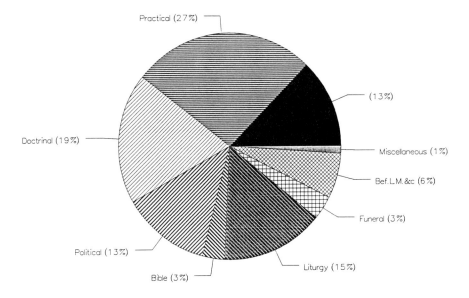

Figure 3   Church of England 1688–1753

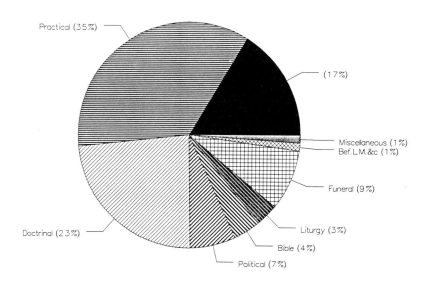

Figure 3A   Dissenters

liturgy was of greater significance in the Church of England than among the non-conformists who were keen to expatiate on the specific doctrines that set them apart from the mainstream of English religious and political life. Likewise, funeral sermons, usually printed in memory of ministers, probably helped to preserve a sense of identity among dissenting communities. The greater number of blank subject references may mean that non-conformists published more 'regular' than 'occasional' sermons.[12] Last, but not least, it is worth noticing that, although 'practical' issues were the major concern for all Churches, the trend was even more noticeable in the dissenting pulpit. The growing sympathy with this moralist strain may be explained by the tradition of 'affectionate religion' that moderate dissenters like Isaac Watts and Philip Doddridge were keen to identify with.[13]

Thus, the printed corpus of eighteenth-century sermons may be divided into three main categories of ethical, political and doctrinal texts. It should be borne in mind, however, that such a collection only reflects the impression that the churches and, often, the establishment wanted to convey, rather than the reality of regular preaching, which can only be glimpsed at from manuscript sources. Published sermons represent the tip of the iceberg.

It was common practice for many a clergyman to use the same text several times. For instance, the manuscripts of John Sharp (1723–1792), vicar of Hartburn, prebendary of Durham and archdeacon of Northumberland reveal that this minister, who performed his professional duties most conscienciously – and, as far as we know,[14] practiced what he preached – may not have composed more than fifty sermons within the space of thirteen years. However, he used them repeatedly for another thirty-one years. It is reasonable to assume, from the evidence to be drawn from his notes,[15] that he stopped writing sermons in 1761, whereas he preached over 2,800 times altogether, to his death in 1792. At the beginning of his career, he had carefully built up a personal collection of sermons that he kept for future use. For each text, he first wrote a draft then corrected it.

12 On the notions of 'regular' and 'occasional' sermons, see Harry S. Stout, *The New England Soul: Preaching and Religious Culture in Colonial New England* (Oxford UP, 1986) 4–5.
13 Isabel Rivers' limpid book, *Reason, Grace and Sentiment: A Study of the Language of Religion and Ethics in England 1660–1780 Volume I Whichcote to Wesley* (Cambridge UP, 1991) subtly and convincingly contrasts the mainstream 'religion of reason' with the sensibility of the dissenters' 'affectionate religion.'
14 Although John Sharp was a member of a famous ecclesiastical dynasty (his grand-father had been archbishop of York and his father, also a prebendary of Durham, preceded him in the archdeaconry of Northumberland), biographical information about him is rather scarce, as if his youngest abolitionist brother Granville had stolen the limelight from him. Yet 'Dr Sharp's' writings and the few known portraits exude confidence. When he succeeded his father as one of the Lord Crewe Charity trustees, he was very active in many philanthropic pursuits for which, to this day, his memory is cherished and respected in Northumberland.
15 I am more than ever grateful to the Durham Dean and Chapter Library for their kind help with my investigations into the Sharp corpus. Not only have they been of great assistance in this respect since 1980 at least, but they offered generous hospitality, unfailing support and useful advice when I was on sabbatical leave in the Easter term of 1992.

On one occasion he even sent a copy to his father, who suggested a few stylistic alterations. Our author then proceeded to write a fair copy, in his best hand-writing, onto a small booklet, about the size of a modern notebook. Sometimes the pages were numbered, but the text was always interleaved, in order to allow enough room for the author to add miscellaneous notes and corrections on the right-hand side. On the fly-leaf of each booklet, the number of the sermon was written meticulously. John Sharp also carefully noted the date and place of preaching. On average he waited for a year to elapse before he repeated the sermon in the same parish, although he did not scruple to use it in different places in the meantime, therefore exerting his influence over a wide area. Probably unbeknown to him, he was thus partly following such advice as the famous Northampton dissenter, Philip Doddridge, would give: 'Do not preach the same sermon over too often either in the same or different places. It hurts a man's reputation.'[16]

A repertoire of approximately fifty sermons was sufficient to cover the needs of a whole liturgical year. Some texts, however, were used far more often than others. The record is held by number 15, on sincerity, which was delivered 205 times from 1749 to 1792. It is difficult to know whether it was popular with the congregation or with the preacher or both, but there is evidence of a method of trial and error in the development of the repertoire. The later sermons are much less heavily corrected and annotated than the earlier compositions. It is note-worthy that John Sharp was not an isolated case. The same method can be documented for other preachers such as Thomas Green, rector of Woodchurch, Cheshire,[17] or more famous authors like Laurence Sterne or John Wesley, who meticulously kept a sermon book too.

The one text that John Sharp did publish, a charity sermon for Newcastle Infirmary,[18] is not significantly different from the manuscript version, number 32, on the 'Pool of Bethesda' (Jn V,6–7) as the draft title shows. Indeed, the hand-written copy looks as though it had been prepared for the printer, with none of the author's standard abbreviations for such words as 'should', 'would', 'could', 'which', and a slightly dissimilar use of underlining, in order to highlight words that will be printed in italics rather than signal syllables that need particular emphasis. Yet the printed version displays a more consistent capitalisation policy. Furthermore, a less trivial alteration may be noticed: the typical alternative quotation (Mt VIII,16–17) and introduction have disappeared, unless, of course, they were added to the written notes at a later stage. One might feel tempted to argue

---

16 Philip Doddridge, *Lectures on Preaching, and the Several Branches of the Ministerial Office: Including the Most Celebrated Ministers among Dissenters, and in the Establishment* (London: Ogle, Duncan, and Co., 1821), p. 74.

17 'Sermons and Miscellaneous Papers', Liverpool University Library, LGP 855.

18 *A Sermon Preached at St Nicholas's Church in Newcastle, Before the Governors of the Infirmary, For the Counties of Durham, Newcastle, and Northumberland, On Wednesday June 24, 1752. Being Their First Anniversary Meeting, Appointed for Returning Thanks to Almighty God for the Singular Success He Hath Given to this Charity; At which a Collection was Made for the Benefit of the New Building. Published at the Request of the Governors* (Newcastle upon Tyne: I. Thompson, 1752 [Durham University Library, Bamb. G .V.10/1]).

from such slight discrepancies that the printed corpus is representative of all the eighteenth-century sermon output, or that published and manuscript discourses complement each other. After all, publishing the text of this 'occasional' weekday sermon for the benefit of the Newcastle Infirmary did not prevent John Sharp from preaching it regularly elsewhere at least another forty times in the next thirty-eight years. Moreover, the author's approach to benevolence is typical enough of the many contemporary 'charity sermons': assistance to the sick results from a Christian duty, though it is necessary to 'look out for the most worthy Objects',[19] 'to whom *Superiority of Misery* gives the *unenvied Claim* of being *first Relieved*'.[20] The author praises the good management of the infirmary, due to the 'strictest *Oeconomy* of Benevolence'[21] and hopes that a new building will enable the governors to admit a larger number of patients.[22]

The only circumstance in which John Sharp had sought his father's advice about a sermon draft had been, precisely, when he was about to address another charitable institution, the society commonly called 'the Sons of the Clergy',[23] as if preaching on such special occasions were of particular importance. The father's answer, suggesting that the text be Timothy rather than James, reveals a keen sense of competition and originality:

> I cannot but prefer this latter text out of Timothy, as being equally well suited to
> ye Discourse that follows, as being a new choice of a text, (for I never remember
> it being made use of,) and as exempting you from a comparison of your sermon
> with an excellent one of Vicar Turner's, now in print, on Ja.I.27. and yet fresh in
> peoples memories.[24]

Although Thomas Turner's sermon to the 'Sons of the Clergy' at Newcastle dated back to 1731,[25] Thomas Sharp, writing twenty years later, assumed that it would be easily remembered, all the more so as it was still available in print. Two different sets of rules thus seemed to have been applicable for published and unpublished sermons. The latter appealed to more ephemeral memory, the former deserved greater elaboration, as Thomas Sharp had advised his son upon entering holy orders:

> . . . if you take a Curacy in the Country, . . . your own compositions, natural &
> unstudied and made both as plain and as instructive as you can make them . . .
> will do them more real good, than any printed sermons that you can meet with;
> and will tend to give yourself an habit of an easy & perspicuous manner of

---

[19] *Ibid.*, p. 6. Page numbers will be quoted from the printed edition rather than from the manuscript for easier reference.
[20] *Ibid.*, p. 10
[21] *Ibid.*
[22] *Ibid.*, p. 17.
[23] MS sermon no. 27, for which there are two drafts, one with Thomas Sharp's annotations.
[24] MS letter from Thomas Sharp to John Sharp, Whitton Tower, Aug. 21 (n.d. [1751]), NRO:452/C3/33.
[25] See Letsome (and Cooke).

writing, which will not easily be lost in your more laboured compositions for better audiences.[26]

Indeed, John Sharp's collection of manuscripts differs from the printed corpus in several respects. No funeral oration is included, although it is difficult to believe that no funeral service was ever taken in a forty-four-year ministry. Hardly any political sermon[27] and *a fortiori* no address to a politically important audience is to be found here. However, a homily primarily intended for Palm Sunday, though occasionally used 'on the [anniversary of] Kings Coronation' reminds the audience that 'Crowned Heads . . . are made for their Subjects, & not their Subjects for them . . . for Princes are Gods Viceregents upon earth.'[28] Although the major trend, i.e. the latitudinarian taste for 'practical' sermons, is emphasized, one comes across unusual themes, such as quarrelling,[29] duelling or even the prevention of cruelty to animals.

Besides, distinctions between sermon categories are more blurred than the historian of the genre might like. The text cannot be understood without reference to its Biblical context, so many an introduction raises the issue of hermeneutics. Furthermore, the discourse takes root in the liturgy ; hence the very atypical ratio of occurrence for the word 'day',[30] often in the clause 'as you have seen in the gospel for the day', for instance, suggesting stylistic differences between published and unpublished discourse. Reference to the liturgy or the interpretation of the Bible is so intertwined with other matters that one sometimes wonders whether they represent the central theme.

In spite of such differences in emphasis, both printed and manuscript sermons conveyed the same latitudinarian outlook, based on rational religion and the happiness of moral life. One of the recurrent themes was the idea that individual happiness can only depend on good social order, which in turn relies on individual virtue. Man is a political animal, it is not good that he should be alone. Hence the constant insistence on the notion of social contract and the need to contribute to the common good. In this respect, the ethics preached in eighteenth-century sermons was only individualistic in so far as private virtues were recommended for the welfare of the whole body politic.

---

[26] MS letter from Thomas Sharp to his son [John], Durham, Nov. 22.1748, NRO: 452/C3/33.

[27] Except, perhaps, for number 14, though its authorship has yet to be proved,and it does not provide detail of dates and places of publication.

[28] MS sermon no. 46, primarily for Palm Sunday, was also used at Houghton le Spring 'on the Kings Coronation Oct.22–1758'.

[29] This theme does not appear in Letsome or Cooke.

[30] A forthcoming concordance on the Sharp corpus shows that the word 'day' is among the most common word-types in the sample analysed so far. This is a significant difference from other eighteenth-century sermons, as exemplified by a corpus of early political sermons, a transcript of which has kindly been passed on to me by professor Neumann from Göttingen, or by Laurence Sterne's sermons, as the concordance made by Kenneth Monkman shows.

John Downes, for instance, began his 1742 sermon before the Society of Cutlers in Sheffield with a description of the sad predicament of a lonely man:

> Nay, indeed, the consideration of Man left alone, totally destitute of a Partner, Companion, Friend of Fellow, is, though an imaginary scene, so gloomy and disconsolate, that it would be quite cruel to draw the Curtain without changing it for a better.[31]

He goes on with the picture of a solitary man on a desert island, a well-known theme in an age that produced over two hundred works of prose fiction exploiting the imaginary voyage idea. In his Robinson Crusoe-like situation, man is

> . . . cast upon an unpeopled island, far from his own country and Kindred, and even from his own Likeness; banished all human sight of Converse, and doom'd to live in perpetual Solitude. What uneasy thoughts and Apprehensions must incessantly haunt and pursue him in his forlorn and uncomfortable Situation? Yea what Fears, yea what Doubts, yea what Despair? one while expecting to perish from want of Provision, another for want of Protection; now to be famished, now again to be devoured; for Fancy would supply the Place with Monsters, if Nature had not, and imaginary Perils as effectually destroy the Peace of his Mind as real Dangers.[32]

The description follows the conventions of the imaginary voyage genre, where the shipwreck victims cannot return to normal, civilised society without going through the ordeal of fear. Like the man depicted here, the castaways have to fight the material dangers of the unknown island and overcome the fear of the fall of man and the wrath of God, before they can start a new life. The preacher now turns from the desert island to civilisation:

> But let us dwell no longer upon this disagreeable and dismal Prospect, but turn our Eyes to man in his social State. And what a blessed Change is this! From viewing him before weak and impotent, defenceless and destitute, we now see him strong and sprightly, secure and happy, not borne down with the Evils, but enjoying all the Comforts and Satisfactions of Life; not oppressed, but assisted by his Neighbour; not naked, but *clad delicately*; not starving, but *faring sumptuously*; not seeking a Retreat in Dens and Caves, but building stately Houses for his more easy and delightful Residence; not arming either through Jealousy or ambition, to secure himself or to molest others; but *sitting peacably under his own vine, and eating his own figtree, and drinking the waters or his own Cistern.*[33]
>
> Under the happier auspices and Protection of society we may behold towns and Cities, and Kingdoms, rising up out of the barren Wastes and unpeopled

---

31 John Downes, *A Sermon Preached in the Old Church in Sheffield, in the County of York, on Thursday, the 26th of August, 1742. Before the Society of Cutlers There Incorporated: And Published at the Request of the Body* (London: J. Clark, 1743) pp. 14–15.

32 *Ibid.* p. 15

33 *Ibid.*, pp. 19–21.

Deserts; Arts and Sciences out of Ignorance and Error, Light out of Darkness; Harmony out of Discord; and Order out of Confusion . . .

Such are the Blessings and Advantages arising from Society, such the Mischiefs and Miseries from the Want of it.

The first paragraph ends with an interesting quotation of the prophet Micah (Mic IV,4) that was to be used time and again in the political sermons preached against the Jacobite rebellion of the '45. Like his colleagues three years later, the preacher brings a significant change to the Scripture passage. Whereas the biblical text describes the latter days when the nations of the earth shall come to Jerusalem and 'they shall sit every man under his vine', eighteenth-century preachers consistently quoted the verse in the present tense, thus identifying the situation of contemporary Britain with the prophetic role played by doomsday Zion. As they also compared Britain with the Garden of Eden or the promised land that 'floweth with milk and honey' (Lv XX,24), it can safely be assumed that they, long before William Blake, considered England as the new Jerusalem. The theme is to be found repeatedly in the corpus, so it cannot be the fruit of one isolated author's imagination, but rather the reflection of a commonplace idea of the age.[34]

The close interconnection of politics, religion and economics, a recurrent theme in the sermons of the time, is noticeable. The preachers were proud to live in a country that provided the appropriate background – political freedom and religious toleration – for free trade to develop harmoniously. Hence their eagerness to defend the Hanoverian cause against the threat of the Jacobite rebellion in 1745. The orators had a clearcut view of the world. There was, on the one hand, a constitutional monarchy that could guarantee the individual's inalienable rights to think and trade as he pleased. On the other hand, Catholic countries whined under the threefold burden of arbitrary power, religious persecution and economic oppression. The constant interference of theology, politics and economy enabled the bishop of Chester, Samuel Peploe, to draw an unexpected parallel between taxation and transubstantiation:

> The chief Agents in this Rebellion may make fair Promises, but no one will believe them, but they who have Faith to believe Transubstantiation. Do they tell us they will ease us for our Taxes? But will they not rather impose much heavier upon us?[35]

Whether he was right in assuming that taxes would necessarily increase if the

---

[34] It may be worth remembering in passing, and in contrast, that in the 1980s the same passage was an inspiration for young East German Christian pacifists whose motto was the immediately preceding verse alluding to the days when 'they shall beat their swords into plowshares' [Mic. IV,3].

[35] Samuel Peploe, *Popish Idolatry a Strong Reason Why All Protestants Should Zealously Oppose the Present Rebellion. A Sermon Preached in the Cathedral Church of Chester, On Sunday, the 13th of October, 1745. The Mayor and Corporation Being Present* (London: John Rowley, 1745) p. 14.

Stuarts were restored to the throne is irrelevant here. What is important is the relationship between religious controversy and economic theory.

The virtues recommended for the good management of the nation's wealth were industry and frugality. The theme was particularly common in the sermons preached for the benefit of charitable institutions that were designed to care only for the 'good' 'honest and industrious poor'. On the other hand, the poor who were deemed responsible for their plight through their own fault, viz. their reluctance to work, were not worthy to be relieved of their misery. Idleness was the root of all evil, and the work ethic the prevailing ideology, as had been the case in most European countries from the sixteenth century. Throughout the age of the Enlightenment, there was a low wage policy, and it was a common assumption that the lower classes, or 'the lower orders' as they were often called, should have just enough money to ensure their subsistence. Thus health was the capital of the poor who could hardly provide against the risk of disease or old age. The cutlers that John Downes had been addressing did not stand much higher on the social ladder. The preacher felt the need to remind the audience that they should save in order to be able to stand against a possible reverse of fortune. The idea fits in perfectly with the traditional themes of moral preaching, with its condemnation of luxury and the vanity of all human enterprises:

> The Dangers which you ought more particularly to provide against are Dearth, Sickness, bodily Accidents, or a Stagnation in Trade. Not that such Events are to you more certain than to others, but the Consequence more mischievous. The most wealthy Merchant is liable to the same contingencies; but when they happen, the Evil is not the same. If Sickness seizeth his Body, his Bread is got and prepared to his Hand. The loss of Limb is not the Loss of Living. If his Sheaf is barren, his Magazines are full. He need not be concerned for one bad Year, because he hath laid in a Supply for many. But now these Calamities to the Man who earns his daily Bread by his daily labour, who hath no Hoard to flee to, no Fortune or Friend to depend on, are inevitable Ruin . . .
>
> And now one would think an Exhortation to Frugality should to you be quite needless. That Wages so dearly earned should of course be carefully used. . . . But I should flatter you to say there are not some amongst you who, though they have the Diligence of the Bee, yet want the Providence of the Ant; who profusely spend what they have painfully got; who disperse in Riot what they have gather'd with Sorrow . . . By which wretched ill Husbandry they reduce themselves to great Straits and difficulties; are obliged to submit to the severest Terms which shall be imposed upon them; to comply rather than to starve; to become the Property of, or rather a Prey unto the greedy, griping Dealer; and thereby are not injurious to themselves, but to the whole Manufacture; and take the likeliest Means to work its utter Ruin and Subversion.[36]

In an age when smallpox was endemic, infant mortality high, life expectancy short, and navigational instruments rather crude, when there were no anaesthetics

---

[36] John Downes, p. 28.

or welfare state, it was obviously easy to play on the theme of the vulnerability of earthly possessions and social status. The borderline between ease and misery could be very thin indeed and a sudden stroke of misfortune was enough to shatter painstakingly achieved security.

Any such event – be it disease, shipwreck, fire, or natural disaster – would then be regarded as 'a providence'. The hand of God was behind it, and the victim could only resign to his/her fate, however apparently unfair, and repent for his/her sins in order to try and avoid, through reformation of manners, another occurrence of the visitation of the wrath of God. Those were the terms in which the preachers interpreted past and present disasters, such as the Great Fire of London, the 1720 plague in Marseilles, and in the 1750s, an endemic 'plague on the cattle', as well as the two London tremors, not to mention the major Lisbon earthquake in which 10,000 people were said to have died. So these terrible events provided the orators with two main themes, theodicy and ethics. England was particularly affected by the Lisbon earthquake, for fear that the tragedy should have unfavourable repercussions on her trade. The title of a sermon preached on the subject, *God's Voice in the Earthquake: Or a Serious Admonition to a Sinful World*, adequately sums up the characteristic approach to the problem. So does the Scripture text chosen for the occasion: Is. XXVI,11 'Lord, when thy hand is lifted up, they will not see: but they shall see, and be ashamed for their envy at the people; yea, the fire of thine enemies shall devour them'. In the first part, the preacher wants to explain why a merciful God should allow such calamities to happen. His answer is that

> GOD is obliged, (with Reverence I speak it) for the vindication of His own most *just* authority, to put to – His HAND – and to make his POWER known; – to have Recourse to His STRANGE WORK, as the last Method left HIM, to put a STOP to the *reigning* Wickedness of Men; – I mean – to execute His THREATENED JUDGMENTS, that *the Inhabitants of the World* may see the Obliquity of Sin, and *learn Righteousness* [Es XXVI,9].[37]

He then proceeds to remind the congregation that death, and the earthquake, are great levellers reducing all men to their original state of naked misery:

> These were oblig'd to flee *into* the Fields and Woods – naked *and* destitute! – they who, *before*, were so delicate, perhaps, as to be almost afraid of setting their *Foot* upon the Ground – Now exposed to HUNGER and THIRST – to the INCLEMENCY of the Seasons – and THEMSELVES on a Level with the meanest of their VASSALS; *even* the KING himself acknowledges (as one of the Accounts tells us) that HE remains in a Tent – *without* House – *without* Servants – *without* Subjects – *without* Money – *without* Bread.[38]

[37] Nathanael Dodge, *God's Voice in the Earthquake: or, a Serious Admonition to a Sinful World. A Sermon, Preached in the Parish Church of Sheffield, On December 7, 1755* (York: C. Ward) p. 8.
[38] *Ibid.*, pp. 11–12.

The natural conclusion is a call for repentance and reformation of manners. The themes are consistent with the moral preaching of the age – the need for industry, frugality, temperance and worship:

> Let the Common Trader, who may, perhaps, labour under some Difficulty, by the Interruption of Trade, see the HAND of GOD in this EVENT. – Let *him* consider his SINS, and put away *far* from him, all *Deceit* and *Injustice*, and every other *evil* thing. – Let *him* pursue his business with Industry, and depend upon GOD for a blessing. Let *him* use the *Means*, which God hath given him, with SOBRIETY – look *well* to his own family, and *provide things honest in the Sight of all Men* – Let *him* not *dare* to spend his Profits upon his Lusts, in rioting and Drunkenness, in Chambering and Wantonness, *nor* in any Kind of Wickedness – Lest the Day of the LORD come upon *him* before *he* be aware.
>
> And, let all of us, considering the Judgments of GOD, descend into our own Hearts, and see what that *accursed* thing, IN US, is, which hath contributed, to the drawing down of this CALAMITY upon the Nation; and, let us put it away, as soon as we find it. . . .[39]

Thus public and private happiness could be explained by God's interference with the course of history. Nothing but sincere repentance and reformation of manners could assuage God's anger at the nation's sins. The idea is in keeping with the traditional condemnation of the evils of the age, sabbath-breaking, swearing and drinking, so vividly illustrated by Hogarth's famous prints.[40] The preachers' emphasis on the need to give up immoral habits not only mirrors the Enlightenment's optimistic view of human nature and its inherent belief in progress; it also implies that man cannot be justified without the works of faith. Strangely enough, the charity sermons mentioned earlier insisted on the importance of good works.[41] It may therefore be interesting to try and analyse the definition of faith underlying the interpretation of the Christian doctrine as construed in the eighteenth-century pulpit.

The preachers believed in the supremacy of Reason as much as their contemporaries, so they advocated the practice of 'natural' religion worshipping a Supreme Being, creator of heaven and earth, as could be inferred from the design of nature and the moral law believed to be imprinted in every man's heart, since even the good savage of the extant voyage literature had a notion of good and evil. Consequently, science could only help religion, its natural ally. The recently invented telescopes and microscopes granting man better knowledge of the infinitely small and the infinitely distant objects of nature only reinforced the traditional physico-theological proof of the existence of God.

---

[39] *Ibid.*, pp. 23–4.
[40] But it can be argued that some of England was already de-christianised, or rather non-christianised, although the classic study by E.R. Wickham, *Church and People in an Industrial City* (London: Lutterworth Press, 1957, 6th edn 1969) has been questioned and probably needs qualification.
[41] Historians of ideas have, at long last, begun to analyse this phenomenon; see, for instance, Isabel Rivers, *Reason, Grace, and Sentiment*, I, 75–7.

However, natural religion could not explain the specific doctrines of the Christian faith in the resurrection of the crucified Christ. So the preachers had to develop a two-tier theology. First, reason leads to the natural belief in the Supreme creator and legislator. But then revelation has to supplement the deficiencies of natural religion. Therefore faith does not contradict reason; they are complementary, although one should never forget that faith is based on reason, as John Sharp repeatedly underlined:

> Nothing can be an article of Faith that is contrary to Reason. The Deity himself thô omnipotent cannot work contradictions forasmuch as he is a Being of Infinite Perfection. But it does not follow that a thing is contrary to Reason because it is contrary to the Ordinary Laws of Nature. Faith and Reason though they have their distinct Provinces, are by no means incompatible, but when properly directed mutually assist each other; And add light to and strengthen the Christian Cause, & conspire together in the advancement of Religion & Virtue.[42]

The delicate balance between faith and reason can be lost if one side is more weighed than the other. Indeed, close study of the corpus shows that some preachers defended natural religion more vigorously than others. The ratio of revealed to natural religion varied enormously from one sermon to another. There was a wide range of opinions on this point, from the almost deist to the methodists who swang back to the supremacy of faith. None, however, denied the importance of reason.

This context made it possible for biblical criticism to develop. If reason was the supreme criterion of judgment in religious matters, not in contradiction with faith, then rational examination of the Scripture text – the main source of revelation in the protestant tradition the preachers were so proud to belong to – could only be profitable:

> Our Regard for the Scriptures provided it be not a superstitious one, cannot be too great; And whenever we examine them fairly & without prejudice, the Sense will generally determine, what parts of them are to be taken literally, & what passages are to be understood in that beautiful Allegory with which Oriental Languages so much abound.[43]

Indeed, the pioneers who paved the way for the development of biblical criticism worked in Georgian England, not in late eighteenth-century Germany as is commonly believed.[44] The most prominent of them was the Hebraist Robert Lowth, who campaigned for a revision of the Authorised Version.[45] The influence

---

[42] MS sermon no. 24.
[43] John Sharp, MS sermon no. 24.
[44] This has been discussed in *Reading the Text: Biblical Criticism and Literary Theory*, ed. Stephen Prickett (Oxford: Basil Blackwell, 1991): see my chapter on 'England and France in the Eighteenth Century'.
[45] The only monograph so far on the Hebraist is by Brian Hepworth: *Robert Lowth* (Boston, 1978). For an extended discussion of the revolutionary impact of Lowth's lectures, see

of this new approach to hermeneutics can be felt in the sermons of his contemporaries, where many clumsy attempts at textual criticism are to be found. To quote but one example, John Sharp examines the description of the Deluge in Genesis VII and concludes that the author of the text, still named as Moses, wanted to convey the universality of the phenomenon through the repetition of 'all' and 'whole'.[46] This represents a modern attitude that considers the Bible, not as an infallible narrative literally transcribing the word of God, but rather as a collection of human, hence fallible, interpretations of Revelation. However, the preacher was quick to confine rational criticism within carefully defined borders, for fear of opening the door to excessive criticism and unbelief:

> And if we allow ourselves to take such unwarrantable Liberties in explaining
> the meaning of passages in Scriptures, we sh^d never know when to stop or what
> to depend on ; and an handle w^d be given to Freethinkers & Atheistical persons
> to deny the Superintendance or Interposition of a Supreme Being in the affairs
> of Mankind.[47]

The balance between faith and reason could be very fragile, once the supremacy of the latter was granted. Rational criticism, if pushed to its logical conclusion, could question the authority of revelation. The danger of a theology where reason proves the existence of the God of philosophers, before faith can reveal the God of Isaac, Abraham and Jacob, is precisely that it might lose its top tier.[48] This is probably why most of the corpus is more or less socinian, which in turn explains the methodist reaction against the prevailing latitudinarian trend.

One may conclude that eighteenth-century sermons need reappraisal. For all the ambiguity of the preachers' social and political outlook in an age when control of the pulpit was as important as control of the media nowadays, they also contributed to developing the idea of provision for the medical and educational needs of the less fortunate members of society. Last but not least, even though the crucial issues of democracy and tyranny, toleration and persecution are not raised in the same terms as at the time of the Jacobite rebellion when the Huguenot refugees were still a living image of religious persecution in a regime of absolute monarchy, even though our reaction to wars, riots and earthquakes cannot be the same, and atheism is different and more widespread than in the Augustan age, one may say that eighteenth-century English preachers can still enlighten us with their quest for rational faith and fear of 'enthusiasm', i.e. fanaticism.

Stephen Prickett, *Words and the Word: Language, Poetics, and Biblical Interpretation* (Cambridge, 1986) 41–3 and 105–17.

[46] MS sermon no. 23.

[47] *Ibid.*

[48] I have shown this elsewhere: 'L'Apologétique dans la prédication anglaise au XVIIIè siècle', *Apologétique 1680–1740: Sauvetage ou naufrage de la théologie?*, ed. Maria-Cristina Pitassi (Genève: Labor & Fides, 1991) pp. 73–99.

HANS OTTE

Christian Poor Relief
between Enlightenment and Revival in
the Cities of Northern Germany

Poor relief serves very well to illustrate the interdependence between church and society, as poor relief depends on similar social challenges and religious laws. This thesis at least is valid for the Christian religion, because Jesus Christ instructed his disciples that charity must be shown to the poor. Since the time of Jesus the church has again and again tried to fulfil that claim, and new kinds of Christian poor relief have been introduced ever since.[2]

For a closer look at this question I have chosen a limited period, the time between the Enlightenment and the Evangelical revival. During that period changes are evident: in 1750 the church and the clergy participated in the local management of the poor in nearly every territory and city; in 1850 in most cities this regular participation had been abolished. A beggar in 1750 could expect to get some money at his churchdoor, in 1850 he would run the risk of being sent back to a municipial official, who would examine him carefully. This was not simply a bureaucratic change, it also indicated that the predominance of the church in the management of the poor had ended.[3] Other organizations were now in charge. In a situation like this Christians had to look for new forms of social help to fulfil the commandments of their Lord. And they found new forms, which proved to be successful. The new organizations, which were created in the nineteenth century, still continue in the social work of the German churches.[4]

---

[1] I am grateful for the comments made on the occasion of the conference 'Crown and Mitre'; special gratitude is due to the Dr Bill Jacob for his suggestions to improve my translation.

[2] Cf. Michael Brocke et al., 'Armenfürsorge', in Theologische Realenzyklopädie, vol. 4, pp. 10–40.

[3] The best survey on the policy of poor relief in Germany during this period offer C. Sachsse and F. Tennstedt, Geschichte der Armenfürsorge I (Stuttgart, 1980). A more general view is presented by C. Lis and H. Soly, Poverty and Capitalism in Pre-industrial Europe (Hassocks, 1979), pp. 131 seq.

[4] There is no recent book on the history of Christian poor relief in early modern Germany. E. Gatz, Kirche und Krankenpflege im 19. Jahrhundert (Paderborn, 1971), deals exhaustively with the Roman-Catholic church.

In dealing with this problem it is necessary to note that Germany in 1750 was a rural country; the majority of the people lived in villages or country-towns, working as peasants or small craftsmen. Politically Germany was divided into more than 360 territories, most of them second- or even third-class states, governed by princes. A beggar in 1750 walking from Brunswick to Hamburg had to cross five or six borders; an unemployed person in 1850 would still have to cross three borders, where today there are no borders at all. Most of the cities, the beggar would pass through, were Protestant, as in northern Germany the Reformation was successful nearly everywhere. But in each city the relationships between local government and church authorities were differently defined: in some towns the magistrate had full authority in governing the church, in others the magistrate and the clergy were subject to princely authority; in some towns the clergy and the churchwardens had obtained some rights in the late-medieval period to govern and administer their local church. I doubt whether a beggar, knocking at a church door would have noticed these differences, but each reform, which touched some rights of the church, modified this complicated framework of relations between church and local authorities. The same goes for poor relief, too.

In discussing this theme we must be selective, as we cannot visit each city of Northern Germany, unlike the beggar who could visit a lot of towns to collect more money. Therefore I have chosen three examples, three towns with different political and ecclesiastical constitutions and of different sizes – Hamburg, a metropolis in Northern Germany; Brunswick, the capital of a small duchy; and Osnabruck, a town, in which the Catholic and the Protestant denominations were in competition with each other. In consequence I have not dealt very much with Catholic poor relief, as this system was of no great importance in northern Germany.

Steps to a Secularized Poor Relief

Hamburg

Hamburg in 1790 had about 120,000 inhabitants and was the greatest city in the northern part of the Holy Roman Empire.[5] Shaped by the harbour which served as an entrepot for its major trade, especially between western Europe and Russia, this centre of production, money and ideas supplied northern Germany with all of these items. The close connections with western Europe facilitated the reading of new French or English literature in the original language by the urban intellectual elite, and Hamburg newspapers were praised as very well informed.

As a free city Hamburg was politically independent of the princes who reigned in northern Germany. The city was governed by a small group of 24 men, called

---

5   Cf. F. Kopitzsch, 'Zwischen Hauptrezeß und Franzosenzeit 1712–1806', in W. Jochmann and H.-D. Loose (eds) *Hamburg: Geschichte der Stadt und ihrer Bewohner I* (Hamburg, 1982), pp. 366 seq.

the senate. The senate could not reign autocratically; in important questions it needed the consent of the citizens. Important questions requiring negotiation included not only treaties with foreign sovereigns but also regulations in religious affairs.[6]

The citizenry was divided into five parishes and the parishoners elected in several stages their leading representatives, called deacons and subdeacons.[7] Together with their speaker, the Oberalten, the deacons and subdeacons formed the mouthpiece of the citizenry. Thus all members of these bodies had a dual function: in the political domain they represented the city in negotiations with the senate, in the ecclesiastical domain they controlled the parishes. But only a few inhabitants of Hamburg could participate in this system: only 5% of the inhabitants had a full citizenship with the right to vote; city employees, clerks of foreign sovereigns, non guild-craftsmen, non-Lutherans, non free-holders and others were excluded.

For those with intellectual and political interests there was a small substitute in bodies originally formed as literary societies and clubs. In the last third of the century these societies became a meeting point for the discussion of political affairs. People, who met in them, wanted to engage in practical enlightenment.

At this point the German Enlightenment differs considerably from the shining example of the French Enlightenment. Above all the German Enlightenment was interested in projects for practical reform; poor relief was of as much interest as reform of the hymn books or agricultural innovations. In this regard the enlightened were not so much interested in fighting the church as reforming it.[8]

In Hamburg the centre of these practical efforts was the Patriotic Society.[9] This served as the meeting point of members of the senate and representatives of the citizenry as well as intellectuals without political rights. The reformers, who met in the Patriotic Society, had originally supported the poor on a private basis,[10] but in 1786 began a broad campaign for a complete reform of the public poor relief.[11]

---

6 For the religious constitution of Hamburg see J. Whaley, *Religious Toleration and Social Change in Hamburg* (Cambridge, 1985), pp. 8 seq.
7 The names 'deacon and subdeacon' for these laymen are typical of the church-constitutions (Kirchenordnungen) in the tradition of Johann Bugenhagen, which were accepted by many Lutheran churches in Northern Europe. They indicated that the reformation had to some extent renewed the medieval unity of church and community.
8 Cf. K. Scholder, 'Grundzüge der theologischen Aufklärung in Deutschland', in F. Kopitzsch (ed.), *Aufklärung, Absolutismus und Bürgertum in Deutschland* (Munich, 1976), pp. 294 seq.
9 Cf. F. Kopitzsch, *Grundzüge einer Sozialgeschichte der Aufklärung in Hamburg und Altona* (Hamburg, 1982), pp. 331 seq. Idem, 'Die Hamburgische Gesellschaft zur Beförderung der Künste', in Rudolf Vierhaus (ed.), *Deutsche patriotische und gemeinnützige Gesellschaften* (Munich, 1980), pp. 71 seq.
10 These first attempts were strongly supported by members of the Lutheran ministery, cf. J.A. Guenther, 'Versuch einer Geschichte der Gesellschaft in den ersten 25 Jahren . . .', in *Verhandlungen und Schriften der Hamburgischen Gesellschaft*, vol. 1 (Hamburg, 1792), p. 79 footnote.
11 For the history of poor relief in Hamburg in this period cf. M. Lindemann, 'Producing

In fact, the traditional system of poor relief in Hamburg was not doing well. There were three pillars of social relief: in the first place, there were public funds and benefactions in favour of the poor; in the second place, there was a workhouse, and in the third place there was private charity. In the workhouse, founded in 1614–22, vagrants were required to work at spinning, and the sick could expect to be supplied with rather basic medical care. Private charity helped those paupers, who got insufficient relief from the public funds. Most of these funds, benefactions and grants were administered by the church, that is the clergy or – more often – the deacons. In addition the deacons distributed the money collected during Sunday services. Thus the organization of poor relief fitted with the local parish system. But this system lacked the capacity to assess whether the needy qualified for relief. Especially during times of economic depression, Hamburg acted as a magnet for the rural poor, who were immigrating into the city and seeking employment. Large numbers of vagrants, journeymen and refugees, looking for charity, were passing through Hamburg.

The crowds of beggars were a strong argument for a fundamental reform of the system of poor relief. The enlightened pioneers of reform in the Patriotic Society were convinced that the whole system was inadequate.[12] During their early work in private charity they had learnt that the conventional wisdom about poverty was wrong. Up to their time poverty had seemed primarily to be a moral defect, caused by laziness or drunkeness. Therefore it had seemed wise to engage the church in dealing with this problem, e.g. nearly all workhouses had had their own chaplain, to help to reform lazy folk. Now this moral view of poverty was losing its plausibility for the enlightened. For them poverty was caused by a lack of work and low incomes, which did not suffice for any subsistence. To fight poverty successfully, economically effective help was necessary and the divided and rival agencies of welfare administration had to be united and concentrated in one strong body. 'Concentration of all forces' was their catchphrase.

Setting aside the new opinions about poverty, the enlightened concept of education made the necessity of reform plausible. First, changes of attitude would be obtained more easily by approval and good example than by fear and punishment. Second, education to work was successful only when the poor no longer needed any charity, since alms seduced them to laziness. Giving away private alms was a sort of misconceived benevolence, which would seduce the poor into deeper misery. Instead, the enlightened wanted a more rational treatment of the poor. A misguided Christian charity was not required, but a precise plan for fighting

---

Policed Man: Poor Relief, Population, Policies and Medical Care in Hamburg 1750–1806', D.Phil. (Cincinnnati, 1980). E. Braun and F. Kopitzsch (eds), *Zwangsläufig oder abwendbar? 200 Jahre Hamburgische Allgemeine Armenanstalt . . .* (Hamburg, 1990).

12 Cf. J.G. Büsch, *Schriften über das Armenwesen . . .* (Hamburg, 1792), pp. 67 seq. and 212 seq. The enlightened discussion about this point is presented by M. Zachau, *Zwangslaeufig oder abwendbar. Auffassungen von Armut in Hamburg . . .* (Hamburg, 1988), pp. 19 seq.

misery. Inadequate people should be assisted at every stage of life, from charity schools to allowances for housing or dependants to sick-benefits and cheap funerals. Those, who were able to work would be provided with tools and material for work at home. Such single steps were not new, what was new was the combination of all of these stages in a well worked out system. The confidence that, in this way, self-induced poverty would come to an end was also new.

Three members of the Patriotic Society, a professor of mathematics, a merchant and a member of the senate prepared a plan for the future administration of charitable relief, and offered it to the senate and citizenry. With few alterations the plan was adopted, and the new poor administration, called the 'poor institute' ('Armenanstalt'), started in 1788.[13] The city was divided into 180 districts, containing roughly equal numbers of paupers. This division ignored old boundaries of the parishes, because the new system did not pay any regard to ecclesiastical concerns. Each district was controlled by overseers, who visited the needy regularly and registered all information about the paupers on printed forms. If an overseer recommended someone for support, the administrative board of the poor institute had to give its approval. As noted above, there were different ways of providing help: goods, supplementary benefits and loans. No one was forced to work, but the benefits were paid at a rate so low that the paupers needed to work to survive. For example, children above six years got no support, but might go to an industrial school, where they had to work for two-thirds of the time, while the rest was devoted to teaching.

The money the administrative board could spend was raised by a weekly subscription by the inhabitants, from some small surcharges and fines and from the money the parish churches had to deliver. The Sunday collection and half of the income of every parish church was required to be delivered to the administrative board of the poor institute.

The administrative board was the heart of the whole system. Its members were five senators, ten overseers and two leading deacons ('Oberalten'), all of whom were elected for life. No seat was allocated to a pastor. For the inventors of this system the integration of the city's government was a primary concern. Religious funds which were independent legal entities were not touched. If pastors or curates took part in the administration of such a fund, they were furthermore regarded as taking part in poor relief, for the money, granted by such a religious fund, was taken account of by the administrative board of the poor institute in making subsidies to paupers.

This short survey shows that the church no longer had any specific function in this form of social policy. A highly developed city like Hamburg could organize its administration of poor relief without the help of the clergy. Nevertheless, the

---

13 'Neue Armen-Ordnung der Kaiserl. Freyen Reichsstadt Hamburg . . . publicirt den 3. 9. 1788', in C.D. Anderson (ed.), *Sammlung Hamburgischer Verordnungen*, vol. 2 (Hamburg, 1789), pp. 341 seq.

system of the old 'corpus christianum' was not abolished entirely. Poor relief was limited to members of the established Christian denominations (Lutheran, Roman Catholic, Reformed); Jews or Mennonites were not included.[14] Moreover, involvement as overseer and or member of the administrative board was regarded as a Christian duty. The senate praised the new engagement in poor relief as 'Christian patriotism'.[15] Some years previously Catholics and Reformed had been granted freedom of public worship;[16] now the intelligentsia of Hamburg praised the working of the poor institute as an example of the cooperation of all Christians in their home town. Thus we can say the first generation of members in the administrative board did not want to act as members of a special Christian denomination, but as good Christians.

Brunswick

Brunswick with its 27,000 inhabitants was considerably smaller than Hamburg. As a place of residence of the duke of Braunschweig-Wolfenbüttel it had a different social structure.[17] The ducal court was the centre of fashionable society, and the inhabitants of Brunswick, earning their living as officials, craftsmen and merchants, were often dependent on him. In 1679, the duke had conquered the town and had suppressed the authority of the municipial magistrate. Therefore political power in Brunswick was in the hands of the Duke's government; the representatives of the citizens had no political weight. Up to the conquest of the city, the magistracy and its offices had been recruited from the leading families, now only a few less important positions of the city were left to them. Among these were the ecclesiastical offices, i.e. the representatives of the parishes and the deacons. The deacons had lost any political function, but remained responsable for collecting money in church and acting as guardians of the poor.

At the end of the eighteenth century the leading intellectuals of Brunswick argued for a reform of the poor relief, along the lines of the celebrated welfare system of Hamburg.[18] The arguments were the same as in Hamburg: Even though the money, which was spent for a sufficient support of the poor, was continually increasing, there were lots of beggars filling the streets. Being close friends of the reformers in Hamburg, the group influenced by the Enlightenment in Brunswick chose the same means to spread the idea of reform. Articles in newspapers and magazines informed the public that the old fashioned system of Brunswick was

---

[14] W. von Melle, *Die Entwicklung des öffentlichen Armenwesens in Hamburg* (Hamburg, 1883), p. 88.

[15] Cf. 'Ankündigung einer am Bußtage . . . in allen Kirchen anzustellenden öffentlichen Sammlung milder Gaben', in Anderson (ed.), *op. cit.*, vol. 2, p. 140.

[16] Whaley, *op. cit.*, pp. 145 seq.

[17] R. Moderhack (ed.), *Braunschweigische Landesgeschichte im Überblick* (Brunswick, 1979), pp. 159 seq.

[18] P. Albrecht, 'Die Übernahme der Prinzipien der Hamburger Armenreform für die Stadt Braunschweig', in C. Sachsse and F. Tennstedt (eds), *Jahrbuch der Sozialarbeit 4* (Hamburg, 1981), pp. 181 seq.

inadequate; the Hamburg system, by contrast, worked efficently and adequately maintained the poor.

The journalists and intelligentsia, who were engaged in this debate, were members of a famous enlightened society, the Grand Club, which even included some members of the ducal court. Although members of this important club had drawn up the reform, it failed in its first attempt. The suggestion of taking over the model of the Hamburg poor institute did not meet with the approval of the leading guardians of the poor. It is not very clear why they rejected the plan, but it was dropped.[19]

After a while, but without any new debate, the duke entered the scene. He became interested in the problem of poor policy and commissioned a member of his privy council to deliver an opinion about better means of organizing poor relief.[20] In his statement this privy councillor, a member of the Grand Club, dealt mainly with the question of how to transfer the regulations of the Hamburg poor relief system to Brunswick. He recommended the centralizing of all welfare funds and introducing overseers and a central administrative board according to this admirable example.

Very soon after the delivery of this opinion and in accordance with its principles, the new poor institute in Brunswick was established. The churches had to surrender the money which they had formerly spent on the poor, and the administrative board was established as an autonomous public authority. The duke and his government tried to realize the ideal of an enlightened police-state. The government had to control everything, but was obliged to care for its subjects. This care included an adequate maintenance of the poor. Therefore the church had to surrender its traditional funds and had to withdraw from this sphere of work, as the further involvement of the pastors and the deacons in this system of poor relief was regarded as inadequate.

There seems to have been no resistance by the clergy to this new welfare system of poor relief. Some pastors, being members of the Grand Club, even helped to promote the reform by preaching and writing articles. One group, however, resisted the reform, the deacons. After handing over the money and funds to the administrative board, they lost direct contact with the recipients of the alms. Until this time they had distributed the money themselves and thus symbolized generosity and control. Now they lost this possibility of showing their social status and their symbolic power in the city. But this was an aim of the reform: poor relief was to become part of a rationalized bureaucracy treating every subject equally. One pastor, however, picked up this point in a sermon. He argued, in favour of the traditional deacons, that the new overseers of the poor were not chosen on account of their ecclesiastical functions. Therefore it was to be feared that soon there would be a lack of morality among the overseers, which some wicked paupers would

---

[19] *Idem*, 'Die Reform der Braunschweigischen Armenanstalt nach Hamburger Vorbild', in E. Braun and F. Kopitzsch (eds), *op. cit.*, pp. 173.

[20] *Ibid.*, p. 174.

exploit by attempts at blackmail, as soon as they would become aware of it.[21] But all this grumbling did not succeed once the duke had decided to establish the reform.

It is worth asking, why the deacons of Hamburg had not opposed the reform. I presume that it was the effect of the different political situation. In Hamburg the deacons kept their political function as representatives of the citizenry; therefore they had no special interest in retaining their ecclesiastical function. In Brunswick the deacons, who had lost their political functions in former times, now had to resign that part of their ecclesiastical functions which showed their importance for the urban society. This obviously caused annoyance.

Osnabruck

Another example of the enlightened reforms of poor relief is Osnabruck. This small town of 8,000 inhabitants had a rich past and was the capital of a formally independent episcopal principality.[22] Alternately a Catholic and a Protestant were elected as prince-bishop by the chapter of the cathedral. Since 1764 a son of King George III, Prince Frederick, duke of York had reigned.[23] The social structure of Osnabruck corresponded to that of Brunswick, with one important difference: the prince-bishop did not live in Osnabruck, but in London or, more often, in Bath. More than a half of the inhabitants of Osnabruck were Protestants, the others were Catholics. Catholics were excluded from membership of the town council, but they were supported by the Catholic chapter of the cathedral. The town was ruled by the magistrate, who acted as head of the Protestant churches in the city. The prince-bishop was not allowed to prescribe anything to the magistrate in ecclesiastical matters. The situation was rather intricate, but it had been eased by growth of the Enlightenment. Détente between both denominations seemed possible, after the enlightened plea for toleration had done its work. The system of poor relief, however, was divided and complicated, as the magistrate could not impose his will on the Catholics and the chapter of the cathedral. Poor relief was part of the canon law and in this regard both denominations had their different ways. Thus a cunning beggar could walk from a Protestant deacon to a Catholic guardian of the poor and could expect money or other forms of charity from each.[24]

In this situation the enlightened critics did not fail to be heard. First a Protestant pastor demanded reforms, evidently based on to the well known Hamburg example. Some years later, a Patriotic Society of the Friends of the Poor was

21 J.H. Schiller, *Armenpredigt. Am Sonntage Invocavit in der Brüdern Kirche gehalten* (Brunswick, 1806), pp. 19–20.
22 L. Hoffmeyer and L. Baete, *Chronik der Stadt Osnabrück . . .*, 3rd edn (Osnabruck, 1964), pp. 84 seq. *Osnabrück: 1200 Jahre Fortschritt und Bewahrung* (Nürnberg, 1980), pp. 192 seq.
23 On details of government and bureaucracy in Osnabruck see C. van den Heuvel, *Beamtenschaft und Territorialstaat* (Osnabruck, 1984), p. 145 seq.
24 L. Hoffmeyer, 'Die Fürsorge für die Armen, Kranken und Waisen in Osnabrück', in *Osnabrücker Mitteilungen*, vol. 51, 1929, pp. 66 seq.

founded. Its board included the Protestant pastor, one of the magistrates, one Protestant church-warden and – perhaps the most important member of the board – a Catholic pastor. This group proposed a plan for a wholesale reform, which was adopted.[25] But it took nearly nine years to achieve it. At first the negotiations between the Catholic chapter of the cathedral and the magistrate delayed any successful development, then the troubles of the Napoleonic era did their work. Finally disputes arose among the citizenry over the question of which denominational funds should be surrendered. Nevertheless, in the end an agreement was achieved. The Protestants had to hand over the fixed income of their funds to the administrative board of the new poor institute. The Catholic funds remained independent, but they paid in a proportion of the money, which was spent on the Catholics by the poor institute. The management of the poor institute was organized according to the Hamburg system. To the administrative board of the poor institute were coopted one Lutheran pastor and a Catholic priest. But the magistrate, who could propose members of the administrative board, remained a Protestant body, therefore the impact of the Protestants was much greater. The church and clergy were not pushed away from the public management of the poor, they were integrated into it.

Intermediate conclusions
The enlightened organizations for poor relief did not need the administrative help of the church and its staff any longer. In the greater cities, the church was driven back to its preaching duties. This development was not simply caused by copying the celebrated Hamburg example, but was generally the result of a social development, which started in the late medieval period and was accelerated by the Reformation in the cities. In the long term, the church ceased to include all society and changed to become one social group among others. It is obvious that this tendency was not a continously successful development. The example of Osnabruck shows this clearly. In the rural regions this development took even longer. But the case of Osnabruck demonstrates the social role of the church: divided into two denominations, both acted for different social groups, who were simply defending their claims.

    For the pastors these changes meant a restriction of their duties. It is surprising, that they accepted this restriction without any complaint. In Hamburg there was no discussion on this point at all, and in Brunswick most of the pastors – as opposed to the deacons – supported the reform. And just as much support was given by the leaders of enlightened opinion among the clergy in Osnabruck. Perhaps the pastors were lazy and were happy to be relieved of some parts of their work. But I think, the main cause for their support of the reform was their agreement with the enlightened principles of the reform, and secondly their

---

[25] Hoffmeister, *loc. cit.*, p. 68. F. Molly, 'Die Reform des Armenwesens in Stadt und Stift Osnabrück . . .', D.Phil. (Münster, 1919), pp. 20 seq.

concept of the church. This will be understood when we look at the academic discussion about the concept of the church. At that time, before the turn of the century, this concept was rarely discussed, neither in theology nor in jurisprudence. The ruling theology, the so-called neology, which was very closely affiliated with deism and accepted most of the enlightened principles, did not reflect on the institutional framework of the church. To these theologians the existence of an institution, which guaranteed the preaching of the gospel, was sufficient.[26] The church was simply defined as a community of teachers and auditors, the favourite name for the pastors was 'teacher of religion' – a term, which was strictly rebutted by Neo-orthodoxy later on. To the Neologians teaching meant preaching, not acting as a social worker. Thus pastors joining administrative boards, which dealt with poor relief, seemed to be very praiseworthy, as they spent their leisure time on a patriotic work, but they were not carrying out a genuine duty of their office.

To accept the cooperation of the clergy in poor relief as a hobby for some pastors was not a suitable way for the future of Christian poor relief. A new treatment was necessary, which made a new practice of ecclesiastical actions conceivable. But to achieve a new practice, there was still a long way to go. I will describe the first steps in my second section.

Initial stages to new forms of Christian poor relief

Hamburg

The new organization of poor relief was a success at first. During the first decade after establishing the poor institute, Hamburg was economically booming and therefore the administrative board had sufficient money to spend, as subscriptions and collections in favour of the poor were adequate.

But even more successful was the publicity for the poor institute. By articles in newspapers, leaflets and magazines writers praised the new model of poor relief. One reformer published a small booklet for the British reader,[27] which had several editions and was later on translated into German. But above all, success meant emulation of the Hamburg poor institute in many other towns, not only in Germany, but also in Austria, Denmark and in France. But in these countries this kind of institute failed, and similarly it did not work well in Hamburg, when a greater depression set in after 1803.[28] As long as the hand-made products of the

---

26 H. Otte, *Milde Aufklärung* (Göttingen, 1989), p. 80 seq. For the Protestant canonic law of the Enligthenment cf. K. Schlaich, 'Kollegialtheorie' (Munich, 1969), pp. 97 seq., 219 seq.

27 *Account of the Management of the Poor in Hamburgh since the Year 1788. In a letter to some friends of the Poor in Great Britain* (Edinburgh, 1795). Translated by Johann Joachim Eschenburg: *Über Hamburgs Armenwesen. Aus dem Englischen* . . . (Brunswick und Hamburg, 1796).

28 Cf. B. Mehnke, *Armut und Elend in Hamburg* (Hamburg, 1982), pp. 97 seq.

lower classes were marketable, financing was no problem. But when the market weakened, a huge organization, which got most of its money by self-imposed subscriptions and collections would run into trouble. In times of economic crises such an organization was overburdened, especially when the wealthy reduced their subscriptions, and more people laid claim to money from the poor institute. After 1806 therefore, the payments of the poor institute were reduced, the workhouses and the loan-office were closed and never re-opened. Later on, it was agreed that the poor could only once get the necessary money for medical cure or clothing. The reduced payments remained low after 1814, after the breakdown of the Napoleonic empire.

New arguments were found for this cutting back. Too much help would seduce the poor to laziness.[29] They would then hope to get continous support from the administrative board and would not try seriously to get a job or earn money themselves. The close connections between Great Britain and Hamburg make it likely that the ideas of Malthus were spread and soon be appreciated. In the debate about the future of the poor institute, the new members of the administrative board argued that more and more people would become impoverished, if the poor institute returned to the former level of payments. In consequence, further beggars would be attracted, and less money would be available to be spent on an individual family. The lower classes would be seduced into getting married earlier and they would never learn thriftiness, if they did not learn the meaning of real need from their own experience. A spokesman in this debate presumed that the poor often did not possess the ability for much education, therefore the poor institute should not be concerned about the personal attitudes and education of the poor. This demand was not completely realised, but the lessons in the charity-schools were further reduced. These schools concentrated on simple reading, hand-skill training and religion. As one member of the administrative board pointed out: there is a need for 'training for the poor but not so, that they are dissatisfied with their social status'.[30] This debate made clear, that the administrative board of the poor institute had given up the pretence to care for the bodies and minds of the poor, now it intervened only in absolute distress.

The voluntary reduction of the work of the poor institute opened the way for new initiatives. These were often started by Christians, who were followers of the so-called revival.[31] Impressed by the misery of the poor, they wanted to show the power of their faith even in these instances, where anyone else would give up. In northern Germany the revival was no mass-phenomenon. After Napoleon's fall this movement started by personal contacts between friends, letters or small meetings. Biblicists, pastors, who were followers of the old orthodoxy, pietists and Moravians came together. Later, young theologians, who had come in contact with the romantic movement, became involved with the revival, and when these

[29] Zachau, *op. cit.*, pp. 47 seq.
[30] C. Godeffroy (1834), quoted by Zachau, *op. cit.*, p. 62.
[31] Cf. I. Lahrsen, *Zwischen Erweckung und Rationalismus* (Hamburg, 1959), pp. 49 seq.

theologians had obtained a parish church, they gathered some of their parishioners in societies for mission and later for welfare work.

In Northern Germany this movement took shape with the help of English Christians: news about the London Mission Society was read in Hamburg, and personal contacts were made with the agents of the British and Foreign Bible Society, especially Dr Robert Pinkerton and John Paterson.[32] In this way Christians in the established Lutheran church learnt new means of promoting knowledge of the bible. As a result of these efforts, new forms of Christian organizations were accepted by church and society.

The field of social work was not the first battle-field of the revival.[33] Its partisans were interested in mission, mission both in foreign countries and at home. Bible societies were being founded after 1814, the Lower Saxony Society for the Spreading of Edifying Tracts was founded in 1820 and a missionary society started in Hamburg in 1821. The first steps towards social work followed the British model: In 1825 the pastor of St George's parish church, Johann Wilhelm Rauterberg (1791–1865), a strong revivalist, founded a Sunday-school. The pupils of this school could not attend the normal charity schools as they had to earn money for their parents. The pastor estimated that about 10% of all children in his parish had never entered a school.[34] This was a result of the reduction in the public poor relief. To support the parents of these children, a visiting circle was founded, which tried to help the adults by advising about morality and distributing gifts. One member of this visiting circle was J.H. Wichern (1808–1881).[35] He had studied theology, but had not yet received a clerical living, therefore he had joined the teaching-staff of the Sunday-school. During his visits he very carefully noticed the miserable situation of the poor. In 1833 he decided with some friends to found a rescue-home for children. Wichern abandoned attempting to help the adults, because he saw no chance for a fundamental improvement in their situation. He wanted to save the children from the misery and immorality of their parents.[36] To make the education more effective, Wichern planned to build a 'village of salvation', containing several small houses, not huge barracks; about 10 children were to live in each together with one of Wichern's assistants, who had to play the role of a paterfamilias. It differed from the public poor institute in that Wichern did not permit the use of any compulsion, therefore he had to use more pedagogical expedients, e.g. music, special celebrations etc.[37]

---

[32] W. Gundert, *Geschichte der deutschen Bibelgesellschaften im 19. Jahrhundert* (Bielefeld, 1987), pp. 113 seq.

[33] Later on, when the social work of the revivalists had proved to be a success, they often used this success to argue that they were fulfilling God's commandments.

[34] Lahrsen, *op. cit.*, p. 70.

[35] M. Gerhardt, *Johann Hinrich Wichern*, vol. 1 (Hamburg, 1927), pp. 117 seq. H. Talazko, 'Johann Hinrich Wichern', in M. Greschat (ed.), *Gestalten der Kirchengeschichte*, vol. 9/2 (Stuttgart, 1985), pp. 44 seq.

[36] This confidence in education was part of the enlightened inheritance of the revival.

[37] Cf. Wichern, 'Jahresbericht', in P. Meinhold (ed.), *Sämtliche Werke*, vol. 4/1 (Berlin, 1958), pp. 130 seq. and 150 seq.

The basis for the village was an estate, called 'Das Rauhe Haus'. It was given to Wichern by a member of the senate, affiliated with the evangelical movement, in 1833. At first there was only one house, but twelve years later five houses had been built. The construction was done by the boys of the 'Rauhes Haus' with the help of professional craftsmen and Wichern's assistants. Since Wichern was an able publicist, his small institute grew quickly, and twenty years later there were six such institutes with rescue-homes in northern Germany. In particular Wichern's assistants, whom he called brothers, spread the idea of Wichern's means of helping the poor. Wichern organized a special training for them with lessons in theology, pedagogics and principles of social work. Wichern had to procure employment for the young men he was training, so he began a wide correspondence, which was often the beginning of similar projects in other towns in Germany.

At about the same time, a second initiative started in Hamburg, which at first had no direct connections to Wichern's own work. Its founder was a young upper class lady, Amalie Sieveking, whose father had lost his money, so that she had to earn some of her own by teaching.[38] An unmarried woman, she wanted to make her contribution to the propagation of the gospel. She planned to found a Protestant order of women; one of her patterns was the Catholic St Vincent de Paul, the founder of the Sisters of Charity. Probably, she had also heard of Elizabeth Fry; later on she even visited her in London. But her first plan failed. When she published a call to young ladies in a newspaper to join her in living together, she got no response. The well educated daughters of Hamburg recoiled from her reputed mysticism and obscurantism. But Amalie Sieveking was not demoralized. During the cholera epidemic (1831) she worked at the cholera hospital and very soon won the respect of the doctors and of the sick. By the end of the epidemic she was in charge of the hospital attendants. At that time, she developed another project, a society of women, who would voluntarily and gratis visit the infirm. While working at hospital she had learnt where the public poor institute had failed. Therefore she founded the Female's Society for the Provision of Poor Relief and Nursing, which started its work in 1832. The members continued to live with their families, and during their leisure time they went to look after the sick or helpless poor at home. There they attended to the health, the cleanliness and – last but not least – the morality of the three or four families, whom they visited. Sieveking once said, 'the members of the Female Society have to be better informed than the overseers of the poor can be.'[39] Because of that the Female Society was able to support the relief of the public poor institute with additional help. The motto of the Female Society was that those who were in need of special help should get it.

Sieveking tried to achieve a closer link with the administrative board of the

38 E. Haupt, *Amalie Sieveking als Gründerin des weiblichen Vereins . . .* (Berlin, 1933), pp. 13 seq., 19 seq.
39 Quoted by R. Postel, 'Sieveking', in M. Greschat (ed.), *Gestalten der Kirchengeschichte*, vol. 9/1 (Stuttgart, 1985), p. 237.

public poor institute, but the board refused. Most of its members feared the Christian claim of the society. The public poor institute did not wish to be connected with a particular church party or denomination.[40] This shows that the poor institute was losing its Christian character and becoming more secularized. But Sieveking accepted this decision without any opposition, as she knew, that the work of her society was essential for the poor relief in Hamburg. 'The poor institute can only give an absolute minimum', she said once, 'our society, however, can give a maximum, so that one can expect an essential beneficial effect on the pauper'.[41]

The Female Society spread very quickly throughout Germany. Ten years after its foundation, there were 15 societies in other towns. Obviously the Female Society responded to social challenges: the first challenge was the situation of upper class women, who lacked a profession, but sought convenient employment without having to abandon their families. The second challenge was the situation of poor relief, which provided a major opportunity for such societies. The liberal view about poor relief had reduced its provision to an absolute financial minimum, now all help above this minimum depended on private generosity. In this situation societies such as Sieveking's Female Society or J.H. Wichern's Rauhes Haus were shining examples of Christian poor relief. In these societies Christians made a new approach to poor relief, after the churches had lost their former prominence in this field.

Brunswick and Osnabruck

A short look at Brunswick and Osnabruck will give a preciser picture.

Because of its identification with the principles of an enlightened police-state, the poor institute of Brunswick had absorbed the particular provision of ecclesiastical poor relief. During these years the economy of Brunswick was less disturbed than the economy of Hamburg, and industrialization with a fast growing population started later.[42] Therefore the poor institute did not fall into such a great crisis. Thus the necessity to improve the provision of help by the poor institute was less urgent and the enthusiasm of new Christian societies to help the poor developed later. After the Napoleonic era Christian societies were restricted within narrow limits; even the church was opposed to them. The only one permitted was the Bible Society started 1815, because it was supported by the Duke's relatives.[43] In the following years some pastors succeeded in founding a society to provide candidates for confirmation with bibles and clothes.[44] But this began as a

---

40 E. Haupt, *op. cit.*, pp. 27 seq.
41 *Ibid.*, p. 35.
42 Cf. P. Albrecht, Die 'Braunschweigischen Armenanstalten', Dipl. Arbeit (Hamburg, 1966), pp. 16 seq. Moderhack, *op. cit.*, p.
43 J. Beste, *Geschichte der Braunschweiger Landeskirche* . . . (Wolfenbüttel, 1889), pp. 572 seq., 665. W. Gundert, *op. cit.*, pp. 113–114.
44 Cf. Albrecht, *loc. cit.*, pp. 225 seq.

sub-society of the Bible Society and only had a limited aim. Thus it could not give much help to supplement the poor-institute. Nevertheless it proved a form of organization, which had an important future. When the revolution in 1848 had eased the foundation of societies, some theologians belonging to the revivalists started a rescue home, based on the model of J.H. Wichern.[45] Other institutions followed very soon, and Brunswick thus followed the development of other towns in northern Germany.

In Osnabruck progress was slower. The Protestant poor relief had not been destroyed or simply disappeared, it had been integrated into the public poor institute, and the Catholic poor relief had a loose connection with this institute. Therefore there was an institutional framework for Christian social services, which made it unnecessary to create special institutions for Christian poor relief. When a Female's Society was founded,[46] it did not lose the character of a society to provide upper-class women with opportunity to use their leisure time for many years. The social commitment, which was set free by the revival, was vastly absent. The popular evangelical pastor C.F.A. Weibezahn (1804–1844) had supported several initiatives of Christian societies, but in the social field these societies had little success or changed their character to a more humanitarian attitude.[47] Because Protestants could invest their social interests in the public poor institute, there was no need for them to found new and separate Christian societies. Not until after 1870 were special Protestant welfare societies developed. In 1870 the principles of public poor relief were changed by law. Poor relief became a municipal responsibility without any involvement by the churches. This opened the door for separate Protestant welfare societies, which were thereafter founded in Osnabruck. Up to that time the mixed system of municipal and ecclesiastical poor relief had blocked this development.

Conclusions

Our short survey has a rather paradoxical result. In Osnabruck, where up to 1870 the ecclesiastical poor relief was never totally abolished, the revivalists were unable to cultivate fields of special social welfare. In the cities, where the ecclesiastical poor relief had been dropped in favour of a public poor institute, the Christian social services flourished.

The first explanation of this phenomenon is the reference to the different beginnings of industrialization in these cities. Hamburg started earlier than

---

[45] St Leonhard-rescue home (1852); cf. J. Kühne, *Geschichte der christlichen Liebestätigkeit im Herzogtum Braunschweig* (Brunswick, 1903), pp. 31 seq.

[46] State archives Osnabruck, Rep. 3b IV 1706.

[47] Cf. H. Koch, *Heimat für Kinder* (Osnabruck, 1990), pp. 22 seq.

Brunswick or Osnabruck. But as northern Germany was one social region connected by a common market, the economic differences cannot be the only cause.

A second explanation is a sociological argument. Social systems, which were too large to administer with calculable costs, had to reduce, otherwise they would break down. Such reductions took place within the enlightened poor institute of Hamburg opening the way for the special poor relief of the revivalists.

Their success in this field had some prerequisites, which should be noted: the increasing misery of industrialization required more help than the public poor relief agency could afford. As the established church was unable to provide an organization which could promote any help, the Christians who were conscious of the misery were forced to use the new method provided by the Christian societies.

Some revivalists presumed that their system of poor relief could replace the poor relief system. They were impressed by the idea of Thomas Chalmers, but no city had seriously tried to establish a parish poor relief according to Chalmers' model. A voluntary system, which was backed up by small groups of the middle and the upper classes could not solve the problems of industrialization. It could only mend some of its defects, but this was quite important.

In general, the Christian societies of poor relief presupposed the existence of public poor relief. This made the work of the social revivalists easy, as they could specialize. In this way they found a purpose for the society as a whole, which could not be denied. Therefore most of these societies, which were founded in the last century, continue their work even today.

Finally I want to look at the point of the societies again. This paper has covered a lot of ground: it started with the enlightened societies, which pleaded for the abolition of specificly ecclesiastical poor relief. Subsequently, specificly Christian societies were the first to try to supplement the public poor institutes. The development of modern social services was pushed forward by societies. It is not unimportant that the revival adopted this particular social form for Christian purposes. This was made possible by the British friends of the revivalists; they had shown how to manage those Christian societies. One often forgets today that organizations like these societies are part of our common heritage, as well as the bible and some buildings. In this respect the German Christian societies owe much to the British ones. I think, it is worthwhile mentioning this connection, because it may provide a basis for further cooperation between British and German Christians.

NIGEL ASTON

The Dean of Canterbury and the Sage of Ferney: George Horne looks at Voltaire*

'But before I begin, I must drink a couple of Bumpers of Champaigne, that I may be a match for the little man – And now, my dear Philosopher, have at you –'.[1] With this mockingly familiar greeting the Rev. Dr George Horne, masquerading as Nathaniel Freebody Esq., commenced the most savage of assaults on Voltaire's religious views in the columns of the *St James's Chronicle* in the winter of 1766–67. Beneath the banter lay the serious awareness of the Sage of Ferney's proven capacity to damage the credibility of the Christian Church and its faith. Voltaire's predilection, especially in later life, for Anglicanism as an Erastian model has been made clear by Dr Graham Gargett[2] but, as Horne's comments indicate, the sympathy was not always mutual. Voltaire's apostrophe to English tolerance and latitudinarian theology[3] in the aftermath of his enforced exile in England between 1726 and 1729 might have suited the intellectual climate of the 1730s when traditionalists in the Church of England were on the defensive,[4] but three decades later the High Church party had recovered ground.[5]

By that date Voltaire's notoriety as an anticlerical sceptic was well established

* I wish to thank the British Academy for the award of a small personal grant which allowed me to undertake much of the research for this article. I am also grateful to Graham Gargett, Sheridan Gilley, John McManners, Bertram E. Schwarzbach, F.C.G. Todd and the 'Crown & Mitre' conference participants at Canterbury in September 1992 for their suggested improvements to earlier versions of this paper.

1 'The Miscellany', *St James's Chronicle*, 3–5 Feb. 1767.
2 Graham Gargett, *Voltaire and Protestantism* (Studies on Voltaire and the eighteenth century, Vol. 188) (Oxford, 1980), pp. 231, 399–411, 435–52, 473–4. See, for instance, his esteem for Bishop Berkeley, father of Horne's close friend George Berkeley, a fellow member of the Canterbury Chapter in the 1780s. André-Michel Rousseau, *L'Angleterre et Voltaire (1718–1789)* (Studies on Voltaire and the eighteenth Century, Vols. 145–147) (3 vols, Oxford, 1976), I. 132; Gargett, *supra*, p. 435.
3 The opening of the fifth letter in the *Lettres philosophiques* is the classic statement: 'Un Anglais, comme homme libre, va au Ciel par le chemin qui lui plaît', ed. René Pomeau (Paris, 1964), p. 42.
4 J.C.D. Clark, *English Society 1688–1832* (Cambridge, 1985), pp. 303–6; Stephen Taylor, 'Sir Robert Walpole, the Church of England, and the Quaker Tithe Bill of 1736', *Historical Journal*, 28 (1985), 51–77, esp. 75.
5 As A.-M. Rousseau puts it: 'L'Angleterre avait fait sa crise de "free-thinking" au début du

among its members, reflecting the extensive degree of English interest in his writings and those of other major French *philosophes*.[6] When it came to a riposte, what High Church clerics sought was a defender of orthodoxy whose talents as a polemicist came close to matching those of the enemy, an ironist who could turn Voltaire's own weapons against him in the cause of correct belief. The Oxford Tory, George Horne, was the apologist who most nearly fitted the bill. With an informed interest in every issue of public controversy in British politics from the 'Jew Bill' of 1753 through to the outbreak of the French Revolution, he contributed to most of those that affected the interests of the established Church, and did so in an inimitable style that establishes him as a leading member of the Anglican counter-Enlightenment.

The threat posed by Voltaire and the other French *philosophes* occupied a good deal of Horne's attention as he made his way up the Church. And yet, in the end, what could have been a fascinating public exchange between a Dean of Canterbury and the Sage of Ferney never took place. In the last twenty years of his life down to 1778 Voltaire had other causes and other enemies to claim his attention, and his interest in England was perhaps not what it had been as a younger man. Horne, too, found, adversaries nearer home.[7] There are robust challenges to the French Enlightenment scattered throughout his sermons, unpublished letters and commonplace books, but his only sustained public attacks on Voltaire or any other *philosophe* were contained in some anonymous newspaper articles of 1766–67 and 1771. Even these failed to provoke any reply from their victims. At one stage Horne seems to have contemplated what he thought would be 'a very valuable work' – *The history of Infidelity* – but nothing came of it;[8] his talents as a controversialist made the pamphlet and the sermon more suitable media than any systematic refutation set out in a long, scholarly tome. There was nothing in his output on the substantial scale of Robert Findlay's *A Vindication of the Sacred Books from various misrepresentations . . . of Voltaire* (1770), a work which Horne knew well.[9] Horne against Voltaire was an oblique combat of occasional shots fired from a distance rather than a direct engagement, but no less fascinating for that.

Horne's qualifications as a defender of Anglicanism were instrumental in securing

siècle. En prenant là ses modèles, Voltaire accusait plus d'une génération de retard'. *L'Angleterre et Voltaire*, III. 664.

6　Ronald S. Crane, 'The Diffusion of Voltaire's Writings in England, 1750–1800', *Modern Philology*, 20 (1923), 261–74; Bernard N. Schilling, *Conservative England and the Case Against Voltaire* (New York, 1950), p. 350, n. 74.

7　See Nigel Aston, 'Horne Against heterodoxy: the defence of Anglican beliefs in the late Enlightenment', *English Historical Review*, (forthcoming).

8　Cambridge University Library [C.U.L. thereafter], Add. MS 8134, B/1/319, heading 9 of a projected sermon against infidelity.

9　The full title was *A vindication of the Sacred Books and of Josephus, especially the former, from various misrepresentations and cavils of the celebrated M. de Voltaire* (Glasgow, 1770). Robert Findlay, D.D. (1721–1814), was a minister of the Church of Scotland, and Professor of Divinity in the University of Glasgow, 1782–d.

his promotion in the Church. Born in 1730 into a Kentish clerical family (his father was vicar of Otham), he had mixed from an early age in circles suspicious of Whig Low Churchmen and their allies. As a young Oxford don in the 1750s, his career prospects outside the University were slight until the translation of Thomas Secker to the archbishopric of Canterbury in 1758 and, above all, the accession of George III two years later. Thereafter, he received ample recognition. In the University he held the Presidency of Magdalen College from 1768 to 1791 and was in office as Vice-Chancellor from 1775 to 1780. His connection with the Chancellor of the University, the Prime Minister Lord North, brought him the Deanery of Canterbury in 1781 and, in 1790 he was promoted by the younger Pitt to become Bishop of Norwich. Horne was in poor health when he accepted a mitre, and he died a mere eighteen months later.

From first to last Horne was a controversialist engaged in the service of his High Church beliefs. He cut his teeth in the 1750s as the able exponent and defender in both sermons and pamphlets of John Hutchinson, a natural philosopher who insisted that modern physics could be validated in the Pentateuch and was highly critical of the inadequate grounding of Isaac Newton's findings in the scriptures.[10] In Horne's hands, the less viable portions of 'the famous Mosaic philosopher's'[11] thought were put aside in favour of Hutchinson's general usefulness against Whig divines whose emphasis on natural religion seemed to leave little scope for revelation. Horne retained Hutchinson's esteem for the Bible as the highest form of knowledge which made clear God's purpose for mankind through Christ's redemptive work,[12] seeing this as one of the foundations of Anglican orthodoxy, upheld and transmitted by the Caroline divines and Non-jurors.[13]

Horne was the formidable enemy of every form of religious belief that ran counter to Trinitarian Christianity. Despite what appeared to be the successful resistance of the established Church to the Deist challenge, Horne never felt that her adherents could for a moment relax.[14] Before the end of the 1750s, he detected

---

10 For Hutchinsonianism see Albert J. Kuhn, 'Glory or Gravity: Hutchinson vs. Newton', *Journal of the History of Ideas*, 22 (1961), 303–22; Robert E. Schofield, *Mechanism and Materialism. British Natural Philosophy in an Age of Reason* (Princeton, N.J., 1970), pp. 122–4; C.B. Wilde, 'Hutchinsonianism, Natural Philosophy and Religious Controversy in Eighteenth Century Britain', *History of Science*, 18 (1980), 1–24.

11 William Jones, *Memoirs of the Life, Studies, and Writings of the Rt. Rev. George Horne, D.D., late Lord Bishop of Norwich* (London, 1795), p. 9.

12 For his deep love of the Bible see the comments of Mrs Felicia Horne, 29 Mar. 1772. Her husband would, he claimed, spend 1000 years with pleasure in the study of scripture. C.U.L. Add. MS 8134/I/2.

13 The Caroline tradition of holiness, Biblical and patristic learning, and love of the Church as a divine institution, remained an important influence in Georgian High Churchmanship. This is one of the central points in the late F.E. Mather's *High Church Prophet: Samuel Horsley and the Caroline tradition in the Georgian Church* (Oxford, 1992).

14 Horne took to heart the exhortation of his teacher, George Watson, Fellow of University College: 'Let us all then, in our several stations, and each of us according to his ability, strive to recover what is diminished of the dignity of the Church of England'. 'A Seasonable Admonition to the Church of England' [Jude, 5]. Preached before the University of

the regrouping of her enemies at home and abroad with the French *philosophes* in the vanguard. He was not alone in his suspicions. Typical of concern in intellectually conservative circles was the *Annual Register*, which in 1762 referred to a 'club of pretended sages' who seem 'to have formed a sort of confederacy against the cause of Christianity, and are not a little anxious about making proselytes'.[15] This identification of a plot corresponded closely with Horne's reading of the situation. He and his close friend and future chaplain, the Rev. William Jones, were to spend much of their lives trying to outflank the British counterparts of the French *philosophes*. Men such as Archdeacon Blackburne of 'A Confessional' fame,[16] Hume, Gibbon, and Priestley, whom Horne regarded as at best bent on altering some of the key tenets of the creeds in favour of Arianism or Socinianism, at worst extirpating outright belief in God.[17]

Links between French and English philosophers might be hard to prove, but Horne was in no doubt that the French apologists for heterodoxy had drawn on previous critics of the religious status quo in England and encouraged new ones in their turn.[18] Voltaire had known contacts with rational Christians like the Arian cleric and commentator on Newton, Samuel Clarke;[19] then there was his praise for

Oxford at St Mary's, 29 May 1751, in *Watson Redivivus. Four Discourses written Between the Years 1749 and 1756*, ed. John Matthew Gutch (London, 1860), p. 74.

[15] *Annual Register*, 5 (1762), 48; cf. J. Briggs, *The Nature of Religious Zeal, in Two Discourses* (London, 1775), part II, passim.

[16] Francis Blackburne (1705–87). Archdeacon of Richmond, 1750–d. Sympathetic to Socinians and anxious for reform of the Thirty-Nine Articles.

[17] At least British philosophers, however pernicious their writings to Horne's mind, retained some tincture of a belief in a Deity. Thus Joseph Priestley deplored the atheism he claimed to find in philosophical circles on a visit to France in 1774. *The Present State of Europe compared with Ancient Prophesies* (London, 1794), pp. 22–5. He accused unbelievers (among whom he included Voltaire) of hypocrisy in attacking Christianity in a covert manner, 'pretending to believe what they really wish to undermine'. *Letters to a Philosophical Unbeliever* (2nd edn, 2 vols, Birmingham, 1787), II.178–9. See also the Preface to Vol. II, xii–xiii, and generally Seamus Deane, *The French Revolution and Enlightenment in England, 1789–1832* (Camb., Mass., 1989), pp. 160–62. For Gibbon's objections to their preaching 'the tenets of atheism with the bigotry of dogmatics' see his *The Autobiographies of Edward Gibbon*, ed. John Murray, (London, 1896), p. 204.

[18] For Voltaire and the English deists see David Lévy, *Voltaire et son exégese de Pentateuque* (Studies on Voltaire and the eighteenth century, Vol. 130) (Banbury, 1975), pp. 123–8; Norman L. Torrey, *Voltaire and the English Deists* (Oxford, 1930), pp. 199–206. Horace Walpole's friend, William Cole, was another cleric who saw early on how French authors had drawn on the English Deists. *Journal of my Journey to Paris in the Year 1765*, ed. Francis Griffin Stokes (London, 1931), p. 25. The theme is a commonplace of the sermon literature of the 1790s, especially those of Horne's great friend, William Jones of Nayland. Bernard N. Schilling, *Conservative England*, p. 233.

[19] 'cet homme d'une vertu rigide et d'un caractère doux', Best. D. 963 [Letters of Voltaire are cited by reference to the number given to them by Th. Besterman in his revised complete edition (51 vols, 1968–77)]; Rousseau, *L'Angleterre et Voltaire*, I. 133–4; W.H. Barber, 'Voltaire and Samuel Clarke', in *Voltaire and the English* (Studies in Voltaire and the eighteenth century, vol. 179) (Oxford, 1979), pp. 47–62; Gargett, *Voltaire and Protestantism*, pp. 427–34.

the Socinians in the 1760s and 1770s because of the way they had purged their creed of of Christological claims which were an affront to an enlightened faith.[20] Such plaudits had arisen primarily out of a Genevan context, but it mattered little to conservative Anglican divines like Horne and Bishop Samuel Horsley. They saw English Socinians and their sympathisers as outright heretics, the declared enemies of the establishment in both Church and State.[21] This chain of contacts among infidels all tended most dangerously towards instilling a decline in Christian values among the wider population. The faithful had to be put on their guard: 'The enemies of Religion are awake, let not her friends sleep'.[22] It was the task of the clergy to rally their people and warn of the threat: '. . . in times when erroneous and noxious tenets were diffused, all men should embrace some opportunity to bear their testimony against them'.[23]

In this respect, Horne was determined not to be found wanting, and he had a historic perspective which was of some comfort. He tended to interpret modern heterodoxy as primarily the revival of the heresies against which the early Fathers of the Church had fought and won, observing that 'Heresies seem, like comets, to have their periodical returns':[24] those whom Jones called 'the new Epicureans and Sceptics' were ransacking the 'magazines of ancient impiety' and merely adding 'modern subtleties' of their own.[25] And, if they were reviving old objections, Horne and Jones reasoned, what better way to meet them than by recourse to answers formerly given?[26] Quite apart from the infidelity they were spreading, Horne deplored the private moral character of most of the *philosophes*, and ascribed it largely to their false beliefs. His comment on reading of Diderot's frustration at imprisonment in Vincennes in 1749 was characteristically terse. It showed, he wrote, the 'great difference between the patience of a Xian and a philosopher'.[27]

20 R.E. Florida, *Voltaire and the Socinians* (Studies in Voltaire and the eighteenth century, vol. 122) (Banbury, 1974), pp. 256–7.
21 Mather, *High Church Prophet*; Aston 'Horne against heterodoxy', *E.H.R.* (forthcoming).
22 [George Horne], *A Letter to Adam Smith* (2nd edn, Oxford, 1777), p. ii. Privately, Horne contrasted clerical inactivity with the energy of their opponents: 'While the assailants are thus employed, the garrison is taken up in morning visits, driving company, & card parties'. C.U.L. Add. MS B/7/16, 1 Jan. 1788. '1787. No. II. 20th Book. Common pl (ace)'.
23 George Horne, *Sixteen Sermons on Various Subjects and Occasions* (London, 1793), p. 170. No. 7, Rom. X.13, 'Christ the object of religious Adoration, and therefore very God', delivered before the University of Oxford, 14 May 1775.
24 Magd. Coll. Oxford MS 534, no. cxix.
25 *Sermons on Various Subjects & Occasions by the Rev. W. Jones*, ed. W.H. Walker (2 vols, London, 1830), no. 25, 'The Difficulties and the Resources of the Christian Ministry in the Present Times', Matt. 28. vv. 18, 19, 20, II.388. Preached 31 May 1791, on the occasion of Horne's only Visitation as bishop of the Norwich diocese.
26 *Ibid.*, II.391. The response in France was similar. The General Assembly of the Clergy in France meeting 1770 ordered new editions of Tertullian, Origen, and Lactantius to counter the heterodox publications of the previous decade. P. de Crousaz-Cretet, *L'Eglise et l'Etat ou les deux Puissances au XVIIIe siècle (1715–1789)* (Paris, 1893), p. 286.
27 C.U.L. Add. MS 8134/B/7/1, reading from *Life of Voltaire*, trans. G. Monke, p. 359.

Other leading writers of the French Enlightenment with the honourable exception of Montesquieu[28] received no more sympathetic treatment. Rousseau, for instance, was characterised as 'a genius brilliant as a comet, but, like that, eccentric and portentous!'.[29] But of all the *philosophes* it was for Voltaire – 'the Lucian of the Continent' as Jones called him in a vivid phrase – that Horne reserved his main fire. Here was a man who had devoted a very long life to disseminating irreligion throughout Europe, and with unbecoming levity of tone had 'scoffed at every part of the dispensations of grace and Providence'.[30] He more than anyone represented in his person the spirit of infidelity, and it was difficult to counter. Horne knew that Voltairean obliqueness both hindered the defenders of orthodoxy trying to establish his meaning, while quietly sapping the faith of his readers. By imposing irony on the literal sense of language, Voltaire disguised an insidious but effective assault on orthodoxy.

It was typical of Horne the polemicist that he judged it vital to know his enemy's manner of thinking before publishing a response. He read extensively in Voltaire, and the extent and exactness of his knowledge was commensurate with his recognition of the damage Voltaire's publications could inflict. This awareness dates from the early 1760s when Horne was turning away from the first phase of his career as a known Hutchinsonian, and Voltaire's output was becoming more than ever overtly anti-religious. Horne was thus writing against fairly recent works quickly diffused and usually available within a year in an English translation. He paid particular attention to a clutch of publications of the middle 60s: *Traité sur la tolérance* (1764), *Dictionnaire philosophique portatif* (1765), *La philosophie de l'histoire* (1766), *Lettre au J.-J. Pansophe* (1766), *Le Philosophe ignorant* (1767), and *L'Ingénu* (1768).[31] Their provocative character helped mould his own vigorous replies. He occasionally misrepresented Voltaire and sometimes missed the point entirely, but as a rule his comments were pertinent enough.

In his reading Horne was especially struck by what he saw as Voltaire's impatience and his capacity for vitriolic *ad hominem* abuse of those who dared to answer him, especially if they were in holy orders. Horne felt a sense of professional solidarity with the clerics who, as a pamphleteer, Voltaire tended to lump together. He noted with horror, 'the torrent of fury and abuse poured forth by

---

28 See Horne, *Sixteen Sermons*, no. 4, Titus II, 11, 12, 'Influence of Christianity on civil society'.

29 Horne, *Discourses on Several Subjects*, III. 131, no. 7, 'The Duty of Self-Denial', Matt. XVI. 24.

30 Jones, *Sermons*, II. 388.

31 The dates given are those of the first English translation, and are based on Rousseau, *Voltaire et l'Angleterre*, III, bibliography of Voltaire's writings in translation. It was thus to his predictable consternation as an Oxford High Churchman that Horne discovered that Hobbes was a favourite of Voltaire's from a reading of *The Ignorant Philosopher. With An Address to the Public upon the Parricides imputed to the Families of Calas and Sirven* (London, 1767).

Voltaire against his opponents, mostly because, as friars and clergymen, they defended religion against his sneers and scoffs'.[32]

Despite the formidable provocation, Horne tried to be fair. He was ever ready to admit 'in the fullest terms, the brilliancy of this author's abilities' just as he was Rousseau's, but at the same time he admitted that he could not help 'marking, and pointing out to others, this deplorable use of them'.[33] He found there to be something essentially perverse about their misapplication. At least it could serve as a terrible warning:[34]

> I conceive that John James [i.e. Rousseau], and another Person [Voltaire], who shall be nameless, have been permitted to write, in order to shew us how far it is possible for Authors to misapply, in different ways, those Talents with which God hath entrusted them; that men of Genius may hear and fear, and be upon their Guard.

Horne's watchfulness never lost an opportunity of restating the connection between Christianity and authentic philosophy,[35] and of denigrating the rupture that Voltaire and his allies were trying to effect. They were confusing superstition and enthusiasm, which all could deplore, with the true foundations of a scriptural faith which had withstood the test of time. By their own writings, the *philosophes* stood condemned for superficiality, and Horne used a favourite passage in Bacon to cite against them: 'A little philosophy may make a man an infidel but a great deal infallibly brings him back to faith & truth'.[36] But these apostles of infidelity had gone too far astray to take notice of the voice of truth. Not content with misleading the public, they were denying them the comforts of salvation by their campaign against Christianity, forgetting that: [37]

---

32 C.U.L. Add. MS 8134/B/7/1.
33 Horne, writing as 'Clericus', in the *General Evening Post*, 12 Sept. 1771. Cf. *Sixteen Sermons*, no. 4, 'The Influence of Christianity on civil society', p. 110n. 'When one considers, for what end such talents were given, and to what purpose they have been, for so many years together, applied . . .' His friend, William Jones, went further. He concluded that Voltaire was a '*Theomachist*'. He 'hated the truth, knowing it to be such, and braved the authority of Heaven itself: or, in the words of Herbert, that he was a man,
> Who makes flat war with God, and doth defy,
> With his poor clod of earth the spacious sky.
[Church-Porch, verse 9, line 53], Jones, *Memoirs of Horne*, p. 131. And see also John Mainwaring, *Sermons on several Occasions, preached before the University of Cambridge* (Cambridge, 1780), p. lxviii: 'One almost trembles to consider the character of that man. The horrid misapplication of such high talent coolly persisted in from the first use of reason to the latest moments of his long life'.
34 'The Miscellany', *St James's Chronicle*, 3–5 Feb. 1767.
35 As opposed to the correlation between modern philosophy and unbelief. Horne, *Sixteen Sermons*, no. 12, 'The Character of True Wisdom', p. 289.
36 C.U.L. Add. MS 8134/B/8/111, '1788. No. III. [21st Bk.]
37 George Horne, *Considerations on the Life and Death of St John the Baptist* (Oxford, 1769), p. 35.

It is this religion which enlightens the understanding with true knowledge, . . . [that] it procures us the only solid happiness there is in this world, and opens a way to the felicities of the next.

Horne's advice to deists and atheists alike was straightforward: 'They should believe, upon sufficient evidence, and trust God for the rest',[38] and that sufficient evidence was the Bible. His position here was directly at odds with Voltaire's. Horne's epistemology rested on scripture. He regarded the Bible as the highest form of knowledge, a unique exposition of divine meaning for man to obey rather than subject to critical scrutiny. His insistence that the events treated therein (even apparently contradictory ones) had a spiritual dimension that found fulfillment in Christ was directly at odds with Voltaire's approach.[39] The latter was at pains always to judge the Bible like any other book. In fact he thought it was much more dangerous and wicked than most books, especially the Old Testament, and he took pleasure in pointing out every sort of inconsistency and implausibility.[40] This was underscored by a sense of the limitations inherent in the Bible as a historical narrative which Horne could not share.

These basic differences in approach resulted in a wholly negative perception of Voltaire's work on the Bible. Both men were formidable scriptural scholars, and had an extensive knowledge of patristic texts and Church history, but Horne's perception of Voltaire's essentially destructive purpose prevented him, quite as much as any French theologian, from admitting the validity of his insights.[41] The contrasts between the two men were quite overwhelming. Horne laid great stress on the integrity of the patriarchs of the Old Testament, especially Moses, whose divine mission he viewed as second to Christ's own.[42] By contrast, Voltaire's disparagement of Moses was notorious.[43] He argued that the Pentateuch was unknown to the Prophets since they never quoted from it, let alone mentioned a constituent book by name.[44] Horne was adamant that no one could vilify the Old Testament without impugning the Gospel, and rested his case on the basis that 'Xt and ye apostles vouch for it as ye word of God'.[45] Voltaire agreed. He never lost an opportunity of discrediting the Old Testament while yet prepared to argue that

---

[38] Magd. Coll., Oxford, MS 534, no. 553.

[39] When any descriptive expression in the Old Testament was less than clear, Horne advised that interpretation should be through 'the faithful mirror of the New Testament'. *Ibid.*, MS 449, f. 61.

[40] Bertram Eugene Schwarzbach, *Voltaire's Old Testament Criticism* (Geneva, 1971), pp. 143, 174, 254. Jones, himself a Biblical scholar with an interest in metaphor as well as holding to a basically typological line, ascribed Voltaire's criticism of the Bible to 'vanity and perverseness', *Memoirs of Horne*, p. 130.

[41] Schwarzbach, *supra*, argues that Voltaire's Biblical criticism is more acute and profound than scholars like Pomeau have allowed.

[42] [Horne], *Letters on Infidelity*, pp. 150–1, 155.

[43] Voltaire wrote frequently on Moses in the later 1760s, especially in *Examen important de Milord Bolingbroke* (1767), and in *Dieu et les hommes* (1769).

[44] Schwarzbach, *Voltaire's Old Testament Criticism*, p. 78; Lévy, *Voltaire et son exégese*, passim.

[45] C.U.L. Add. MS 8134/B/319, Heading 11 of a projected sermon.

even if one did accept its veracity, it in no sense led to the fulfillment of the divine law in the shape of Christianity.[46]

Voltaire's distrust of dogmatics gave shape to a deistic faith broadly similar to other versions current in Enlightenment circles in both England and France.[47] Horne viewed such a religious outlook with disdain. He deprecated deism as an inadequate explanation of God's character and purpose because of its complete reliance on natural theology and its affinity with materialism. News that the latter had come into philosophical vogue did not much surprise Horne. He heard in 1764 that 'the great men in France were, most of them, deep in materialism', and found it an explicable development.[48] As far as he was concerned deists and materialists alike were adherents of a false philosophy that took no account of man's true nature: religion without REDEMPTION is no religion for a FALLEN creature,[49] he preached at the age of twenty four and he never shifted from this insistence. As a Hutchinsonian, Horne laid much of the blame for the neglect of revelation at the door of Voltaire's hero, Newton,[50] whose pervasive influence on mainstream English theology in the first half of the eighteenth century has been strongly argued by Margaret Jacob.[51] Horne's private sense of the damage that Newton had done to the cause of Christianity was acute. Whatever Whig apologists like Samuel Clarke had claimed, Horne believed that the marginalisation of revelation in Newtonian natural philosophy had given a major impetus to infidelity.[52]

In his response to the writings of Voltaire and other *philosophes*, Horne revealed himself to be quite the opposite of the ponderously scholastic churchman whose works invited ridicule. He was sharp-witted, sprightly, and able to wound with effect. When the time came to reply, Horne's tone invariably had the same good humour that marked his personal life. This was a man who, in his daughter's words, united 'so much real religion with so much cheerfulness, humour – and I may add *fun*'.[53] He was aware of the value of courtesy but not for its own sake so

---

46 Schwarzbach, *Voltaire's Old Testament Criticism*, p. 19.
47 Rene Pomeau, *La Religion de Voltaire* (revised edn, Paris, 1969), pp. 395–427 for some of the characteristics of Voltaire's belief. The subject is also well-treated in Z. Lauer, *The Mind of Voltaire. A Study in his 'Constructive Deism'*, (Westminster, Maryland, 1961).
48 Horne to Jones, 6 June 1764, quoted in *Gentleman's Magazine*, Aug. 1793 (63), 688.
49 George Horne, *Two Sermons Preached Before the University of Oxford* (Oxford, 1755), pp. 20–1.
50 Gargett, *Voltaire and Protestantism*, pp. 425–7; Pomeau, *La Religion de Voltaire*, pp. 209–17; Edouard Sonet, *Voltaire et l'Influence Anglaise* (repr., Geneva, 1970), pp. 116–38; Martin S. Staum, 'Newton and Voltaire: constructive sceptics' (Studies on Voltaire and the eighteenth century, vol. 62) (Geneva, 1968), pp. 29–56.
51 See Margaret Jacob, *The Radical Enlightenment: Pantheists, Freemasons and Republicans* (London, 1976); *The Newtonians and the English Revolution, 1689–1720* (Hassocks, 1976).
52 Jacob, *The Radical Enlightenment*, p. 97; Jones, *Memoirs of Horne*, pp. 20–22; Kuhn, 'Glory or Gravity', pp. 311–12, 315–16
53 Magd. Coll. MS 1028, f. 5, Felicia Hole's (Horne's youngest daughter) account of her childhood. Cf. Samuel Parr, no political friend of Horne's, who said he united 'a playful

that it led to an opponent holding on to his arguments. 'Best way', Horne noted, was 'to be civil and courteous, but nothing further'.[54] To a remarkable degree, his appreciation of what made an effective controversialist coincided with Voltaire's. Sheer scholarship could not be enough. Horne was mindful that, in any controversy, overwhelming an opponent with superior learning could never alone be effective in silencing him. Other weapons had to be pressed into service to confound the heretics, and Horne was blessed with them to an extent which makes him one of the key Anglican polemicists of the second half of the century.

Horne shared with Voltaire a supreme gift for irony.[55] He could thus depict Voltaire as 'a modest, peaceable man'[56] prior to attacking both his beliefs and his character. And D'Alembert's comments to Frederick the Great about his fear of death was glossed by Horne with the words 'Such are the faith, hope and love of a modern philosopher!'[57] Horne's sense of irony was so developed that one of his critics in the *St James's Chronicle*, while allowing the aptness of a comparison with Lord Bolingbroke, accused him of over-reliance on it and a corresponding tendency to forget that orthodoxy should be 'grave and solemn'.[58] Horne could never have agreed. Like Voltaire he appreciated that geniality, even playfulness, could be deployed in polemic to deadly effect, and he wanted to be an accessible author. To write 'in a concise and lively way' best suited 'the taste and turn of the present age'[59] by retaining the interest of that wider public to whom both writers were so anxious to appeal and win over.[60] Ridicule had an important role in any response to Voltaire, given that, as Horne's friend, William Jones, rather unfairly put it, their adversary resorted to abuse rather than reasoned criticism:[61]

> . . . as Voltaire had treated religion with ridicule instead of argument, and had done infinite mischief by it, justice required that he and his friends should be treated a little in their own way.

fancy with a serious heart'. C.U.L. Add. MS 8134/N/8. 'Character of the late Bishop of Norwich by S. Parr'.

54 Horne was noting what often happened in Parliament, 4 Jan. 1788. C.U.L. Add. MS 8134, B/7/18.

55 Horne found it impossible not to enjoy the skill with which Voltaire's shafts found their mark so long as the target was not Christianity. He was willing to cite both *Candide* and Rousseau's *Confessions* in support of the irksomeness of being idle. Magd. Coll., MS 534, no. ccclxxxvi. Jones, *Memoirs of Horne*, 'Essays and Thoughts on Various Subjects and from Various Authors', pp. 330–1. Cf. Advertisement to *The Philosophical Dictionary for the Pocket written in French by A Society of Men of Letters*: 'Where he [Voltaire] does not intermeddle with religion, he is very entertaining, and oftentimes instructive'.

56 *St James's Chronicle*, 13–15 Jan. 1767.

57 C.U.L. Add. MS 8134/B/8/114, '1788. No. III.' [21st Bk], 28 Dec. 1788.

58 Letter from 'Misomountebank' in *St James's Chronicle*, 14–16 Apr. 1767.

59 [Horne], *Letters on Infidelity*, p. 2. For his insistence on the value of brevity in controversy, see 'The Duty of Contending for the Faith', 1 July 1786, *Sixteen Sermons*, pp. 402–4.

60 For Voltaire's intended reader see J.R. Monty, *Le style polemique de Voltaire* (Studies on Voltaire and the eighteenth century, vol. 44) (Geneva, 1966), pp. 13, 193.

61 Jones, *Memoirs of Horne*, p. 125.

Horne knew and approved of the response of two authors, Nonnotte and Bergier, to the main Enlightenment writers and the 'eminent service' they had done, and their works undoubtedly inspired his own response.[62] He applauded the 'civil language' of their criticism, in such contrast to Voltaire's sneers and abusiveness.[63] The use to which the ex-Jesuit, Claude-François Nonnotte (1711–93), put his skills as a historian, was certainly noticed to good effect by Horne. Nonnotte's principal work, *Les Erreurs de Voltaire*, published in two volumes at Avignon in 1762, set out to discredit Voltaire's scholarship.[64] Nonnotte's rather ponderous style contrasted unfavourably with Horne's, but it did not stop him winning a wide readership as its republication no fewer than eight times over the next eight years indicated.[65] His success may well have encouraged Horne to believe that he could be no less effective in undermining Voltaire's reputation as a Biblical scholar.[66] The abbé Nicolas Sylvain Bergier, canon of Notre-Dame, was another talented defender of the Catholic faith.[67] He had made his mark with a book directed against Rousseau's 'Vicaire savoyard' chapter in *Emile*, called *Le Déisme réfuté par lui-même* (1765),[68] and this was certainly the sort of polemic to catch Horne's eye, as were Bergier's monthly ripostes (June 1766 – November 1767) to forty seven major articles in Voltaire's *Dictionnaire philosophique portatif*.[69]

It was of little concern to Horne that both Nonnotte and Bergier were Catholic authors. Horne took no comfort from the fact that the shafts of the Sage of Ferney were directed primarily against the Catholic Church in France,[70] and its powers as a corporate institution able to function with quasi-autonomy in a monarchical state. If Voltaire pointed in preference to an Erastian settlement, such as he perceived the English one to be, this was not how Horne saw it. While a staunch defender of the Church-State alliance, like most High Churchmen he saw it as one

---

62 Horne, *Letters on Infidelity*, pp. 300–1. Jones reported on the extent to which 'the learned of the English and Roman persuasions' could agree 'against our new philosophers'. [William Jones], *Observations in a Journey to Paris, by way of Flanders* (2 vols, London, 1777), I. 178.

63 C.U.L Add. MS 8134/B/7/1.

64 A. Monod, *De Pascal à Chateaubriand: les defenseurs du Christianisme de 1670 à 1802* (Paris, 1916), pp. 381–2, and n.

65 Charles Simond, *Les AntiVoltairiens* (Paris, 1889), p. 263n.

66 *Ibid.*, p. 263n; Pomeau, *La Religion de Voltaire*, p. 344.

67 'Il faut convenir que M. l'abbé Bergier est un homme très superieur aux gens de son métier . . . Il a de l'erudition et même de la critique'. Baron F.M. de Grimm, *Correspondance littéraire, philosophique et critique*, ed. Suard (17 vols, Paris, 1813–14), VII. 225. See also R.R. Palmer, *Catholics and Unbelievers in eighteenth-century France* (New York, 1939), pp. 96–102; Alfred J. Bingham, 'The Abbé Bergier: An eighteenth century Catholic Apologist', *Modern Language Review*, 54 (1959), 337–50; 'The Earliest Criticism of Voltaire's *Dictionnaire Philosophique*', *Studies in Voltaire and the eighteenth century*, 47 (1966), pp. 15–38; Monod, *De Pascal à Chateaubriand*, pp. 421–2; Lanfrey, *L'Eglise et les philosophes au XVIIIe siècle* (Paris, 1855), p. 16.

68 Monod, *De Pascal à Chateaubriand*, pp. 421–3.

69 Bingham, 'The Abbé Bergier', p. 341.

70 Cf. Rev. William Cole's concern at anticlerical feelings in France, especially as directed against the regular clergy. *Journal of my Journey*, p. 27.

of mutual respect and advantage in which the Church's role as the guardian of
religious truths and the visible agency of grace was fundamental.[71]

Unlike many of his countrymen, he did not applaud what he read in the *Traité
sur la tolerance* (published 1763) of Voltaire's efforts for religious toleration in the
wake of the cases of Calas and later De la Barre. Voltaire might deplore the
revocation of the Edict of Nantes and shudder at the Inquisition, but Horne did
not let this side of his adversary's character weigh in the balance on his behalf. He
shared William Jones's suspicion that Voltaire's zeal against persecution was 'at
bottom nothing but spite against Christianity, and tenderness to blasphemy. He
sees no evil in persecution when good Christians are the objects of it'.[72] Nor did
Horne welcome the damage done to the standing of the Gallican Church from
Voltaire's campaign against *l'infâme*.[73] Rather Horne possessed an underlying sympathy for its predicament as a model of the vulnerability of all organised religion.
As far as he was concerned, the French opponents of orthodoxy were merely the
vanguard of an army of infidels at work in every state whether Catholic or
Protestant, a force dedicated to the destruction of Christianity and the institutions
which the faith had fostered,[74] working to replace it with 'a system of universal
scepticism'.[75] 'Popery', Horne opined, 'may be bad; but irreligion is not better'
offering a cautionary tale of a Catholic convert whom his friends had sent to
Ferney for a 'cure'. The predictable result was that the young gentleman returned
home 'a confirmed infidel' ready to write against the faith.[76]

That was precisely the course that Voltaire was taking himself in the early
1760s. The inception of his campaign against *l'infâme* was signalled by the publication of a devastating attack on the Bible in the *Sermon des Cinquante*[77] which
coincided with Horne starting work on what he called his 'evangelical comment'
on the Psalms.[78] He found himself immensely moved by 'the truly great and
glorious things contained in those wonderful hymns',[79] and these labours in the
cause of encouraging the devotions of the faithful sharpened his awareness of
Voltaire's contrary intent. So did publication of the Complete Works of Voltaire in
English between 1761 and 1765.[80] His disapproval of the increasingly dominant

71 Horne, *Discourses on Several Subjects and Occasions* (5 vols, 4th edn, London, 1804), II.
   160, no. 6 'The Unspeakable Gift', Eph. IV. 7, 8 June 1757, Whit Tuesday; III. 123, no.
   6, 'The Duty of Praying for Governors', Canterbury, 25 Oct. 1788.
72 [Jones], *Travels*, II. 181.
73 Schilling, *Conservative England*, pp. 211–12.
74 *Ibid.*, p. 216.
75 Jones, *Sermons*, II. 388.
76 [Horne], *Letters on Infidelity*, p. 73. He probably had the example of Gibbon in mind.
77 Schwarzbach, *Voltaire's Old Testament Criticism*, p. 18; Pomeau, *La Religion de Voltaire*, pp.
   184–9.
78 Published in 1776 as *Commentary on the Psalms* in 2 vols. Cf. Arnold Ages, 'Voltaire et les
   Psaumes, un livre admiré', *Revue de l'Université d'Ottawa*, 36 (1966), pp. 61–5, which
   points out Voltaire's admiration for the Psalms and their inspiration on his own writing
   and style.
79 Horne to George Berkeley, 16 Sept. 1763, B.L. Add. MSS 39311 (fo. 141).
80 36 vols appeared between 25 Feb. and 1 Mar. 1765 [ed. T. Smollett, M.D.T. Franklin].

anti-religious strain within the Enlightenment enterprise on the continent grew all the stronger and he told Jones of his wish that 'Johnson would mount his dray-horse and ride over some of these fellows'. It was a reflection of the esteem that Samuel Johnson had acquired in High Church circles, but he never took up the challenge. Instead it was left for Horne to respond not, as Jones observed, 'mounted upon a dray-horse' but on 'a light courser, to hunt them fairly down'.[81]

Horne was by no means the only Briton who had come to deplore Voltaire's influence. Goldsmith might praise his humanity, virtue and attainments in Letter 43 of *The Citizen of the World* in 1763 on hearing a false report of his death,[82] but a decreasing number echoed this view, especially if they were clergymen.[83] After publication of *Candide* in 1759 Voltaire moved to attack more explicitly the fundamentals of religious faith by identifying the Bible and the Church as the sources of superstition and tyranny.[84] This shift of strategy in the early 1760s marked a decisive break for Voltaire, and was barely anticipated in the 'histories' of the previous decade, except perhaps in the introduction to the *Essai sur les moeurs* on the 'philosophie de l'histoire'. Quite suddenly the danger posed by Voltaire to orthodoxy in Britain became apparent to the faithful,[85] and provoked a counterattack. Thus the Scottish professor, Robert Findlay, took issue with Voltaire's biblical scholarship in his *Philosophy of History*, and was surprised at the extent of public interest in the debate.[86]

This topicality was not lost on Horne. He had read most of Voltaire's historical studies of the 1750s which focus on the evils inflicted on their fellows by religious men and they seemed to him crude in their psychological understanding.[87] This served to confirm his opinion that Voltaire, like so many critics of religion, had the most superficial understanding of its immutable character:[88]

. . . it [religion] does not change with the changing tempers, dispositions, and interests of mankind, in different times and places.

He was personally unimpressed by Voltaire's inability to see manifestations of religious zeal as anything more than fanaticism usually motivated by wickedness,[89]

There was another edition in 14 parts brought out between 1779 and 1781 edited by the Rev. D. Williams, H. Downman, and W. Campbell. Full bibliographical details are in Rousseau, *Voltaire et l'Angleterre*, III. 978–81, 986–88.

81 Jones, *Memoirs of Horne*, pp. iii, iv.
82 Rousseau, *L'Angleterre et Voltaire*, II. 587. For Goldsmith's complicated attitude to Voltaire and his writings, see *Ibid.*, II. 578–88.
83 Schilling, *Conservative England*, pp. 3–4, 209–10; Rousseau, *L'Angleterre et Voltaire*, III. 617–19, 850–1, 869.
84 J.R. Monty, *Le style polémique de Voltaire* (Geneva, 1966), p. 12.
85 Among them Bishop Warburton, John Wesley and Mrs Montagu. The latter was in no two minds about Voltaire – 'This creature is a downright rebel to his God'. *Letters of Mrs Elizabeth Montagu* (4 vols, London, 1813), IV.185–6.
86 Findlay, *A Vindication*, pp. iii–v.
87 Monod, *De Pascal à Chateaubriand*, p. 381.
88 [Horne], *Letters on Infidelity*, p. 40.
89 Pomeau, *La Religion de Voltaire*, p. 273.

but he was well aware that this insidious message would find an English audience. It was brilliantly embodied in the *Dictionnaire philosophique portatif* (1764–69), where a range of theological subjects are surveyed by Voltaire in a philosophical and rational manner calculated to offend the faithful.

Horne was one of numerous English readers who were catered for by a translation within the year, which he approved but seems to have had no part in.[90] This was a collective enterprise undertaken by a self-proclaimed 'Society of Men of Letters' who, in their advertisement to the volume, made clear that they wanted to be first to undertake the translation of the *Dictionnaire* lest someone else had done it first 'who would perhaps have been glad of opportunity of spreading its errors'. To make doubly sure the unwary reader was protected from the snares of Voltaire, the 'Men of Letters' added their own Notes intended, as the title page put it, to refute 'such Passages as are in any way exceptionable in regard to Religion'.[91] But even the protective shield of annotation could not conceal Voltaire's underlying hostility to Old Testament Judaism in order to sap the basis of the Gospel.[92]

Having read the book, Horne argued that a very different conclusion could be drawn from this collection of 'the follies and absurdities of mankind', one which counted against the '*sufficiency of the light of nature*' on which the *philosophes* set so much store and reminded men of their need for salvation.[93] He found the argumentative strategy of the book unpersuasive and Voltaire guilty of unfairness to Christian theologians and historians. Nothing in particular was to be proved by 'Collecting the slips, blunders, absurdities of commentators & defenders, so endeavouring to depreciate their labours & render them contemptible & religion thro' them',[94] and yet such cataloguing was seen by Horne as Voltaire's 'grand battery' in the *Dictionnaire*.[95] For Voltaire to search the Scriptures, the Fathers and the course of Church history generally for corruption, obscenities and absurdities,[96] and argue that these things counted decisively against Christianity was unpersuasive; even if it was conceded that they were largely the product of 'ignorance, superstition, and enthusiasm'[97] they could not in themselves invalidate the

---

90   The full title was *The Philosophical Dictionary for the Pocket. Written in French by A Society of Men of Letters, and translated into English from the last Geneva edition, corrected by the Authors. With Notes, containing a Refutation of such Passages as are in any way exceptionable in regard to Religion* (London, 1765).

91   See also the 'Advertisement' to the book.

92   Schwarzbach, *Voltaire's Old Testament Criticism*, p. 78.

93   [Horne], *Letters on Infidelity*, p. 40.

94   Heading 5 of notes for a sermon 'We are not Ignorant of his Devices', C.U.L. Add. MSS 8134/B/1/318.

95   *Letters on Infidelity*, p. 40. Cf. Horne, *Sixteen Sermons*, no. 4, p. 110n. 'Influence of Christianity on Civil Society': 'This is the method invariably pursued, in the numerous novels, and other tracts of Voltaire'. Horne also identified Hume in his *Natural History of Religion* as guilty of the same ploy.

96   See Voltaire to Helvetius, 4 Oct. 1763, B. 10618: 'Il y a une belle histoire à faire, c'est celle des contradictions. . . .'

97   Magd. Coll., Oxford, MS 534, 'Thoughts on Various subjects', p. 48, no. cxxxviii. See also no. cxxxiii. Cf. *Letters on Infidelity*, p. 40, where Horne argued that religion was not 'to be

Christian religion. That, as Horne contended, was a divine institution, whose truths no amount of human sinfulness could undo. To an appreciable degree, this riposte came close to an effective a refutation of Voltaire's finding that religion had done mankind much harm.

Confident that Voltaire could be rebutted, Horne's circle were greatly alarmed at the damage the *Dictionnaire philosophique portatif* was likely to inflict on orthodoxy, not least from its risible treatment of sacred subjects, and its praise of deviations from Nicean Christianity like the Socinians. It was accordingly decided to issue a formal reply. Horne's friends deemed it essential to protect 'weak people' from the perplexities raised by men like Voltaire who were so apt to raise 'difficulties about the parts' of religion.[98] In this respect he represented a greater danger than did outright atheists, and demanded rather than invited refutation. The original scheme seems to have been for Horne's friend and arch-Hutchinsonian, William Jones, the Rector of Pluckley in Kent, to undertake the task, but he was privately advised by Archbishop Secker in the summer of 1766 to postpone any such plan.[99] Archdeacon Blackburne's *The Confessional* calling for changes in subscription to the Thirty Nine Articles had come out in the meantime, and a reply to this work was to have the first priority. Secker's involvement indicated the high level of concern in the Church of England at the threat Voltaire's *Dictionnaire* letter posed to believers everywhere: Voltaire's fierce criticisms of the doctrines and practices of the Gallican Church could so easily be applied to the tenets of Anglicanism.

Jones was ruled out, but Horne considered the situation so critical that he was prepared to defy Secker's prohibition by writing anonymously. He could not resist the opportunity that came his way when in 1766 the quarrel between Rousseau and Hume errupted in the columns of the *St James's Chronicle*.[100] The very public dispute generated a correspondance in the newspaper on both sides of the question.[101] Horne found it impossible not to get embroiled. This was precisely the sort of opening for which critics like him had been waiting, and his pleasure was heightened when on 8 April 1766 a loose English translation of Voltaire's *Lettre au*

charged with the guilt of practices, against which it protests in every page. No demonstration in Euclid can be clearer than this'. Cf. Voltaire to Damilaville, 26 Dec. 1762, B.10046, 'La théologie m'amuse: la folie de l'esprit humain est dans toute sa plenitude'.
99 Samuel Horne (his brother) to Berkeley, 17 July 1766, B.L. Add. MS 39311 (fo. 179). Instead the archbishop gave Jones careful guidelines within which to execute a reply to Blackburne's *Confessional*.
100 Margaret Hill Peoples, 'La Querelle Rousseau-Hume', *Annales Rousseau*, 18 (1927–28), 1–331 has the texts of many of the letters that appeared in the *St James's Chronicle* on the subject in 1766 and 1767. See also J. Churton Collins, *Voltaire, Montesquieu and Rousseau in England* (London, 1908), pp. 233–8; Louis-J. Courtois, *Séjour de Rousseau en Angleterre (1766–1767)* (Geneva, 1911); Henri Roddier, *J.-J. Rousseau en Angleterre au XVIIIe siècle* (Paris, 1950), pp. 259–306; Ronald Grimsley, *Jean-Jacques Rousseau: A Study in Self-Awareness* (Cardiff, 1961), pp. 199–204; Rousseau, *L'Angleterre et Voltaire*, I. 251–8; Edward Duffy, *Rousseau in England* (Berkeley, 1979), pp. 24–7.
101 See Peoples, 'La Querelle Rousseau-Hume', pp. 240–44, and App. b, pp. 307–20.

Dr Pansophe was published denouncing Rousseau's unbelief.[102] Horne revelled in the public wranglings of the *philosophes*:[103]

> Rousseau, it seems, says Voltaire, does not believe in God; and Voltaire affirms Rousseau to be undermining Christianity. Voltaire calls Rousseau an Infidel, and Rousseau insists upon it, that Voltaire is an Atheist. And then, for poor Mr Hume, what Voltaire thinks of him, or he of Voltaire, we know not at present: But Rousseau declares him to be 'worse than an Infidel', and he [Hume] tells us, Rousseau is ran mad with Pride.

This was the tone that Horne adopted from the moment of his debut in the *St James's Chronicle* on 30 December 1766 in the guise of 'Nathaniel Freebody Esq.' As such he produced a regular column called 'The Miscellany', and it lasted well into the the spring of the following year. Horne used 'The Miscellany' to good effect against every enemy of orthodoxy who came into his sights (liberal Anglicans as well as French *philosophes*), and never deployed his gifts as a wry humorist to better effect. In the issue of 13–15 January 1767 he drew up the twelve heads of an imaginary indictment of Hume by Rousseau, and then the sixth and seventh issues of the 'Miscellany', published for 3–5 and 10–12 February, Horne gave to the public what he claimed to be 'a very great curiosity', a Confession of Faith by Voltaire as it appeared at the end of his *Lettre au Dr Pansophe*. The likelihood of Voltaire's authorship was fairly high,[104] and it was too tempting a document for Horne to ignore. Even if he turned out to be wrong the benevolent deism of its contents appeared a neat general summary of 'the sentiments of the Voltaire's, the D'Alembert's, and others on our own side of the water'. He lambasted it so ferociously to the extent that Voltaire stood accused 'of almost every crime under Heaven' as some correspondants on 'Nathaniel Freebody's' column complained. One, writing from Oxford, pointed out that Horne had 'endangered the Heads of some of our best Friends in aiming your stroke at our enemy'.[105]

Horne commented on every clause of Voltaire's 'Confession'. He thus cited Voltaire's insistence that 'I love him [God] and serve him, as well as I am able, in men, my Fellow Creatures and his Children'. Horne's superscription was quite damning: 'Videlicet, by breaking his Laws, and blaspheming his Revelations; by setting a glorious example of Infidelity and Profligacy, and encouraging all nations and Languages to follow it'. Again, Voltaire was quoted as claiming that, *inter alia,*

---

102 *Ibid.*, pp. 74, 197–99. The *Lettre au docteur J.-J. Pansophe* appeared concurrently in French and English versions. There is a summary and translation in *Gentleman's Magazine*, 36 (1766), 563–66. For the original see *Mélanges de Voltaire*, ed. van den Heurel (Paris, 1961), pp. 849–57.

103 Issue 3 of the 'Miscellany', *St James's Chronicle*, 13–15 Jan. 1767.

104 Rousseau attributed it to Voltaire, who denied his authorship and gave it to either Bordes or the abbé Coyer. *Oeuvres completes de Voltaire* (54 vols, nouvelle édition, Paris, 1877–85), vol. 17, 17 ff.

105 See, for instance, Solomon Freemind, 21–24 Feb. and 3–5 March 1767, and Philospurnius, issue of 12–14 Mar. These arguments seem to have carried weight with Horne. At any rate Nathaniel Freebody's 'Miscellany' ceased in the summer of 1767.

everyone deserved divine mercy 'who does Justice, who comforts the Miserable, who relieves the Poor, who is no Bigot, serves God as He himself requires, and fulfills the Law'. Horne saw this exposition as humbug, a specious claim to moral respectability from someone who had forfeited every claim to it by his undermining of the Christian faith. For Voltaire to state 'Vice, Knavery, and Slander are the only Iniquities I know of' stung Horne deeply as his response showed: 'And yet there is not a man in Europe, whose Knowledge in that way is more extensive'. Horne hinted at even darker crimes:

> Be not deceived, my dear Philosopher, nor attempt in vain to deceive us. It will puzzle your own dear self to frame a Law, fit to appear in Public, which will not condemn you. What then will become of you, when tried by the all-perfect Law of the Most High?

This suggestion of repentance to Voltaire in his old age was one that appealed to Horne, though he considered its likelihood uncertain: 'Whether, after sinning with an high hand, till seventy, he will, or can repent, is another Question'. Yet it was an awesome theme that even made Horne put aside an ironical mode in favour of a direct exhortation to Voltaire to adopt a Christian life:

> Divest yourself of Passion and Prejudice; reform your manners; cease to do Evil; learn to do well; consider, you are now well stricken in years; Death is near, and Judgment will follow. Repent, and you will soon believe, take my word for it.

Horne gave up his persona as Nathaniel Freebody in midsummer of 1767, but he returned in a new guise – 'Clericus' – in a different newspaper, the *General Evening Post,* four years later. His targets were various, among them the publications of Voltaire subsequent to the *Dictionnaire philosophique* also claimed his notice. In the issue of 12 September 1771 he wrote at length about a translation of Voltaire's *L'Ingénu,* a book with rather Rousseauian theses on the emotions which had appeared in English under the title *Pupil of Nature.*[106] Horne put satire aside in favour of an unambiguous warning to intending readers. It was, he admitted, 'a pleasing and amusing tale', but deplorably concluded by representing faith and virtue 'in a ridiculous and contemptible light'. This was an exaggeration, but Horne was convinced that Voltaire had an underlying malevolent purpose. He certainly underscored the differences between the two of them as to what constituted appropriate subject matter for humour:

> To satirize, with wit and humour, the Vices and follies of mankind, is one thing; but to burlesque and convert into smut an institution of God [marriage], held in reverence through the whole Christian world, is another.

Though his contributions to the newspapers ceased in 1771, Horne was ready to use the pulpit to defend orthodoxy, and in so doing revealed that his dislike of

---

106 This was the second English translation of *L'Ingénu,* appearing in spring 1771. Other reviews were more favourable. See Rousseau, *L'Angleterre et Voltaire,* III. 604.

the French Enlightenment did not preclude an admiration for Montesquieu. In a sermon at Oxford Assizes on 4 March 1773 on the 'Influence of Christianity on civil society'[107] Horne quoted liberally from Book 24 of the *Esprit des lois* to drive home his argument that Christianity was essential as a restraining influence in civil society and that, *pace* 'the celebrated sceptic' Bayle, there was nothing to stop Christians from forming a durable government.[108] And Horne took obvious satisfaction in quoting from Montesquieu against the technique employed so devastatingly by Voltaire in the *Dictionnaire philosophique portatif* and elsewhere:[109]

> It is a false way of reasoning against religion, to collect, in a large work, a long detail of the evils it has produced.

Despite feeling able to deploy arguments first set out in the 'masterly manner' of Montesquieu against Voltaire's technique, Horne continued to be troubled by the latter's role in fanning the spread of infidelity. In the 1770s, when President of Magdalen College, Oxford, Horne drew up in note form the heads for a sermon provisionally entitled 'We are not ignorant of his devices' that aimed to counter Voltaire's objections to Christianity decisively.[110] This did not shrink from noticing such classic objections to the faith like as wars, persecutions, and the prevalence of vices of every sort, and how some chose to accuse God of injustice for the way 'earth quake [and] pestilence slay indiscrim:'.[111] Without giving much exact details about his arguments, Horne felt he could answer these charges and, in so doing, give the public the 'character of Voltaire compleat'. The Sage of Ferney would be presented as a warped mind, bent on 'Ridicule, scorning, reading with a view to sneer'. Horne was ready to concede that Voltaire had perfected the 'art of conveying ridiculous ideas of ye most sacred things', but it was specious to present this technique as in any sense a 'test of truth'.[112] Horne intended to finish with a flourish and, as he put it, 'carry the war into the enemy's quarters, & shew what infidelity is, whence it arises & c.'[113]

This interesting adumbration of a sermon remained only in note form. Certainly, it does not appear as planned in any of Horne's published sermons. Pressure of business after 1775 as Vice-Chancellor, not least in defending the privileges of the Church of England against the growing lobby which wanted to abandon subscription to the Thirty Nine Articles, kept Horne from giving his attention to infidelity on the wider stage. It was not until after his promotion to the Deanery of Canterbury in 1781 that he returned to combatting irreligion. His next publication, *Letters on Infidelity*, appeared in 1784 and shows how willing he was to adopt

---

107 *Horne, Sixteen Sermons*, no. 4.
108 *Ibid.*, pp. 93, 101, 109–10. An argument Voltaire might well have accepted.
109 *Ibid.*, p. 110 and note.
110 C.U.L. Add. MS 8134, B/1/317–19, undated.
111 *Ibid.*, B/1/317.
112 *Ibid.*, B/1/319.
113 *Ibid.*

tactics first deployed by Enlightenment writers whenever he judged them effective, as here where he deliberately opted for an epistolary format.[114]

His book was directed primarily at David Hume's *Dialogues on Natural Religion* and various Grub Street unbelievers, but he could not resist taunting the shade of Voltaire, possibly encouraged by the publication in 1782 of a vituperative, anonymous attack on Voltaire's antagonism to the Christian religion, *The History of the Life and Writings of . . . Voltaire.*[115] Horne took his ground on two familiar themes: the Jews and the reliability of the Bible. Once again he stressed the sophistication of Jewish civilisation and general culture as revealed in scripture against Voltaire's charge of 'inurbanity'.[116] He also looked closely at one Old Testament text, Judges XI. 24, which concerned the sacrifice of Jephthah's daughter, a subject wide open to Enlightenment critiques. Horne claimed Voltaire had 'amused himself much' and kept going 'Like a shuttle-cock', particularly in chapter twelve of the *Traité sur la tolérance* (in English translation) where Voltaire had pointedly noted that the Bible had talked of Jephthah being filled with the spirit of God though Augustine and other Fathers had condemned his action[117]. Controversy centred on the exact rendering of the verse 'Wilt not thou possess that which Chemosh thy god giveth thee to possess? So whomsoever the Lord our God shall drive out from before us, them will we possess'. Stung by Voltaire's implication that the Jews like the Romans acknowledged local divinities, Horne accused his 'little man' of relying exclusively on the Vulgate translation when 'any modern schoolboy would have informed thee better' about the meaning of the Hebrew. The moral was clear:

> Are we to give up our Bible, and pin our faith upon the slant of such a man as this?[118]

In the last years of his life the campaign against Priestley took first priority,[119] and any hopes that Horne may have entertained of producing a comprehensive history of infidelity or a large scale refutation of Voltaire receded. But his fascination with the French Enlightenment (and Voltaire in particular) continued and he found time in 1786 to make extracts from L.M. Chaudon's edition of Voltaire's

---

114 [Horne], *Letters on Infidelity* (2nd edn, Oxford, 1786), p. 2. As he told his friend 'W.S.' [William Stevens] in the introductory letter, there was 'no reason why a method practised by Voltaire (and so much commended by d'Alembert) *against* religion, should not be adopted by those who write for it'.

115 The work contains old charges rehashed. The full title is *The History of the Life and Writings of Mr Arruet de Voltaire, from a Collection Published in France in the Year 1781.* There is no corresponding title in the Bibliothèque nationale catalogue.

116 [Horne], *Letters on Infidelity*, pp. 204–7. Cf. heading 7 in C.U.L. Add. MS 8134, where Horne planned 'A true account and vindication' of the Jews. This has its parallels in Bergier's articles on the Jews before Jesus. Ex. info Dr Bertram E. Schwarzbach.

117 The references are to pp. 136 and note, and 139–40 of the first English translation of 1764 which Horne used, *A treatise on Religious Toleration occasioned by the Execution of the Unfortunate John Calas.*

118 Horne, *Letters on Infidelity*, pp. 237–8.

119 See Aston, 'Horne against heterodoxy', *E.H.R.* forthcoming.

Memoirs[120] in his Common Place Book. What he discovered there reinforced the impression of his opponent he had gained over the previous quarter century: Voltaire, as Horne saw it, carried immorality over from his life into his writings. He read of and deplored the terror Voltaire experienced if he thought death was near (as in 1745) and his willingness to withdraw 'the dangerous pieces he had published'. Horne also censured his pretended conversion to gain admission to the Academy, the satirising of friends he had previously commended, and cheating booksellers by denying 'his own works continually in ye most solemn manner'.[121]

But none of this prevented Voltaire's influence holding firm in the decade after his death, much to the Dean of Canterbury's consternation. In 1787 Horne noted with some foreboding the appearance of a forty two volume edition of Voltaire edited by Beaumarchais (the 'Kehl' edition),[122] and took some small comfort from learning that the plan for an edition in vellum covers had pushed up the price to 200 guineas which would in itself deter readers.[123] At Christmas that year, Horne had obtained a copy of a *Life* of Voltaire, written in a hostile vein by T.I. Duvernet in Geneva and translated by G.P. Monke,[124] a Royal Navy Lieutenant ekeing out his half-pay after the end of the American War of Independence: Horne supplemented the book's unflattering picture of the Sage of Ferney with his own mordant thoughts in his Common Place book.[125]

In the last three years of his life Horne saw the outbreak of the Revolution in France as a posthumous triumph for Voltaire. It confirmed his own worst fears about the destructive potential of the French Enlightenment on national institutions as much as beliefs. In an anonymous pamphlet of 1790 arguing against the desirability of relaxing the Test and Corporation Acts in favour of Protestant dissenters, he made it clear that he saw Voltaire's pernicious influence at work in

---

120 The full title is *Historical and Critical Memoirs of the Life and Writings of Mr de Voltaire, interspersed with numerous anecdotes relative to the Literati of France*. It is allegedly based on a French original entitled *Mémoires pour servir à l'histoire de M. de Voltaire*.

121 '19th Book. 1786 Common place'. C.U.L. Add. MS B/5/6–9. Horne had first raised the charge of Voltaire's disowning a work when writing in 'The Miscellany', *St James's Chronicle*, 3–5 Feb. 1767. He alleged in the same place that Voltaire had sold the copy of a work to six different booksellers.

122 It actually ran to 70 octavo volumes (1785–89). Subscriptions were sought on a wide basis and the prospectus was translated into English. G. Barber, 'Voltaire and the English: Catalogue of an exhibition' (Studies in Voltaire and the eighteenth century, vol. 179), pp. 161–92, at p. 189.

123 *Ibid.*, 'II. 1787. No. I. 18th Book. Common pl(ace) Book and family memorandums', C.U.L. Add. MS B/6/21. Horne's friends were delighted that George III did not follow other European rulers and subscribe to it. As George Berkeley said, 'I am sure His Majesty has shown himself a real Christian in not doing it; and I have no doubt God will publicly reward him for it'. *Sermons* (London, 1799), p. iv.

124 The full title is *The Life of Voltaire; with Notes Illustrative and Explanatory*. Trans. G.P. Monke, Lieut., R.N. It is dedicated to the Prince of Wales and the other Princes.

125 C.U.L Add. MSS 8134, B/2/6, f. 21, 15 Apr. 1787.

France beyond the grave inspiring the Revolutionaries. The risk of the contagion affecting even elite institutions in Britain could by no means be discounted:[126]

. . . though superstition be a very bad thing, I hope never to see the British National Assembly possessed by the spirit of – VOLTAIRE.

Horne's fears for his own country were groundless. He died in January 1792, but as Britain and France drifted into war, the denunciation of the French Enlightenment which he had made so much his own theme was thundered forth afresh from scores of pulpits. Preachers everywhere led by William Jones and Horne's old colleague in the controversy with Priestley in the previous decade, Bishop Samuel Horsley, echoed Horne closely when he accused 'the accursed crew of French philosophers' of aiming to overthrow the whole worship of God and efface his name from the world.[127]

Horne had always regarded the whole enterprise of Enlightenment as at best unnecessary when measured against God's revelation, at worst perverse and mischievous. In his lifetime he never formally lent himself to the conspiracy theory of the Revolution that became fashionable in the late 1790s,[128] but his surviving writings make it clear that he expected nothing but disaster and disappointment to be the fruit of the destructive attacks launched on Christianity by Voltaire and his disciples. It saddened Horne that, in Jones's words, 'Our own nation has drank deep of the deadly draught',[129] but so much was to be expected from sinful men. At least he with Horne had tried to show the public the errors of Voltaire as one who 'seeketh wisdom & findeth it not',[130] and their efforts undoubtedly paved the way for the widespread public acceptance of the intellectual conservatism of the 1790s. Indeed, as Owen Chadwick has pointed out, by 1815 Horne's view of Voltaire had effectively won out in England, and would retain its currency until at least the 1860s.[131]

In Horne's hands, couched in irony and expressed with a good humour that still entertains, the vitality of traditional Christianity continued to appeal against late Enlightenment blandishments. The Dean of Canterbury needed no champagne to make out his case against Voltaire that not a little utilised the same techniques that

---

126 [George Horne], *Observations on the Case of the Protestant Dissenters with Reference to the Corporation and Test Acts* (Oxford, 1790), p. 19.
127 Samuel Horsley, ed. H. Horsley, *Sermons* (3 vols, London, 1816), III. 332, 'App. to Sermon of Jan. 30, 1793'. For the odium with which the term 'philosopher' was held by the outbreak of the Revolution and the alleged complicity of such in its origins see Schilling, *Conservative England*, pp. 220–1.
128 Robert Hole, *Pulpits, Politics and Public Order in England, 1760–1832* (Cambridge, 1989), pp. 153–6.
129 Jones, *Sermons*, II. 388.
130 Biblical quotation, head nine in projected sermon. C.U.L. Add. MS 8134, B/1/319.
131 Owen Chadwick, *The Secularisation of the European mind in the nineteenth century* (Cambridge, 1975), p. 147. See also S.B. Deane, 'John Bull and Voltaire: the Emergence of a cultural cliché', *Revue de littérature comparée*, 45 (1971), pp. 582–94.

the Sage of Ferney himself found so effective against *l'infâme*. Amid the criticism there was a degree of name-calling, but that is explicable given the anger and frustration orthodox clerics like Horne felt at Voltaire's status and output. Horne saw himself as engaged in essentially a clearing operation in favour of truth, and it was supremely worth undertaking:[132]

> Religion is the gift of God to man. If some have perplexed and confounded its doctrines, others should labour so much more diligently to disintangle and clear them.

---

[132] Horne, writing as 'Clericus', in the *General Evening Post*, 12 Sept. 1771.

DAVID BEBBINGTON

Holiness in Nineteenth-Century British Methodism

The quest for holiness was fundamental in the thought of John Wesley. It was an aim that had to be sought by each Christian since, according to the book of Hebrews, holiness was a state 'without which no man shall see the Lord'.[1] Wesley's spiritual biography was an enduring search for sanctification. He came to believe that justification by faith was its necessary condition, and so, from around the time of his evangelical conversion, that principle was incorporated in his teaching. Sanctification nevertheless remained basic: justification was in a sense incidental.[2] The priorities were reversed in the Methodist movement he created. Methodists proclaimed justification by faith, the theological formulation of the experience of conversion, with sanctification as only a supplementary goal. Yet something of Wesley's passion for holiness was imparted to Methodism. Respect for the founder ensured that the doctrine remained a significant feature of the movement during the nineteenth century.

Methodist sanctification teaching took a particular form. By contrast with other evangelicals whose roots were in the Reformed tradition, Methodists held that there was a distinctive state of holiness attainable on earth. Entire sanctification did not have to wait, as the Calvinists taught, until the moment of death, but was available in the ordinary course of life. Many Methodists laid claim to a decisive experience beyond conversion that was variously called 'full salvation', 'perfect love', 'a clean heart' or, in the later nineteenth century, 'the second blessing' or 'the higher life'. Such high aspirations were possible because the movement accepted a circumscribed – if common-sense – understanding of sin. It was defined by Wesley as 'a voluntary transgression of a known law'.[3] An act, that is to say, was sinful only if it was deliberate and deliberately sinful. Breaches of the divine law committed in ignorance or error were merely 'infirmities'. So restricted a definition made lofty

---

[1] Hebrews 12.14.
[2] The standard work is Harald Lindström, *Wesley and Sanctification* (London, [1946]). For a succinct exposition, see A. Skevington Wood, *Love excluding Sin: Wesley's Doctrine of Sanctification* (Occasional Paper No. 1 of the Wesley Fellowship) (n.p., n.d.).
[3] Wesley, 'A Plain Account of Christian Perfection' [1766–89], in Frank Whaling, ed., *John and Charles Wesley* (The Classics of Western Spirituality) (London, 1982), p. 329. This document contains Wesley's authoritative view of the doctrine.

spiritual attainments come within range. Nevertheless Wesley believed that, like justification, sanctification could be forfeited. There was no guarantee of its retention, and Methodists sometimes spoke of repeatedly losing and regaining a clean heart. It was attained, whether for the first time or subsequently, through gradual spiritual progress that normally culminated in the reception of entire sanctification in an instant. Although Wesley was prepared to admit exceptions, he found that his followers usually testified to entering the state of perfect love at a particular point in time. After that juncture it was still possible to grow in grace, for, as Wesley insisted, there was no spiritual state that could not be improved. The perfection of the believer was not absolute, like the perfection of God, but only relative, for it was the condition of a human being. It therefore had to be received by faith as a gift of God. Here Methodists diverged sharply from Calvinists, who taught that sanctification, unlike justification, called for effort. For Wesley's followers, however, full salvation was no human achievement, but simply, as one of their hymns put it, a 'rest of *faith*'.[4] Nineteenth-century Methodists inherited a very specific body of teaching about holiness.

How far was the theory embodied in life? James Obelkevich has rightly suggested that relatively few Methodists of the first half of the nineteenth century received the experience. Only three out of a sample of one hundred Primitive Methodist obituaries for 1830 and 1850 contain any reference to entire sanctification.[5] Nevertheless there did exist a number of early nineteenth-century Methodists who bore memorable witness to it. A fascinating instance is Samuel Hick, a Yorkshire blacksmith, whose only published sermon was called 'Entire Sanctification'. Printed posthumously at Barnsley in 1831, it faithfully reproduces Hick's Yorkshire dialect. 'Naw', he tells us, 'I'm kummin to't *varree best paaart*! for I'm suer I can sa summat about *sanktefekashun*, for I love it t'best of awl.' He recounts how he had doubts about the doctrine until one day he was walking through a wood. Seeing two trees that had been felled, he noticed that the stump of one had been left in the ground and that young trees were growing out of it. 'Ah! thinks I to mee sen, naw, this is just like a man in a justeefide state – t'oud stump o' his evel nater reemains, an fresh evels spring up too trubbel him.' The other tree had its roots torn out of the earth so that it could not grow again. 'I sed too mee sen, naw this tree's just like a man in a sanktefide state – the fibers wor kutton, at bun him to t'wurld – t'hearth wor noa longer abowt his rooits – "the world was crucified to him, and he to the world." '[6] The Lord, he was sure, had made use of the trees to teach him what he had long desired to know. Sammy Hick clearly felt the experience vividly and preached it powerfully.

In the second half of the century, holiness teaching went into decline. It was already fading by the 1850s. 'It is to be feared', wrote a contributor to *The Wesleyan Methodist Association Magazine* in 1854, 'that this privilege of the

4   *Ibid.*, p. 314.
5   James Obelkevich, *Religion and Rural Society: South Lindsey, 1825–1875* (Oxford, 1976), p. 233n.
6   Samuel Hick, *Entire Sanctification: A Sermon . . .* (Barnsley, 1831), pp. 11–13.

believer, is not presented to our people so fully and forcibly as necessary, nor as in days gone by; and there are few people in the present day who make a profession of its enjoyment.'[7] He was echoed two years later by a Free Methodist minister in Beverley, Yorkshire. Full salvation, he feared, had 'almost gone from the church and from the pulpit'.[8] As though in confirmation, several obituaries for the Wesleyan Methodist Association in the early 1850s still contain references to the experience having been gained earlier in the century, but by 1869 there are no equivalents.[9] A similar pattern is evident among the Primitive Methodists. When, in the mid-1870s, a zealous connexional evangelist preached the message of perfect love at Shotley Bridge in County Durham and Tunstall in Staffordshire, local officials were delighted. They told the visitor that, though they had not listened to such teaching for a long time, it was what they had regularly heard some forty or fifty years before, that is around 1830.[10] It is clear that both doctrine and experience were much rarer in the second half of the century than in the first. It will be useful to explore the reasons for the decay.

Popular objections form one major category of explanation. There is evidence of a persuasion within Methodism that to raise the standard of holiness too high was a mistake. It was thought to operate as a deterrent: members felt that they would not be able to sustain a life of sanctity and so did not seek it.[11] It was even believed to be an obstacle to conversion: people would not embark on the Christian life at all for fear of what would later be expected of them.[12] Methodist evangelists therefore sometimes played down entire sanctification. Outsiders suspected that it was all a farrago of hypocrisy, and many Methodists agreed.[13] The leading Primitive Methodist exponent of full salvation in the later nineteenth century, George Warner, was said to be marked by a 'brusqueness of manner',[14] and other advocates of the doctrine seemed less than saintly. Thus a Wesleyan local preacher in Manchester who concentrated on sanctification teaching in the early years of the century was also noted for his severity from the pulpit and for his aversion to instrumental music. When at one chapel a violin struck up after he had given out a hymn, he cried out sternly, 'stop that squeak!'.[15] Such angularity did nothing to adorn his doctrine. Multitudes, according to a biography of William Clowes, the early Primitive leader, 'satisfied themselves with sanctimonious cant, and pharisai-

---

7   *The Wesleyan Methodist Association Magazine* [hereafter *WMAM*], February 1854, p. 83 (J.M.).
8   *The Revivalist* [hereafter *R*], May 1856, p. 73 (William Braimbridge).
9   Comparing *WMAM* for 1853–54 with *The United Methodist Free Churches Magazine* [hereafter *UMFCM*] for 1869.
10 J. Stephenson, *The Man of Faith and Fire or, the Life and Work of the Rev. G. Warner* (London, 1902), pp. 165, 172.
11 Richard Treffry, jun., *Memoirs of the Life, Character, and Labours of the Rev. John Smith* (London, 1832), p. 231.
12 *WMAM*, August 1853, p. 358 (Edward Wright).
13 *Benjamin Hellier: His Life and Teaching*, ed. by his children (London, 1889), p. 298.
14 Stephenson, *Warner*, p. 273.
15 *WMAM*, Februray 1854, p. 83 (J.M.)

cally boasted of a holiness which they never possessed'.[16] Why should other folk wish to join in such a charade? There were Methodist apprehensions, furthermore, of lapsing into the extravagances that had disfigured the early history of the movement when, in the 1760s, George Bell had claimed to be more perfect than the unfallen Adam.[17] In the excitement surrounding the rise of the Bible Christians in the West Country, one of their female preachers told William O'Bryan, the connexional leader, that she possessed 'a blessing far superior to the being only cleansed from all sin; this I call being sealed to the day of redemption'.[18] O'Bryan, who had formerly held similar views, was now alarmed that exaggerated claims would bring the whole movement into disrepute and actively discouraged her. Such fears of 'third-blessingism' were to dog nineteenth-century Methodists. The consequence was an element of popular unwillingness to pursue even the second blessing.

A second reason for the decay of holiness teaching was the almost inevitable process whereby over time it was gradually toned down. The doctrine was restated in terms more acceptable to others who did not maintain Wesley's position about entire sanctification. The classic case was *The Tongue of Fire*, published in 1856 by William Arthur, a Wesleyan connexional official who mixed widely with other evangelicals. He does urge his readers to obtain a second blessing, but he wraps up the experience in urbane and genteel phraseology.[19] A perusal of his book would be unlikely to rouse its readers to a crisis of discovery. Likewise Benjamin Hellier, a Wesleyan college tutor at Richmond and then Headingley, wrestled in private with holiness teaching and in public smoothed away its sharp edges. Can we, he asked in an address to lay preachers in 1886, be sanctified in a moment? In true academic fashion his answer was yes and no. We may give ourselves to God as never before, he argued, but the process of sanctification is not the work of an hour.[20] That was to diverge from Wesley, who had held that sanctification was indeed instantaneous. In a similar way biographies became more oblique in their treatment of the subject. Thus John Rattenbury, who was celebrated in the 1840s for his expositions of entire sanctification, was commemorated in a work published in 1884, five years after his death. The memoir recounts his ability as an evangelist, alludes to his preaching on heart purity and mentions his personal sanctity but explains nothing about the nature of his experience or teaching on the

16 William Garner, *The Life of the Rev. and Venerable William Clowes* (London, 1868), p. 411.
17 W. Stephen Gunter, *The Limits of 'Love Divine'* (Nashville, Tenn., 1989), pp. 225–6.
18 Henry Freeman, *A Memoir of the Life and Ministry of Anne Freeman*, 2nd edn (London, 1828), pp. 29–30, quoted by Deborah M. Valenze, *Prophetic Sons and Daughters: Female Preaching and Popular Religion in Industrial England* (Princeton, N.J., 1985), p. 152 (Ann Mason).
19 This is to modify the judgement expressed in D.W. Bebbington, *Evangelicalism in Modern Britain: A History from the 1730s to the 1980s* (London, 1989), p. 153. I am grateful for advice on this topic to the Rev. Dr N.W. Taggart, whose biography of William Arthur is about to appear.
20 *Hellier*, pp. 312–13.

theme of holiness.[21] The qualities of deceased Methodists were increasingly described as in a eulogy of a New Connexion Sunday school teacher from Stone, Staffordshire, in 1850: 'his conduct and character were unblemished'.[22] Conduct and character, matters for which human beings were themselves responsible, were replacing full salvation, a supernatural endowment. It was perhaps part of a process of the routinisation of charisma, whereby early spiritual leadership in the Methodist societies was supplanted by something more commonplace. The distinctive experience of the movement was steadily fading away.

In the third place the decline of entire sanctification was bound up with the decay of corporate religion in Methodism. The experience of perfect love often came in a group context in the earlier years of the century. To call its attainment 'following my leader' would be unfair, but undoubtedly an element of imitation eased people towards the crisis. So much is clear from an account by the minister, John Smith, of happenings at Bassingham Wesleyan Chapel, Lincolnshire, in 1829:

> I preached at half-past one from, 'Create in me a clean heart, &c.' We then had a good lovefeast. Just as I was about to give out a verse, and commence a prayer-meeting, a fine young man got up, and told us he had some time ago lost a clean heart, but that he had been powerfully acted upon again during the sermon, &c. I was on the point of speaking to him, when he said, 'God cleanses me again!' It went like an electric fluid. I said, 'Now you see the cleansing power of God is in the chapel: you that want a clean heart may have one.' One man exclaimed, 'I have got it;' and looking round, added, 'you may all have it.' We began to pray, and the meeting did not conclude till I went to preach at six o'clock. I was told that thirty-three obtained entire sanctification . . .[23]

Community expectations were powerfully reinforcing the message of the preacher. Many parallels could be drawn. A Manchester lovefeast held in 1827 roused a Wesleyan woman to seek holiness of heart once more;[24] and testimonies to cleansing from all sin by fourteen Liverpool members of the Wesleyan Methodist Association in 1837 stirred a minister to press on after entire holiness, which he duly discovered at a subsequent band meeting.[25] Consequently the decline of such corporate exercises undermined the transmission of higher religious experience. Attendance at class meetings, the weekly groups where leaders would enquire into the spiritual progress of ten or so members, fell away in the later nineteenth century.[26] Lovefeasts, whose purpose was testimony over a simple meal, became

---

21 H. Owen Rattenbury, ed., *The Rev. John Rattenbury: Memorials* (London, 1884), spec. pp. 43, 45, 96.

22 *The Methodist New Connexion Magazine* [hereafter *MNCM*], July 1850, p. 331 (of John Earp).

23 Treffry, *Smith*, p. 286.

24 *UMFCM*, February 1858, p. 78.

25 *WMAM*, March 1853, pp. 137–8 (of E.W. Buckley).

26 H.D. Rack, 'The Decline of the Class-Meeting and the Problem of Church-Membership in Ninetenth-Century Wesleyanism', *Proceedings of the Wesley Historical Society*, 39 (1973–74), pp. 12–21.

less frequent and in many places disappeared during the Victorian years.[27] Most crucially band meetings, which were select classes designed specifically for those seeking perfect love, went into eclipse. Although their decline has not yet been documented, it was evidently more widespread and more rapid than that of the ordinary class meetings. In places such as Scarborough on the Yorkshire coast where bands still existed in the 1880s, testimonies to full salvation were still heard at them.[28] In general, however, band meetings were rare by that date. The decay of entire sanctification is closely associated with the disappearance of the meetings that formed its institutional vehicle.

Underlying the other factors, fourthly, was a fundamental social process, the advance of respectability. Greater national prosperity, markedly affecting all ranks by mid-century, meant higher material standards. It also created more opportunities for upward social mobility. Methodists tended to press upwards, out of the mass of the common people into the strata of the middle classes. Even the Primitive Methodists, who could boast the highest share of working-class attenders, rose in the social scale during the Victorian era. Although only 4% of Ashton-under-Lyne Primitives in the period 1850–70 were lower middle-class, by 1890–1910 the proportion had reached one quarter or more.[29] Those aspiring to better things were eager to conform to the conventions of the rank above them. The consequence was deplored by a holiness enthusiast in 1872. 'Unfortunately for the power of the Church', he lamented, 'there is often little sacrifice made, and far too little distinction between the life of moral worldliness and the life of many Christian professors.'[30] Entire sanctification savoured too much of fanaticism to be popular in late nineteenth-century suburbia. In the increasingly private world of the Victorian middle classes, public testimony to a clean heart seemed entirely out of place. Holiness began to be commended, even by its keenest advocates, as a private matter. 'Religious experience', ran an article on 'Why ought I to be holy?' in 1856, 'with all its advantages, is a *personal* matter; if I am pious, I am so for myself'.[31] The contrast with the uninhibited corporate religion of earlier in the century could hardly have been more stark. With self-improvement ousting spiritual fervour, the prospects for holiness teaching were bleak. As Methodists became respectable, so distinctive beliefs about sanctification were discarded.

In the light of the powerful forces ranged against it, the survival of holiness doctrine is perhaps more remarkable than its decline. Why then did it persist? One reason is that it was inescapably part of the Methodist deposit of faith. It was present, first and foremost, in the hymns that most vividly expressed Methodist popular piety. Throughout the nineteenth century connexional hymn books

27 Frank Baker, *Methodism and the Love-Feast* (London, 1957), pp. 56–7.
28 *Holiness Advocate* [hereafter *HA*], September 1887, p. 137 (G.W. Palliser).
29 Clive D. Field, 'The Social Structure of English Methodism: Eighteenth-Twentieth Centuries', *The British Journal of Sociology*, 28 (1977), p. 209.
30 *The King's Highway* [hereafter *KH*], December 1872, p. 399 (W.G. Pascoe).
31 *R*, April 1856, p. 54.

contained blocs of verse on holiness, most of it written by Charles Wesley. Methodists loved to sing 'O for a heart to praise my God':

> A heart in every thought renewed,
>   And full of love divine,
> Perfect, and right, and pure, and good –
> A copy, Lord, of thine!³²

It was possible for nineteenth-century congregations, like their twentieth-century successors, to use the words without discerning their reference to entire sanctification, but where the flame of holiness still flickered such oil would help to fuel it. Similarly the teaching was embodied in the sermons of John Wesley studied by local preachers, while candidates for the ministry were questioned explicitly on the subject. Wesleyan theologians defended the doctrine, sticking close to their founder's views. It is expounded in Richard Watson's *Theological Institutes*, the summa of early nineteenth-century Methodism,³³ and was the theme of two lectures delivered annually by John Hannah, the first tutor, from 1834 onwards, of the Wesleyan Theological Institution.³⁴ Agar Beet, soon to be theological tutor at Richmond, published a book on holiness in 1880,³⁵ shortly after W.B. Pope had treated the subject in his *Compendium of Christian Theology*. Pope, it has to be admitted, is not entirely faithful to the tradition since, by contrast with Wesley, he holds that true holiness is unconscious.³⁶ Yet Pope still teaches the possibility of the extinction of sin in the life of the believer. The doctrine was therefore largely sustained by the Wesleyan magisterium. Furthermore the reading of books discussing full salvation was still encouraged in the later nineteenth century: Wesley's *Plain Account of Christian Perfection*, the writings of his assistant John Fletcher of Madeley and the lives of Methodist preachers who had enjoyed the experience such as William Bramwell and William Carvosso. Each of these literary sources is repeatedly cited by those who were drawn to holiness teaching in the late Victorian years.³⁷ Entire sanctification was clearly what Methodists were supposed to believe.

The survival of the teaching, secondly, was buttressed by its association with revivalism. Although revivalism was probably never absent from Methodist bastions such as Cornwall, in the sense of the deliberate encouragement of mass conversions by specific techniques it was largely introduced from America. The leading Wesleyan exponent, John Smith 'the Revivalist', a minister who died in 1831, was equally celebrated as a preacher of holiness.³⁸ The techniques became

---

32 Franz Hildebrandt *et al.*, ed., *A Collection of Hymns for the Use of the People called Methodists* (The Works of John Wesley, Vol. 7) (Nashville, Tenn., 1983), p. 491.
33 Richard Watson, *Theological Institutes*, 14th edn, 4 vols (London, 1865), 4, pp. 138–49.
34 John Hannah, *Introductory Lectures on the Study of Theology* (London, n.d.), lectures LVII and LVIII.
35 J. Agar Beet, *Holiness as understood by the Writers of the Bible* (London, 1880), spec. pp. 53–4.
36 W.B. Pope, *Compendium of Christian Theology*, 2nd edn, 3 vols (London, 1880), 3, p. 56.
37 *KH*, 1872–74.
38 Treffry, *Smith*.

commoner in the 1850s, particularly among the Free Methodists but also in the circle of the young New Connexion minister William Booth, later the founder of the Salvation Army. The vigorous missions promoted by the Free Methodists and by Booth were given publicity in *The Revival*, a journal that also advocated entire sanctification. Revivalism and holiness, both expressions of Methodist zeal, seemed natural partners. Later the example of the Salvation Army, itself an ardent holiness organisation in its early years, prodded individual Methodists towards the same combination. George Clegg, a Wesleyan Halifax millowner, for example, had his life transformed through an address on holiness by a Salvation Army Hallelujah Lassie and so became a supporter of two mission halls in the town, a Home for Women Evangelists and a leading advocate of entire sanctification.[39] A succession of American visitors repeated the same blend down the century: Lorenzo Dow (from 1805), James Caughey (1840s and 1850s), Dr and Mrs Palmer (1850s and 1860s) and J.S. Inskip with two companions (1880).[40] By teaching entire sanctification in tandem with conducting revivals, they did much to sustain the holiness tradition.

It is also clear, in the third place, that the doctrine persisted because it proved flexible. In America, it has been argued, there was a shift during the nineteenth century in the understanding of the reception of a clean heart that put greater emphasis on the role of the Holy Spirit,[41] but that was not the nature of the change in Britain. Already in the early nineteenth century references to the agency of the Holy Spirit were common. The experience of a Bible Christian woman in Cornwall in 1817 was recounted five years later as 'God by His Holy Spirit filling her soul with joy unspeakable';[42] and a Liverpool minister recorded in an 1838 diary entry, 'Bless the Lord, he has baptized me with his Spirit.'[43] In this respect there was continuity into the late nineteenth century, when such language was still employed. The crucial change, promoted by Caughey and the Palmers, was a rejection of the traditional belief that entire sanctification, to be real, must be consciously experienced. There was no need to feel any different. Holiness could be claimed immediately by anyone, since it was no longer, as in Wesley's day, expected to be the climax of a long quest drawn out over months or years. Caughey urged faith as the condition of purity, 'faith in a promise, a naked faith, stripped of all feeling . . . a *voluntary* act of the mind'.[44] Faith could be exercised at the behest of the will. The reformulation was not merely a means of maximising numbers entering full salvation, for it was also a recasting of the doctrine in terms

---

39 I.E. Page, *A Long Pilgrimage with some Guides and Fellow Travellers* (London, 1914), p. 237.
40 John Kent, *Holding the Fort: Studies in Victorian Revivalism* (London, 1978), chaps 1, 2 and 8. *The Revival*, 15 July 1880, p. 13.
41 Donald W. Dayton, 'The Doctrine of the Baptism in the Holy Spirit: its Emergence and Significance', *Wesleyan Theology Journal*, 13 (1978), pp. 114–23.
42 *The Arminian Magazine*, December 1822, p. 382 (of Damaris Hooper).
43 *WMAM*, March 1853, p. 138 (of E.W. Buckley).
44 *Earnest Christianity illustrated: Or, Selections from the Journal of the Rev. James Caughey* (London, 1857), p. 152. Cf. Kent, *Holding the Fort*, pp. 315–24.

of the diffuse Romanticism of the period that stressed the power of the will. The newer style of holiness teaching, especially in Mrs Palmer's version as the 'rest of faith', appealed to the rising taste of the age. Younger generations were drawn to entire sanctification in its new guise during the last three decades of the century. From 1872 there was a fresh journal, *The King's Highway*, to spread the teaching, and from 1885 an annual Methodist Holiness Convention at Southport to act as an institutional focus.[45] It was all part of a broader holiness movement that swept English-speaking evangelicalism in the later nineteenth century. The main British expression, the annual Keswick Convention, cultivated a similar sub-Romantic spirituality.[46] Adaptation gave the holiness message a new lease of life both inside and outside Methodism. Its transmutation is a major explanation of its persistence to the end of the century and beyond.

The distribution of instances of entire sanctification, though often harder to pin down precisely than the reasons for its decline and continuance, can nevertheless be analysed in terms of denomination, social class, geography and gender. The denominational distribution was widespread for there is evidence of cases of full salvation from all the main Methodist connexions. The doctrine was maintained even in tiny splinter groups such as the Magic Methodists of Delamere Forest in Cheshire. James Crawfoot, their leader, was said to include the subject 'in nearly every discourse'.[47] It was likewise present among the Protestant Methodists of Leeds, another small body. A workman in their ranks named Abraham Holt enjoyed the experience soon after his conversion but lost it in a struggle with doubt. Afterwards, however, 'the Holy Spirit again filled his soul with the perfect love that casteth out all fear, and from this time to the end of his life he walked in constant fellowship with God'.[48] Entire sanctification was probably least looked for in the New Connexion, whose literature tended to describe Christian experience in a more restrained way than the publications of the other denominations. Thus the obituaries in the 1850 volume of *The Methodist New Connexion Magazine* contain only one instance of an aspiration after a clean heart together with a more complex case in which a profession of the experience seems not to have been understood by the obituarist, even though he was the man's minister.[49] The obituaries in the volume for the following year include no reference to entire sanctification at all. Although the phenomenon appears to have been weakest in the New Connexion, it was present in all the branches of Methodism.

Distribution by social class also appears to have been general. In the early years of the century a majority of recorded instances was from the common people.

---

45 *To the Uttermost: Commemorating the Diamond Jubilee of the Southport Methodist Holiness Convention, 1885–1945* (London, 1945), p. 15.
46 Bebbington, *Evangelicalism*, chap. 5.
47 George Herod, *Biographical Sketches of Some of those Preachers whose Labours contributed to the Origination and Early Extension of the Primitive Methodist Connexion* (London, [1855]), p. 269.
48 *UMFCM*, July 1858, p. 377.
49 *MNCM*, July 1850, p. 326 (of John Spencer); October 1850, pp. 444–5 (of David Fox).

Obituaries often attribute the experience to workmen, artisans and smallholders, the predominant Methodist constituency of the period. Typical were David Fox, a shoemaker of Batley in Yorkshire, and W. Drummond, a millhand at Middleton in Lancashire.[50] But there were exceptions in a higher station of life such as Joseph Massingham of Norwich, who acted as private secretary to members of the Quaker Gurney family, or John Brown of Newcastle-under-Lyme, Staffordshire, who rose to become overseer, guardian of the poor, chief constable, a borough councillor and trustee to the burgesses.[51] A brother and sister, Christopher and Margaret Dove of Leeds, who in the 1830s both entered Christian perfection (remarkably) at the age of eleven, came from what was clearly a leisured family possessing several servants.[52] Later in the century, cases from rather higher up the social scale seem to have been relatively more numerous. Among the prosperous businessmen who now became leading figures in the holiness movement was Cuthbert Bainbridge, the son of the founder of a Newcastle-upon-Tyne warehouse and department store, who gave much of the money that established *The King's Highway*.[53] Earlier on, however, when the teaching was at its strongest, working men and their families were the commonest recipients of perfect love. At that time it represented a genuine strand of popular culture.

The geographical distribution reflects the firm grasp of the experience in the industrial workforce. There are far more recorded instances from the north of England than from the south of the country. That is only to be expected on account of the greater strength of Methodism in the north than in the south. Yet it does appear to have a deeper significance in the light of evidence from the south of lukewarmness and even hostility towards the doctrine. When, in 1820, John Smith transferred from the north of England to Brighton, he was dismayed by the attitude there to entire sanctification: 'in this part', he noted in his diary, 'those who profess it are opposed, and considered to be in a dangerous error'.[54] There were exceptions in the south, Cornwall being the chief. Methodism enjoyed its highest population density there, and religious excitement was usually close to fever pitch in 'the county of revivals'. It was in Cornwall, for example, that William Carvosso, perhaps the most celebrated lay exponent of full salvation, flourished for sixty years.[55] Yet the north was the stronghold of the doctrine. There is evidence that, despite official opposition, the traditional teaching lingered at least until the 1880s at Scarborough among Wesleyans and Primitives alike.[56] Likewise the lay supporters of the revitalised doctrine at the Southport Holiness

---

50   *MNCM*, October 1850, p. 441. *WMAM*, October 1853, p. 486.
51   *UMFCM*, June 1869, p. 376. *The Primitive Methodist Magazine* [hereafter *PMM*], February 1850, p. 77.
52   Peter M'Owan, *Memoir of Christopher Dove, jun., of Leeds* (London, 1837), pp. 36–40. Peter M'Owan, *The Two Doves: Or Memoirs of Margaret and Anna Dove* (London, [1839]), p. 20.
53   T.H. Bainbridge, *Reminiscences*, ed. Gerald France (London, 1913), pp. 55–6.
54   Treffry, *Smith*, p. 133.
55   *A Memoir of Mr. William Carvosso . . . written by Himself* (London, n.d.).
56   *HA*, January 1884, p. 20; August 1884, p. 88.

Convention were gathered chiefly from the northern counties – from Southport itself, Leeds, Edgeworth, Weardale, Halifax, Goole, Newcastle-upon-Tyne, Manchester and Birkenhead.[57] Entire sanctification clearly put down deeper roots in the north than in the south.

Distribution by gender is particularly difficult to estimate. A high proportion of the recorded instances was male, but that is only to be expected. Officials tended to have obituaries, and officials were usually male. Consequently what is striking is the large number of women whose experience of a clean heart is commemorated in the connexional magazines. On occasion there could be more women than men: *The Primitive Methodist Magazine* for the first half of 1850, for example, records only two male cases but four female cases. Such women were commonly among the most powerful advocates of the experience. Elizabeth Bramall, a Primitive Sunday school teacher and choir member from Bredbury, Cheshire, who died in 1849 at the age of twenty-one, 'often . . . bore scriptural and satisfactory testimony concerning the cleansing power of Jesus' blood'.[58] Again Mary Moffett, an Association Methodist from Carlisle who entered the experience at about the time she was widowed in 1828, gave practical illustration to her message by visiting the sick and advising penitent sinners.[59] Holiness opened the way for women to speak in public. Mrs Palmer and Mrs Booth are the best known, but there were many others for whom bearing testimony to the experience seemed sufficient reason for ignoring the normal male monopoly of platform work in the later years of the century. The Southport Convention, for example, had women speakers;[60] and there was the intriguing figure of Sophia Chambers, who lived near Maidstone in Kent. After being converted through the Primitives at seventeen, she migrated to the Wesleyans to avoid becoming a prayer leader. She received entire sanctification in the 1870s through a series of special meetings in the town, and, after frustration in trying to promote the cause among the Wesleyans, left in 1882 to create a new denomination, the Holiness Church. It fostered congregations in Kent, London and Yorkshire, issued a magazine and seemed likely to imitate the success of the holiness denominations that were growing in America at this time. It was very much Sophia Chambers' organisation. When she died in 1887, it took only three years to collapse entirely.[61] Not only, therefore, were women probably participants in the holiness tradition in disproportionate numbers, but also the experience could project them into positions of prominence. Entire sanctification was sometimes liberating for women in more senses than one.

What were the other effects of the doctrine? It has been suggested that it reinforced the standard evangelical code of renunciation,[62] and that was undoubtedly the case. Thomas Waugh, a Wesleyan missioner at the end of the

---

57 *To the Uttermost*, pp. 15, 20.
58 *PMM*, February 1850, p. 127.
59 *UMFCM*, April 1858, p. 212.
60 *To the Uttermost*, p. 21.
61 *HA*, 1884–90, spec. March 1887, pp. 33–7.
62 Kent, *Holding the Fort*, p. 317.

century, remarked that he had never known a person 'filled with the Spirit' who played cards for money, or who patronised the theatre, the music hall and the ball-room.[63] 'Are not billiards unquestionably bad?', demanded George Warner, an equivalent of Waugh among the Primitives. He recounted how a Wesleyan lady had desired a clean heart for many years, but a passion for novel reading had stood in her way. Warner directed her to burn the novels – which she duly did.[64] Holiness zealots usually opposed cricket, football, smoking and, towards the end of the century, strong drink. Sanctification teaching helped to boost the total abstinence movement within Methodism.[65] Nevertheless there was a dimension of the holiness message that pointed towards a certain breadth of social outlook. It was expected that the sanctified Christian would extend his impeccable standards to his place of work. Thus, for example William Holdsworth, a Bradford trades-man who died in 1852, was said to have been marked by 'strict integrity'.[66] 'Entire sanctification', lay preachers were told in 1886, 'means that a man will be perfectly upright in all his business transactions, even in buying and selling horses, and in paying income tax.'[67] Soon the Wesleyan social gospeller Hugh Price Hughes was interpreting the doctrine of sanctification as meaning that the Christian must show a loving concern for the weak and the poor.[68] Holiness teaching, for all its narrowing effects, also helped to ensure that religion was carried into society at large.

A second possible impact of the doctrine that deserves consideration was its role in favouring theological conservatism. It might be supposed, in fact, that it would promote obscurantism. There was nothing, however, intrinsically anti-intellectual about entire sanctification. 'This baptism of the Holy Spirit which I have re-ceived', wrote a Wesleyan minister in 1825, 'instead of superseding study, fits me for, and impels me more to, it.'[69] Others similarly recorded that holiness and learning were entirely compatible. Nor was the doctrine tied as closely as it was in America to conservative trends of theological opinion in the late nineteenth cen-tury. In the United States the holiness movement was associated with the rise of premillennialism, the belief that Christ will return in person before the millen-nium that was to form the ideological cement of Fundamentalism.[70] In Britain, however, premillennial teaching was rare in holiness circles. It was heard from

63 Thomas Waugh, *Twenty-Three Years a Missioner* (London, n.d.), p. 142.
64 Stephenson, *Warner*, pp. 109, 164.
65 Kent, *Holding the Fort*, pp. 317–19. The point should not, however, be exaggerated: in 1872 I.E. Page, one of the leaders of the revitalised holiness movement, still made temperance principles an open question. *KH*, June 1872, p. 195.
66 *WMAM*, February 1853, p. 89.
67 *Hellier*, p. 311.
68 Hugh Price Hughes, 'The Christian *Extra*', *Ethical Christianity* (London, 1892), p. 15; 'The New Commandment of Christianity', *The Philanthropy of God* (London, 1892), p. 18.
69 John M'Owan, *A Man of God: Or, Providence and Grace exemplified in a Memoir of the Rev. Peter M'Owan*, ed. George Osborn (London, 1873), p. 56.
70 George M. Marsden, *Fundamentalism and American Culture: The Shaping of Twentieth Century Evangelicalism, 1870–1925* (New York, 1980), chs VIII–XI.

James Wood on the platform of the Southport Convention in 1897,[71] but in general the advocates of entire sanctification still accepted the traditional postmillennial eschatology of Methodism.[72] Christian effort, it was believed, would bring in the millennium before the second advent. W.G. Pascoe, one of the group responsible for *The King's Highway*, for instance, could refer to the work of the churches culminating in 'the latter-day glory'.[73] Furthermore, entire sanctification was not identified with biblical inerrancy. Holiness speakers were usually ambiguous in their comments on biblical criticism. It had unsettled some, admitted Thomas Waugh, but it had helped others.[74] Although holiness teaching did not foster obscurantism, there are nevertheless signs that it did stiffen belief in a more general way. In a survey of leading Bible Christians at the turn of the twentieth century, for example, only one of the sixty-six personalities, Arthur Hancock, is identified with entire sanctification. Hancock is also described as 'orthodox to the very core', concentrating on the three Rs of ruin, redemption and regeneration.[75] It seems likely that holiness did reinforce basic convictions, but not through being yoked with any other specific doctrines.

A third effect of eagerness for full salvation was to help sustain the energy of the overall movement. Methodism, in common with evangelicalism as a whole, was profoundly activist, but in the case of Methodism entire sanctification was one of the motors that sustained its dynamic. Those enjoying the experience of a clean heart were both the elite corps and the shock troops of Methodism. They were often noted for their unusual degree of devotional commitment. Thus Mary Easingwold, a Primitive from near Hull who died in 1849, was celebrated for praying privately seven or eight times a day.[76] The teaching often provided the most earnest evangelists. It was a commonplace that there was a connection between holiness and conversions.[77] The truly holy were commonly revered, with special power being attributed to them, as in the early church. John Rattenbury was recalled as 'a holy man, sanctity was essentially wrought into his being, it pervaded his speech, sat on his countenance, dominated his life'. 'Herein', went on the author of the recollections, 'lay the secret of his marvellous power in prayer and preaching'.[78] The reputation of such figures made the curious flock to see

71 Eliza A. Wood, *Memorials of James Wood, LL.D., J.P., of Grove House, Southport* (London, 1902), p. 276.
72 I.E. Page, ed., *John Brash: Memorials and Correspondence* (London, 1912), pp. 174–7, 185–8.
73 *KH*, December 1872, p. 399.
74 Waugh, *Twenty-Three Years*, p. 69. Cf. D.W. Bebbington, 'The Persecution of George Jackson: A British Fundamentalist Controversy', in W.J. Sheils, ed., *Persecution and Toleration* (Studies in Church History, Vol. 21) (Oxford, 1984), p. 429.
75 W.J. Mitchell, *Brief Biographical Sketches of Bible Christian Ministers and Laymen*, Vol. 1 (Jersey, 1906), pp. 248–9.
76 *PMM*, February 1850, p. 124.
77 *The Irish Evangelist*, 1 December 1875, p. 143 (William Arthur). I am grateful for this reference to the Rev. Dr N.W. Taggart.
78 Rattenbury, *Rattenbury*, p. 96.

them, as much as to watch Simeon Stylites in the fifth century. The crowd would hear their message and conversions would follow. Consequently entire sanctification was a contributor to Methodist church growth; and conversely the fading of the doctrine in the later nineteenth century was one of the factors behind the slackening rate of growth of the Methodist denominations at that time. Holiness was a good index of the vigour of the movement.

The long-term effect of holiness teaching was determined by the pattern of its development in the last quarter of the century. As in the United States, it spread beyond Methodism and, in the distinctive Keswick form, it became the orthodox spirituality of conservative evangelical Anglicans. In substantially its Methodist form it was the *raison d'être* for a range of holiness bodies of which the Salvation Army became by far the largest. There were also, apart from several lesser organisations, the Holiness Church, the Faith Mission, the Star Hall and the Pentecostal League that eventually gave rise to the International Holiness Mission and the Calvary Holiness Church.[79] By contrast with the American movement, however, Methodism in Britain retained most of its holiness enthusiasts within its own ranks. In 1874 a crucial decision was taken not to create an organised holiness movement within Methodism.[80] If one had been established, it might well, as in the United States, have come into conflict with the denominational authorities and eventually have triggered a mass separation. As it was, the bulk of the readers of *The King's Highway* and attenders of the Southport Convention remained loyal Methodists into the twentieth century, when two other foci for their allegiance, the journal *Joyful News* and the training centre Cliff College in Derbyshire, tied them into the structures of Methodism. Cliff College became the anchor of conservative Evangelicals in twentieth-century Methodism, a sect within the denomination.[81] Consequently there was no large holiness sector outside Methodism in British religion during the early twentieth century. In America, on the other hand, by 1907 there were already twenty-five holiness groups, some of them burgeoning into sizeable organisations.[82] From this seedbed grew the vast American Pentecostal denominations. In Britain the tiny holiness base dictated that indigenous Pentecostalism would remain a small and marginal force. One of the chief contrasts between British and American religion in the twentieth century has been the different scale of classical Pentecostalism. That divergence flows directly from the continuing vitality of the tradition of entire sanctification within British Methodism.

79 Faith Mission: I.R. Govan, *Spirit of Revival: The Story of J.G. Govan and the Faith Mission* (Edinburgh, 1938). Star Hall: J. Rendel Harris, ed., *The Life of Francis William Crossley* (London, 1900), ch. 5. Pentecostal League: Jack Ford, *In the Steps of John Wesley: The Church of the Nazarene in Britain* (Kansas City, Mo, 1968), pp. 90–5.
80 *KH*, November 1874, p. 391.
81 J.I. Brice, *The Crowd for Christ* (London, 1934).
82 Robert M. Anderson, *Vision of the Disinherited: The Making of American Pentecostalism* (New York, 1979), p. 37.

YVES-MARIE HILAIRE

Catholicisme politique ou catholicisme social? Réflexions sur le mouvement religieux des laïcs 1860–1914

ENGLISH SUMMARY

At a time when in Rome, from Pius IX to Pius X, authoritarian and centralising tendencies were reinforced, it was paradoxical to see the spread in Europe of a strong catholic movement in which lay people were particularly numerous. Being in opposition to the ideologies of the time, such as liberalism, 'scientisme', secularism, the catholics set up counter-societies against a worldly background. Yet, according to the situations of the different countries, the catholic movement took different forms. In Belgium and Germany catholicism was strongly marked by politics. This model, which was copied in the Netherlands and in the Austro-Hungarian monarchy, was not adopted at that time by the Latin countries. On the other hand, the latter were influenced by the catholic 'social' movement of which the Encyclical letter *Rerum Novarum* (1891) was either the cause or the incentive. After 1918 this movement would bring in Italy the soil in which Christian democracy would grow; in France and Italy it would largely extend beyond Christian democracy and influence the whole of political society.

Les travaux récents de chercheurs de plusieurs pays européens sur le mouvement catholique et notamment le mouvement religieux des laïcs, les recherches accomplies à l'occasion des colloques commémorant le centenaire de l'Encyclique *Rerum Novarum* sur la question sociale ont attiré l'attention sur une période marquée certes par des débats politico-religieux autour du cléricalisme, du libéralisme ou de la démocratie, mais caractérisée aussi par une participation accrue des laïcs au mouvement religieux qui prend alors son essor. L'économiste Anatole Leroy-Beaulieu observe ce dernier fait à propos de la genèse de l'encyclique *Rerum Novarum* et de celle du Ralliement: 'A aucune époque, les laïques n'ont eu plus d'influence dans l'Eglise; naturellement, avec les laïques, devaient pénétrer dans le sanctuaire les préoccupations du dehors'.

Cette observation peut sembler paradoxale à propos d'une époque 1860–1914, dominée par le poids de la question romaine, l'intransigeantisme de la Papauté, de Pie IX à Pie X en passant par Léon XIII, intransigeantisme bien mis en valeur par

Emile Poulat, une époque qui voit l'apogée d'une Eglise des oeuvres apparemment bien cléricales. Cependant, cet intransigeantisme s'avère fécond, la formulation de la doctrine sociale et politique par Léon XIII, formulation qui tient compte des réalités du temps, rencontre un assez large écho, et un mouvement catholique puissant (bien mis en valeur lors du congrès de Leuven en 1980), prend son essor avec une participation accrue des laïcs encadrés par un clergé entreprenant. Les catholiques discrédités par les idéologies à la mode, libéralisme, scientisme, laïcisme, construisent des sociétés, des contre-sociétés qui s'insèrent dans le monde.

La terre d'élection de ce mouvement catholique est connue grâce aux observations de la sociologie religieuse historique. Il s'agit généralement des pays de chrétienté de cette époque: l'Europe 'lotharingienne' d'abord, la plus grande partie de la Belgique, le sud des Pays-Bas, la Rhénanie, la Bavière, l'Autriche, une grande partie de l'Italie du Nord et du Centre; accessoirement les régions de chrétientés du Nord-Ouest en Espagne, de l'Ouest armoricain et du Sud-Est du Massif central en France et les métropoles à bourgeoisie catholique entreprenante comme Lyon et Lille-Roubaix-Tourcoing.

Cependant, le mouvement catholique peut se constituer sous deux aspects différents: sous l'égide ou en prolongement d'un parti catholique – et on a alors un catholicisme politique, bien étudié par Jean-Marie Mayeur dans son livre très documenté *Des partis catholiques et la démocratie chrétienne XIXe-XXe siècles*; ou bien dans le cadre d'institutions et d'associations catholiques sociales – et on a alors un mouvement catholique social dont l'émergence a été bien observée dans un autre ouvrage de Jean-Marie Mayeur: *Catholicisme social et démocratie chrétienne, principes romains, expériences francaises*. Tandis que les partis catholiques apparaissent vers le milieu du XIXe siècle, le mouvement catholique social, qui a commencé aussi au milieu de ce même siècle, se définit et prend son essor vers 1900 dans le sillage de l'encyclique *Rerum Novarum*.

Pourquoi le catholicisme politique prédomine-t-il dans certaines nations et le catholicisme social dans d'autres? Nous allons essayer de répondre à cette question en observant d'abord quelques exemples de nations où le catholicisme politique l'emporte, puis des exemples de nations où le catholicisme social influence principalement le mouvement religieux.

Le catholicisme politique

Le catholicisme politique apparaît au XIXe siècle dans deux types de pays: une nation nouvellement fondée à constitution libérale précoce, la Belgique et une nation en gestation, les états allemands, dans lesquels les catholiques sont souvent minoritaires. Ce catholicisme politique implique des partis confessionnels.

'La liberté comme en Belgique'

L'état indépendant belge moderne est issu de la révolution de 1830, dirigée contre le régime autoritaire hollandais et préparée par une union des catholiques et des libéraux. La révolution belge est influencée par les idées de Lamennais et influence à son tour les catholiques libéraux francais de Lamennais à Montalembert, en passant par le Marquis de Regnon qui publie un journal intitulé la 'Liberté comme en Belgique'. En effet, la constitution belge de 1831 instaure le régime parlementaire et les quatre grandes libertés représentées ensuite par des statues sur la place de la Liberté à Bruxelles, liberté des cultes, liberté d'association, liberté de presse et liberté d'enseignement. Les Eglises sont séparées de l'Etat, mais aidées par l'Etat. Dans le prolongement des libertés communales de l'Europe du Nord, vivaces depuis le Moyen-Age, la Belgique est fondée sur les libertés, et les condamnations pontificales du libéralisme, de *Mirari vos* (1832) au Syllabus des erreurs (1864), ont un effet limité dans ce pays, n'influencent pas beaucoup les hommes d'état responsables.

Les deux forces constitutives de l'état belge, les catholiques et les libéraux, forment des partis qui rivalisent pour le pouvoir. Tandis que l'Eglise catholique est dirigée par une suite de cardinaux de grande envergure, la franc-maçonnerie anime le libéralisme. La question scolaire est l'enjeu d'âpres débats. Le parti catholique qui est au pouvoir en Belgique, de 1884 à 1914, pendant une période où en France les anticléricaux dominent au Parlement et au gouvernement, doit s'adapter à l'évolution progressive vers la démocratie et le suffrage universel. Il s'appuie alors sur un puissant mouvement catholique social de type professionnel qui se met en place à partir des années 1880 et qui multiplie les oeuvres sociales: sociétés de secours mutuel, caisses d'épargne, banques populaires, sociétés d'habitations à bon marché, ligues agricoles, syndicats d'ouvriers et d'employés... Les catholiques intransigeants, formés sous Pie IX et déroutés par certaines orientations de Léon XIII, s'investissent dans l'action sociale fortement encouragée par l'encyclique Rerum Novarum (1891): les congrés sociaux de Liège des années 1886, 1887, 1890, ont précédé cette encyclique et ont, dans une certaine mesure, contribué à sa préparation.

Le modèle allemand

En Prusse, puis en Allemagne, la naissance et le développement du parti catholique, le Zentrum (centre), sont provoqués par la nécessité de défendre les droits et les libertés des catholiques minoritaires contre les interventions d'un roi luthérien dans la vie de l'Eglise catholique (affaire de Cologne 1837–1840) et contre une administration dominée par les protestants et tentée d'établir une léglislation religieuse régalienne, profitable à la Réforme. Les catholiques, réveillés par l'affaire de Cologne, réunissent au lendemain de la révolution de 1848, le premier Katholikentag et fondent en Prusse, à partir de 1852, un groupe parlementaire qui prend le nom en 1859 de Zentrum. Un autre parti catholique apparait également dans un état où le prince est protestant, ainsi dans le Grand Duché de Bade en 1869 sous le nom de Katholische Volkspartei.

L'unité allemande met à l'épreuve les catholiques, car elle se fait dans le cadre de la conception prussienne de la 'Petite Allemagne' au détriment de la conception bavaroise et autrichienne de la 'Grande Allemagne' soutenue par la majorité des catholiques. Le Chancelier Bismarck, qui a réalisé l'unité allemande, prend prétexte de l'émoi suscité chez les protestants par le vote de l'infaillibilité pontificale au Concile de Vatican I pour tenter d'imposer une unification religieuse de l'Empire allemand au profit des protestants présentés comme réellement 'civilisés'. C'est le 'Kulturkampf'. Le Reichstag vote les lois de mai 1873, 1874 et 1875 qui persécutent les catholiques. Ceux-ci réagissent dans le cadre d'un grand parti politique confessionnel le Zentrum créé à l'échelle allemande dès 1870 et utilisent toutes les libertés modernes pour se défendre: liberté de la tribune parlementaire, de presse, d'association et bien sûr d'élections. Conduits par un groupe d'hommes politiques de talent menés par Windthorst, ils gagnent des sièges aux élections. Au nom des droits des minorités, Windthorst refuse alors la tentation de l'antisémitisme dans laquelle s'engage une fraction des luthériens. Finalement, Bismarck doit céder, changer d'alliance parlementaire, faire abroger les lois anticatholiques et faire voter avec l'appui d'une partie du Zentrum la législation sociale la plus moderne d'Europe pour prendre de vitesse la progession des socialistes.

Le Pape Léon XIII, malgré ses réticences vis-à-vis d'un parti d'esprit indépendant, en fait plus allemand que romain, est amené à tirer les leçons du conflit en publiant en 1888 l'encyclique *Libertas*, premier texte pontifical dont le titre reprend la devise guelfe et qui explique que les libertés modernes présentent certes des dangers, mais aussi des avantages. C'est un véritable aggiornamento de la pensée catholique sur les libertés politiques qui ont permis au Zentrum de sortir victorieux du Kulturkampf.

Le Zentrum n'a pu gagner qu'en s'appuyant sur un important mouvement social catholique encouragé par l'archevêque de Mayence Ketteler (1850–1877). Le Zentrum doit tenir compte des intérêts des différentes classes qui le soutiennent, des nobles silésiens aux ouvriers rhénans. Comme en Belgique, le mouvement social catholique, en place avant l'encyclique *Rerum Novarum*, vient renforcer l'action du parti politique.

D'autre part, les membres du Zentrum qui veulent être catholiques bavarois, badois, rhénans, hanovriens, mais aussi catholiques allemands restent toujours menacés par une surenchère nationaliste qui sait exploiter le mythe de Luther, véritable chrétien allemand, et qui les accuse d'être plus romains qu'allemands. Fidèles à l'Allemagne pendant la guerre de 1914–1918, les catholiques sont, comme les autres Allemands, très éprouvés par la défaite de 1918. Après les drames effroyables que l'on connaît, Konrad Adenauer parviendra à partir de 1949 à reconstruire une Allemagne fédérale autour du parti politique chrétien démocrate qui réunit cette fois catholiques et protestants qui se sont rapprochés au cours de l'épreuve et dans la Résistance.

Inadéquation ou échec du catholicisme politique dans plusieurs pays

Les modèles belge et allemand ont été imités dans quelques pays voisins, comme les Pays-Bas (parti catholique) ou l'Autriche-Hongrie (parti chrétien social), mais ils ne sont pas transposables partout, malgré la séduction qu'ils ont exercée sur certains esprits en France, de Montalembert à Albert de Mun. En effet, dans certains pays, ils n'ont guère de raison d'être, dans d'autres ils se heurtent à des obstacles qui empêchent leur naissance ou entravent leur développement. La première catégorie comprend les nations anglo-saxonnes, le plus souvent à forte majorité protestante, marquées par le libéralisme politique et l'évolution vers la démocratie; la deuxième catégorie comprend les nations latines où l'anticléricalisme rejette le gouvernement des curés et l'intrusion de l'Eglise catholique dans la politique.

Pour nous en tenir à l'Europe, la Grande-Bretagne à très forte majorité protestante, mais à pluralisme confessionnel accusé, connaît au XIXe siècle une libéralisation dans le domaine religieux avec l'abrogation des mesures d'exception contre les catholiques promulguées jadis sous la pression de la foule (no popery). Les Irlandais catholiques, en combattant pour leur liberté, contribuent à cette libéralisation. L'influence des non-conformistes, des chrétiens sociaux anglicans et des catholiques sur les classes populaires explique pour une part les limites de l'antichristianisme dans le peuple. Le cardinal catholique Manning, qui a réclamé des réformes sociales, est choisi comme l'un des arbitres lors de la grande grève des dockers de Londres en 1889. L'importance du christiansime social ne saurait être sous-estimée en Grande-Bretagne, notamment dans la formation des premiers lecteurs travaillistes, comme l'a justement souligné Hugh MacLeod. Dans le pays qui a expérimenté et fait progresser de façon décisive les libertés politiques, les différents partis n'excluent pas au XXe siècle les candidats catholiques.

Dans les pays latins où la majorité de la population reste rurale, l'éclosion ou le développement des partis catholiques se trouve entravé par la vigueur de l'anticléricalisme qui s'oppose au cléricalisme, à l'intervention du clergé dans la vie politique et qui combat l'Eglise du Syllabus hostile aux libertés modernes. L'Italie aurait pu constituer une exception avec l'écho rencontré par le mouvement néoguelfe de Gioberti à l'époque romantique, mais le conflit entre le nouvel état italien et le Saint-Siège à propos de la question romaine, très vif dès 1860, entraîne le *non expedit*, l'interdiction signifiée par la papauté aux catholiques italiens de participer à la vie politique. Cependant, un très important mouvement catholique remplace et précède un parti catholique qui commencera à s'ébaucher à fin de notre période.

La France et l'Espagne présentent des histoires comparables dans ce domaine. Pourtant, les tentatives de parti catholique n'ont pas manqué. D'abord, sous la forme de groupes de pression parlementaires. En France, à propos de la liberté de l'enseignement, Montalembert en crée un qui gagne les élections de 1846 sous la Monarchie de Juillet et en anime un autre qui fait voter la loi Falloux en 1850. Sous le Second Empire, au corps législatif, Keller est l'un des leaders d'un groupe de pression qui oblige Napoléon III à défendre le pouvoir temporel du Pape. En 1885, sous la IIIe République, Albert de Mun tente de constituer un parti catholique. Il est découragé par le pape Léon XIII qui préfère un rapprochement entre les catholiques et les républicains modérés, solution qu'il met en avant lors du Ralliement en 1892.

En Espagne, à la même époque, Pidal y Mon, fondateur de l'Union catholique en 1881, se heurte aux profondes divisions des catholiques espagnols et aux réticences du pape Léon XIII, qui la aussi préfère une certaine entente entre les catholiques et les modérés. En réalité, en France et en Espagne, l'union politique des catholiques est rendue difficile par la virulence de l'anticléricalisme, comme le prouvera encore en France le demi-échec de l'expérience tentée par Jacques Piou avec l'Action libérale populaire entre 1902 et 1914, mais cette union est profondément entravée par une querelle de légitimité sur la dynastie ou le régime politique: carlistes en Espagne, qui livrent trois guerres civiles à la dynastie rivale, légitimistes puis monarchistes non ralliés en France. Interprétant à la lettre l'intransigeantisme doctrinal du *Syllabus* des erreurs, ces légitimistes vont inventer en Espagne en 1880 un parti 'intégriste' (ils créent le mot) et vont rallier en France le mouvement d'Action Francaise de Charles Maurras au début du XXe siècle.

En revanche, cet intransigeantisme, qui est le plus souvent stérile en politique, se révèle fécond en matière sociale, comme Emile Poulat et Jean-Marie Mayeur l'ont démontré. En effet, le catholicisme social n'est pas issu du catholicisme libéral, mais il provient d'un catholicisme intransigeant, encouragé par Rome, hostile au libéralisme, et allant à la rencontre de certaines aspirations du peuple. Un catholicisme populiste socialement réformateur est inspiré, dans la ligne du *Syllabus*, de *Rerum Novarum* à *Quadragesimo Anno*, par une réflexion intransigeante face aux errements de la société moderne. Rejetant à la fois le libéralisme et le socialisme, il préconise le développement des communautés intermédiaires entre l'individu et l'Etat (communautés intermédiaires qui sont le fondement du principe de subsidiarité proposé par l'encyclique *Quadragesimo Anno* et inscrit dans le traité de Maastricht).

Le catholicisme social au xixe siècle

Le catholicisme social se cherche et se définit à la fin du XIXe siècle. Le mouvement catholique précède les définitions théoriques. Il éclot en Allemagne dès 1848, apparaît en Italie en 1875 avec l'oeuvre des congrès et des comités catholiques, se dessine en France à partir de 1873 avec les congrès catholiques et l'oeuvre des cercles catholiques d'ouvriers, se constitue en Belgique en 1868 avec les Fédérations des cercles et associations catholiques et en 1884 avec l'Union nationale. Cependant, les événements se précipitent autour de 1890, peu avant la parution de *Rerum Novarum*, sur un fond d'importants mouvements sociaux qui ont pour conséquence la montée du socialisme: création en Suisse des Fédérations d'associations catholiques en 1887–88, constitution en Allemagne du Volksverein für das Katolische Deutschland, Association populaire pour l'Allemagne catholique en 1890, création de la Ligue démocratique belge par Georges Helleputte en 1891, après les congrès internationaux d'oeuvres sociales de Liège de 1886, 1887 et 1890. Cette participation active des laïcs à la vie de l'Eglise justifie l'observation de l'économiste Anatole Leroy-Beaulieu qui a été citée plus haut.

L'encyclique *Rerum Novarum*, qui parait le 15 mai 1891, est un document attendu et bien accueilli, comme l'ont montré les colloques tenus à l'occasion du centenaire en 1991. Son impact a été considérable.

Les évêques présentent l'encyclique dans leurs mandements, insistent sur son opportunité, la diffusent dans leurs diocèses, mais leur interprétation de ce texte reste souvent un peu courte, comme Jean-Dominique Durand l'a souligné pour la France lors du colloque de Rome en 1991.

Le mouvement catholique social reçoit de l'encyclique une justification et une forte impulsion. En France, dans un premier temps, les abbés démocrates prennent la direction du mouvement et répandent les idées nouvelles par la tribune parlementaire, la presse, les conférences populaires et les congrès. Le plus célèbre d'entre eux est l'abbé Lemire, élu député d'Hazebrouck en Flandre en 1893. Il le restera 35 ans, jusqu'à sa mort. Il milite inlassablement pour le vote des lois sociales, la protection du bien de famille, les jardins ouvriers. Une presse démocrate chrétienne naît alors à Lille, à Bordeaux, à Paris, à Lyon, à Montpellier, à Rennes où paraît en 1899 le journal le plus durable, l'Ouest-Eclair de l'abbé Trochu, ancêtre de l'actuel Ouest-France.

Cependant, ce mouvement démocrate-chrétien se politise à travers ses multiples congrès, et prépare les élections de 1898 que les catholiques perdent. Cette politisation n'est pas sans risque, car, dans le climat de l'affaire Dreyfus, elle entraîne une participation à l'agitation nationaliste et antisémite, et met l'accent sur les revendications cléricales avec l'appui des organes de la presse intransigeante, les nombreuses *Croix* locales qui prolifèrent alors. Une dérive antisémite analogue se produit chez les chrétiens sociaux autrichiens conduits par le bourgmestre de Vienne Karl Lueger. En France, les républicains s'inquiètent et réagissent en formant en 1899 le bloc des gauches qui reprend la politique anticléricale avec le gouvernement de Waldeck-Rousseau.

Le pape Léon XIII, voyant le danger de cette politisation excessive, qui concerne plusieurs pays, esquisse alors un mouvement en retrait: par l'encyclique *Graves de Communi* (janvier 1901), il définit la démocratie chrétienne comme une bienfaisante action sociale et la limite au domaine social. En France, les abbés démocrates divergent alors: tandis que l'abbé Lemire poursuit son activité politique, les abbés Six et Dehon privilégient l'action sociale et laissent le domaine politique au laïc Jacques Piou et à son parti l'Action libérale populaire.

*L'éclosion d'un mouvement catholique social en marge de la politique
au debut du xxe siècle*

Pour comprendre ce qui se passe au début des années 1900, il convient d'observer deux pays où le catholicisme politique est interdit, l'Italie, du *non expedit*, ou contesté, la France. Le début du pontificat de Pie X accentue la réorientation esquissée sous Léon XIII. La crise et la disparition de l'Oeuvre des Congrès provoquées par Rome permettent à Pie X de réorganiser le mouvement catholique. L'encyclique *Il fermo proposito* adressée aux évêques d'Italie le 11 juin 1905 a une grande importance: elle est d'abord la charte de la première Action catholique appelant les laïcs à participer à l'apostolat; elle prévoit l'organisation d'unions sociales, populaires et dans un autre domaine d'une union électorale; elle encourage les catholiques 'à se préparer prudemment et sérieusement à la vie politique' et annonce donc la fin prochaine du *non expedit*.

L'ampleur du mouvement catholique italien dans les classes moyennes, l'enracinement populaire de son action sociale avec le développement du crédit à bon marché, des caisses rurales, des syndicats agricoles (en Vénétie et en Lombardie notamment), sur les territoires de l'ancien Empire d'Autriche, permettent de comprendre pourquoi ce catholicisme social engendrera plus tard un puissant catholicisme politique lorsque Luigi Sturzo, puis Alcide de Gasperi seront sortis de l'intransigeantisme étroit et auront réussi la synthèse entre le mouvement de réforme sociale et les libertés modernes, entre le catholicisme social et le catholicisme libéral.

La situation de la France est différente sous le gouvernement du très anticlérical Emile Combes (1902–1905), mais si le mouvement francais n'a pas la même ampleur que celui d'Italie, ses expériences ne sont pas négligeables pour la définition et l'orientation du catholicisme social.

Le catholicisme social francais est alors très influencé par les modèles belge, allemand et italien. Cependant, il présente son originalité. Comme Jean-Marie Mayeur l'a montré, c'est vers 1900 que Georges Goyau et Max Turmann fixent et tentent de définir le vocable 'catholicisme social' qui fera fortune pendant les deux tiers du XXe siècle. L'enseignement du catholicisme social est assuré dans quelques Facultés et séminaires, principalement à la Faculté catholique de Lille avec Eugène Duthoit qui formera des centaines de militants. Les grandes institutions du catholicisme social se mettent en place. En 1903, l'Action populaire des Jésuites est créée à Lille, puis elle s'installe à Reims en 1904; elle publie une revue, des ouvrages et ses fameuses brochures jaunes qui atteignent les jeunes militants catholiques du Sillon et de l'Association catholique de la jeunesse francaise. Une étude récente a montré que 70 brochures sur 300 concernaient les femmes et notamment les ouvrières: ces petits livres présentent une description saisissante de l'exploitation du travail féminin et proposent des remèdes pour améliorer la condition féminine. L'Action populaire est à l'origine d'une série de campagnes contre le sweating system, pour la suppression du travil de nuit.

Les *Semaine sociales* créées en 1904 par des laïcs sont une université itinérante où les participants échangent des expériences, recoivent une formation sociale et se voient proposer des réformes sociales. Elles inspirent très vite des réalisations analogues en Italie et en Espagne, pays où le mouvement social catholique prend aussi son essor à cette époque.

A un moment où l'Eglise fait appel aux laïcs pour remplacer les religieux expulsés, notamment dans l'enseignement privé, à un moment où apparaissent les ligues de femmes – en 1901, la ligue des Femmes francaises, en 1902 la ligue patriotique des francaises (celle-ci aura 600,000 adhérentes en 1914) la jeunesse s'engage dans le combat social. En 1900, Henri Bazire, président de l'Association catholique de la jeunesse francaise, déclare que les membres de son mouvement sont sociaux parce que catholiques, et l'ACJF tient régulièrement de grands congrès sociaux où sont proposées des réformes qui seront votées dans les trente prochaines années. L'ACJF a 140,000 membres en 1913–14. Le Sillon de Marc Sangnier veut réconcilier l'Eglise et les ouvriers, l'Eglise et la démocratie, et une grande amitié unit ses membres issus de toutes les classes sociales. La condamnation du Sillon par Rome en 1910 entravera le mouvement social sans le faire disparaître. Le début du siècle voit l'essor du syndicalisme d'inspiration chrétienne dans les milieux agricoles. La seule Fédération agricole du Nord de la France a en 1913 une presse influente et 10,000 syndiqués. Les évêques eux-mêmes prennent position. En 1902, 74 evêques déclarent: 'Plus que la question cléricale, c'est la question sociale qu'il faut résoudre'.

Les députés catholiques dans le climat tendu de l'expulsion des congrégations et de la Séparation, ne cessent de proposer des lois sociales: retraites ouvrières, organisation et représentation professionnelles, repos dominical, limitation du travail de nuit, salaire minimum des ouvriers à domicile. Des catholiques parlementaires font voter les premières mesures familiales, notamment en 1909, l'institution d'un congé de maternité après la naissance, et participent à l'élaboration des lois sur le logement populaire, la construction des habitations à bon marché.

Issus de mouvements de défense religieuse et d'une volonté de reconstruction sociale, catholicisme social et catholicisme politique – celui-ci sous la forme de la démocratie chrétienne – vont marquer l'histoire du XXe siècle en Europe. Le catholicisme social confronté aux rudes problèmes du monde du travail inspire un vaste mouvement social chrétien pendant les deux premiers tiers du siècle. Le catholicisme social de type allemand a formé les trois hommes politiques démocrates chrétiens qui ont construit l'Europe des six devenue aujourd'hui celle des douze, Konrad Adenauer, mais aussi Robert Schuman et Alcide de Gasperi. Le catholicisme politique – ou la politique d'inspiration chrétienne, là où catholiques et protestants sont réunis – a connu un essor inégal en Europe après la Seconde guerre mondiale. Son développement a été beaucoup plus accusé en Italie et en Allemagne où il a présidé à la reconstruction et à la transformation de ces nations, qu'il ne l'a été en France où le pluralisme politique des catholiques est enraciné. L'Espagne qui a connu la dictature de 1936 à 1975 présente un cas à part, mais le problème du catholicisme politique devrait pouvoir y être étudié avec sérénité.

Si le catholicisme ou le christianisme politique est aujourd'hui à l'épreuve dans beaucoup de pays, n'assistons-nous pas, autour de l'encyclique *Centesimus Annus* de 1991, à une certaine renaissance de l'inspiration catholique sociale qui, selon la définition proposée par Charles Flory est plus 'un esprit et une méthode qu'une doctrine'. De même que 'la Bible n'est pas un livre de recettes', selon la formule inscrite dans le programme de la Christliche Democratische Union (CDU) catholicisme social et christianisme social invitent les hommes et les femmes à user dans les meilleures conditions possibles de leur liberté.

CLYDE BINFIELD

A Working Memorial?
The Encasing of Paisley's Baptists[1]

I

Victorian architectural competitions were minefields. They made, marred or exploded the reputations of assessors, competitors and premiated alike. They were always fraught and sometimes rigged. Their great virtue was the publicity which they provided for the profession and its patrons. There was not a building type without its competitions. Consequently there were some famous chapel competitions: for Spurgeon's Metropolitan Tabernacle, for example, or Henry Allon's Union Chapel, Islington, or St James's Congregational Church, Newcastle, or The Thomas Coats Memorial Baptist Church, Paisley.[2]

Although it was nine years before the result of the Paisley 'Baptist Chapel Competition' could truly catch at the breath of all who surveyed it, the competition itself hit the pages of *The Builder* and *The British Architect* in 1885.[3] The proposed church was to be a working memorial to Thomas Coats, the Paisley sewing-thread manufacturer, who had died in 1883. This explained the cost at

1 Earlier and shorter versions of parts of this paper have appeared in C. Binfield, 'Towards an Appreciation of Baptist Architecture', K.W. Clements ed., *Baptists in the Twentieth Century* (London, 1983), pp. 126–27; C. Binfield, 'Thomas Coats Memorial Church, Paisley', *Proceedings of the Summer Meeting of the Royal Archaeological Institute in Glasgow in 1986* (London, 1986), pp. 28–30; C. Binfield, 'Coffee Kirk Sundays', *Landscape*, October 1988, pp. 26–29. For further help in the preparation of this paper I am particularly indebted to Mr Ian Gow, Mrs Phyllis Hastings, Mrs MacGregor, and Mr George Thallon.

2 See R.H. Harper, *Victorian Architectural Competitions. An Index to British and Irish Architectural Competitions in 'The Builder' 1843–1900* (London, 1983); C. Binfield, 'The Building of a Town Centre Church; St James's Congregational Church, Newcastle Upon Tyne', *Northern History*, vol. xviii, 1982, pp. 155–182; C. Binfield, 'A Chapel and its Architect: James Cubitt and Union Chapel, Islington, 1874–1889', Diana Wood ed., *Studies in Church History, 28: The Church and The Arts* (Oxford (Blackwell), 1992), pp. 417–447.

3 *The Builder*, vol. xlix, 1885, pp. 4, 49, 86, 113, 186–9; *The British Architect*, 24 July 1885, pp. 43–44.

Plate VII   Thomas Coats Memorial Baptist Church, Paisley

(a) General view of the exterior

(b) General view of the interior

which competitors were to set their sights (£20,000); it explained the style, which was to be Gothic with tower and spire; and it explained the size, since it was to seat some 800 people. It also explained the shape. Because those people were believed to be connoisseurs of music as well as preaching, the choir and organ must be as carefully placed as the pulpit. Because they were Baptists there must be the appropriate arrangements for believer's baptism by immersion and that meant not just a baptistry but convenient retiring and dressing rooms for those who were to be baptised. There must be rooms for minister and deacons and there must be halls to hold the social genius of these Baptists. Then there was the site. That was potentially commanding and certainly demanding, since it was hillside and not hill top. Here was such an opportunity as might make or crown a career.

Nine architects were invited to compete: one from Edinburgh, three from London and five from Glasgow.[4] The assessor was Glasgow's James Sellars.[5] *The British Architect* gave his report on six of the designs, those by the Londoners J.P. Seddon, Arthur Billing and Charles Bell, by the Glaswegians J. Burnet and Son and John Hutchison, and by Edinburgh's Hippolyte Blanc. Of the six, Seddon was the best known.[6] He was a Goth to be reckoned with though Dissenting Gothic was hardly his forte. In that respect Charles Bell was the soundest practitioner. He was a veteran competitor with a strong line in chapels; his Old Independent at Haverhill in Essex, a domineering essay in a spired Greek Cross built largely by another textile family, the Gurteens, had been opened in 1884.[7] Of the Scots, Burnet and Son had the soundest base and the most distinguished future: Glasgow's Barony Church would be built in 1886 and the Burnet son, who became Sir John, would stamp London and Edinburgh as firmly as his father had stamped Glasgow.[8] Two others of the competing practices were also springboards for futurity. In the 1870s C.F.A. Voysey had been articled to Seddon and by 1885 John Hutchison's office included the young Charles Rennie Mackintosh.[9]

The prestige of the competition was thus not in doubt. The Coats family was politically, economically and philanthropically influential and it was about to become powerful. Given the vigour of Glasgow's architectural profession, there was spice in the battle between Glasgow, Edinburgh and London. There was also a challenge in the commission's Baptistness. For cost, its only rival apart from the Metropolitan Tabernacle was James Cubitt's recent Church of the Redeemer,

---

4   Harper, *op. cit.*, p. 133.
5   For James Sellars (1843–88), see R. Dixon and S. Muthesius, *Victorian Architecture* (London, 1978), p. 266, Elizabeth Williamson, Anne Riches and Malcolm Higgs, *The Buildings of Scotland: Glasgow* (London, 1990), wherein his Glasgow work can be charted.
6   For John Pollard Seddon (1827–1906) see Dixon and Muthesius, *op. cit.*, p. 266.
7   For Charles Bell (d.1899), see Harper, *op. cit.*, p. 187; *Congregational Year Book*, 1885, p. 251.
8   For John Burnet (1814–1901) and Sir John James Burnet (1857–1938) see A.S. Gray, *Edwardian Architecture: A Biographical Dictionary* (London, 1985), p. 128–131; see also *D.N.B.*.
9   Gray, *op. cit.*, p. 362 (sub 'C.F.A. Voysey'); *ibid.* p. 249 (sub 'Charles Rennie Mackintosh').

Hagley Road, Birmingham, completed in 1882;[10] and as a symbol it had no rival for here was to be a Baptist cathedral (was not its minister a true bishop?) commemorating a Christian family which had made its way by Baptist principles in a town whose economy might warm to their expression but in a country which was ungrateful ground. As a British statement this was to be a notable church; as a Scottish statement it was to be extraordinary. No wonder the assessor trod delicately as Agag, and even so found it very hard not to see the planned memorial as Presbyterian.

The competitors rose to the drama of the moment.[11] Their drawings were of the highest artistic excellence.' Their seating ranged from the 800 of Burnet and Blanc to Bell's 971; the furthest their hearers could sit from their pulpits ranged from the eighty feet of Hutchison and Blanc to Bell's 110 feet; the height of their spires rose from Blanc's 183 feet and Seddon's 185 feet to the 250 feet of Billing and Burnet. As for the cost, Blanc estimated £19,000 for either of his plans A and C; his plan B, like those of his rivals, was put at £20,000. Sellars could not agree. He thought that Billing's £20,000 would prove to be £34,894 and that Blanc's would be £25,489; Hutchison, Bell and Seddon would work out at over £22,000; the closest would be Burnet at £21,559.

The churchiest architect produced the churchiest design. Seddon's most notable feature was an octagonal chancel round which were grouped the retiring rooms and vestries for minister and choir (there was a separate building, also octagonal, for the deacons) and in which, facing each other in apsidal recesses, sat the choir, which Seddon seemed to see as a vast body, eighty-two strong. This did not impress Sellars. Such a choir was 'greatly in excess of the necessities of a Presbyterian [sic] church,' and the whole arrangement was unsatisfactory. He was dubious about the acoustics. He noted that the retiring rooms could only be reached through the church ('nor are there any lavatories or other conveniences in connection with these apartments'). As for the halls beneath the church, they remained, for all their modish electric lighting, 'not well arranged, and . . . ill lighted.' On the other hand the pulpit, organ and baptistery were central features, the ambulatories in the aisles conduced 'greatly to the comfort and convenience of the congregation,' all of whom at least had a good view of the pulpit even if they could not hear its occupant. And the whole was in 'a good type of Gothic architecture.' It would be 'simple and dignified. The detail is vigorous, yet refined and the ornate parts are well relieved by plain surfaces'; and none of this precluded an interior as ready for rich ornament as funds or the Coatses might allow. Neither did it preclude separate schools. For these Seddon proposed a building of university grandeur, its Gothic learnedly transposed into French Renaissance.

Seddon's lively chancel terminated a standard nave and transepts. Billing's plan

---

10 It cost £17,340; see C. Binfield, 'Towards an Appreciation of Baptist Architecture', *op. cit.* p. 125; T.W. Hutton, *The Church of the Redeemer, A History 1882–1957* (Birmingham, 1457), pp. 2–16; J.M. Gwynne, *The Chronicles of Our Church* (Birmingham, 1902), pp. 73–86.

11 The following account is drawn from *The British Architect*, 24 July 1885, pp. 43–4.

Plate VIII   Thomas Coats Memorial Baptist Church, Paisley

(a) The pulpit

(b) The baptistry

was similarly routine and it had some of the same drawbacks. His retiring rooms, too, led from the chancel and they too were approached only from the church, though at least they had lavatories. His acoustics, too, worried Sellars, in part because his chancel and transepts were so deep and in part because of his side pulpit in the angle of chancel and west transept. And since his choir sat in front of the chancel and his baptistry was at the back of the chancel, his church's most distinctive architectural and confessional feature would be invisible to most of the congregation. In short, the 'arrangement of the plan generally does not recommend itself to me as being suitable for a Presbyterian [sic] Church'. As for the building as opposed to the plan, its proportions would be noble and its grouping effective 'but it is oppressed with decorative detail not always in the best taste.' There was also the question of the roof:

> . . . while I cannot agree with the author's opinion, . . . that a really Gothic church cannot be considered properly finished without having a stone-groined roof, it is undoubtedly the most permanent kind of roof, and should be preferred.

That meant a great deal of money. Billing had stuck at £20,000 but the assessor's 'measurements and calculations give a different result,' which was three-quarters as much again.

By contrast Charles Bell had his feet firmly on the ground. Sellars liked Bell's drawings, his proportions and the refinement of his details. He also approved of his acoustics, his heating and his ventilation. The basement halls, too, were 'fairly well arranged and lighted.' He had, however, two very sensible criticisms. The first was about Bell's baptistery. This was properly prominent in front of the central pulpit; but when not in use it was to be boarded over, to provide a rostrum for the deacons' seats. This was common practice in up-to-date English Baptist churches, but for Sellars 'This arrangement is not satisfactory.' The other criticism was a palpable hit, targeted at all Dissenting Gothic, for Bell's practical plan did not fit his exterior. That is to say, the form, which was Early English, did not follow the function, which was that of the Dissenting use: a columnless nave facing an apsidal chancel of the same width (round which were grouped all the necessary ancillary rooms), with a central pulpit from which were described the curves of the congregational seating. Here was a decidedly non-churchy plan, stressing 'the comfort and convenience of the congregation in relation to the preacher, and *vice versa.*'

This leaves the three Scotsmen, Hutchison, Burnet and Blanc. Hutchison was the mixture as before: nave, aisles (i.e. passages), transepts and chancel, with the necessary rooms grouped round the chancel, the pulpit in the centre of the chancel arch and the baptistery set in the chancel's end. Sellars liked the acoustics, the retiring rooms, the basement halls, the Gothic and the drawings. He found it all tasteful, dignified, and unoriginal.

For originality Sellars looked to Burnet. Burnet was not perfect. His retiring and ancillary rooms were too small and his lavatories were inconvenient and inadequate. So was his main entrance. He too had succumbed to the rear baptistry and the centre forward pulpit, so that the one concealed the other. But against this were the wide nave and short transepts, the fine acoustics, the excellent basement halls and, above all, the noble *architecture*. For Burnet planned to have a detached tower and spire in line with the east transept. Sellars fell for 'the largeness and simplicity of its parts', the 'comparatively simple, always vigorous, and occasionally bold' detail, the richness of the chancel with its marble, its Derbyshire spar, its Mexican onyx and its alabaster. 'I am able to speak with almost unqualified approval . . . No more dignified architectural composition will be found in the whole series of designs submitted.'

Burnet's entry might have won the day in any other competition but it was Hippolyte Blanc, the Edinburgh man, who carried Paisley.[12] There can be little doubt that he was the most suitable choice.

For a start Blanc landscaped his design, setting it back in its hillside on a series of terraces. Next he provided three variants, A, B and C. Each had nave, aisles, (passages only), transepts and chancel but B had a shorter, wider nave which brought the congregation closer to the preacher and C made a prime feature of the crossing of nave and transepts, which turned the space into an octagon with a circular rhythm of pews. Sellars opted for B ('better for a Presbyterian church,' he persisted). B worked well acoustically; its necessary rooms were convenient and had lavatories; its baptistery was given the central position under the chancel arch, with the pulpit to westwards. Sellars paused only at the elevations, for B had twin towers with spires at its south end ('quite unworthy of the other parts of the design') while A's tower bestrode the church's great crossing, its stone-ribbed crown striking a superbly memorial note. If B had Sellers's suffrage internally, A won hands down externally:

> The drawings show that the author is familiar with the best examples of Gothic art in our own country . . . The central tower, surmounted by the open lantern, forms a fitting and graceful crown to a beautiful edifice.

II

Despite his name and origin, Hippolyte Jean Blanc (1844–1917) was Scottish born and bred. He was the essence of the Edinburgh architectural establishment, Tory in politics and antiquarian by inclination. His publications reflected this: papers on 'Medieval Abbeys: their place as Schools of Art', or 'The Arts of the Monastery', or 'Scottish Ecclesiastical Architecture in the Fourteenth and Fifteenth Centuries', brought up-to-date by his passion for photography. There was nothing arcane in his practice. Restorations were outweighed by his institutional and municipal work, with public halls, public baths and public libraries culminating in the colony for a thousand patients at West Bangour for the Edinburgh and

---

12 For Hippolyte Jean Blanc (1844–1917) see *The Builder*, 30 March 1917, p. 206; *RIBA Journal*, vol. 24, 3rd Ser. April 1917, p. 147.

District Lunacy Board. When it came to churches Blanc worked across the denominational board. The Church of Scotland, the Free Church of Scotland, the United Presbyterians, the Episcopalians and the Evangelical Union all employed him. In Paisley he had already designed St. James's Church (1880) for a Presbyterian Coats, and he was soon to reconstruct Ferguslie Park for Thomas Coats's son, Sir Thomas Glen Coats. He was, in short, the ideal choice for fully-fashioned paternalism.

No visitor to Coats Memorial can escape that paternalism and no thinking visitor will find it easy to reconcile it either with the congregational polity of the Baptists for whom it was built or with the radical understanding of Christian initiation which made them *Baptists* in the first place. Is it, then, a rich family's toy, to be enjoyed and then set aside? 'I can remember as a small boy,' recalled Thomas Coats's grandson in a reminiscence which sheds incidental light on James Sellars's perplexity as to plans A and B and on Blanc's handling of the consequent diplomacies,

> seeing side by side two models of churches prepared by Mr. Blanc, the interior of each illuminated by electric light . . . The one had twin towers recalling the cathedral of Notre Dame in Paris. The other, with its crown tower, reminding one of St. Giles' Edinburgh, was the one chosen.[13]

One of Thomas Coats's cousins made no bones about the high-minded high-handedness of his kinsfolk, so ready to be at one with Notre Dame or St Giles:

> we shall be translated to a building every stone, every curve, every pillar and arch of which have been conceived and constructed with the idea of affecting, as far as art can, the hearts and souls of men Godward. I believe this building is acknowledged to be the finest example of medieval ecclesiastical Gothic architecture which has been erected in this country since the Reformation, and it is perfectly equipped and adapted for its purpose. All this magnificent transformation has been accomplished without the slightest effort on the part of the Church. By the fairy wand of filial piety swaying and directing the resources of labour and art, the change has been effected, without our lifting our little finger or contributing one farthing towards its production. The founders could do no more. They have done their part. The dress of the Bride is there; the apparel is gorgeous. Everything which can materially signify purity and love and high endeavour and holy aspiration will be waiting and ready. Is the Bride going to shew herself worthy?[14]

Man must propose if he is to be true to his nature, but God disposes nonetheless; therein lies the motor of church life. Paisley man, however, had posed some cruelly sharp questions for one group of God's people. Manipulation by words, whether Godward or not, was already their occupational hazard as Baptists. Now

[13] *The Thomas Coats Memorial Church, Paisley Jubilee Book 1944* (Paisley, 1945), p. 10.
[14] G[eorge] H[olms] C[oats], *An Ideal Baptist Church: A Lecture Delivered in the Baptist Church, Storie Street, Paisley, 2nd April, 1894* (Paisley, 1894), pp. 4–5.

they were to be manipulated by stone. Their options for future action were to be sumptuously constrained by bounds no longer of their own making. A dead man's family had set the agenda for their future worship and church life. Could that possibly be a recipe for Baptist life? The competing architects, none of them Baptists, had wrestled with the bones of the problem and their solutions spoke first to the emotions. That was natural and safe. Their Gothic idioms, their towers and spires, were sure reference points, even for Scottish Baptists, but they served no practical, working use, however satisfactory their aesthetic, memorial appeal.

Yet even at the level of the emotions this memorial to paternalism is a markedly rational creation. It is without doubt a cathedral, a Baptist St Giles, 220 feet from the tip of its crown to the High Street pavement, grandly appropriating France and Germany as well as medieval Scotland, commanding the hillside into which in fact it nestles, holding Paisley in its view, keeping Paisley Abbey in its place and upstaging every other Paisley church. It is breathtaking in its completeness and its quality. Its tiled lavatories were like reception halls. In its vestibule are fonts, but since this is a late-Victorian Baptist church they are neither fonts nor stoups for holy water but fountains for drinking water to slake thirsts caused by gas lighting. That combination of richness with convenience is echoed in the traceried screens which separate the transept aisles from the ambulatory, for these screens are glazed in the clearest crystal, essays in merciful deception for the eye and draught exclusion for the neck. The pews are of oak, the first ten of them exported from Scandinavia since only there could wood of the right length be obtained. They have kneeling boards for any worshippers who might dislike the Nonconformist crouch and when they are unbolted from the floor they can be moved for easy cleaning. Nothing jars. Burnet's Mexican onyx and Derbyshire spar have their counterpart in Blanc's pulpit of marble from Languedoc and alabaster from Staffordshire. That dates from 1910, and like Blanc's lectern of 1904 it is of cathedral richness. So too, though few cathedrals were built with such things in mind, are the umbrella stands, the radiator cases and the gasoliers – these last turned now into electroliers and electrolabra. So is the door furniture, the hinges and the handles and the massive studs. There are niches in the stonework so that when the main doors are opened wide they fit flush against the walls, studs, hinges, handles and all. And there is the colour: the oak barrel vault of the nave in contrast with the pulpit's gold and blue-greys; the chancel ceiling alive with angelic musicians; the vestibule mosaics; all of it richly dimmed now. Only in the windows is there no colour, for there is no painted glass since only clarity should celebrate so grand a space.

The church's admirers praised its harmony and form. Purists might be disturbed by its decorative eclecticism and some, mindful that even churches sprang to life when touched by the contemporary Glasgow style, might regret a Gothic which is too scholarly to be free; save that later Victorian Free Gothic slips very easily into modishness unless released by genius. All, however, must applaud the fruitful tension between the cathedral Goth and the Arts and Craftsman in this architectural proof text of the liberty for which intelligent patronage can find room.

With that patronage we are back to the fact that the 'name of Coats is inseparably linked with the Memorial Church.'[15] The opening service, in May 1894, was almost a memorial service (admission by ticket, with Paisley's M.P. and Provost in attendance) for Thomas Coats, now eleven years dead.[16] His widow had opened the east transept door with a golden key and then she and her family were escorted by the architect to their seats in the west transept. That service was conducted by Richard Glover of Bristol, the weightiest of English provincial Baptists, but the afternoon service was taken by Oliver Flett, the new building's minister, whose wife was Thomas Coats's first cousin once removed, and the evening service was taken by her brother, Jervis Holms Coats, who ministered at Govan.[17] The opening service was choral, with a robed choir, sixty strong, thus putting key parts of the architect's brief to an immediate test. There remained the problem of maintenance. Three weeks earlier the church members had agreed to conditions proposed by the Coats family.[18] The church's polity, that is to say its conditions of membership and communion and the ordering of its worship and meeting, was unaffected. It was what the church did in the new memorial that exercised the Coatses, for the 'church buildings and property remain in the hands of the Family.' They paid for its upkeep, they appointed and paid the caretakers, they met the expenses of organist and choir, and they had the right to use the new building on weekdays for 'organ recitals and other musical services of a religious character.' That, of course, referred to the naved church; the halls beneath were to be for social meetings or Bible classes but not for mission or Sunday school work – those were firmly restricted to the church's former premises.

Their mission accomplished, it might seem that the commemorating family went the inevitable way of all prosperous flesh. A baronetcy came to one of Thomas Coats's sons and a barony (taking its name from its new holder's ball-roomed-baronial place in Aberdeenshire) to another.[19] A granddaughter married an English duke.[20] A third son combined the family disease of yachting with art collecting. His collection of Dutch old masters and the Hague and Barbizon schools was one of the most important to be amassed by that turn-of-the-century

---

[15] *Jubilee Book, op. cit.*, p. 18.

[16] D.D. Hair, *The Thomas Coats Memorial Church. Notes Historical and Descriptive* (Paisley, 1930), pp. 14–15.

[17] For Richard Glover (1837–1919), who had ministered in Glasgow 1861–69, minister of Tyndale Chapel, Bristol 1869–1911, President of Baptist Union 1884, see *Who Was Who, 1916–1928*, p. 413; for Oliver Flett (d.1894), minister at Paisley from 1860, see *Jubilee Book, passim* esp. pp. 10, 49, 72, 78–9; G.H. Coats, *Rambling Recollections* (Paisley, 1920), pp. 78–80; for Jervis Holms Coats (1844–1921), see *Jubilee* passim; *Rambling Recollections*, pp. 56–62; *Who Was Who 1916–1928*, pp. 208–9.

[18] *Jubilee*, p. 69.

[19] For Sir Thomas Glen-Coats Bt., M.P., (1846–1922) see M. Stenton and S. Lees, *Who's Who of British Members of Parliament*, vol. II 1886–1918 (Hassocks, 1978), p. 138; his brother, George Coats (1849–1918) was created 1st Baron Glentanar in 1916.

[20] Lilian Coats (d.1946), second daughter of the 1st Baron Glentanar, married the 5th Duke of Wellington (succeeded 1934, died 1941) in 1909.

phenomenon, the art-collecting Scottish industrialist. It rivalled those of his friend, Sir William Burrell, and of his kinsman-by-marriage, T.G. Arthur.[21]

In that respect, Thomas's line, the Coatses of Ferguslie, were no doubt simply following the stylish ways of his brother's line, the Coatses of Auchendrane. The family's first title, a knighthood, had come in 1869 to Thomas Coats's elder brother, Peter Coats, who had ceased to be a Baptist in 1843. The Scotch baronial of Sir Peter's Auchendrane provided the precedent for his nephew's Glen Tanar and to his unbounded civic philanthropies his descendants added yachting and hardline fishing, Roman Catholicism and Toryism, marriage to the débutante of the season in 1922 and horticultural journalism and game shooting in later years.[22]

III

The contexts for this variably consecrated paternalism were Paisley, weaving and Scottish Baptist. Within these contexts, there developed polity, worship and relationships as well as buildings. What was their *tone*? It can be detected, artfully no doubt but affectionately, in two generations of reminiscence.

Paisley's Baptists were born in secession from a congregation of Independents. Another Paisley congregation of Independents also issued in a Baptist secession. That was in 1797. The seceders reconstituted themselves in 1798 and continued in Pen Close (hence the seceders were the Pen Folk) until 1819. Although their awkward Calvinism separated them from everybody and they remained quite distinct from the Storie Street Baptists, whence sprang Coats Memorial. secessions from the Pen Folk enlivened Storie Street with some of its dominant characters. John Taylor, weaver and Pen Folk elder from 1799 to 1805 was Storie Street's elder from 1819 to 1842, his family intermarrying with the growing Storie Street network.[23] The Pen Folk, like Storie Street's folk, were practised exhorters and it was held that Storie Street's debating atmosphere owed much to seceders from Pen Close. Their memorialist, writing after the death of their last survivor and sensibly skirting their doctrinal quirks so that he could get to their strength of character, seized on three Pen facets. The first, from a manuscript sermon of 1817, began in terms that most congregationalists would have echoed in 1917:

---

21 William Allan Coats (1853–1926); see R. Marks, *Burrell, A Portrait of a Collector* (Glasgow, 1983), pp. 60, 72, 79.

22 For Major Archibald James Coats (1916–1989), 'a legendary figure in the shooting world', see *Daily Telegraph*, 24 August 1989; for Mrs Dudley Coats (Audrey James), see P. Ziegler, *Mountbatten: The Official Biography* (London, 1985), pp. 50–60; for Peter D. Coats (1910–90), horticultural journalist, see *The Independent* 11 August 1990; for Sir Stuart Auchincloss Coats Bt., M.P., (1868–1959), Private Chamberlain of the Sword and the Cape to four Popes, see M. Stenton and S. Lees, *Who's Who of British Members of Parliament*, vol.III 1919–1945 (Brighton, 1979), p. 69.

23 *Jubilee* pp. 32, 34, 36, 37. His granddaughter, Georgiana Taylor (1852–1927) married Professor Joseph Wilson Coats (1846–99); see [Olive and Victoria Coats], *Dr. and Mrs. Joseph Coats: A Book of Remembrance* (Glasgow, 1929).

The text is, 'Where two or three is gathered together in my name, there am I in the midst of them.' This is the charter of Christian brotherhood and equality. When the Lord spoke those memorable words, he gave to every band, however small, of his followers, who might at any future time gather to worship him, their inalienable law. He did not place their right in the keeping of any Presbytery or Synod; nor did he give any control or supervision into the hands of Bishop or priest whatever. The charter is Divine, and gives its duties and privileges to each gathering of worshippers without the intervention of council . . .[24]

The second is the memorialist's own gloss of 1871:

Democratic government is the only one that is in harmony with a gospel brotherhood, because it alone recognises the divine declarations in their simplicity, 'All ye are brethren,' and '*One* is your Master, even Christ.' Presbytery in any form ignores that brotherhood, because it involves a self-perpetuating order of men to whom the laity is, to some extent, subservient; whilst Episcopal and Papal rule exclude the brotherhood altogether, and make the Church to consist of its officials, – reminding me of the regiments we formed in our boyhood which were wholly composed of corporals, captains, and colonels. Democracy, however, is obnoxious to the great ecclesiastical trades-unions of Christendom, whose chief use in our day resembles that of custom-houses, whose officers levy a tariff on the products of the earth bound heavenward, prohibit *unsound* articles, and consign them to destruction.[25]

The third facet concerns those whose gender precluded them from public exhortation though in no other sense from serious discussion: 'the wives of the Pen . . . those quiet, sensible, queen-like mothers, who, in the very maturity of repose, sat during the intervals of worship in the cozy nook of the meeting-house.' The point about them was this:

the children of each family were enjoined to call every matron in the connection 'Aunty'. I had half-a-dozen Aunty Jeans, and as many Aunty Maries and Aunty Margarets . . . Those who have not experienced the benefits arising from the use of this name, cannot know the humanising power it had over our young hearts . . . More than fifty years have passed, and yet, when I meet the descendants of the Aunties of the Pen Kirk, I feel the old kindly affections welling up strong within me, and I would gladly do them service . . .

That humanising element is too often omitted from analyses of sectarianism. Transposed from Pen Close to Storie Street it makes sense of building and society alike.

As Pen Close was recalled in 1871 'By One Who Knew Them,' so Storie Street was recreated fifty years later in G.H. Coats's *Rambling Recollections*.[27] In his mind's eye the east end of its upper room was dominated by

24 *Reminiscences of the 'Pen' Folk By One Who Knew Them* (Paisley, priv., 1871), p. 27.
25 *Ibid.*, p. 9.
26 *Ibid.*, pp. 9–11.
27 G.H. Coats, *Rambling Recollections* (Paisley, priv. 1920).

a big gaucy pulpit . . . a big four-barrelled affair, with room . . . for four elders
at a time – panels up at the back, with hat pegs and a bookboard and cushion in
front for the Bible and hymnbook.[28]

Storie Street's topography was complicated. The big pulpit reared above a
smaller one with a well-cushioned seat for the precentor. To its left was a secondary
bench, where the precentor moved 'when any brother who could not give the
"word of exhortation" without his notes ousted him.'[29] To its right was the
hymn-tune rack (Stroudwater, Caroline, St Marnock's, Marksworth, St George's
Edinburgh) and to its front again was a red plush upholstered desk, flanked by
brass holders for the tune's name which the precentor would hold aloft as appropriate. There too were the music book, the tuning fork and the spittoon, 'indis-
pensable for the clearing of the precentor's throat.'[30]

Thus the landscape extended from the gaucy pulpit, for the plush-upholstered
desk was in turn fronted by the railed-in table seat reserved for deacons and
non-officiating elders. So to the table in the centre. This in fact was the baptistery's
portable top, edged by sloping book boards. The room had a central passage
between pews whose sittings, ten a side, were free. For baptism the table top was
removed and candidates for baptism followed the presiding elder up temporary
steps, over the edge and into water 'cold to freezing point in winter.'[31]

The room worked or, rather, was made to work, a fact confirmed by the Storie
Kirk Love Feast (or 'Coffee Kirk') held between Sunday services in the downstairs
meeting room, Storie Street's equivalent of the Pen wives' 'maturity of repose.'[32]
What began for church members was extended to church children and what began
with kail broth and mild ale was gentled to Johnstone's essence, biscuits, cheese,
bread and mustard. 'We sat on the forms, with our coffee jugs on the sloping
school desks, and sometimes they slid off.'[33] Coffee Kirk's liturgy was grace, food,
fellowship, and then news of members. It was the cement of community, and
Coats Memorial, with its upper-room cathedral and its banqueting hall beneath,
was designed to perpetuate it. But somehow that did not happen:

> There is little hope of these practices being revived . . . under the conditions as
> they at present exist in the magnificent buildings called the Thomas Coats
> Memorial Church![34]

Yet for some the heart of the matter was transformed rather then obliterated.
One minister recalled for the jubilee of those magnificent buildings his own
formation in them: the choir on the opening day, in which he sang; the first
baptism, with him baptised; the building 'that spoke of the eternal things all about
us;' the naturalness of what was

---

28 *Ibid.*, p. 119.
29 *Ibid.*, p. 120.
30 *Ibid.*
31 *Ibid.*, p. 121.

32 *Pen Folk* p. 10.
33 *Rambling Recollections* p. 138.
34 *Ibid.*, p. 139.

stately, dignified and moving. It made Christian worship unique, and proved that the influence of the church service could be the greatest moral and spiritual instrument in the world.[35]

That testimony suggests that these memorial buildings *worked as buildings for Baptists*, that they grew from Storie Street rather than that they sucked in Storie Street.

IV

This brings us to the Baptistness of Paisley's many-septed Coatses and in particular to the published lecture which George Holms Coats gave in April 1894 so that Storie Street might be better prepared for its new working memorial. Coats called it *An Ideal Baptist Church*.[36] It contains all the traditional sense, the radicalism, the directness of the Storie Street mentality as distilled through his engaging prejudices. It explains the new Baptist cathedral. Coats lectured at unequal length under seven heads: The Entrance into Church, Prayer, Praise, Giving, Religious Freedom, Baptism and Brotherliness.

The Entrance into Church was about the Voluntary: 'the opening part of our Church service is, not the prayer or hymn, but the Voluntary, and . . . every one should be seated before it begins.'[37] *Prayer* homed in on the new church's kneeling boards: 'In an Ideal Church, the worshippers will not "hunker," but reverently kneel.'[38] *Praise* went to town on the choir. Choristers were truly priests, set apart for the sacrifice of praise. The choirmaster should be 'one who unites the qualities of artist and Christian gentleman,' fit for his 'high and holy' office as he applies 'the refining influences of art to the nurture of those emotional feelings which form so important a part of human experience – of brotherly life.'[39] And they should look the part. The new church aimed architecturally at form and colour above all in the chancel, the singing place. There George Coats reached a minefield:

> It seems rather strange that no church would think of interfering with a choir even though the ladies wore the most gaudy and vulgar costumes and the men dressed as lady-killers and sported light kids and diamond rings; and yet, were these ladies and gentlemen to dress in surplices, which are the plainest of all costumes, they would be very apt to interfere.[40]

He selected his arguments with care:

> I have been informed that most of the nurses in our Infirmaries – many of whom are ladies by education, and have been brought up in what is called good society – offer no objection to the uniformity of dress which they assume.[41]

[35] *Jubilee* pp. 131–32.
[36] G.H. Coats, *An Ideal Baptist Church: A Lecture* (Paisley, 1894).
[37] *Ibid.*, p. 8.
[38] *Ibid.*, p. 9.
[39] *Ibid.*, p. 12.
[40] *Ibid.*, p. 14.
[41] *Ibid.*

Coats got away with it. The choir unanimously agreed to wear surplices, and though the matter came to church meeting the church declined to interfere. And so to *Giving*. This too must be bound up with active worship:

> Instead of putting one man at the door to watch the plate, I would put several men at each door to watch for the wayfarer, the dissolute, the poor, and the needy, and who would with kindliest tone lead them to the best seats in the house . . .
>
> There is . . . special music written for what is called the Offertory. The meaning of an Offertory to Protestants is the Collection, and music is written for it . . . an aid to the devotional act of contributing to the necessities of the poor . . .[42]

Thus the act of giving in worship would truly become 'a sacrifice – a sacred deal – a sacrament, a sacred act of the mind' and he imagined the plate passing 'from hand to hand like a communion-cup, knitting hearts together in common sacrifice for the well-being of others.'[43]

With *Religious Freedom, Baptism* and *Brotherliness* Coats came to what he and his hearers would have agreed was the heart of the matter. The first of the three gave him the opportunity to urge his hearers to cast out all fear 'of the discoveries of science, of the anathemas of the orthodox or the tattle of Mrs. Grundy':

> As all Baptists ought to know, each of our churches is independent . . . It is rather difficult to make Presbyterians understand that the Baptist Union is not the Baptist Church . . . that whenever an attempt has been made, even by so great a name as that of Spurgeon, to touch the inviolable liberty of each congregation, it has been utterly defeated, so that each Baptist Church has as one of its fundamental principles a constitution within itself embracing all the power which is wielded by Presbytery, Synod, and General Assembly: and any one, priest or layman, can, without consulting any man or body of men, start a church tomorrow and call it a Baptist Church. Every individual church enjoys this freedom . . . in accordance with order and decency and the progress of thought and culture.[44]

That was simple. *Baptism* was less so. In the new church Baptism was an architectural matter: in modern Presbyterian churches the font was to be found prominent in front of the chancel; in many modern American Baptist churches the baptistery was 'as prominent and ornamental as the font in other churches.' So now at Paisley, as the Presbyterian church 'has conspicuous the sacramental font, [we] shall have conspicuous the emblematic baptistery.'[45] The stress was on 'emblematic,' for Coats had a keen weather eye on current moves within Presbyterianism

---

[42] *Ibid.*, pp. 16–17.
[43] *Ibid.*, p. 18.
[44] *Ibid.*, pp. 21–22. The reference to Charles Haddon Spurgeon, of the Metropolitan Tabernacle, is to the Downgrade Controversy: see 'Charles Haddon Spurgeon, 1834–92', *D.N.B.*
[45] *An Ideal Baptist Church*, pp. 19–20.

to assert 'the efficacy of the sacraments' and so, firmly denying that Baptism was a *sacrament*[46] and thus enjoyably refuting 'an utterly false dogma of the Roman Church' that Presbyterians and Episcopalians alike had taken on board, he could contrast their 'narrow, meagre view of God's spirit-baptism with that which it shall be the pride and joy of an Ideal Baptist Church to hold aloft.'

> The Church must be satisfied that this great fact had taken place in his being, and then he shall be recognised as a Freeman, the baptismal bath shall be there, so that, if he desire it, he shall be permitted to act in outward symbol, a material representation of the great spiritual change which has taken place within him.[47]

Baptism ended in *Brotherliness*. Here the homely spirit of Coffee Kirk, most vulnerable by its very homeliness to the splendours in store, flooded upon him. Fellowship at the Lord's table greatly worried Coats if it were held to have any sacramental significance. 'In our Ideal Baptist Church some attempt will be made to return to more rational ways. Let us, if necessary, continue the present service . . . In this, as in baptism, there is no mystery, no sacerdotalism. But . . . an Ideal Baptist Church will revert to the primitive form':

> True socialists, communists, were they. And all this was brought about not by any other way than this, by the brethren meeting frequently and enjoying a social, brotherly, holy meal together – by introducing family life into the Church. They were . . . drawn into intense fellowship . . . This is Christ's gospel; this is the business of a Church.[48]

In this at least Coats Memorial might be Storie Street or even Pen Close.

V

Did the new building help that business? Did it reflect the totality and intensity of the Paisley Baptist experience? It is on the answers to those questions that the success of this working memorial must be judged.

Certainly here is drama, carefully articulated, larger than life but never frightening and never unreasonable. Thus the Wagnerian stairway rising from the carriage sweep to the suite of front doors disguises a false basement of surprisingly light yet still dramatically Gothic halls and retiring rooms of the sort necessary for the daily activities of such a congregation, reinterpreting the spirit of Storie Street's Coffee Kirk Sundays, with T.G. Abercrombie's quietly stylish but sensible Sunday schools a street or so away for more strenuous activity.[49] This is the reason, not the

---

[46] *Ibid.*, p. 24.
[47] *Ibid.*, pp. 26, 28, 29.
[48] *Ibid.*, pp. 32–33.
[49] T. Graham Abercrombie, who was also the architect of the Coats-aided Royal Alexandra Infirmary, drew up plans for the schools in 1905; they were built 1909–10 for £8,152, and opened by Winifred Glen-Coats (d.1947); *Jubilee*, pp. 85–86.

excuse, for the building's height. It is an engineering challenge fit for the most up-to-date architect, as the building's careful, complex buttressing amply demonstrates.

So the drama unfolds in successive acts. The Sunday worshipper, expectant from the challenge of the steps, crosses the vestibule, an intense space, richly confined. Under his feet is the mosaic of the lamb. Above his head are monograms of Thomas Coats's family, in almost the sole recognition of their grand benefaction. So into the main church, the people's space. Here is a place for proclaiming the Word, hence the careful positioning of the pulpit so that the preacher can survey each individual, and be surveyed. Hence the convex metal cap in the pulpit's canopy and the thirty-nine acoustic wires stretched high above the pews across the nave's front three bays. Hence the significance of the glazed screen, excluding all breezes save those of the Spirit. Hence the sermons in alabaster carved on the pulpit or high on the chancel's north wall: Jesus and Paul, John and Isaiah; the woman at the well, and the Good Samaritan, and Christ and the little children, the Adoration of the Magi, the Last Supper. Here too is a room for Protestant drama, symbolic certainly, sacramental perhaps: the table and the open baptistery, the former with a seated Christ carved on its top, the latter in marble with its purpose pointed by the chancel's central carving. This is of Christ's baptism, as might be found in Chartres. It is in alabaster. It is drama which might be oratorio, scored for a cathedral choir, fifty strong. Here the choir, though side-stalled, manages to be congregational too because the organist sits behind what looks like an altar but is in fact the console. Thus he faces choir and congregation alike, controlling them alike. The only other worshipper placed so strategically is the minister when in the pulpit.

The vestries are reached quickly and easily across the ambulatory behind the chancel. Their grandeur, though faded, is undeniable. The electrolier in one of them brings out a touch of Mackintosh. There are the remains of stencilling on the walls. The washbasins here too are like fonts. The electric fires are dramatically ineffective. And there is one most important Baptist touch. Two of the rooms are period-panelled and generously chimney-pieced, meticulously equipped as baptismal changing rooms, for the panelling folds out, rather as in an expensive outfitter's.

The total cost has been estimated at £110,000; so much for the competitors' £20,000 or the assessor's £25,000.[50] In this it was certainly a sport among contemporary Baptist churches. Yet it is hard to see how its architect could have been more sensitive, given his brief, to his memorial's working needs.

Twenty-five years on from his lecture and four years out of fellowship George Holms Coats was no longer so sanguine about the effect on 'a church whose traditions were laid and built up on the basis of congregational liberty and independence.'[51] Nonetheless Coats Memorial has outlived the firm of Coats, at least

---

50 That is the implication of *Rambling Recollections*, p. 123.
51 *Rambling Recollections*, p. 272.

in Paisley. By 1985 the firm had moved out of the town, abandoning the mills and Ferguslie and retaining a presence only in Anchor Mills, which had belonged to the Clarks, the Coatses' great Presbyterian rivals; but there were still Coats descendants in membership at Thomas Coats's Memorial.

STEWART J. BROWN

The Campaign for the Christian Commonwealth in Scotland, 1919–1939

The First World War had a shattering effect on the optimism of the nineteenth century, with its faith in rational progress through industrial capitalism, free trade and parliamentary institutions. Throughout Europe, there was a turning away from the orthodoxies of nineteenth-century liberalism, which now seemed to have placed too much emphasis on individual rights and aspirations at the expense of communal identity and collective security. The Great War brought unprecedented slaughter – an orgy of mechanized killing. But it also brought unprecedented levels of economic planning and collective action – a new sense of community and comradeship – that many hoped would renew and elevate post-war societies. The European churches shared to a considerable extent in this turning towards collectivism and community. The churches had been heavily involved in the war efforts of their respective countries, appealing to the God of Battles and sanctioning war aims. As the war came to an end, many church leaders looked for a new social order that would build on the lessons of war-time cooperation, and be a fitting memorial to those killed and maimed. In post-war England, the emphasis on corporate Christianity found expression in the Christendom Group and in the growing influence of Anglo-Catholicism. In Germany, it contributed to the rise of German Christianity, with its emphasis on the immanence of God in German history. In Scotland, it found expression in a campaign to achieve the Christian commonwealth.

The idea of the Christian commonwealth in Scotland was rooted in the Reformation, when John Knox and the reformers had sought to apply the model of Calvin's Geneva at a national level. In the Reformed social ideal, church and state were to cooperate for the establishment of a righteous social order, characterised by a corporate discipline enforced by the church courts and the godly magistrate. The righteous commonwealth would ensure that all inhabitants – the elect and the reprobate alike – obeyed the laws of God and practiced charity toward one another, for both the glory of God and the well-being of society. The church would control education, poor relief and the enforcement of Christian morals, while the civil magistrate would be responsible for protecting property, punishing serious offenders and defending the realm from foreign enemies. Within the commonwealth, the basic ecclesiastical and civil unit was to be the parish, conceived as a small, largely self-contained community in which inhabitants would know one another and share a common Christian life. As there was one God and one truth, so there should be one national church, representing the Christian conscience of the commonwealth, guiding the civil magistrates and accepting responsibility for the Christian nurture and discipline of the population.

The idea of the Christian commonwealth was never achieved in sixteenth and seventeenth-century Scotland, in large part because of the refusal of the crown and landed classes to concede so much power to the church courts. During the eighteenth and nineteenth centuries the unity of the Scottish national church was broken by three major secessions, in 1733, 1761 and 1843, which had resulted from disputes over patronage and the relation of church and state. Along with the fragmentation of the national church, the parish system of the Church of Scotland was largely overwhelmed by the concentration of population in large towns and cities, and by the growth of religious Dissent. Control over poor relief and education passed to the state, while the church courts lost power to enforce moral discipline. Scottish society became religiously pluralistic, and the influence of the national church steadily waned. During the later nineteenth century, there was a prolonged campaign to disestablish the Church of Scotland. Nonetheless, the Church of Scotland survived as an established church, and many Scots held to the idea of a Christian commonwealth centred upon a revived and reunited national church. In the aftermath of the First World War, a significant number of Scottish Presbyterians embraced the hope that they could achieve this idea – that they could reunite the national church and transform Scotland into a Christian commonwealth, both for its own spiritual and temporal good, and so that it might stand as a model for other nations to follow. The leading figure behind this movement was the Revd Dr John White (1867–1951), minister of the Barony Church, Glasgow, architect of the Church Union of 1929. and the dominant churchman in inter-war Scotland. This essay will trace the efforts of the mainstream Presbyterian churches to achieve the Christian commonwealth in inter-war Scotland. It will explore the response of the national church in one of the smaller nations in Northern Europe to the great hopes raised during the war, and consider how the disillusionment, industrial unrest and international tensions of the inter-war decades led to changes in the church's conception of the Christian commonwealth.

I

Scottish society suffered devastating losses in the First World War. An estimated 110,000 Scots were killed, and tens of thousands more shattered in body or mind. Amid the horrors of war, however, many within the two main Scottish Presbyterian churches – the established Church of Scotland and the voluntary United Free Church – embraced the hope that a new social order would emerge out of the ordeal. In 1916, the General Assemblies of the two churches formed special 'commissions on the war', to explore the meaning of the struggle for Christians.

The first reports of the Church of Scotland Commission, which appeared in May 1917, portrayed the war as a visitation from God, both judicial and redemptive in its nature. On the one hand, the visitation was God's judgement on the selfish materialism of pre-war civilisation; on the other, the visitation summoned all the nations of Europe to corporate repentance. In particular, God was calling the Scottish nation to reject laissez faire capitalism and radical individualism and to seek to reconstruct society on the principles of equality, brotherhood and cooperation: 'Never again' was to be the church's 'watchword' as she contemplated the chaos of pre-war society.[1] In the final months of the war, the two Presbyterian churches conducted jointly a series of conferences on housing and industrial organisation, published studies of social problems, and sought to work closely with the Coalition Government's Committee on Reconstruction, which was formed in April 1917.[2] Church and state, it was believed, would advance together to create the Christian commonwealth.

The hopes of post-war reconstruction were raised still further with the revival of the movement for Presbyterian church reunion. The church union movement began in the 1890s, with negotiations which led in 1900 to the union of the two largest non-established Presbyterian churches to form the United Free Church. In 1909, formal negotiations for union were opened between the United Free Church and the Church of Scotland, which promised to bring the large majority of Scottish Christians together in a restored national church. The union movement was inspired largely by the ideas of efficiency and collectivism that were current in the 1890s, and by the need for a more effective home mission among the industrial working classes. Though temporarily halted with the beginning of the war, the union negotiations were revived in 1917, as the two churches prepared to assume a role of leadership in post-war reconstruction.[3]

With the end of the war, the Church of Scotland and United Free Church together entered into the work of building the new social order. In April 1919, the churches cooperated in the National Mission of Rededication, summoning congregations to pledge themselves to work for the supremacy of Christ in all spheres of national life.[4] At its first post-war meeting in May 1919, the General Assembly of the Church of Scoland transformed its Commission on the War into a permanent Church and Nation Committee, instructed to guide the work of building the Christian commonwealth in all its aspects, including the social and industrial. At the close of the Assembly, the Moderator, Professor W.P. Paterson of Edinburgh University, called on the Scottish nation to 'covenant together' in the work of

---

1   *Reports on the Schemes of the General Assembly of the Church of Scotland* (1917), 723–58.
2   *Reports on the Schemes of the General Assembly of the Church of Scotland* (1918), 619–33; *Reports* (1919), 631–35; W.P. Paterson and D. Watson (eds), *Social Evils and Problems* (Edinburgh, 1919).
3   R. Sjolinder, *Presbyterian Reunion in Scotland* (Stockholm, 1962); A. Muir, *John White* (London, 1958), 83–175, 191–6.
4   D.C. Smith, *Passive Obedience and Prophetic Protest: Social Criticism in the Scottish Church 1830–1945* (New York, 1987), 359–60.

reconstruction.[5] The war had been a victory for the rights of Belgium and other small nations, and Christian Scotland was destined to play an important part in the new European order.

Even as Paterson spoke, however, the war-time unity was collapsing, and post-war Scottish society was proving to be far different from that envisaged by the church's Commission on the War. The final months of the war had witnessed a dramatic increase in industrial unrest, with war-weariness and divided responses to the Bolshevik revolution in Russia contributing to the social tensions. The general election of November 1918 brought victory for the Conservative party, which now dominated the Coalition Government. The Government immediately began dismantling the war-time economic controls and limiting or scrapping the reconstruction proposals. Not reconstruction, but a rapid return to the pre-war economic system became the Government's aim.[6] The Liberal party, which had dominated pre-war Scottish politics and represented Scottish national identity and aspirations, was now fragmented. Politics became increasingly divided along the lines of social class, between a Conservative party representing the propertied classes and a Labour party representing the working classes. The class divisions in Scotland were deepened by the economic stagnation that followed the war, with high unemployment and falling wages confronting the men returning from military service.[7] Presbyterian leaders were unclear about how to respond to the divided society of the early 1920s. For the churches to cling to their war-time pledges to work for radical social and industrial reconstruction based on cooperation would be to set themselves against the stated policies of the Conservative-dominated Coalition Government and align themselves with the Labour opposition. This would not be acceptable to middle-class Presbyterians, who provided most of the financial and organisational support for the churches and who had little sympathy for labour politics. In the event, church leaders decided to follow the Government's lead and withdraw from the call for social and industrial reconstruction. The church-sponsored conferences on questions of social reform and the aspirations of labour ended in 1921. The Church of Scotland's Church and Nation Committee and the United Free Church's Church Life and Social Problems Committee ceased calling for reform of the social and industrial system, and concentrated instead on the need to improve personal morality as the means to bring about the amelioration of social conditions.[8] Church leaders did not

---

5   W.P. Paterson, *Recent History and the Call to Brotherhood: Address delivered at the Close of the General Assembly, May 29, 1919* (Edinburgh, 1919), 32.
6   R.H. Tawney, 'The Abolition of Economic Controls, 1918–1921', *Economic History Review*, xiii (1943), 1–30; P. Abrams, 'The Failure of Social Reform, 1918–1920', *Past and Present*, 24 (1963), 43–64.
7   M. Fry, *Patronage and Principle: A Political History of Modern Scotland* (Aberdeen, 1987), 136–39, 147–8, 165–7.
8   S.J. Brown, 'Reform, Reconstruction, Reaction: The Social Vision of Scottish Presbyterianism, c.1830–c.1930', *Scottish Journal of Theology*, 44;4 (1991), 507–11.

relinquish their hopes to revive the social influence and authority of the national church, but they did begin to modify their idea of the Christian commonwealth.

The key figure in redefining the social ideal of the churches in post-war Scotland was John White, who emerged as the acknowledged leader of Scottish Presbyterianism during the early 1920s.[9] Born the son of a flour merchant in the small West of Scotland village of Kilwinning in 1867, White had studied at Glasgow University, where he was influenced by the Hegelianism of Professor Edward Caird. Ordained to the ministry of the Church of Scotland in 1893, he served as parish minister in Shettleston and in South Leith, before being called to the prestigeous Barony Church, Glasgow, in 1911. As a minister, White was committed to the parish system, including regular house-to-house visiting, Sunday schools, literary societies, cycling clubs, and the distribution of coal and groceries. A Tory paternalist, he believed the church should work to alleviate poverty and unemployment through charitable action within parish communities, rather than call for large-scale reforms of the social order.[10] During the First World War, he had been a fiercely patriotic preacher, and served with notable courage for over a year as a chaplain on the Western Front. It was as a tireless and practical worker for church union that White emerged to leadership within the church. Cultivating connections with influential Conservative politicians, White played a leading role in securing the parliamentary acts of 1921 and 1925, which cleared the way legally and financially for the established church to proceed to union with the United Free Church. He also took a major part on the Church of Scotland's Commission on the War, and became joint-convener of the Church and Nation Committee created to oversee post-war reconstruction.

Under White's leadership, the social policies of the Presbyterian churches during the 1920s took two major directions. First, the churches ceased their criticism of the economic and political order, which effectively meant that they gave tacit support to the revival of competitive industrial capitalism with its accompanying social inequalities. Secondly, the churches became associated with an exclusive national religion, with strong racial and sectarian aspects.

White and other church leaders, including Lord Sands and Alexander Martin, worked to ensure that the Presbyterian churches would no longer criticise the system of industrial capitalism or appear to favour the aspirations of organised labour over other sections of society. The proponents of the social gospel within both the Church of Scotland and the United Free Church, men like Colin Gibb, Malcolm MacCallum and J.D. Robertson, were marginalised and effectively silenced during the early 1920s. In 1925, White's leadership in the Church of Scotland was recognised when he was appointed Moderator of the General Assembly. In his closing address to the Assembly of 1925, he defined his views on the proper response of the church to the post-war industrial strife and economic

---

9 The standard biography is A. Muir's *John White*, a largely uncritical life that omits certain key events and movements. There is also much valuable material in the large collection of John White Papers at New College Library, Edinburgh.

10 Muir, *John White*, 51–65.

deprivation. The church, he argued, must be concerned with all aspects of social life. However, it should also avoid pronouncements that might appear to be taking sides in the industrial conflict. Its role should be that of mediator, seeking to reconcile a divided society through appeals to Christian charity and personal morality: 'the social message of the Gospel can only become a social force as it becomes the rule of individual hearts'. Further, the church had to recognise that it had no technical competence to speak on economics – 'which is a science for experts and in which it has no authority'. Its mission was to proclaim the 'governing principles of human value and human comradeship' to the Scottish people, while leaving specific questions of social justice to the state. The church must refuse to be made a 'judge and divider' among men, but should concentrate on defining a religious consensus that would unite the nation. It should concentrate on improving its own institutional 'efficiency', especially in the parish ministry.[11] This was, in many respects, a reasonable position – especially if the church is conceived of as essentially a clerical institution, controlled by ministers who lacked expert knowledge in politics and economics. It is less reasonable if the church is conceived of as the community of believers, including businessmen, labour leaders and politicians. White's policy restricted the sphere of the church's action, placing politics and economics largely outside its province. This could mean leaving the social order to be determined by the exercise of brute power rather than of righteousness, while the church focused on the 'efficiency' of its parish structures.

The ambiguities in White's position were made apparent during the General Strike of 1926, which created a national crisis in the final weeks of his moderatorial year. Early in May 1926, most unions in Britain went out in support of the coal miners, who had been locked out for refusing to accept wage reductions made necessary by the withdrawal of state subsidies to the industry.[12] As retiring Church of Scotland Moderator, White sought to give substance to his vision of the church as a force for social reconciliation; he condemned the General Strike as misguided and dangerous, but promised that once the strike was ended, the church would exercise its influence to mediate a just and lasting settlement of the dispute in the coal fields. The General Strike was called off after nine days. A few days later, the National Union of Scottish Mine Workers sent a deputation to the General Assemblies of both major Presbyterian churches to appeal for the churches' aid in mediating a settlement. It now became clear, however, just how far the churches had moved from their war-time promises of a new industrial order. Few members of the two General Assemblies were prepared to do more than express a vague sympathy for the miners or the labour movement. The Revd John Harvey, the Moderator of the United Free Church General Assembly, had described the defeat of the General Strike as a 'victory for God', and this attitude was widely shared in both churches. The miners' deputation was allowed to speak to the two Assemblies,

[11] J. White, *Efficiency: Address delivered at the Close of the General Assembly, May 25. 1925* (Edinburgh, 1925), 22–3, 39–40.
[12] S.J. Brown, ' "A Victory for God": The Scottish Presbyterian Churches and the General Strike of 1926', *Journal of Ecclesiastical History*, 42;4 (October 1991), 596–617.

but only after being informed that the church had no competence to consider questions of economic or political justice. White made a half-hearted appeal to both the miners' union and the Scottish Coal Owners Association to accept the church's mediation. The miners' union accepted the church's offer, but the owners refused – reminding White of his own axiom that the church had no competence to speak on economic matters. White then dropped the offer and the churches remained silent as the miners were defeated and forced to suffer reduced wages and the victimisation of union leaders. Church leaders made no further attempts to mediate in industrial disputes during the inter-war years. The churches remained silent while power was allowed to prevail in the industrial order, and they now largely restricted their social mission to providing charity to some of the individual victims of capitalism.

While Presbyterian leaders were withdrawing from their war-time promises of social justice through industrial reconstruction, they were turning to a new vision of the Christian commonwealth – one in which consensus would be built, not upon shared sacrifices or Christian teachings, but upon an exclusive, racial nationalism. In 1923, the Church and Nation Committee of the Church of Scotland, under White's co-convenership, summoned the Scottish nation to unite in a campaign directed against the approximately 600,000 Roman Catholics of Irish descent who were living in Scotland.[13] The movement had its origins among the church courts in the West of Scotland. It arose in part from opposition to the Education Act (Scotland) of 1918, which provided state assistance for Catholic schools, and in part from fear and hostility felt by many middle and upper-class church members towards the growing strength of the Labour party in the West of Scotland, where Labour received valuable support in the general election of 1922 from the Catholic community. In 1923, the Church and Nation Committee presented a special report on Irish immigration to the General Assembly. This report described the Scoto-Irish Catholics as an alien race, which was corrupting the values and lowering the moral character of the Scottish nation. Scoto-Irish Catholics refused to accept the moral authority of the national church and aroused resentments among native Scots. Scotland was becoming a nation divided against itself, and might well be losing God's favour. For God, the report asserted, 'placed the people of this world in families' and 'the nations that are homogeneous in Faith and ideals, that have maintained unity of race, have been ever the most prosperous, and to them the Almighty has committed the highest tasks, and has granted the largest measure of success in achieving them'. Further, most of the industrial unrest that so troubled post-war Scotland could be attributed to the presence of this alien race. Scoto-Irish Catholics, it was argued, took employment from native Scots, and depressed wages by their willingness to accept a lower standard of living. They were a major force behind the Labour organisation in the

---

13 For the story of the Presbyterian campaign against Irish immigration in the inter-war period, see S.J. Brown, ' "Outside the Covenant": The Scottish Presbyterian Churches and the Irish Catholic Community in Scotland, 1922–1937', *Innes Review*, 42;1 (Spring 1991), 19–45.

West of Scotland, and they fomented industrial unrest. In short it was this alien presence, and not the system of industrial capitalism, that was to blame for Scotland's post-war economic stagnation, and it was the sacred duty of the national church to confront this 'menace' and 'preserve Scotland for the Scottish race'.[14] After 1923, the Church of Scotland organised a national campaign against the Scoto-Irish Catholic community, collecting statistics, issuing reports, holding public meetings and sending petitions and deputations to the Government. The Church of Scotland secured the support of the United Free Church and together the two churches demanded legislation to restrict Irish immigration into Scotland, and to deport any Catholic of Irish descent who received poor relief or state medical care, or who had a prison record. Further, the churches called on employers to employ only native Scots, which would have the effect of forcing Scoto-Irish Catholics either to leave voluntarily or to apply for relief and thus be deported. The campaign was open in its racism. Writing on behalf of the Church and Nation Committee to Sir John Gilmour, Secretary of State for Scotland, in 1926, White referred to the Scoto-Irish Catholics as an 'inferior race', who by their very presence lowered the moral character of the Scottish nation and created social unrest.[15] In organising the campaign, White and his supporters evidently hoped to define a cause that would unite the propertied classes and working classes behind the authority of the national church. The church would revive the war-time national consensus, now against the 'enemies' within, who one prominent Church of Scotland minister described as more sinister foes than the Germans in the recent war.[16] White also believed he was giving his church a leading place in an emerging world movement for the achievement of racial purity. 'To-day there is a movement throughout the world', White had asserted confidently in the *Glasgow Herald* on 15 April 1929, 'towards the rejection of non-native constituents and the crystallisation of national life from native elements'.[17]

In October 1929, the union of the Church of Scotland and the United Free Church was at last achieved. The united church included some 200 congregations, 200 chapels and mission stations, nearly 200 ministers, and an estimated total membership of 2,150,000 – out of a population of about 5,000,000.[18] White was hailed as the chief architect of the union, and his leadership was recognised by his appointment as the first Moderator of the General Assembly of the united church. In his opening address to the Assembly, he proclaimed that the urgent task facing the united church was to secure 'the moral, social and religious well-being of the people of Scotland'. Now that the national church had ended its divisions, it would be able to mobilize its resources and radically improve its 'efficiency' as an

14 *Reports on the Schemes of the General Assembly of the Church of Scotland* (1923), 749–62.
15 *Reports on the Schemes of the General Assembly of the Church of Scotland* (1926), 619.
16 The Revd Duncan Cameron, Church of Scotland minister of Kilsyth, cited in the *Paisley Daily Express*, 27 October 1927.
17 *Glasgow Herald*, 15 April 1929.
18 [J.W. Stevenson, ed.], *The Call to the Church: The Book of the Forward Movement of the Church of Scotland* (Edinburgh, [1931]), 36–7.

evangelising force. The two principles for which the united church stood, White maintained, were national religion and the territorial ministry. First, the Church of Scotland represented the Christian conscience of the nation, uniting social classes, influencing legislation and defining Christian values. Secondly, it maintained an effective parish ministry, organising the population into close-knit parish communities under the authority of the national church.[19]

Not everyone, however, shared White's confident view of the church union and the approach of the Christian commonwealth. Some were disturbed by the church's withdrawal from most of its war-time promises for a new social order based on greater equality and cooperation, and by its unwillingness to question the existing economic and political order. They felt the national church had become too closely tied to the propertied classes, and insufficiently sympathetic to the needs and aspirations of the working classes. In 1930, for example, the Edinburgh journalist, G.M. Thomson, published a critical response to the claims of White and other proponents of church union. The church, Thomson maintained, could no longer be termed a national institution, as it had come to represent only one section of society, and that the most conservative and unthinking section of the middle class: it had been reduced to 'a class organisation: the Scottish middle class in a black frock coat and top-hat, masquerading as a national Church'. The church union, Thomson argued, represented simply a 'shortening of its line of defence', and few were convinced that it marked a significant event in the nation's history.[20] There was too much truth in Thomson's critique. Bold and decisive action would be needed if the church hoped to build upon the church union and achieve a genuine national consensus for the Christian commonwealth.

II

As first Moderator of the General Assembly of the united national church, White proclaimed that one priority for the church would be to continue the campaign against the combined 'menace' of Roman Catholicism and Irish immigration. He had hoped to be able to announce to the first General Assembly of the united church that the Government had agreed to introduce legislation to restrict Irish immigration. The Government, however, had decided to resist Presbyterian pressures and declined to support any legislation. White now announced that the united church would carry on its efforts to rouse the Scottish people against the 'alien' minority. The Catholic presence, he argued, complicated the home mission task of the national church: as aliens in both race and religion, they could never be made part of the Christian commonwealth and would always remain an obstacle to the evangelisation of the nation. Further, he maintained, Catholics in Scotland were becoming 'aggressive' – working openly to convert the Scottish nation to

---

[19] J. White, *Address to the General Assembly of the Church of Scotland* (Edinburgh, 1929).
[20] G.M. Thomson, *Will the Scottish Church Survive?* (Edinburgh, 1930).

Rome.[21] In 1931, the General Assembly transferred the anti-Catholic campaign from the Church and Nation Committee to a new standing committee, the 'Church Interests Committee', which was to concern itself exclusively with anti-Catholic and anti-Irish agitation. This Committee was not only to coordinate the agitation within the church, but was also to unite other Scottish Protestant denominations behind the national church's anti-Catholic campaign. Ministers were instructed to report to the Committee on Catholics residing in their parishes, including their numbers and racial composition. After 1933, moreover, the Committee cooperated with the 'International League for the Defence and Furtherance of Protestantism', an anti-Catholic organisation based in Berlin.[22]

The united Church of Scotland opened its post-union campaign for the Christian commonwealth with the Forward Movement, which was intended to inform and mobilise the people of Scotland. Twelve commissions, with over 200 members, were set up in 1929 to explore different aspects of the church's mission. Their reports were presented in a volume, *The Call to the Church*, which was distributed for discussion within specially formed congregational study groups. In October 1931, a Congress of some 2500 delegates was held in Glasgow. This Congress was followed by ten regional 'Missions of the Kingdom' conducted throughout Scotland. The emphasis of the Forward Movement was on the need to improve the efficiency of the church, and particularly on the need to revive the parish system as a means of creating Christian communities under the direction of the national church. Ministers and elders were to supervise the moral and spiritual development of parish communities through regular house-to-house visiting, while every member of the church was to join in the work of parish agencies – literary societies, youth groups, Sunday Schools, charity societies – for the work of national evangelisation. Scottish parishes would once again become the foundation stones of Scottish national life, shaping a Christian consensus based on communal benevolence and individual self-help. Through the revived parish system, the church would also reduce the intemperance, gambling, sexual immorality and lack of parental authority that church leaders argued lay at the root of nearly all Scotland's social problems.[23]

Despite strenuous efforts by the organisers, however, the Forward Movement proved a disappointment, failing to arouse much enthusiasm for the reunited national church among a population increasingly suffering the effects of the world economic depression.[24] The local Missions of the Kingdom were continued for two years, though with less than satisfactory results. Much of the problem lay in the conservative content of the Forward message. Some participating ministers – for example, George Macleod of Govan – did try to convince the Movement's

21 *Glasgow Herald*, 21 January, 26 February 1930.
22 Brown, ' "Outside the Covenant" ', 37–9.
23 [Stevenson, ed.], *The Call to the Church*, esp. 37–73; J.A. Steele, ed., *The Congress Message: Report of the Forward Church Congress at Glasgow, October 1931* (Edinburgh, [1931]); *Reports of the General Assembly of the Church of Scotland* (1932), 1243–8.
24 A.R. Fraser, *Donald Fraser of Livingstonia* (London, 1934), 303–7.

organisers that the church needed to put aside excessive concern for personal morality and sabbatarianism, and openly confront the larger economic and political problems of the day.[25] For the most part, however, the Forward Movement avoided criticism of the economic and political order; it pressed for the idea of a Christian commonwealth based on closely-knit parish communities, while showing little sensitivity for religious and ethnic minorities. In one of the key papers at the Glasgow conference, for example, the popular preacher and future Moderator, James Black of St George's West, Edinburgh, focused on 'the astounding indifference of the Christian Church to the whole Jewish problem'. Jewish efforts to assimilate into the life of Christian nations, Black argued, had failed: 'they remain, in large part, an undigested element in the cultural civilisation into which they enter', while their control over international finance and the new film industry made them a growing threat to Christian society.[26]

In the country as a whole, meanwhile, economic conditions continued to worsen, and unemployment became the urgent and desperate national issue, with the humiliation of the 'means test' adding to the misery of the unemployed and their families after 1931. Individual clergymen and congregations struggled bravely to ease the plight of the unemployed through soup-kitchens, reading rooms and clothing societies at the parish level.[27] Witnessing the pain of families struggling on the dole, some within the church grew uncomfortable with the accepted position that the church should not speak on economic and political issues.[28] In a special report on unemployment to the General Assembly of 1932, the Church and Nation Committee suggested that the church should press the Government to take a more active role in the struggle against unemployment: 'the principle of laissez-faire, that self-interest and free competition are sufficient guides in industry, has disintegrated for the present, and the logical alternative is conscious direction, planning, and control'.[29] In the discussion of the report in the General Assembly, however, it became clear that such views did not have the support of the majority of the Assembly, and that for many, unemployment resulted primarily from the individual moral failings of the unemployed. When J.M. Munro, a minister in industrial Falkirk, introduced a motion criticising the harshness of the 'means test' used to determine eligibility for benefit, he was answered by Isaac Low, an elder of Bishopriggs, who argued that the unemployment problem was primarily related to the moral decline of the labouring orders: 'if the spirit of independence and self-help were as strong now in the character of

[25] G.F. Macleod, 'The Call to Crucifixion', in Steele (ed.), *The Congress Message*, 45–54.
[26] J. Black, 'The Kingdom and the Jew', in Steele (ed.), *The Congress Message*, 187–94.
[27] For example, Charles L. Warr, minister of St Giles, Edinburgh, described the efforts in his urban parish in his autobiography, *The Glimmering Landscape* (London, 1960), 144–6. See also, L. Cameron, *Opportunity My Ally* (London, 1965), 124–31.
[28] See, for example, J.W. Stevenson, *Christ and the Economic Crisis* (London, 1932), 35–45, in which the young Church of Scotland minister described the existing economic system as a 'denial of God'.
[29] *Reports of the General Assembly of the Church of Scotland* (1932), 504–12.

the people as it had been fifty years ago, fewer people would apply for help'. Low's speech was received with applause, and Munro was forced to withdraw his motion in favour of a compromise motion simply urging the Government to apply the means test 'with wisdom and Christian discernment'. The Assembly decided that the church would take only 'limited measures' to alleviate the misery of the unemployed through recreation clubs and moral support.[30] The Church Interests Committee, meanwhile, continued to condemn the presence of Irish Catholic aliens, who were allegedly taking employment from native Scots.[31]

In 1932, White, having been made sole convener of a newly created Board of Home Mission, announced a new campaign to build upon the work of the Forward Movement and help to revive a sense of purpose in the Church of Scotland. This was a national campaign for Church Extension, directed to building parish churches and halls, particularly in the new housing areas being developed on the edges of the cities and larger towns.[32] The Church Extension campaign was, for White, a logical development from the Forward Movement, with its emphasis on reviving the parish ministry.[33] It also looked back to the celebrated Church Extension campaign of the 1830s, when under the leadership of the Evangelical Churchman, Thomas Chalmers, the Church of Scotland had built over 220 new parish churches through voluntary contributions.[34] The first Church Extension campaign of the 1830s had been a response to the increase of population, especially in the towns and cities, that had accompanied the industrial revolution. The new Church Extension campaign, as White conceived it, was a response to the diffusion of population from the urban centres to new housing areas on the peripheries, a diffusion made possible by the motorcar, electricity and telephone. Initially, White called for the raising of £180,000 to build thirty churches and twenty church halls in the new housing areas. The money was to be collected by the church as a whole, with every congregation expected to contribute substantial amounts to the central fund. The churches, as they were built, would organise the new housing areas into close-knit parish communities, under the guidance of the national church. In building the new churches, no consideration was to be given to the average income levels in the housing area: the campaign would collect funds to build churches in both affluent leafy suburbs and council housing estates. The sole concern was to ensure that those moving to the new housing areas would not be lost to the church.[35] White acknowledged that in one sense Scotland already had enough churches. The problem, he argued, was that

---

30 *Proceedings and Debates of the General Assembly of the Church of Scotland* (1932), 270–87; Smith, *Passive Obedience and Prophetic Protest*, 369–71.
31 *Acts, Proceedings and Debates of the General Assembly* (1937), 382–5.
32 For a full account of the Church Extension campaign, see Muir, *John White*, 285–95, 321–334.
33 *Scotsman*, 22 December 1933.
34 For a comparison of the Church Extension initiatives of the 1834 and 1933, see 'Thomas Chalmers and John White: History Repeating Itself', *British Weekly*, 24 August 1933.
35 *Acts, Proceedings and Debates of the General Assembly of the Church of Scotland* (1934), 180–81.

existing churches could not be moved with the shifting population. Some historic churches in areas of declining population would therefore have to be closed, as new churches were erected.[36]

Retiring from the full-time parish ministry in 1934, White devoted his energies to the Church Extension campaign, travelling extensively to collect funds and dedicate new churches and halls. He worked to ensure that his campaign had priority over all other schemes of the church, including overseas missions, and he directed harsh public criticism towards ministers and congregations, including those in deprived urban areas, who did not contribute to the scheme.[37] The slogan for the campaign became 'the Church in the Midst', signifying the aim of restoring the church to a central position in the life of communities.[38] Church Extension would become a cause to unite the nation. The campaign also promised to revive cooperation between the state, which was building much of the new housing, and the national church, which would organise the new areas into Christian communities. Church Extension, White argued, might be the last opportunity to revive the Christian commonwealth, before large sections of the population became lost to the church. Despite his urgent appeals, money came in slowly, and it was not until 1936 that the initial goal of £180,000 had been reached. White immediately launched another campaign to raise a further £90,000.[39] The housing act of 1935, he argued, promised to move another one million people, so that nearly a third of the population of Scotland would have been rehoused since the War, in what he described as the greatest social revolution in Scotland's history.[40] It was providential design, White believed, that the church union of 1929 had been completed before this massive migration of population.[41] Among the supporters of the campaign was the Glasgow minister, George Macleod, who in 1938 founded the Iona Community, a brotherhood based on the island of Iona. One of the aims of the Community was to help prepare ministers for the new Church Extension charges, and the Community initially had White's blessing.[42]

Others were not so enthusiastic. From the beginning of the campaign, some had objected to collecting money for Church Extension in the midst of an economic depression, when so much of the population was suffering unemployment and deprivation.[43] Ministers and congregations in badly affected urban areas objected to being pressed to contribute to building churches either for working-class people fortunate enough to be re-housed or, as was often the case, for middle class neighbourhoods which already had tennis clubs and golf courses.[44] City

---

36 'Church Extension', *Scotsman*, 16 November 1933.
37 Muir, *John White*, 323.
38 *Ibid.*, 329.
39 *Reports to the General Assembly of the Church of Scotland* (1938), 359–60.
40 *Acts, Proceedings and Debates of the General Assembly* (1938), 190.
41 Muir, *John White*, 335.
42 R. Ferguson, *George Macleod* (London, 1990), 128, 139; Muir, *John White*, 362–3.
43 Muir, *John White*, 287–8.
44 See, for example, the letter to the editor from an 'East-Side Minister', *Glasgow Herald*, 17 August 1936.

congregations were often struggling with debt and declining membership, and it was small comfort for them to learn that they were probably to be made redundant. Further, the new housing areas were often not far from existing churches. Would it not be better for people to travel back to the historic churches, which might then have a mixture of social classes, than to create new churches in areas where the social classes were often segregated? While few were prepared to challenge White's authority openly, the flow of contributions began to dry up. In 1939, White reported that the movement had completed seventeen churches with halls, one church without a hall and seventeen halls, while another seven churches were under construction – an impressive effort given the economic conditions, but well below the thirty churches and twenty halls which he had proposed to build in 1933.[45] Further, the campaign was having difficulty collecting the supplementary £90,000 White had called for in 1936. There were, to be sure, strong arguments for the Church Extension campaign. A large proportion of the Scottish population was being rehoused during the 1930s and new parish churches were needed in the new housing areas. However, in White's hands the campaign could appear backward-looking and triumphalist – concerned primarily with restoring the authority and discipline of the national church over the new communities. With society struggling desperately with the problems of unemployment, mass deprivation and class divisions, many congregations simply had few resources to spare for such a campaign.

While efforts to achieve the Christian commonwealth were failing in Scotland, the increasing international tensions were throwing shadows over the church's aspirations to exercise an increased influence outside Scotland. The church union of 1929 had made the Church of Scotland perhaps the largest Reformed Church in Northern Europe, and Scottish Presbyterian churchmen had hoped to exercise international leadership. Following the union of 1929, White had argued that a 'new interdenominationalism' was finding expression alongside the 'new internationalism' embodied in the League of Nations, and that the Scottish church union would provide a model of Protestant ecumenism to the world.[46] In the event, the vision of international and interdenominational cooperation quickly faded in the early 1930s, amid the world depression and the rise of the totalitarian states.

Concerns over the darkening international scene found expression in the debate over pacificism, which increasingly divided the Church of Scotland after 1933, as a section within the church raised questions over whether any national goal could be worth the horrors of another general European war. The issue of pacificism served to revive the memories of the Great War and the broken promises of reconstruction. It also drew the church back into debate of political questions. The General Assembly held its first major debate on pacificism in May 1933 when J.W. Stevenson, the young minister of Coulter and a member of the Scottish

---

[45] *Acts, Proceedings and Debates of the General Assembly* (1939), 199.
[46] J. White, *Reunion and International Friendship* (Oxford, 1930), 5–9.

Ministers Peace Group, introduced a motion to the effect that Christians could never condone modern warfare with its technologies of mass destruction directed against civilian populations as well as combatants. John White, a staunch opponent of the pacificists in the church, was recovering in the south of England from a serious attack of pneumonia and was not present in the General Assembly that year. In White's absence, the task of answering Stevenson's motion was taken up by Professor W.P. Paterson of Edinburgh University and Charles L. Warr, minister of St Giles, Edinburgh, who argued in the course of a three-hour debate that a Christian nation must be prepared to defend international law, as Britain had so clearly done in 1914. The motion was remitted to the Church and Nation Committee for consideration.[47] White was present when the issue was debated again the following year and he succeeded in convincing the Assembly to reject the arguments of the pacificists and recognise the principle of a just war. None the less, the pacifists remained a strong force in the church, and they forced further debates on war and peace in the Assemblies of 1935–38, raising questions about national interests and international justice.[48]

As probably the largest Reformed Church in Northern Europe, the Church of Scotland sought to exercise European leadership, particularly through its Continental Committee. As a whole, the church was slow after 1933 to recognise the dangers in the National Socialist state in Germany, or to see the corrupting influences of the pro-Nazi 'German Christian' movement. From May 1933 the church's Continental Committee, under the convenership of Professsor W.A. Curtis of Edinburgh University, expressed concern over the Nazi regime's church policies, including the 'Aryan Clause' and the threats to the independence of the German church. The General Assembly, however, declined to issue an open protest or express public support for the 'Confessing Church' movement.[49] The Scottish church was in fact divided over the meaning of events in Germany. When in its report of 1934 the Continental Committee strongly criticised the Nazi regime and expressed sympathy for the Confessing Church, the report was immediately attacked from the floor of the Assembly by Scottish supporters of the German Christian movement. For David McQueen, an elder from Paisley, the Nazi regime's church reforms had been inspired largely by the Scottish church union of 1929, and the Scottish church should support their efforts to defend Christian civilisation against godless communism. The German Christians, he argued, were also following the example of the Church of Scotland in seeking to identify themselves with the aspirations of their nation and to cultivate close relations with the state. McQueen's call for a united front with the German Christians was received with applause in the Assembly, and on White's motion the church agreed to send a deputation to express friendship and a desire for closer

47 *Acts, Proceedings and Debates of the General Assembly* (1933), 34–50.
48 *Acts, Proceedings and Debates of the General Assembly* (1935), 301–2; (1936), 324–28; (1937), 293–302; (1938), 320–22.
49 *Reports to the General Assembly of the Church of Scotland* (1934), 812–15; *Reports* (1936), 740–41; *Reports* (1938), 716–17.

relations with the German state church.[50] By the following year, Nazi moves to control the German church were becoming more blatant, but still the Assembly declined to do more than remit the matter to a Committee. For Professor W.P. Paterson of Edinburgh University, a former Moderator, matters in Germany 'were not quite so black as they were often painted' and 'the Hitler regime had checked the militant atheism associated with continental Communism'.[51] Scottish divinity students continued to study at Nazi-controlled universities, ignoring warnings from the Confessing Church, and in November 1936, *Life and Work*, the official magazine of the Church of Scotland, published a favourable account of the German Christian church in Hitler's retreat at Berchtesgaden.[52] By 1937, the tide of opinion had turned, and the Church of Scotland began to show some support for the Confessing Church. Karl Barth was invited to present the Gifford Lectures at Aberdeen University in 1937–8 and was awarded an honorary D.D. from St Andrews in 1937, while Dietrich Bonhoeffer was invited to present the Church of Scotland's Croall Lectures for 1940, the outbreak of war preventing their delivery. None the less, the church committees maintained an official silence toward the German church struggle, and the matter received relatively little attention in the General Assembly.

In September 1939 the outbreak of war with Nazi Germany marked the end of an era in the Church of Scotland. The programmes associated with John White's leadership had been clearly failing during the later 1930s. The campaign against Irish Catholic immigration, which had been steadily waning through the 1930s, was finally dropped in 1939. Financial contributions to the Church Extension campaign had been falling off, and there was declining enthusiasm for the vision of a Scotland of small, largely self-contained parish communities under the authority of the national church. The pacificist movement had forced the church to debate the pressing issues of national and international politics, while friendship with the Nazi-controlled German state church was clearly seen to be misguided by the later 1930s. Above all, the crises of the 1930s – of unemployment, mass deprivation, the rise of fascism – had convinced many church members that the church must engage in meaningful social criticism, and that it could not restrict its message to personal morality and personal salvation.[53]

In May 1940, the Church of Scotland General Assembly appointed a 'Commission for the Interpretation of God's Will in the Present Crisis', which became known as the 'Baillie Commission', after Professor John Baillie of Edinburgh University, its convener and dominant intellectual force. Significantly, despite his leading role on the comparable Commission during the First World War, John White did not become a member of the Baillie Commission. In its first report in May 1942, the Baillie Commission called on the church to take a more active role

---

50 *Acts, Proceedings and Debates of the General Assembly* (1934), 62–70.
51 *Acts, Proceedings and Debates of the General Assembly* (1935), 381–4.
52 D. Shaw, 'The Kirk and the Hitler Regime', *Life and Work* (April 1983), 26–7.
53 For the growing discomfort with the axiom of non-interference in economic and political matters, see W.R. Forrester, *The Lost Provinces of Religion* (Edinburgh, 1937).

in political and economic matters, to work for social justice, greater social equality and industrial reform. 'The truth is', the report asserted, 'that there is no single issue which it is safe to relegate entirely to the expert specialisation of . . . political and economic knowledge'. If the church lacked sufficient knowledge, it should work to attain it: 'it is certain that there is much more we could know if we cared to know it'.[54] The report of 1942 was a clear challenge to the policies pursued during the 1920s and 1930s, and it helped prepare the church to participate in the creation of the social welfare state after 1945.

III

The interwar years were largely a time of drift and disappointment for the Church of Scotland. The period had begun amid hopes of a new social order to emerge out of the shared sacrifices of the Great War. Scotland would become a Christian commonwealth, uniting its people under the moral and spiritual direction of a reunited national church, and providing leadership to the Reformed Churches of Europe. The period had ended with the hopes of the church union and Christian commonwealth largely in ruins, and the influence of the Church of Scotland greatly reduced at home and in Europe. Part of the cause for the failure lay in the times. A bleak period of world economic stagnation and acute international tension, the inter-war years did not provide fertile ground for raising Christian commonwealths in small nations. Much of the reason for the church's disappointing record, however, lay in the idea of the Christian commonwealth that White and his supporters sought to achieve.

First, their idea of the Christian commonwealth was based on an exclusive idea of a national church, one that called for a racial and cultural homogeneity. The national Church of Scotland was to represent a Scottish national character, and include among its teachings a 'scientific' racism in which the separation of the races was part of the divinely-ordained natural order. The national church was to confront the Scoto-Irish Catholic minority with crusading zeal as a 'menace' to the covenanted commonwealth. The campaign against the Scoto-Irish Catholic community revealed the darker side of national religion – and it failed to gain the support of either the Government or the majority of the Scottish people. Despite years of reports, meetings, petitions and deputations, the Church of Scotland could not bring the state to legislate against Irish immigration or the Scoto-Irish community in Scotland. Nor did the Church have much success in attracting Scottish working-class support for its campaign, despite its claims that the Scoto-Irish Catholics were taking employment from native Scots and reducing living standards.

Second, the goal of organising the population into close-knit communities under the shared direction of church and state – of reviving the ideal parish system

---

[54] *Reports to the General Assembly of the Church of Scotland* (1942), 419–93.

– proved to be unrealistic in a pluralistic society characterised by the growth of centralised government, large industry and an increasingly mobile population. The Church Extension effort of the 1930s was a reasonable and in many respects a necessary response to the development of the new housing areas, and it represented probably the most lasting achievement of the era of White's leadership. However, it also failed to reverse the decline of the parish as a social and political unit. With the development of transportation and communication, more and more people worked and enjoyed leisure pursuits outside the parish. Further, while the parish remained the basic administrative unit of the national church, it was no longer the administrative unit of the State. The Local Government Act of 1929 had abolished the parish council and parish educational authority (both of which had been dominated by church representatives) – part of a long movement toward centralised state control of social services.[55] The Church Extension campaign of the 1930s, moreover, contained an element of Presbyterian triumphalism, an assumption that the national Church of Scotland had only to improve the efficiency of its parochial institutions in order to restore its rightful social authority. There was little sensitivity to, or even recognition of, the realities of religious pluralism.

Finally, the Church of Scotland failed to make its voice heard as the Christian and moral conscience of the commonwealth. The church's sphere of influence was greatly reduced by the axiom embraced by White and other church leaders in the 1920s that the church should not speak on economic and political matters. Further, the church was inconsistent in its application of that axiom – as, for example, when it pressed for legislation on Irish immigration, while declining to appeal to the Government on behalf of the miners or for more generous treatment of the unemployed. Nor did the church speak out boldly against the continental dictatorships or in support of the Confessing Church movement in Germany. Part of the difficulty lay in the nature of the Presbyterian system – a representative system of church government which could tend to reflect the opinions and prejudices of the majority of Church members. Presbyterian ministers were very much under the influence of their largely middle-class congregations, while the upper church courts, especially the General Assembly, gave considerable influence to wealthy lay elders. For most of the period, church leaders seemed more concerned with defining social policies that would have the support of the majority of ministers and elders, than with interpreting social issues in the light of Scripture or the historic confessions. It was an era when the faculties of divinity in Scotland's historic universities exercised relatively little influence on the life or policies of the church, and also when the church received little support from Scottish intellectuals. It was perhaps significant that Scottish writers of the 1930s, among them Hugh MacDiarmid, Lewis Grassic Gibbon and Neil Gunn, tended to seek a

55 J. White, 'Devolution as Safeguard of Democracy', *Glasgow Herald*, 27 December 1947; C.G. Brown, ' "Each Take Off their Several Way?" The Protestant Churches and the Working Classes in Scotland', in G. Walker and T. Gallagher (eds), *Sermons and Battle Hymns: Protestant Popular Culture in Modern Scotland* (Edinburgh, 1990), 80–1.

revival of Scottish community based on a Celtic or Jacobite past, rather than to look back to Presbyterian and Covenanting traditions.[56] There was nothing comparable in Scotland to either the Christian Sociology movement in England or the drift of English intellectuals back to the Church of England during the 1930s. The Second World War brought new leaders and a new voice of constructive social criticism to the Church of Scotland. The church's Commission for the Interpretation of God's Will in the Present Crisis encouraged more active involvement of the church in the political and economic life of the nation, and prepared the church to assume a role in shaping the pluralistic social democracy that emerged after the war. The policies of the 1920s and 1930s represented the final attempt to revive the Christian commonwealth under the authority of the Church of Scotland, demonstrating the limits of ecclesiastical authority in twentieth-century society and the need for new conceptions of the church and its mission.

---

[56] M.G.H. Pittock, *The Invention of Scotland: The Stuart Myth and the Scottish Identity, 1638 to the Present* (London, 1991), 134–49.

IAN MACHIN

British Churches and Moral Change in the 1960s

'There is no need to prove that a revolution is required in morals. It has long since broken out, and it is no 'reluctant revolution'. The wind of change here is a gale'.[1] Thus wrote the Rt. Rev. John Robinson, Suffragan Bishop of Woolwich, in his controversial and very widely-read treatise of 1963, *Honest to God*, which attacked what it called 'supranaturalist' theology and 'supranaturalist' ethics. 'Supranaturalist ethics' were seen by Robinson as the morals of the Ten Commandments, received from God on Sinai, accepted by the Jews and endorsed by Christ as part of the Christian religion.[2] Robinson disliked aspects of this morality because he believed that it 'subordinated the actual individual relationship to some universal, whether metaphysical or moral, external to it. The decision is not reached, the judgment is not made, on the empirical realities of the particular concrete relationship between the parties concerned.'[3] The contemporary change to a more empirical ethic, described as 'the new morality', was welcomed by Robinson, who wrote that: 'nothing can of itself be labelled as "wrong". One cannot, for instance, start from the position "sex relations before marriage" or "divorce" are wrong or sinful in themselves. . . . They are not intrinsically so, for the only intrinsic evil is lack of love.'[4] Robinson's opinion was supported by some Christians, for example the contributors to a book entitled *Towards a Quaker View of Sex*, published in the same year as *Honest to God*.[5] But other Christians deplored the opinion. The pope, for example, had first denounced the 'new morality' in 1952. The debate on morality caused ideological division among British Christians, and these divisions were seen in differing attitudes to the various questions of moral change in the 1960s.

Robinson was right in saying that the 'moral revolution' had been long in the

I wish to thank the British Academy for a research grant which assisted the work for this paper.
1   J.A.T. Robinson, *Honest to God* (London, 1963), 105.
2   *Ibid.*, 106–7.
3   *Ibid.*, 112.
4   *Ibid.*, 117–18.
5   A. Heron, ed., *Towards a Quaker View of Sex* (London, 1963), 5ff., 37ff. Cf. J. Weeks, *Sex, Politics and Society: the regulation of sexuality since 1800* (London, 1981), 261.

making. The establishment of democracy in Britain, more or less in 1918, no doubt encouraged demands to remove social restrictions and disadvantages and to promote freedom of choice in morality. The spread of comparative popular affluence, enjoyed by many people in the 1930s and by a much greater number in the 1950s, played an important part in encouraging hedonism and some harmful (as well as many harmless) uses of leisure. A campaign to spread artificial methods of birth control began in the early 1920s; an Abortion Law Reform Association, aiming at legal abortion, was started in 1936; and important Acts extending the grounds for divorce were passed in 1937 and 1938. The relaxation of the law against homosexual practice had long been advocated, and was recommended in the Wolfenden Report of 1957, the Homosexual Law Reform Society being founded consequently in 1958. All of these claims and movements were challenges to traditional Christian morality as it had been built up by church teaching over the centuries. But Robinson was not so convincing in implying that the Ten Commandments were under challenge. For none of them was directly threatened by these developments of opinion, with the single exception of the injunction to keep the Sabbath holy, and this had been a matter of dispute for centuries. Sunday observance as generally practised by the respectable classes in Victorian times was being increasingly disregarded. But in view of Christ's liberal words on this subject, differences of opinion and practice on Sunday observance were surely legitimate. More and more Christians were not thinking it necessary to be obvious Sabbatarians in order to be faithful to their religion. Bishop Robinson himself gave some reason to believe that the commandment not to commit adultery might be under challenge. He said, in giving evidence at the *Lady Chatterley's Lover* trial in 1960, that adultery might not be invariably sinful. But although there seemed to be some calls in the 1960s for the abolition of marital fidelity and even marriage itself (Robinson emphatically did not join in these), there was no widespread or effective advocacy of adultery in the 1960s or later. So, although there were effective challenges to several aspects of the churches' moral teaching in the 1960s, the Decalogue survived that 'swinging' decade generally intact.

However, the churches undoubtedly appeared to be under serious moral challenge in this decade, and to many they seemed to be in an increasingly weak position to withstand the threat because of their numerical decline in membership and attendance. The Roman Catholic Church in Great Britain continued to expand its numbers until the end of the 1960s. But most Protestant Churches had been more or less in numerical decline since the first decade of the twentieth century, though there were exceptions which included the Quakers and (until the mid-1950s) the Church of Scotland. After 1945, British churches were hoping to regain the numerical levels they had experienced thirty or forty years before, but they failed to achieve this object. The 1950s were a decade of stability for the churches, but effective revival did not come. The early evangelistic campaigns of Dr Billy Graham, for example, were very impressive but generally transient in their impact. During the 1960s many British churches experienced unprecedentedly rapid decreases in membership. Numbers of communicants in the Church of England, and membership of the Church of Scotland and of the Methodist,

Congregational, Baptist and some other Nonconformist churches, showed falls which were considerable though differing in extent between one church and another.[6] Among Protestants, only some of the small unorthodox churches showed increases, and in 1970 the estimated Roman Catholic population showed its first drop since the eighteenth century.[7] To some extent unbelief and scepticism were growing. To a larger extent, Christianity was continuing but was becoming 'privatised', its followers maintaining their beliefs but giving scarcely any church witness and perhaps relinquishing any denominational connection, although they probably watched services on television and might have begun to meet for worship and discussion in small groups – the origins of the 'house churches' of the 1970s. There was developing a trend which, by about 1970, left the traditional churches as regular resorts of only a small minority of the population, about ten per cent (and stabilising) in England, perhaps slightly more in Wales, and about seventeen per cent (and declining) in Scotland. There has been no marked upturn in the succeeding twenty years.

Whether they were 'public' (i.e. church-going) or 'privatised', Christians in Britain did not respond in any united way to the moral changes of the 1960s. Nor did society as a whole. Educational opportunity, which encouraged confidence in individual decision, and the assumption of democratic freedom of choice had become too widespread for reactions to be anything but diverse. This was the case among Christians as well as non-Christians, among members of the same church as well as (sometimes) between the official standpoints of different churches. On a very general level there may have been a degree of Christian consensus in reacting to the changes. For instance, when the Roman Catholic Archbishop of Cardiff described the affluent society as 'the effluent society' in 1967, the Anglican *Church Times* said: 'There are thousands of Christians outside the Roman Church who must have said 'three cheers for the Archbishop' on reading of this protest made in the common Christian cause against the excesses of fashionable moral anarchy'.[8] There was an unprecedented example of ecumenical protest, including Roman Catholics, against the sale of pornographic literature at Wigan in 1968.[9] There existed indeed a fairly common Christian concern about the lowering of moral standards;[10] but there was too much difference over the details of moral change for convincing union to develop among Christians on these matters. Some differences were very clear, notably those between the Roman Catholic church and Protestant churches over birth control, abortion and divorce. There were also clear differences of emphasis between more conservative Protestant churches, such as the Free

---

6   R. Currie, A. Gilbert and L. Horsley, *Churches and Churchgoers: patterns of Church growth in the British Isles since 1700* (Oxford, 1977), 129, 135, 144, 151. See also A. Hastings, *A History of English Christianity, 1920–85* (London, 1986), 549–52.
7   R. Currie *et al.*, *op. cit.*, 153, 158.
8   *Church Times*, 3 Mar. 1967, 3.
9   *Ibid.*, 16 Feb. 1968, 11.
10 E.g. debate on motion by the Bishop of Gloucester (Rt. Rev. W.M. Askwith) in Upper House of Canterbury Convocation, 3 Oct. 1961; *Chronicle of the Convocation of Canterbury*, III.6, no. 3 (1961), 486–97.

Church of Scotland, and more liberal ones, but one cannot ascribe a uniform moral view to the membership of one Church.

The moral changes of this era were not limited to Britain but were an American and European phenomenon which spread to other parts of the world. In Britain one of its clearest expressions was the passing of Acts of Parliament which seemed to sanction the permissive trend, though their intention was not to grant general libertarian licence so much as to relieve people who were under a social disadvantage. Because of these Acts and the growth of libertarian social assumptions, the permissive tendency became deeply rooted and continues to permeate our lives at the present day. The legislative measures included the Betting and Gambling Act of 1960, which liberalised the gaming laws and enabled bingo halls and betting shops to be opened; three important innovations in 1967, the *annus mirabilis* of the new morality, comprising the legalisation of abortion, the legalisation of homosexual acts between consenting adults, and the enabling of local health authorities to give advice on contraception; finally the Divorce Reform Act of 1969, allowing divorce on the grounds of breakdown of marriage, without the necessity of proving (as hitherto) a 'matrimonial offence' in the form of adultery, cruelty or desertion, or the incurable insanity of a spouse. But not all such legislation in the 1960s was permissive: the Drugs (Misuse) Act of 1964 forbade the use of both hard and soft drugs for non-medicinal purposes.

In addition to the major instances of liberating legislation, there was the relaxation of the censorship of literature, plays and films. The authority of the Lord Chamberlain's office to censor plays was abolished in 1968, though there had been campaigns to achieve this since before the First World War. Advocates of more freedom in literature – another long-standing cause – obtained a victory in the acquittal of Penguin Books in 1960 for publishing the unexpurgated version of D.H. Lawrence's *Lady Chatterley's Lover*. This encouraged much more freedom in the production of books, magazines and newspapers, though all literature was open to prosecution under the Obscene Publications Act of 1959 if it was thought liable to deprave or corrupt. Censorship of films remained, by the British Board of Film Censors and by local government bodies, but there was a great deal more lenience in its practice from the early 1960s onwards.

The extension of gambling allowed by the Act of 1960 was widely put into effect, so that it was said in 1968 that Britain was becoming 'a gambler's paradise'.[11] Churches were therefore given much cause to continue their attacks on gambling. The General Assembly and the local presbyteries of the Church of Scotland, for example, made repeated efforts to deter members of that church from taking part in all forms of gambling. Included in this ban were church raffles, which were by no means excused in spite of the good causes they were meant to aid and in spite of complaints by church members that such an attempted ban was stooping to triviality and would only make the church ridiculous.[12] The

11 *Reports to the General Assembly of the Church of Scotland, 1968* (Edinburgh, 1968), 498.
12 *Ibid.*, *1960* (Edinburgh, 1960), 341–2; *1961* (Edinburgh, 1961), 446–7, 453.

Edinburgh presbytery of the Church of Scotland stated in 1959: 'Raffling is a form of gambling, the principle of which contradicts the Christian way of life'.[13] This presbytery called on churches to give 'positive instruction in the Christian use of money so that young people, in particular, may be trained to resist all gambling inducements'.[14] Careful stewardship of money was held to be an essential Christian characteristic, and gambling was seen as a form of squandering and a display of covetousness. Whatever method the gambler adopts, reported the Committee on Temperance and Morals to the General Assembly, 'his motive is to get much for little. . . . The Football Pool, the Bingo Club, the Totalisator, the Premium Bond, the bookmakers' odds all seek to exploit this motive. Such an outlook is a denial of the Christian's true calling.'[15] Another report to the General Assembly in 1967 implied that some church members were spending more on a 'mild gamble' than they put in the collection: 'comparatively small sums of money may be spent weekly by many who indulge in a mild gamble, but then 'comparatively small sums' are usually about twice the average giving of the church member to the cause of Christ'.[16] In 1968 there was a new threat to extend gambling – the introduction of a bill in the House of Commons to establish a National Lottery, though this was defeated. The proposal to give further official encouragement to gambling in this way was condemned by the assemblies and newspapers of different religious persuasions, including the Anglican *Church Times* and the Nonconformist *British Weekly*.[17]

The consumption of alcohol was the social issue on which more ecclesiastical energy had probably been spent than on any other since the early nineteenth century. In the 1960s there was anxiety in many Church bodies to prevent the extension of opening hours for public houses, and in some cases to reduce them. The Ayr presbytery of the Church of Scotland, for example, wanted all public houses in Scotland to close at 9.30 in the evening, and of course wanted the ban on Sunday opening to be maintained.[18]

The contribution of alcohol to road accidents was continually stressed, not surprisingly in a period when car driving was rapidly increasing and the number of casualties growing. In 1960 the Archbishop of Wales, the Most Rev. Edwin Morris, told the Governing Body of the Church in Wales that motorists should abstain from alcohol before driving: 'to exercise our freedom in circumstances which may cause us to deprive someone else of the greatest gift of all – life itself –

---

13 Minutes of Edinburgh Presbytery of Church of Scotland (Scottish Record Office, Edinburgh), 3 Feb. 1959, 12.
14 *Ibid.*, 13 Sept. 1960, 265; also 10 Jan. 1961, 330.
15 *Reports to General Assembly of Church of Scotland, 1963* (Edinburgh, 1963), 406–7, 418; *1965* (Edinburgh, 1965), 350ff.
16 *Ibid.*, *1967*, 504.
17 *Ibid.*, *1968* (499), *1969*, 512; *British Weekly*, 7 Mar. 1968 (6), 28 Mar., 1; *Church Times*, 22 Mar. 1968, 1.
18 *British Weekly* (Scottish edition), 10 Mar. 1960, 3; *Reports to General Assembly of Church of Scotland, 1960* (Edinburgh, 1960), 338, and *1961*, 450–1. cf. *Congregational Year Book, 1971–2* 92–3.

is beyond question sinful'. Christians were free to consume alcoholic beverages in moderation, he continued, as was shown by the example of Christ, but 'they must use them responsibly, recognising the danger of excess at all times, and the duty of abstaining from their use when it was unfitting.'[19] In 1960 also the Congregational Union of England and Wales resolved at its Annual Assembly that all citizens should abstain before driving, and that a blood test or a 'breathing apparatus for measuring alcohol-concentration in the body' should be employed.[20] The Road Traffic Act of 1962, which treated the drink and driving problem firmly, was warmly approved; and when in 1965 the Government announced that driving with more than a certain amount of alcohol in the blood would become an offence, the move was welcomed by the Congregational Union.[21] The application of the breathalyser test from October 1967 received emphatic approval from the General Assembly of the Church of Scotland, which hoped that 'the country . . . will not be put off by the high-powered publicity against the test being adopted by the Licence Trade'.[22] Concentration on the drink-driving issue illustrated that churches by the mid-twentieth century were less concerned with trying to prevent the consumption of alcohol than to limit its dangerous excesses. It was generally accepted that there were differences of opinion and behaviour among Christians on the matter of moderate drinking.

New concern shown in the 1960s about drug-taking and tobacco-smoking was similar to the worries about alcohol. Growing addiction to drugs, and the efforts required to restrain it effectively, were repeatedly stressed by church bodies, which called on the Government to take more action.[23] Cigarette smoking began to be regarded as a serious danger to health if it were taken to excess, and the Government's declared intention to prohibit the advertising of cigarettes on commercial television was welcomed.[24]

The weakening of censorship over books, magazines, plays and films was another major moral concern of the 1960s. The legal acceptance in 1960 of the publication of the full version of *Lady Chatterley's Lover*, after a famous trial, aroused sharply differing opinions among Christians. This was most notably the case in the upper reaches of the Anglican hierarchy, where the Archbishop of Canterbury, Geoffrey Fisher, clashed with Bishop John Robinson. Fisher was engaged in this dispute when he received a letter suggesting that the judgement in favour of *Lady Chatterley* should be made the occasion of 'a tremendous witness . . . by all the Christian denominations. What a thrill it would be if a great Christian campaign could be organised and waged against the corruption of much

---

19 *Church Times*, 22 Apr. 1960, 7. Cf. *Reports to General Assembly of Church of Scotland, 1961*, 449.

20 19 May 1960; *Congregational Year Book, 1961*, 82. Cf. *British Weekly*, 28 July 1960, 6; *Reports to General Assembly of Church of Scotland, 1965* (Edinburgh, 1965), 350–1.

21 *Congregational Year Book, 1965–6*, 88.

22 *Reports to General Assembly, 1968*, 496.

23 *Ibid., 1965*, 348; *1967*, 507–8.

24 *Ibid., 1965*, 351.

of the present day life.'[25] Acrimonious divisions which were already developing, however, seemed to prohibit any such united crusade. Bishop Robinson had defended the book at the trial, advising Christians to read it and making the contentious statement that it portrayed 'the love of a woman in an immoral relationship, so far as adultery is an immoral relationship'.[26] Robinson was accused of denying the Commandment against adultery,[27] whereas he seems really to have been saying that it was open to question in some circumstances. Fisher, after warning him that 'I cannot defend you, of course, at all', publicly rebuked him at a diocesan conference at Canterbury on 5 November 1960, in the following terms:

> Inevitably anything he [Robinson] said would be regarded as said by a Bishop whose chief official concern is to give pastoral advice to the people committed to his charge. . . . Anyone must know that in this sexually self-conscious and chaotic age, to speak pastoral wisdom in public on particular questions is extremely dangerous. The Bishop exposed himself to this danger. The Christian fact is that adultery . . . is always a sin, and at present a very prominent, even all pervasive sin. The good pastor will teach his people to avoid both the fact of and the desire for sex experience of an adulterous kind and of fornication also, from the plain undeviating teaching of the Bible, both Old and New Testament. . . . In my judgement, the Bishop was mistaken to think that he could take part in the trial without becoming a stumbling block and a cause of offence to many ordinary Christians.[28]

Fisher's statement was, of course, widely publicised in the press and was greeted with differing Christian reactions. He received a letter of congratulation from Enid Blyton and critical letters from Valerie Pitt.[29] One of his most vehement Christian opponents was a lady at Dundee who wrote:

> I am one – and I am sure there are thousands more – who are horrified at the narrow and moralistic view you express. . . . I am almost ashamed to admit the name of Christian. I am certain that Jesus must squirm at this sort of pitifully inadequate action. YOU – and not the Fine Christians like Dr. John Robinson – are the one who is driving people out of the Church.[30]

Milder criticisms of Fisher were expressed by Dr Edward Wickham, Bishop of

---

25 Ernest S. Heap to Fisher, 15 Nov. 1960; Archbishop Fisher Papers (Lambeth Palace Library), 246, fo. 203.

26 Newspaper cutting *ibid.*, appended to fos 158–9.

27 Rev. L.H. Cuckney (Chief Information Officer, Church House, Westminster) to Fisher, 29 Oct. 1960; *ibid.*, fo. 158.

28 Fisher to Robinson, 3 Nov. 1960, copy (*ibid.*, fo. 160); Fisher's speech at diocesan conference, 5 Nov., *ibid.*, fo. 162; also Robinson to Fisher, 8 Nov. 1960 (*ibid.*, fos 177–81).

29 Enid Blyton to Fisher, 6 Nov. 1960 (*ibid.*, fo. 168); Fisher to Blyton, 17 Nov. 1960 (*ibid.*, fo 204); Valerie Pitt to Fisher, 6 Nov. 1960 (*ibid.*, fo. 169); Fisher to Pitt, 10 Nov. 1960 (*ibid.*, fos 193–5).

30 Mrs Daphne Laing to Fisher, 6 Nov. 1960; *ibid.*, fo. 172.

Middleton, who thought the book could have 'a profound value', and by the President of the Methodist Conference, Rev. Edward Rogers, who did not think that *Lady Chatterley's Lover* could be called obscene.[31] Another well-known Methodist, Dr Donald Soper, told a crowd of three hundred at Speaker's Corner in Hyde Park that he was 'delighted that the book has been reprieved. It is an excellent piece of literature and it is a sincere attempt by the author to present one side of married life'.[32] On the other hand, opponents of the book included the Moderator of the General Assembly of the Free Church of Scotland; Monsignor Gordon Wheeler (Administrator of Westminster Cathedral); and the Temperance and Morals Committee of the General Assembly of the Church of Scotland, which declared the book to be 'pernicious, pornographic, and in some passages positively blasphemous'.[33] One particularly forthright opponent was the Rev. Basil Buckland, Rector of Longton, Stoke-on-Trent, and husband of Mrs Mary Whitehouse's partner in her 'clean up television' campaign a few years later. It was Buckland's view that:

> All of us in the Church [of England] ought to be bitterly ashamed that we, largely through the advocacy of one of our Bishops, but also by our own flabbiness, have allowed a book which glorifies adultery and unrestrained lust to be approved for general reading.[34]

The freedom of publication given to *Lady Chatterley* encouraged the appearance of a great deal of explicit writing and pictorial display, some of it of the 'soft pornographic' kind which was not regarded as harmful enough to be prosecuted under the Obscene Publications Act but was nevertheless fiercely denounced by some religious periodicals. For example, the publicity issued to launch the pseudo-intellectual magazine *Penthouse* in 1965, which claimed to lead 'the struggle for moral and intellectual freedom', was condemned by the *British Weekly* as 'diabolical drivel' and as 'one of the first major steps in a cataclysmic flood of planned pornography'.[35] The *British Weekly* welcomed the end of stage censorship in 1968 only with reservations, for (it said) 'while the pressure for freedom in the arts comes, genuinely, from creative thinkers, writers and producers, it also comes from pornographers and perverts, anxious to cash in on the permissive society, happy to corrupt if it means commercial gain'.[36] Christians, like members of society in general, continued to differ in their attitudes to the new freedom for literature, plays and films, and the controversies produced by this freedom have continued up to the present. Society has not simply absorbed this freedom unquestioningly but continues to argue over it, because society is constantly renewed by fresh

---

[31] *Sunday Dispatch*, 6 Nov. 1960.
[32] *The Times*, 7 Nov. 1960.
[33] *Ibid.*; *Sunday Dispatch*, 6 Nov. 1960; *Reports to General Assembly of Church of Scotland, 1961* (Edinburgh, 1961), 447.
[34] *Sunday Dispatch*, 6 Nov. 1960.
[35] *British Weekly*, 11 Feb. 1965, 1.
[36] *Ibid.*, 3 Oct. 1968, 6.

generations which react in the familiar diverse ways to the new material presented to them.

In the 1960s one of the main threats of this kind to traditional morality was seen as the television set – described as 'the most powerful medium of propaganda that mankind has yet invented'[37] – which had come to occupy the majority of British homes in the course of the 1950s. Television aided religion in one sense, on account of the popularity of televised services, although it was, of course, privatised and not church-going religion which benefited from these. The Catholic *Universe* claimed in 1959 that 'as many as half the population view and hear religious services and talks on Sunday on television and radio'.[38] On the other hand, by the early 1960s the pronounced moral permissiveness in many television programmes, especially in 'experimental' plays produced by the British Broadcasting Corporation, was arousing concern and opposition among Christians of all denominations. The B.B.C. had, over several decades, been a reliable upholder of Christian attitudes in its transmissions, the original Director, Lord Reith, having been particularly responsible for this. But by the later 1950s doubts were arising as to whether this situation would continue. The Roman Catholic Earl of Longford informed the House of Lords in June 1959 that 'the British people have a right to insist . . . that the Christian moral code and the basic religious beliefs of Christianity should be supported and fostered by public services such as the B.B.C. and publicly-supervised services such as those of Independent Television'.[39] Articles in the Nonconformist *British Weekly* repeatedly condemned 'the worship of the sensual' in advertising and entertainment, which it said was 'a degradation of human personality'.[40] In 1961 a Catholic memorandum, written by Archbishop Heenan and two others and presented to a government committee on broadcasting, complained of a frequent 'complete lack of restraint and reticence' in programmes which could seriously infringe 'both modesty and morality'.[41] The Church and Nation Committee of the Church of Scotland said that plays or films which appeared 'to question the sanctity of marriage and family life' should not be broadcast, that all forms of blasphemy should be banned from the air, and that programmes should not do anything to encourage gambling and drinking.[42]

Protests of this kind from church bodies and individuals would perhaps have made little impression on the broadcasting authorities in a secularised society. What did have much more impact was the formation in 1964 of a wider move-

---

37 Peter Kirk, reviewing a book by Mary Whitehouse in *Church Times*, 24 Feb. 1967, 5.
38 *Universe*, 29 May 1959, 10. Cf. figures of listeners to and viewers of religious broadcasts in R. Currie, A. Gilbert and L. Horsley, *Churches and Churchgoers: Patterns of Church growth in the British Isles since 1700* (Oxford, 1977), 235–7.
39 *Universe*, 12 June 1959, 1.
40 *British Weekly*, 11 June 1959, 6. Cf. *ibid.*, 18 June 1959, 6; 17 Sept. 1959, 9; 21 Jan. 1960, 3; 28 Jan. 1960, 9.
41 Copy of memo (Feb. 1961) in Fisher Papers, 261, fo 313 (complete memo, fos 308–22).
42 *Reports to General Assembly of Church of Scotland, 1961* (Edinburgh, 1961), 430; cf. *ibid.*, *1965*, 300 ff.

ment with a decided Christian message, the 'Clean Up TV' campaign of Mrs Mary Whitehouse and Mrs Norah Buckland. This campaign led to the foundation of the National Viewers' and Listeners' Association early in 1965. Both leaders of this association had long been attached to two morally conservative bodies, Moral Rearmament and the Mothers' Union of the Church of England.[43] The association commenced with 300,000 supporters, including about a hundred M.P.s from different parties – 'a strong busy-body minority', in the words of the Director-General of the B.B.C., Sir Hugh Greene, who was the individual most under attack by the association.[44] Members of the working committee of the association included a Roman Catholic vicar-general and a leading Methodist minister, Rev. Kenneth Greet. But the difference of viewpoint among Christians was shown when Greet soon withdrew his support because of what he described as the 'negative' expressions of the association.[45] Another clerical opponent of the organisation wrote that he could not support it because his religion compelled him to defend 'the priceless value of freedom of speech'.[46] In contrast was the opinion of a Birmingham doctor who wrote that Mrs Whitehouse 'deserves the support of all Christians who have the future of our nation at heart'.[47] It was claimed that, by 1967, an improvement had taken place in the moral standard of television broadcasts.[48] But the campaign had also shown the wide diversity of Christian opinions on such matters, just as it had been shown over the publication of certain kinds of literature.

Many supporters of Mrs Whitehouse disliked representations of homosexuality and lesbianism in television drama. The traditional Christian view was to regard homosexual inclinations not as the result of a natural God-given state like heterosexuality, but as unnatural and abhorrent. Nevertheless, there had been a notable softening of these opinions. The recommendation of the Wolfenden Report on Homosexual Offences and Prostitution in 1957, that homosexual acts between consenting adults should be legally permitted, won the support of the Archbishops of Canterbury and York, many Free Church leaders, the Methodist Conference and a Roman Catholic advisory committee, and obtained a narrow majority in the National Assembly of the Church of England.[49] Resolutions against the change however, came from the Church of Scotland and the Salvation Army; and the

43 Mary Whitehouse, *Cleaning up T.V.: from protest to participation* (London, 1967), 19, 23 and ff. For Mrs Whitehouse's motivation and campaigns up to 1980, see also J. Weeks, *Sex, Politics and Society: the regulation of sexuality since 1800* (London, 1981), 277–81.
44 *Church Times*, 12 Mar. 1965, 9.
45 *Ibid.*, 5 Mar. 1965, 1; Whitehouse, *op. cit.*, 52–3. Cf. D. Bebbington, *Evangelicalism in Modern Britain: a history from the 1730s to the 1980s* (London, 1989), 264.
46 Letter from Rev. C.D. Westbrook, *Church Times*, 19 Mar. 1965, 14.
47 Letter from Dr Robert Browne, *ibid.*, 3 Mar. 1967, 7.
48 *Reports to General Assembly of Church of Scotland, 1967* (Edinburgh, 1967), 162.
49 *Hansard's Parliamentary Debates*, vol. 596, cols 388–9, 396; *Tablet*, 6 May 1967 (letter from D. Geraghty).

Baptist Church was stated (by Sir Cyril Black, a Baptist M.P.) to be opposed to the reform.[50]

Support for a change in the law did not mean that homosexual acts were no longer seen as sinful, but only that legal restrictions were inappropriate as a means of preventing them. Those in favour of the reform did not conceive the possibility of granting homosexuals the same freedom and privileges as heterosexuals, for example the right to live as a married couple after a church or a civil wedding. After debating the matter on several occasions during a decade, Parliament finally adopted the Wolfenden recommendations on homosexuality when it passed Leo Abse's private bill of 1967. This was another reform on which Christians continued to differ, even if many previous opponents had come to acquiesce reluctantly in the change.[51]

The well-justified suspicion of growing unchastity among heterosexuals outside marriage was another challenge of the 1960s to traditional Christian moral concepts. These held that sexual relations should be limited to marriage. The coming of relatively 'safe' contraception in the form of the pill, which was generally available by the end of the 1960s, made this a particularly difficult sanction to maintain. In the years since the 1960s Christians seem generally to have acquiesced fairly silently, not in promiscuity but in pre-marital sex between a couple firmly attached to each other. However, as opposed to this manifestation of human relations, which neither the Commandments nor Christ specifically prohibited, the Commandment against adultery has been strongly maintained by Christians. Disapproval of adultery is generally held by society as a whole. Recent opinion polls show large majorities acquiescing in pre-marital sex but equally strong majorities opposed to adultery. The Commandments have generally managed to stand while later ecclesiastical sanctions have been more obviously infringed.

However, during the 1960s the churches were clearly not ready to give any acceptance to pre-marital sex.[52] The Reith Lectures for 1962 were given on the radio by Professor G.M. Carstairs, a medical scientist at Edinburgh University and son of a Church of Scotland minister, though himself a humanist. The lectures were later published under the title of *This Island Now*. Carstairs aroused controversy because his third lecture, on adolescence, condoned pre-marital intercourse, which he regarded as a sensible preparation for marriage:

> It seems to me that our young people are rapidly turning our society into one in which sexual experience, with precautions against conception, is becoming accepted as a sensible preliminary to marriage; a preliminary which makes it more

[50] *Hansard*, vol. 596, cols 461–2; *Reports to General Assembly of Church of Scotland, 1967*, 511.
[51] *Tablet*, 8 July 1967, 742–3; *Reports to General Assembly of Church of Scotland, 1968*, 490–1.
[52] E.g. *Church Times*, 3 Sept. 1965.

likely that marriage, when it comes, will be a mutually considerate and mutually satisfying partnership.[53]

The Temperance and Morals Committee of the Church of Scotland General Assembly, while unanimously acknowledging that the lecture was 'a timely and able analysis of adolescence, written by a specialist in his own field', entirely rejected the statement about pre-marital sex. The committee's report said that Carstairs had produced no evidence that 'unchastity is a better preparation for marriage than the exercise of self-restraint', though the report went on to accuse the lecturer of saying more than he had, such as alleging that 'sexual harmony' was the only basis required for a successful marriage.[54] The General Assembly stressed that 'chastity before marriage and fidelity after marriage remain the true ideal for the Christian'.[55] Carstairs later stated that the letters he had received against his statement (among others which expressed support) included ones from the Baptist Union, the Free Church presbytery of Glasgow, a Catholic Women's Group, and the clergy of the rural deanery of York.[56] He also noted, in respect of the controversy in Scotland, that: 'In the whole of this correspondence, as indeed in the public debate which was waged with some vigour . . . during the weeks following the third lecture, the spokesmen both of the Roman Catholic Church and of the Church of Scotland were among the lecturer's most temperate, charitable, and reasonable critics.'[57]

The General Assembly's reaction was not surprising in view of the worries already existing about the growth of pre-marital sex. In 1960 statistics were produced to show the increase of venereal disease among teenagers which the *Church Times* believed was due to laxity by parents and teachers in instructing children in correct moral behaviour. 'The responsibility lies', said this paper, 'supremely on all those parents and teachers who have so lightly discarded the whole Christian scheme of things. It is no use expecting to pluck the fruits of purity when they have cut the roots of faith.'[58] Teachers claimed, however, that it was difficult to teach moral standards when the media sent out broadcasts which undermined them.[59]

Reactions to the Profumo affair of 1963, in which a government minister resigned after first denying and then acknowledging having had an adulterous relationship with a call-girl (who, because of another of her relationships, was regarded as a security risk to British defence policy), sharply illustrated current concern about moral decay. The scandal had 'encouraged the belief abroad that Britain is finished, not only as a military power but as a moral power' said the

53 G.M. Carstairs, *This Island Now: the B.B.C. Reith Lectures, 1962* (Harmondsworth, 1964), 49–50, also 103–12.
54 *Reports to General Assembly of Church of Scotland, 1963* (Edinburgh, 1963), 410–11.
55 *Ibid.*, 419. Cf. *ibid.*, *1969*, 505.
56 Carstairs, *op. cit.*, 108.
57 *Ibid.*, 109.
58 *Church Times*, 29 Apr. 1960, 3.
59 *Tablet*, 30 Apr. 1960, 403.

British Weekly.[60] The religious press rebutted claims by some politicians that the moral issue had no bearing upon the minister's public role. 'Christians', said the *Church Times*, 'cannot regard moral decadence and corruption in public life as matters of no public concern. Rottenness in high places, lying, sexual licence and the widespread social acceptance of adultery cut at the roots of the nation's life, because they are contrary to the law of God.'[61] These sentiments were reflected in the statements of many church leaders, some of whom linked the incident to what they saw as 'a general moral deterioration in the country'.[62]

A medical threat to the preservation of chastity in marriage was seen in the use of artificial insemination by a donor (A.I.D.) in order to enable a woman to have a child when she was unable to have one by her husband. This practice became legal in 1960; but, although some Christian opinion supported it, it was opposed by many church leaders including Anglicans, Roman Catholics and Methodists. A resolution of the Methodist Conference of 1958 stated:

> The exclusive sexual union of man and wife is the essence of marriage as the Christian understands the mind and purpose of God. To destroy that exclusiveness, therefore, is to thwart the purpose of God. It is because the exclusive union between man and wife is . . . invaded by the giving and receiving of the seed of the donor that A.I.D. is wrong.[63]

A leading article in the *Church Times* urged the medical profession to 'think again whether this artificial and calculated invasion of the sanctity of marriage can possibly be anything but utterly wrong, a thing with which doctors should have nothing to do. And they should ask themselves whether, on this or a host of kindred problems, they really have the right to try to evade the acceptance of moral responsibility for their professional actions. To divide man into two parts, one concerned with morals and the other with technical skills, is to tear a seamless robe of what should be the indivisible integrity of human nature.'[64]

The restriction of birth, on the other hand, was a much larger question which applied to pre-marital sex, the happiness and continuance of marriages, and concern over world population growth. Contraception was an example of a moral issue which caused sharp division between the official attitudes of different churches. By the 1920s, when the Quaker Marie Stopes commenced her determined and largely successful campaign to propagate artificial contraceptive techniques among the population (provided, it was then stressed, that the users were married), Nonconformist churches were making no recommendation on

---

60   13 June 1963, 1, 6.
61   14 June 1963, 3.
62   *Church Times*, 21 June 1963, 20. Cf. a letter from George Goyder, *ibid.*, 14 June 1963, 14: 'I believe the present climate of this country and the tragedy of Mr Prufomo both rise up in judgment against the blind guides of Cambridge [he seems to have been referring chiefly to Bishop John Robinson] who reject the law of God and with it the morality of society in favour of a morality of self-development and social selfishness'.
63   *British Weekly*, 28 July 1960, 6.
64   *Church Times*, 10 July 1959, 8.

contraception but leaving the matter to individual decision. The Church of England was moving in the same direction. The decennial Lambeth Conference of Anglican bishops declared against artificial birth control methods in 1920, but in 1930 the Conference resolved, somewhat hesitantly, that they might be used according to individual discretion. The Conference did not meet again until 1948, when it made no further pronouncement on this subject. In 1958 the Conference declared its approval of artificial birth control methods, describing them as an important factor in 'the wise stewardship of the resources and abilities of the family as well as a thoughtful consideration of the varying population needs and problems of Society and the claims of future generations'.[65] The Church of Scotland did not pronounce officially on the subject until 1960, though previously it had given some favourable attention to the matter. A report of that Church's Temperance and Morals Committee in 1960 commended the use of the available methods of birth control to parents who wished to limit the size of their families for respectable reasons:

> If marriage is first and last intended for the procreation of children, then contraception frustrates that purpose, and so must be deemed unethical. But if marriage be primarily for the enrichment of the life of the home, then it would appear that to limit and space one's family so that the mother has time to regain her strength and the child to enjoy the care and attention which is its birth-right, is to recognise the true dignity of personality.[66]

This committee reported in 1969 that the 'mechanical or chemical means' given to mankind to control the number of births should be accepted as 'a divine call'.[67]

What had thus become a usual Protestant acquiescence in artificial birth control was not, however, agreed to by the Roman Catholic Church. By the 1960s contraception had become a major subject of difference between Catholic and Protestant. The difference had first clearly emerged in the 1920s, when, despite some more favourable indications previously, the Catholic Church committed itself only to sanctioning 'natural' methods of birth limitation, mainly the use of the 'safe' period. There were some sharp conflicts of opinion between Marie Stopes and Roman Catholics, but also some gentler and more reasoned debate between them. Different views on the subject were also expressed in 1959 between Mervyn Stockwood, the Anglican Bishop of Southwark, and the Apostolic Delegate, Gerald O'Hara, when Stockwood defended the Family Planning Association. Archbishop Fisher became involved in this dispute when he thought it necessary to protest to O'Hara for 'rebuking' Stockwood, a bishop under Fisher's and not Roman jurisdiction.[68]

---

[65] Quoted in *Reports to General Assembly of Church of Scotland, 1960* (Edinburgh, 1960), 344.

[66] *Ibid.*, 344–7, 350; also *ibid., 1968*, 492.

[67] *Ibid., 1969*, 506 and ff.

[68] Correspondence of Stockwood and Most Rev. Gerald P. O'Hara, 21 June–3 July 1959 (Fisher Papers, 228, fos 228–31); Fisher to O'Hara, 14 Aug. 1959 (*ibid.*, fo. 237).

In March 1960 the chairman of the Lambeth Conference's Family Planning Group, Bishop Stephen Bayne, said he could see no reason why the new oral contraceptive should be 'an affront to Christian conscience.'[69] The discouragement of the Catholic Church, however, continued to be given to all artificial methods of contraception. Though there was considerable dispute between conservative and liberal Catholics on the matter,[70] the existing official attitude was upheld by the papal encyclical *Humanae Vitae* in 1968. This was the result of long and agonized consideration by Pope Paul VI. He was supposedly a liberal, and his eventual decision caused a storm of liberal Catholic protest, both clerical and lay.[71] The Pope's conclusion apparently represented a triumph for the wish to resist permissiveness. This wish was so emphatic that he repelled pressures openly to sanction individual decision on the matter, and resisted worries about the escalating world population. But the official guidance given in *Humanae Vitae* could not nullify the right of private judgement open to Catholics in matters of personal discipline;[72] and it is probably the case that Catholics have sometimes used this right to disregard the injunctions of *Humanae Vitae*.

Probably no church had a completely uniform view on birth control, however, and there were differences among people who belonged to the same Protestant church. The extent and methods of advertising and propagating birth control techniques were causes of concern, especially when they involved giving contraceptives to the unmarried.[73] The passage of an Act in 1967 enabling this to be done legally caused the Bishop of Portsmouth, the Rt. Rev. John Phillips, to resign from the presidency of his local Family Planning Association. The Act, he claimed, 'assumed that only pregnancy or contraception were open to young people, and nowhere was there any sign that a third choice – chastity – should be considered'.[74] Some Anglicans disliked the message of the 1958 Lambeth Conference in favour of contraception. One of these wrote in a letter to the *Church Times*: 'We have no right to 'plan' the entry of an immortal soul into the world. What we should plan is the wise, temperate and reverent use of the procreative instinct, instead of mutilating and interfering with God's work of creation.'[75] Against this argument appeared another letter in the same paper, which said: 'I am glad that the Church, in an effort to keep in touch with the realities of changing times, has sufficient humility and courage to review the situation regarding family planning'.[76]

Abortion and divorce were other issues which divided Roman Catholic from most Protestant opinion, and Anglo-Catholic opinion also was strongly opposed

---

69 *British Weekly*, 31 Mar. 1960, 1.
70 E.g. *Tablet*, 29 Apr. 1967, 478–85 ('The Conservative Case'), and 6 May 1967, 510–13 ('The Arguments for Reform').
71 Details in A. Hastings, *A History of English Christianity, 1920–85* (London, 1986), 575–7.
72 Cf. *Tablet*, 1 Apr. 1967, 339–40.
73 E.g. *Reports to General Assembly of Church of Scotland, 1968* (Edinburgh, 1968), 492.
74 *Church Times*, 8 Mar. 1968, 1.
75 Letter from Mrs Frances Edwards, *ibid.*, 13 May 1960, 13. Cf. Rev. J.W. Davey to R. Beloe, 2 Nov. 1959; Fisher Papers, 219, fo. 342.
76 *Church Times*, 27 May 1960, 11–12.

to divorce. The division over abortion was much more recent than that concerning contraception. Leaders of the Church of England were reluctant to acquiesce in the demand to legalise abortion until 1967. An Anglican commission in 1964 declared that the foetus was sacred, and that only if the life or health of the mother was at serious risk should abortion be allowed.[77] Michael Ramsey, Archbishop of Canterbury, went beyond this in making concessions to pro-abortion opinion in certain circumstances. At a session of the full synod of the Convocation of Canterbury in January 1967 he proposed that abortion should be permitted if the child to be born was likely to be seriously deformed or defective; if conception occurred as a result of rape; and if the mother were 'totally incapable' of rearing a child.[78] He could not agree fully, however, with David Steel's Termination of Pregnancy Bill of 1967, which gave both more and less than he advocated. The bill allowed abortion under the National Health Service within twenty-eight weeks of conception, if two doctors agreed either that the pregnancy involved risk to the mother's life or to her health or to that of her existing children, or that the child conceived was likely to be seriously handicapped.[79] Among the opponents of Steel's bill were Anglican and Roman Catholic clergy of the Shrewsbury area, who jointly petitioned their M.P. against the measure as being 'unacceptable to Christian Conscience'.[80] Although Archbishop Ramsey decided that he could not vote for the bill, some bishops supported it in the Lords, and the measure went through.

The Church of Scotland's Social and Moral Welfare Committee had recommended, in May 1966, conditions for abortion which were similar to those in the Act. Abortion should be allowed when the mother's life was at risk or if her health might be seriously affected, or where foetal deformity was almost certain. The Methodist Conference's report on abortion in July 1966 was more liberal, adding to these conditions the occurrence of pregnancy as a result of rape and the serious unlikelihood that the mother would be able to bring up a child. Resolutions of other Nonconformist churches were rather less liberal than this. The Free Church of Scotland ironically resembled its long-standing antagonist the Roman Catholic Church in opposing any liberalising of the abortion law, which it said would represent 'another slide down the slope of the permissive society'.[81] A Catholic statement issued by Cardinal Heenan in October 1966, following a meeting of bishops, was that abortion was an 'abominable crime' like infanticide. The official view was supported by many Catholic organisations, and probably most Catholics were strongly against abortion. But Catholic Marxists held that abortion was justifiable in some cases, since life only became 'social and meaningful' after birth.[82] The official Catholic view has been maintained up to the present. The

77 O. Chadwick, *Michael Ramsey: a life* (Oxford, 1990), 154.
78 *Chronicle of the Convocation of Canterbury*, iv.6, 3–6.
79 *Church Times*, 26 May 1967, 1.
80 *Ibid.*, 3 Mar. 1967, 17.
81 Lorna Smith, 'The abortion controversy, 1936–77: a case study in 'emergence of law' (unpublished Ph.D. thesis, Edinburgh University, 1979), 143–6.
82 *Ibid.*, 146.

Society for the Protection of the Unborn Child, formed in January 1967 to resist the abortion bill, is largely Catholic but receives support from members of many other churches.[83] Campaigning by this society has produced the only reversal so far of the permissive legislation of the 1960s (and then only a slight reversal) – the reduction of the period permitted for an abortion from twenty-eight weeks to twenty-four weeks from conception, in 1990.

Divorce was another area in which many Christians found themselves acquiescing, if reluctantly, in a demand for social change in the name of humanitarian freedom. All Churches agreed with the traditional ideal that Christian marriage should not be dissolved. But the ideal could not, of course, be an absolute prohibition, and Christians also agreed that marriage could be terminated in certain circumstances. Over the divorce laws which existed in Britain, however, a clear division had emerged between Churches, notably when the last legal changes making divorce easier had occurred in 1937–8. The Catholic Church held to its view that divorce should not be accepted, but that Catholic marriages could be dissolved by papal annulment. The official Church of England view in the 1930s, still held in the 1960s, was that the grounds of divorce might be extended for the sake of society as a whole, but that the Church should clearly maintain its dislike of divorce and should urge clergy not to marry divorced persons in their churches.[85] Some Anglican societies, such as the Church Union and the Mothers' Union, maintained a particularly strong stand against divorce.[86] The Church of Scotland and Nonconformist churches also did not wish to encourage divorce, but left to the individual discretion of a minister the matter of re-marrying a divorced person.[87]

Efforts were made to liberalise the divorce law during the 1960s, and success was obtained in 1969. An important clause in Leo Abse's unsuccessful bill of 1963 was opposed by leaders of the Church of England, the Roman Catholic hierarchy, and the Free Churches Federal Council, because the clause would have allowed divorce after seven years' separation regardless of whether a 'matrimonial offence' (i.e. mainly adultery, desertion or cruelty) or the incurable insanity of a spouse had occurred, as the existing law required.[88] The clause was withdrawn after what the

---

83 Letter from Norman St John Stevas, a Roman Catholic, in *Church Times*, 10 Mar. 1967, 14, appealing to Anglicans to sign a petition against the bill which was launched by this society. He addressed his appeal 'especially to societies such as the Mothers' Union to help us achieve an aim of one million signatures to the petition', and continued: 'We fully accept the need for a moderate measure of abortion law reform, but we feel that the present proposals amount to abortion on demand and constitute a threat to the principle of the sanctity of human life'.

84 E.g. *Reports to General Assembly of Church of Scotland, 1968* (Edinburgh, 1968), 481–4.

85 G.I.T. Machin, 'Marriage and the Churches in the 1930s: royal abdication and divorce reform, 1936–7', *Journal of Ecclesiastical History*, xiii (1991), 78–81.

86 *Church Times*, 16 Feb. 1968, 14; 8 Mar. 1968, 24; 15 Mar. 1968, 9; 22 Mar 1968, 14.

87 Legal opinion quoted in Minutes of Edinburgh Presbytery of Church of Scotland, 3 Mar. 1959, 30–1.

88 *Tablet*, 6 Apr. 1963, 380; Chadwick, *op. cit.*, 151.

Church Times described as 'an unprecedented essay in Christian co-operation', and in the face of protests from secularists that the Christian 'minority' had no right to enforce its views on the non-Christian 'majority' of society.[89] But soon afterwards the official Church of England opinion was notably relaxed. An Anglican commission on the divorce law was appointed, with R.C. Mortimer, Bishop of Exeter, as chairman. In 1966 the commission produced a report entitled *Putting Asunder*. This proposed that the requirement of a 'matrimonial offence' before divorce was granted should be replaced by 'breakdown of marriage', which should not be accepted without attempts at reconciliation. This proposal received the general support of the Church of Scotland, the Methodist Church and other Protestant churches.[90]

Archbishop Ramsey defended the proposal in the House of Lords, and a report of the Law Commission also recommended that the change should take place. The National Assembly of the Church of England voted in February 1967 in favour of the reform.[91] Ramsey made it clear. however, that he was against divorce by consent and that he thought divorce should still be obtainable only through the law courts.[92] He criticised Leo Abse's Divorce Reform Bill, which finally passed in 1969, because it allowed divorce to take place after five years without the consent of one of the parties, and because he thought that the provision for divorce after two years by the consent of both parties permitted too short a period. Ramsey abstained from the division on the second reading, and the bishops who voted were on different sides. Ramsey's strictures on the measure were far exceeded by the Roman Catholic Lord Longford, who described parts of the bill as being utterly evil.[93] Much Anglican opinion was also opposed to the measure – for example the *Church Times* which said that it struck 'at the root of the institution of marriage as a lifelong and monogamous union. It would make marriage a temporary contract, dissoluble at will'.[94] There were attempts in the next few years to remove the official opposition in the Church of England to the marriage of divorced persons in church, but these were strongly disputed and were unsuccessful.[95] The effects of the Act of 1969 have caused differing and uncertain reactions, for the Act can be held on the one hand to have encouraged the steep increase in

[89] 10 May 1963, 3.
[90] Chadwick, 151–2; *Reports to General Assembly of Church of Scotland 1968* (Edinburgh, 1968), 484–9, and *1969*, 523–4; *British Weekly*, 1 May 1969, 10; *Congregational Year Book, 1968–9*, 92.
[91] *Church Times*, 24 Feb. 1967, 16; *Chronicle of Convocation of Canterbury*, full synod, 11 Oct. 1967 (iv. 7, 269).
[92] Chadwick, 151–2; *Church Times*, 24 Feb. 1967, 12, 16.
[93] Chadwick, 152–3. Cf. Jane Lewis, 'Public institution and private relationship: marriage and marriage guidance, 1920–68', *Twentieth Century British History*, I.3 (1990), 233–5.
[94] 16 Feb. 1968, 12 (leading article).
[95] Chadwick, 153; *Chronicle of Convocation of Canterbury*, full synod, 10 Oct. 1967 (iv. 7, 242–56); *Church Times*, 3 May 1968, 1.

divorces since that time and to have promoted the view that marriage can be temporary, but on the other hand to have given greater facility to the ending of genuinely unhappy marriages.

The spread of permissiveness cannot be equated with the spread of love, and the moral changes of the 1960s have by no means invariably led to the increase of human happiness. In some respects they have clearly produced the reverse. What was created, mainly in the 1960s, was a different moral approach but not necessarily (taken as a whole) a better one. Whether it is better or not, however, 'permissive Britain' has become a permanent institution, not a passing phase, although some of the pornographic and blasphemous excesses of permissiveness were restricted in the 1970s by public protests and rallies and by cases in the law courts.

The churches, undoubtedly challenged though they were, easily survived the 'swinging sixties'. In 1970 they were, in form and structure if not in number of members, in exactly the same position as they had been in 1960. There were obvious divisions of opinion both between and within churches over the changes of the 1960s – between Catholic and Protestant, conservative and liberal Catholic, and conservative and liberal Protestant. But, unlike the contemporary issue of Anglican-Methodist reunion or the later issue of female ordination in the Church of England, moral differences did not threaten to fracture any Church. This was probably because the moral issues of the 1960s were long-standing ones which had for many years been causes of differing opinions between and within churches, so that division on such points had become familiar. The permissive legislation of the 1960s and the wider permissiveness of practice which accompanied or resulted from it, emphasised familiar grounds of internal disagreement on such questions among the churches. Church members were not likely to be driven to secede from their religious body by a moral or social question, whatever they might threaten over a doctrinal issue which seemed much more fundamental. In 1970 the British Churches remained intact, though numerically weaker and more divided than a decade earlier.

INDEX